AF518399

# Religion and Literature: Indian Perspectives

*Edited by*
**Projit Kumar Palit**

**Kaveri Books**
New Delhi-110002

First Published in 2011
ISBN 978-81-7479-119-1



*Published by*
**Kaveri Books**
4832/24, Ansari Road
New Delhi - 110 002 (India)
Tel.: 011-2328 8140, 2324 5799,
Fax: 011-2328 8140
E-mail: kaveribooks@vsnl.com
kaveribooks@gmail.com
Website: www.kaveribooks.com

*Laser Typesetting by :* Deep Graphics, Delhi

*Printed at :* Salasar Imaging Systems, Delhi-110 052

PRINTED IN INDIA

*Dedication*

*To*

*My Parents*

**Mahadev Das Palit**

**Purnima Palit**

# Foreword

I am very much delighted to introduce the present volume entitled, "Religion and Literature: Indian Perspectives", edited by Dr. Projit Kumar Palit, who is the Associate Professor in the Department of History and also the Director of Centre for Indological Studies at Assam University (A Central University), Silchar, Assam.

As many as thirty-three distinguished scholars have articulated on various aspects related with religion and literature in India, in the present volume. I am sure readers would be immensely benefited from the learned exposition of religion as a moral code of our heritage. The strength of this volume rests on the wide variety presented on the subject as well as projcctions of the learned scholars on the theme of this book.

I am confident that this volume will be well accepted by the readers. I congratulate the editor for his sincerity and successful efforts.

**Ravindra Panth**
Director
Nava Nalanda Mahavihara
Nalanda-803 111 (India)

# Acknowledgement

I am happy to announce that my endeavour for the publication of a volume on 'Religion and Literature : Indian Perspectives' which has come out finally for the participation of thirty-three distinguished scholars from India and also abroad.

I am expressing deep regard and gratitude to Professor Rabindra Panth, the Director, Nava Nalanda Mahavihara, Nalanda, Bihar, for his valuable 'Foreword'.

I am also expressing deep regards to Prof. Pranabananda Jash, Former Professor of Visva Bharati University, who has kindly supervised me to complete the work. I am sincerely grateful and indebted to all authors who have contributed their research papers for this volume. I am thankful to Mr. Rakesh Goel of Kaveri Books, New Delhi for publishing this volume within a very short time. Thanks are due to Dr. Subdh Gopal Nandi, Mr. Susanta Kumar De and Mr. Achintya Kumar Mandal of Visva-Bharati Library, for their sincere co-operation. I am also thankful to Visva-Bharati and Assam University Library and all staff members for helping us during this work. I acknowledge my wife Mrs. Susmita Palit Saha, my daughter Poulomi Palit and my elder brother Niranjan Roy for their encouragement and assistance for completing this work.

**Projit Kumar Palit**

# Contents

# Diacritical Marks

System of Transliteration
*Roman equivalents of Deva-nāgari Letters*

| | | | | | |
|---|---|---|---|---|---|
| a | अ | ka | क | da | द |
| ā | अस | kha | ख | dha | ध |
| i | इ | ga | ग | na | न |
| ī | ई | gha | घ | pa | प |
| u | उ | ṅ | ङ | pha | फ |
| ū | ऊ | ca/cha | च | ba | ब |
| ṛ/ri | ऋ | cha/chha | छ | bha | भ |
| e | ए | ja | ज | ma | म |
| ai | ऐ | jha | झ | ya | य |
| o | ओ | ñ | ञ | ra | र |
| au | औ | ṭa | ट | la | ल |
| | | ṭha | ठ | va | व |
| | | ḍa | ड | śa | श |
| | | ḍha | ढ | ṣa/sha | ष |
| | | ṇa | ण | sa | स |
| | | ta | त | ha | ह |
| | | tha | थ | ṃ/ṁ | ं |
| | | | | ḥ | : |

Common words and modern names are usually written without any diacritical marks.

# Contributors

**Anirban Dash**
Assistant Professor
Central Institute of Higher Tibetan Studies
Sarnath, Varanasi-7, U.P.

**Ankur Barua**
The Centre of Buddhist Studies,
The Unviersity of Hong Kong,
Tung Lin Kok Yuen, Hong Kong

**Anupam Jash**
Assistant Professor
Department of Philosophy
Bankura Christian College, Bankura

**Asha Mukherjee**
Professor
Department of Philosophy and Religion
Visva- Bharati, Santiniketan
West Bengal -731235

**B.N.Patnaik**
Former Professor of English and Linguistics
Indian Institute of Technology
Kanpur, U.P.

**Bhagirathi Biswas**
Associate Professor, Department of Sanskrit
Assam University, Silchar

**Bikash Mukherji**
Associate Professor
Department of Ancient Indian History, Culture and Archaeology, Visva-Bharati, Santiniketan
West Bengal - 731 235

**Bimalendra Kumar**
Professor, Department of Pali Buddhist Studies,
Banaras Hindu University,
Varanasi - 210005 (U.P.)

**Debashree Dattaray**
Assistant Professor
Department of Comparative Literature
Jadavpur University, Kolkata, India

**Eknath B. Saharey**
Former Professor
Plot No.114, "VIMAL" Nazul layout,
Po-Bezonbag, Nagpur-440004 (MS)

**Gargi De**
Research Scholar
Ramakrishna Mission Institute of Culture
Kolkata

**Goutam Ghosal**
Professor, Department of English and Other Modern European Languages
Visva- Bharati, Santiniketan
West Bengal - 731235

**H. D. Khobragade**
Research Scholar
K.J.Somaiya Centre for Buddhist Studies,
Mumbai.

**K. Mavali Rajan**
Assistant Professor, Department of Ancient Indian History, Culture and Archaeology
Visva-Bharati, Santiniketan, West Bengal-731235

**Krishnendu Ray**
Reader,
Department of Ancient Indian History & Culture
University of Calcutta

**Lalita Chakraborty**
Associate professor
Department of Sanskrit, Pali & Prakrit
Visva-Bharati, Santiniketan
West Bengal - 731 235

**Mahua Mukherjee**
Professor, Department of Dance
Rabindra Bharati University, Kolkata.

**Md. Sirajul Islam**
Associate Professor
Department of Philosophy & Religion,
Visva Bharati, Santiniketan

**Meem Hai Zaffar**
Professor, Institute of Kashmir Studies,
Kashmir University
Srinagar, Kashmir

**Mohit Chakrabarti**
Former Professor of Education
Vinaya Bhavana, Visva-Bharati, Santiniketan
West Bengal - 731 235

**Muhammad Ismail**
Associate Professor,
Department of Islamic Studies,
Aligarh Muslim University, Aligarh, U.P.

**Nagendra Rao**
Assistant Professor
Goa University, Goa

**Preeti Sharma**
Associate Professor
Department of History & Indian Culture
Banasthali Vidyapith, P.O. Banasthali,
Distt.Tonk, Rajasthan-304022

**Projit Kumar Palit**
Associate Professor, Department of History
Assam University, Silchar

**Pranabananda Jash**
Former Professor, Department of Ancient
Indian History Culture and Archaeology
Visva-Bharati, Santiniketan,
West Bengal-731235

**Raghunath Ghosh**
Professor, Department of Philosophy
University of North Bengal,
West Bengal - 734013

**Sarani Mondal**
Assistant Professor
Department of English
Durgapur Society of Management
Sciences College,
Durgapur, West Bengal.

**Saswati Mutsuddy**
Reader,
Department of Pali
University of Calcutta,
West Bengal

**Sayamtara Jash**
Research Scholar
Ramakrishna Mission Institute of Culture
Kolkata

**Shiuli Ghosh**
Assistant Professor
Department of Sanskrit
Jadavpur University
Kolkata

**Sib Ranjan Misra**
Professor
Department of Economics and Politics
Visva Bharati University
Santiniketan, West Bengal

**Sukumar Bhattacharjya**
Former Professor
Department of History
Visva-Bharati, Santiniketan
West Bengal - 731 235

**Suniti Kumar Pathak**
Former Professor
Department of Indo Tibetan
Visva-Bharati, Santiniketan
West Bengal - 731 235

# Introduction

Human society is, broadly speaking, is an understanding of Religion and Literature. It has occupied a great place in the corpus of knowledge of the ancient Indian Civilization. The Indian civilization can not be examined, interpreted and translated without the help of religion and the literature. It is the traditional philosophical faiths, believes which flow to Indian culture and heritage from generation to generation. Religion and literature were complementary to each other for the enrichment of culture and tradition in India. Religion acts a significant role in creating the greatest literature. The Indian literature reflects Indian culture and civilization consisting of traditional beliefs and faith which is *dharma'* or religion. The word "religion" translates into modern Indo Aryan languages is dharma, which means "law". Throughout classical South Asia, the study of law consisted of concepts such as penance through piety and ceremonial as well as practical traditions. The word 'dharma' is derived from the Sanskrit word 'dhr '. The term of 'dharma' does not mean only religion in its narrow sense but it means a universal approach of life which is 'to bind' in Indian tradition. It signifies the 'law of being' and the 'fulfilment of that law'. The word 'Dharma' is one of the comprehensive terms which are playing a key role in the whole Indian literature. At this point, too, the root of the English word "religion", the Latin religio, was in use only to mean "reverence for the God or the Goddess, careful pondering of divine things, piety" (which Cicero further derived to mean "diligence") Max Müller characterized the religion which was a power structure in human history. Religion is the belief in and worship of a god or goddess, or in general a set of beliefs explaining the existence of and giving meaning to the universe, usually involving devotional and ritual observances, and often containing a moral code governing the conduct of human affairs. Aspects of religion include narrative, symbolism, beliefs, and practices that are supposed to give meaning to the practitioner's experiences of life. Whether the meaning centers on a deity or deities, or an ultimate truth, religion is commonly identified by the practitioner's prayer, ritual, meditation, music, art and literature among other things, and is often interwoven with society and politics. It may focus on specific supernatural, metaphysical, and moral claims about reality (the cosmos and human nature) which may yield a set of religious laws and ethics and a particular lifestyle. Religion also encompasses ancestral or cultural traditions, writings, history, and mythology, as well as personal faith and religious experience.

The development of religion has created in various forms literature at different cultures in India. Sociologists and anthropologists tend to see religion as an abstract set of ideas, values, or experiences developed as part of a cultural matrix. George A. Lindbeck, (*Nature of Doctrine*, Louisville: Westminster/John Knox Press, 1984) defines religion as, "a kind of cultural and/or linguistic framework or medium that shapes the entirety of life and thought... it is similar to an idiom that makes possible the description of realities, the formulation of beliefs, and the experiencing of inner attitudes, feelings, and sentiments." According to this definition, religion does not refer to belief in "God" or a transcendent Absolute. But religion refers to one's primary worldview and how this dictates one's thoughts and actions. Thus religion is considered by some sources to extend to causes, principles, or activities believed in with zeal or conscientious devotion concerning points or matters of ethics or conscience, and not necessarily including belief in the supernatural. Although evolutionists had previously sought to understand and explain religion in terms of a cultural attribute which might conceivably confer biological advantages to its adherents, Richard Dawkins called for a re-analysis of religion in terms of the evolution of self-replicating ideas, or memes, apart from any resulting biological advantages they might bestow. Susan Blackmore regards religions as particularly tenacious memes. Chris Hedges, on the other hand, regards meme theory as a misleading imposition of genetics onto psychology. The Brahmanical religion claims that this religion is not afraid of scientific explorations, nor of the technological progress of mankind. According to them, there is a comprehensive scope and opportunity for this religion to mold itself according to the demands and aspirations of the modern world; it has the ability to align itself with both science and spiritualism. This religion uses some modern examples to explain its ancient theories and reinforce its own beliefs. For example, Hindu monks have used the terminology of quantum physics to explain some basic concepts of Hinduism such as Maya or the illusory and impermanent nature of our existence. Religious belief usually relates to the existence, nature, and worship of a deity or deities and divine involvement in the universe and human life. Alternately, it may also relate to values and practices transmitted by a spiritual leader. Unlike other belief systems, which may be passed on orally, religious belief tends to be codified in literate societies (religion in non-literate societies is still largely passed on orally).Religious belief can also involve causes, principles or activities believed in with zeal or conscientious devotion concerning points or matters of ethics or conscience, not necessarily limited to organized religions.Humans have many different methods which attempt to answer fundamental questions about the nature of the universe and our place in it (cosmology). Religion is only one of the methods for trying to answer one or more of these questions. So religion continues to be recognized in East and Western thought as a universal impulse, many religious practitioners have aimed to band together in interfaith dialogue and cooperation. The first major dialogue was the Parliament of the World's Religions at the 1893 Chicago, which remains notable even today both in affirming "universal values" and recognition of the diversity of practices among different cultures. This century has been especially fruitful in use of interfaith dialogue as a means of solving ethnic, political, or even religious conflict through creating religious literature for mankind. So religion and literature accept the strength of the human emotions of love, fear, curiosity, reverence and they both presume and accept the categorical imperative of the conscience and the freedom and force of the will of man. This volume contains thirty three research papers in different areas of the religion and literature in India which includes the following facets like: Brāhmanical Religion and its literature; Śaivaism and Śaiva literature; Vaisnavism and Visnava literature; Saktism and Sākta literature.; Tantra and Tântric literature; Bhakti Religion and Bhakti literature.; Buddhism and Buddhist literature; Jainism and Jaina literature;. Islam and Islamic literature; Sufism and Sufi literature; Folk religion and Folk literature.

So this volume has emerged as the product of research work with a holistic approach to religion and literature in India and it may be a useful reading for those scholars who are working in this area.

1

# Tantra: A Facet of the Indian Culture Pertinent to Religion and Literature

*S.K. Pathak*

Linguistic equivalene of Anglo-vernacular lexicons compiled in India correspond 'religion' with *dharma*. That requires critical observations. Etymologically *dharma* is derived from the verb-root *dhṛti* meaning to hold, to grasp, to catch suggestively, *dharma* is what a person holds and individually, socially or both. To that extent *dharma* may refer to 'religion' as that is used in Christianity partially. The term 'religion' has been known in India since the eighteenth century when the Jesuits and clergies entered.

After the advent of Christianity in Europe a band of people had been religiously avowed to the teachings of the Jesus Christ. Saint Augustine had been chosen by Pope Gregory and was chosen for convey the message of Christianity to Britain with forty monks. He became the Archbishop of Canterbury till he expired in 604 C.E[1]. In the Middle Ages of the European history, Pope, the head of Roman Cathlic exercised great influence over the political affairs of Catholic countries. So Catholic religion and political administration entered in conflicts. That led to the Reformation and Protestant Church to came in existence for compromise with socio-political affairs as an alternative. In due course the political affairs becomes further 'secular' in order to avoid any scope of interference. Karl Marx commented that 'religion was an opium'.[2] However 'religion' is etymologically derived from the Latin *religion*, Old French 'religion' referring to the practice of sacred rites. Here 'sacred' is a hallowed holiness as safeguarded by reverence. Again 'holy' means what is morally and spiritually perfect. 'Religion' has therefore two basic faders morality and spirituality. Despite that, the human societies cannot escape from their adherence to some faith of theirs whether that is instituted with a particular nomenclature identity or not.

In the case of multiethnic inhabitants of Bharatavarsa (Bangladesh, Bharat, Pakistan, Afghanistan) political governance was not administered usually by collective responsibility either be elected or be group chosen. In the ancient days, the alter procedures had been in vogue, but the political system, later on, gave prominence to 'One-person' leadership in Indian Sociology. Since Kautilya's *Arthashasta* and other *Rajaniti* manuals declared 'the duties of a ruler' as *rajadharma.*[3] Because 'dharma' in Indian understanding is the totality of personhood whether individual or social, whether material or spiritual. The expression *dharma* all over the Indian peninsula means the total way of life. That amounts to both ethics and mannerism in respect to the individual at the personal level and the social level as well. That is generalized as *mānavadharma* in numerous contexts like ethics with multiply manners in household life *saṁsāradharma / gṛhastha dharma* in social life. Those in the life of a renunciation *sannyāsa dharma*; those of a wife *stridharma* or those of a husband *patidharma* at the individual life. *Dharma* is therefore of connotation in the Indian Cultural plurality with reference multiple community ethics since the ancient days. It is to note that 'dharma' is of the neuter and masculine genders in the Vedic language and in Classical Sanskrit. That suggests of the evolution in understanding *dharma* was in different concepts. Generally speaking, *dharma* refers to various social ethics with their lien to manners performed singularly or collectively. (See Appendix) Thus the institutional nomenclatures like Vaidika, Buddha, Jaina, Smārta, Shaiva, Shākta, Vaiṣṇava and so on, speak of separate cults in practice of their institionalised organizations with multiple Objective and missions.

## Scripture and *dharma* Literatures

In the context of Christianity, 'scripture' is significant. That refers to the Bible with or without Apocrypha having no article while that had been formulated in Hebrew as the sayings of the Prophet. The scripture therefore suggests what contains doctrines as those had been laid down in the Holy Bible. The collections in writings of original manuscripts of the Bible-containing of thirty nine in the Old Testament and twenty-seven in the New Testament are regarded as a record of God's teaching to humans. The early translations of the Old Testament from Hebrew were made in Latin and these of the New Testament were in Greek. In due course its English translations demand several critical editions with revised versions, of the New Testament (1881) and those of the Old Testament (1884) that may regarded as the latest.

About to religious literatures, in the case of the Indian Culture the scenario is different. For the Indian pluralistic cultures from the second millennium BCE may be broadly distributed in four facets. Those are:

1) Ancient Vedic facet promoted by the seers who are said have visualized their good sayings *sukta* by their Wisdom eyes *prajñācakṣu* or illuminated vision about the phenomenal world and the Beyond as well. Thereafter the *Sūtra* in the aphoristic style of enunciation of theirs formulated a specific kind of literature descended from the

Vedas, or those had been listened and were preserved in committance of listening in generations i.e. *shrautasutra*.

2) Shramana facet deviated from the Vedic fire-ritual culture with animal sacrifice. Gautama the Buddha, Mahavira the Jina, Ajit Kesakambali and others innovated a separate mendicant culture strata from those of the Vedists by circa 6th century BCE. They decried the *grāma* establishments of the Vedic promoters of the then hydralic culture.

3) Since the Indian peninsula had been uneven topographically of diverse elevisions was remours peoples came and settled. Each group had separate faculties to hold diverse culture strata. Those indigenous but pluralistic patterns of culture developed the extensive peoples facet *lokāyata* (*loka* means people and *āyata* extention.)

4) Again, the Indian indigenous groups of multiethnicity used to reside in diverse uneven elevations of the land under the different natural enclosures. They prefer to be close to the Nature around with alienation and alliance. They did witness the violent aspects and the benign aspects of the Nature and avoided the forms for their livelihood. Thereby they either propitiated the crude wrath of deadly enimical Nature for protection or utilize the friendly associating Nature for bestowing material gain and prosperity. Thus, from the virgin physiolatry, Shamanism had generated and that was modified in socio-spiritual upliftment to extend over the three spheres of this Solar Earth namely the surface, the underground, the ethereal space and above. That extensive culture facet at the macro and the micro levels is known as the Tantra facet of the Indian culture. (*tan* is a verb Sanskrit to extend, to weave)

These facets have cross-culturally negotiated through generations ruled by either Oral dedications or literary pursuits, despite their intellectual criticism to acclaim superiority among the followers of each facet. Those competitions promulgate the cultural diversity in quest of conformity in oneness through the rational understanding among one another.

## Tantra or Tantras

For brievity the discussion is limited to Tantra facet of the Indian cultural heritage.[4] Due to plurality in applications of Tantra, as stated. Tantra appears to be multi pronged Tantra may be applied in multiple methods through its objective is one and the same. Tantra is more applied than theoretical to render good and welfare benefit of the cruel face, if required. Methodologically, the observances of Tantra, otherwise Tantras in practice, hold *kriyātantra* of six kinds, *Ṣaṭkarma*: Those are applied under two broad heads,

i) Observance of tantra deeds for peace and harmony, *shāntikarma* for alliance inprapitiation.

ii) Observance of Tantra deeds in challenge and control over the alien crude force of by five major means like (1) Submitting the rival power *vashīkaraṇa*, (2) Dispelling that force ruthlessly *vidveṣaṇa* (3) Stupifying the reacting force to make inactive *stambhana* (4) attracting the negative force to engage for positive function *ākarsaṇa* (5) destroying the antiforce, if not be submitted being attracted or stupefied *māraṇa*. The order in series are not uniform practice as they depend on the efficacy of the antiforce. These factors are common though the measures vary in many respect. These are more psycho-spiritually subjective than physically objective.[5]

## Co-related steps

Thus, the functional aspects of Tantra are relative generally according to the mental efficiency of the person engaged in Tantra deeds. So its action-faction is regarded as the first step for mental make up. The mental power and capacity prompts to generate efficiency in cultivating Tantra facet primarily for its base which is either alienation or alliance. That is called Action Tantra *kriyātantra*.[6]

Again no action is thoroughly furnished unless the mental aptitude corroborates with the daily routine and proper livelihood with moral conduct and discipline of practitioner engaged in good and welfare of others. Unless the potential power is achieved to combat against the antiforce or to spread harmony and peace around this culture facet becomes of no worth. That stipulated lifestyle in Tantra is specific; it is regarded as *caryātantra* or *ācāratantra* to observe in person. This is essential to the above one.

Next comes the choric of unification in respect to a Tantra practitioner at the individual level. It is a serious step that requires strong determination to achieve the goal. Here unification refers to *Yoga* in Indian Sanskritic languages. That aims to experience no duality or to become the 'united one' by thorough concentration having no defalcation with the Nature around at macro and micro levels.

Lastly, a strong willed person in the best of his or her efficiency experiences to know the miserliness of the ego-centricism of each and every alive beings belonging to the phenomenal universe. That knowledge is named *jñāna tantra* as the Supreme Yoga-tantra in which the practitioner equates to others in order to share the relative suffering. So these four measures in Tantra become co-related and interallied with a common goal though they vary in methods to 'address' the cause of defaulters.

## Methods in applications

As diversities in the nature around the humans appear manifold. Numerous methods in applications are relevant in Tantra. A few among them have been identified so far where as many of them are yet 'unidentified'. Among the Identified Tantra prevailing with the Indian people, the following deserves mention.

(i) Vedicized Tantra distributed in five emanations of the Nature in the Indian Peninsula namely,

a) *Saura Tantra* relating to emanation the Solar power as the Vedist's follow:-

b) *Gāṇapatya Tantra* referring to the emanation of minor bio-physical elements under the special superintendence of theirs as a leader.

c) *Vaiṣṇava Tantra* emanating the natural efficacy in maintenance and preservation of this solar universe totally.

d) *Shaiva Tantra* dealing with the emanation of compatible virtues of the nature around the humans in complacency and fierceness as well, like origin and decay, birth and death etc.

e) Again, *Shākta tantra* in emanation in playing the vital role in creation and destruction for keeping the natural properties in balance of potency manifested with feminity.

These five functional emanations of the primary virtues of the Nature around are regarded as *Pāncadaivata tantra* with reference to the Vedic illuminated emanation of natural elements like earth, water, fire, air and space. In the Vedas, eac̣h *mantra* is related to the illuminated emanations of multiple virtues of what the Vedists discovered then. As already stated Tantra refers to the primitive physiolatrical 'nature-worship' in relation to the 'vital forces' of the physical universe. The Vedists could not leave them aside and developed those criteria after casting their shamanic features and occult empowerment. Tantric emanations co-relate to the Vedic illuminated emanations of physical virtue like Sūrya (Rudra) Gaṇapati, Viṣṇu, Soma and Ambikā as defied in the Vedic expression *devatā*.

The Vedic etymological derivation of *deva* and *devatā* suggests to cast, to throw, to conciliate, to play, to spread, to increase in different context. In Classical Sanskrit those significances leave a room to hold *deva / devata* for the emanated manifestations which are deified in benign or fierce forms to bestow grace or wrath. These ideas have been persisting among the Indians of multiethnic populace with love and awe. Subsequently those emanations in numerous forms manifestated either in non icononic arts or in iconic arts to develop the aesthetic factors of the Indian Culture. So the Buddhists and the Jainas could not escape from these popular ideas and they included them in their respective pantheon of deities in plurality at the populace level. But those are in case idotatry.

An account of the acceptance of Tantra by the Buddhists may date back upto the lifetime of the Buddha, if the *parittā suttas* in Pali Pitakas and in application of *uttarimanussa* super human capacity be regarded as the *Buddhavacana*, sayings of the Buddha. It may not relevant to raise the property of these mentions in Pali Tipitaka here. However it may be presumed that after the Pataliputra Council Tatiya sangiti during the life time Ashaka, the Buddhist recluses entered in different regions of the then Bharatavarsa and in the Indo-Greek kingdom *yonaratta* in the northwest. As and when the Buddhist recluses came in contact of numerous indigenous groups, probably they had to adopt some shamanic rituals and practices in course of alienation and alliance with them. Again, the Buddhists prefer to lay greater emphasis on the Ethics of Altruism in promoting the Bodhisattva ideal from the Ethics of Discipline *Vinaya-Kamma* and that of *Moral Conduct Vinaya siladha*. The Mulasarvastivadins followed by the Sarvastivadins of Mathura and Kāshmira had sponsored the Bodhisattva ideal. A large section of Buddhist Mahasanghikas, later on, the Bodhisattvayāra Buddhists, popularly the Mahāyānists, have innovated two separate methods for becoming Bodhisattva and Vajrasattva. Those are

(a) Method of Pāramitā Practice

(b) Method of Mantra Practice

a) the former lays emphasis on observance of benovalence by donation *dāna pāramitā*, that of moral precepts with adequate discipline *shīla pāramitā*, that of tolerance *kṣāntipāramitā*, that of vigour *viryapāramitā* that of meditation with deep *prajña-parāmitā* centraction *dhyānaparamita* and by experiencing the nature of the phenomenal constituted universe being led by Wisdom. The last one is regarded as the essencelessness of all constituted phenomena belonging to the universe otherwise known as *shūnyatā*.

A Bodhisattva is conversant of it by wisdom, *projña*. All these practices are basically attainable by unification *Yoga*, thorough, one-point concentration of the deep consciousness which is as extensive as the infinite space and is as deep as a great ocean.

b) Also some Buddhist practitioners could find out the efficacy of the psycho-somatic vibrations in muttering specific selected *mantra*, syllables belonging to alphabetic symbols of the languages of North India and South India. Thereafter the Method of *Mantra* muttering practice has been regarded a quicker method to achieve the goal of becoming the Buddha than that by the Method of *Paramita* practice of a Bodhisattva. The practitioner of Mantra method is known as *Vajrasattva* or account of his or her adamantive vow of becoming the Buddha, Awakened one.

## *Bindu* and *Brahmacarya*

A citation goes: *maranam bindu patena jivanam bindu dharanat*. Life promotes by preservation of generic semendrop and death is by the dropping of that.

Despite of Vedicization of Tantra, the Smarta school of the Vedists decline to accept the importance of Tantra. They usually charge Tantra is vulger referring to sex-symbolic erotic rituals by declaring non-elite rustic and barbarous rites of the *anaryajana*, other than the Aryans.[7] They usually decry the symbolic union as the lotus and thunderbold *kamala-kulisha samāyoga*, of the Buddhists. In the *Pāncadaivata Tantra* following the lines of the Vedic plurality suggest (1) matsya (fish), madya (wine), (3) māmsa (mean), (4) mudra (delicious presents like food, ornaments etc.), (5) maithuna (cohabitation) in symbolic internal expediments.[8]

Apparently, these go against the general rules of moral conduct in disciplined lifestyle. A practice of Tantra in the radical approach is regarded retrovertive from the normal domestic life in quest of some wonders and astonishment. While inner course of psycho-somatic advancement towards experiencing the Bliss *annda* within, the disciplined practitioner never deviates from the strict vow of restrain *brahmacarya*, the practice of extensive universality. Here *Brahman* refers to the extension in universality.

Among the Jaina Shramanas instituted by Mahavira the Jina (c.6th cent. BCE) the impact of *mantra* is not disowned. They also cultivated rigoristic vows *vrata* faithfully with five discipine *pancakaṣāya* to narture their basic Ethics of Welfare of humankind through purity of the individual. Alike the Buddhists, they also led emphasis on individual plurality of a person who differs from others physically and mentally. Their doctrine of *anekāntavāda* of plurality in individual soul leaves a room of personal endeavours to uplift by disciplined practices in which the muttance of particular *mantra* syllables becomes an aid to avowedness. So in due course the Method of *Mantra* has been fallowed by a section among them along with Discipline.

## Discipline in practice of *mantra* and *tantra*

Discipline in Tantra and mantra Method is essential and that requires extensively practiced by a person involved. In this Method irrespective of the divisions in the Identified Tantra already dealt above strict measures in preserving the human physiological genetic semen *kayavindu* several moral conducts positive *vidhi* and negative *niṣedha* rules have been laid down as those are laid in all religious institutions like Vedic, Buddhist Jaina etc. In Tantra that is neither ignored nor disobeyed in any respect. Any lapse amounts to failure in life. Retrovertive course of practice demands abnormally the general way. It is regarded as from opposite kind of practice *vāmācāra*. The word in constructed of two words *vāma* (left), *vāmā* (feminality) and *ācāra* (practice). It therefore be interpreted as the left or retrovertive practice or a practice with feminality. Those who are involved in this practice should observe strict moral conducts as follow:

1) He or she must be a brahmacarin, tending to restrain the livelihood with no lapse in Preservation of physiological genetic drops. That is regarded as the primary efficacy of becoming *Brahmcarin* or *brahmacarini*. The Buddhists name that *bodhicitta* for the mental state in Awakening. With awareness the Jainas call it *amethuna*.
2) A 'blind looking' at the belongings of others to have them physically or mentally. The Buddhist term reads that 'not to take unless given' or theft. The Jains also follow that.
3) A hermaphrodite in relation to a woman other than wife, in respect to a householder *tantra* practitioner. For a renunciated person, a woman is matherlike to respect.
4) Observe like a dumb person while others in casting censure on others. In this regard *Merutantra* reads: *paradravyeṣu yo'andhashca parastriṣu napumsaka parapāvade yo mukaḥ sarvadā-vijitendriyaḥ*.

In applications of such strict disciplined procedure it demands repeated elucidations among the Tantra practitioners like Vatuka Bhairava, and the followers of Gorakṣanāth, Sitānātha, Matsendranātha among the Shaivites, the Kanṭhadhāri Shaiva Tantrikas, Sir John Woodroffe in his Shakti and Shakta (1957:537) points out that the retrovertive practices are in vogue with the Shākta *tantra*. The Buddhists and the Jains in modalitics separate from each other. The practice in Shakta *tantra* is named the practice of Five in Realities *pañcatattva*.

*Rudra yamala* condidly describes the *cakra* wheel-discipline for self-examination

1) A competent *yoginī* before a capable *yogī* practitioner be seated in presence of the Master engaged in didaction.
2) Among the other materials, a pot of wine, non vegetarian snacks and pills etc.
3) Melodious tuning of lutes be played on as background music.

The significance implied in the verse is stated as *vāmācāraḥ paramagahano yoginamaphagama* the retrovertive practice is so deep as the efficient *yogin* finds difficult to follow.

The Buddhist counts four states of the practice in wheel *gaṇacakra* and that appears in the four positions of twaining in oneness *yugala* namely (i) To be intimated *sāmīpya* (ii) To close up *sālokya* (iii) To form an unit *sārūpya* and (iv) To be unified *sāyujya*. Depending on threefold disciplinary practices by an initiated person like the mundane behaviours *prapañca-caveyā*, the behaviours having no-murdaneness to fall in decay *nis-praparicacaryā* and, lastly, the behaviours beyond the above two *atinispapañca-carya* a practitioner enters into the last status of the above fourth one having no ascillation vibrative duality in friction to perceive objectively. A state of the fourth Bliss is availed with no knowledge of I-ness and otherness of a person.

A unification here means the union of one with other in oneness. The word *yoga* implies a union or becoming one. Arithmetically, one plus one become two. Tantra teaches spiritually how one plus one is one. That is the case of unification.[9] It is a practical experience to be in four stages as referred above. That requires multiple experiments physically and mentally how to achieve the spiritual oneness prior to demonstrate for becoming competent and capable in self-examination restrained discipline. It is not attainable by philosophy nor by epistemology. Tantra, being one, holds multiple methods how to overcome the notion of plurality, those of duality and those of philosophical absolute monism. So many methods, so many adaptations among the practitioners whether those belong to the identified Tantra or to the Un-identified Tantra become occasionally puzzlesome.

The Saivaites describe such status of experience in the Deep Psyche in a symbolic manifestation of Half-male and half-female *ardhanārīshwara*. The Sramanas like the Buddhists state that a unification in equity of psychic status with no wavering *samatayoga* in the course practice *prajnapaya-samayoga*.

## Cultivation of the human psychic layers

Evidently, the Tantra facet claims its primacy on account of exhaustive cultivation of the human psychic layers with rigors but unfettered. The practitioners of Tantra never enter in philosophical discourse nor epistemological catechism nor logical debating. In most cases a capable never allows to be known to others what she or he performs in a solitary place or inside a close room. That discreet inquiry of the individual mind to extend as much as his or her capability allows is the wonder to them who are unaware. Only the capable one estimates the psychic measures in cultivating one's mind. It holds three major processes for extending one's mental capacity by overseeing the tender neuro-sensibility of his or her comate in the same formulae in practice. In course of cultivation of the psychic field normally a practitioner follow some principles.

1) Willingness to involve in quest of knowledge of reality, what deems fit according to the guide and the incumbent, i.e. *guru* and *shiṣya*.
2) Involvement is determinable through rituals for examining the strong willingness of some events which may be either palatade to hold or not. Despite that, the physiological neuro-muscular tensions must be equamined by strict moral conduct and disciplined restrain as levied on. Those break down and demolish the previous structure of psychic make up in the latent layer of a person's Dearms in that state of may become significant to follow as much as possible. That may be regarded the ploughing on the normal empirical mind.
3) Persistence in psycho-spiritual drive with zeal and vigour in the concentrating psychic oscillations to complacency for a longer duration with the least possible discharge on the functional state of the practitioner's mind enters in the psyche 'Deep Layer' as

much as it concentrates until some vision appears depending on positive or negative norm. A Tantra practitioner claims to be relieved and released from the mental latency.

The above experiment with the individual empirical mind as the practitioner claims to undergo may, record three states.

1) To listen to the guide in thorough mindfulness.
2) To ponder with restrain morally, physically and mentally with no bias.
3) To concentrate fathomlessly what is to ponder until a vision appears.

In description of the vision, oneself finds within own self as if manifested in a form despite of its no form. Thus Tantra becomes wonderous to others as the practitioner achieves the capability of looking within having no real which functions in an average mind. For neuro-muscular psychological exercise to overcome sickness of functional mind of the average, a Tantra practitioner avails a state of complaceant bliss to remain unaltered and pacified in rendering welfare service, as required with undaunted freedom.

## Plurality in the Tantra Literature

As and when the Tantra facet of culture has not been institutional religion like Hinduism, Buddhism, Jainism, Sikhism, Islam or Christianity, some identified Tantra practitioners have left their experiences in the form of treatises for their followers to use. Traditional literatures, belonging some esoters like Vaiṣṇava, Shaiva and Shākta claim that they hold Āgama and Nigama teachings by Viṣṇu, Shiva and Shivani (Pārvati) respectively. Some of them, critically speaking, appear to be with pre-historic materials when Tantra had not been regarded as a separate branch of human learning. In that respect, the Vedicization of Tantra in Indian Sociology is important.

'Agama' refers to a vast literary resource found in Tamil, Prakrit and Sanskrit. Pashupata Sutra of the Shaiva cult (c.4th cent. CE) refers to the treatises which come down from Shri-mahesware in the lineage of masters and their disciples. Among them, *Tamil-agama* otherwise *Dramila Veda* of *Periyapuranam* ascribed to Sekkilar (c.12th cent. C.E.) mentions that Saiva Tantric devout authors account among the Shavites of Tamilnadu since the hoary ancient days. About the Prakrita āgama texts of Tantra the Jainas took measures. Āgamas are distributed in two categories like Vedic and non-Vedic (Appendix). It may be noted that 'āgama' used in the sense of resource. The Sarvastivadin Buddhists[10] and the Jains used 'agama' for Buddha vacana and Jina vacana respectively presumably Agamas as the Tantric Literature suggests the 'resources', prior to their cult-divisions.

Apart from the traditional cultwise divisions of Tantra Literature geographic distributions of the Tantra treatises are to be noted. That is comprehensive to follow the growth. Three are:

i) *Viṣṇukrāntā*: The eastern region of Bharatavarsa from Vindhya mountain to Caṭṭala the easternmost centre on the bank of Karnaphuli river. Obviosly Bangāla (East Bengal) and Ladabhūmi (West Bengal) included. The Ventilation of Shakta esoters.

ii) *Rathakranta*: The northern region of Bharatavarsa from Vindhya mountain to Mahācīna including Kailasa Mansaravara and Nepal.

iii) *Ashvakrāntā*: The southern region of Bharatavarsa including the eastern and the western mountainous ranges along the Bay of Bengal and Arabian Ocean respectively. In this regard, *Mahāsiddhasāra* of late origin (c. 13th cent CE) reads the jurisdiction from the Karatoya river belt to Java island (Javadvipa) in South East Asia.

Similar divisions according the *Piṭha,* seat of accomplishment like *Vidyā pīṭha, Mantrapīṭha, Mudrāpīṭha, Maṇḍalapīṭha* help is to locate. The Bhairava tantra and Yamāla tantra belong to the *Vidyapitha* are said to have developed applied Vidyā. This norm of division is based on the methods of practices differently in which *vidya* is prominent. *Vidyā* in esoter Tantra is significant to denote the perfect knowledge to achieve by sustained efforts to know the knowable. Tantra is an experimental methodology. So *Tantrashāstra*, the treatises on Tantra are numerous and distributed in many lines of practice by pluralistic societies of India either at individual level and at community level.

The classifications with reference to the five major *Shākta* Tantra the *amnāya* and the mother-deities therein are significant to trace their mutuality. Such as,

The Eastern āmnāya: Shrividyā group like Tārā, Tripurā, Bhuvaneshvari, Annapruṇā etc.

The Western āmnāya: Mahālakṣmī-vidya group like Sarasvati deity of speech, Pratyangira, Bhavani etc.

The Sourhtern āmnāya: Bagalāmukhi vidyā group Balabharavi (Vashita) Dhanadalaksmi, Mahisamardini (Mahisaghni)

The Northern āmnāya: Kālikā vidyā group. Mātangitarā, Bhairavi, Chinnamastā Dhūmavatī etc.

The Upper āmnāya: Parāvidyā group Ṣoḍashī.

These five āmnāya: Vidyā traditionally refers to five faces of Shiva. The Master of Letters for pronouncing them in course of muttering *mantra* in correlation between the multiple *mantra*-sounds pronounced through the vocal organs of the animate. Those who count the sixth āmaya *Divyagarna*, a later text regarding the Mother enumerates the accessories for Tantra rituals like the body posture of practitioners, garland, food offerings sacrifice, *mantra* accomplishment, retributory manualite. *Parā vidyā* in Tantra practice is ragarded supreme accomplishment for liberation and oppositely *aparavidya* in Tantra practice devote to the rituals for instrumentation other than esoterism.

Again the *kula* or family divisions are significant[11]. In this respect a large number of Tantra texts of Indian and of Chinese origins are preserved in the Tibetan translations. As regards the compositional structure of the treatises on Tantra whether Buddhistic, Jaina, Pāñcadaivata, or of indigenous groups like Shavara, Kinnara, Gandharva, Yakha, Dāka, Dakini, Gāruḍa etc. noteable distinction are observed.

## Cultural dimensions of Tantra

As one of the four facets of culture in India Tantra has played a multi dimensional role. Some of them are enumerated below.

1) *Material aspect*: Numerous cult worships prevailing among the identified Tantra practitioners have left a spacious scope to multifarious material growth; like temples, icons of deities made of clay, stone, metal, utensils and various accessories, for daily and occasional worship, weaving of clothes and dresses in different colours, crafts of preparing manifold decorative objects made of food, paper, etc.

   Thereby economic growth by commercial marketing among different trade guilds in rural and urban areas appeared in most case. Also, fairs and festivals in connection with Tantric worship occasions promote in high order at the wider level since the ancient days.

2) *Aesthetic enterprises with creative themes*

   As regards the icon-making arts developed among Indians at various levels may claim excellence on account the practice of numerous deity worship recommended by numerous Tantra treatises. That makes a room for aesthetic craftsmanship of multiple order.

3) *Agro-economic development*

   Tantra prescribes seasonal ritualistic deity worship throughout the year in which the agro-economic prosper. Bharatvarsa until the advent of the Europeans was regarded as an agrobased hydraulic peninsula with multiethnic population. Several tantric worshipping occasions have been made among rural agrobased communities with multiple rituals, like worship of cattles, worshipping fests for new crops, worship of forest deities to safeguard the domestic animals like goats, sheep etc.

4) Last but not least, Tantra holds an indigenous therapeutic method. That develops many curative methods with herbal medicines including *Mantra* to recite with some curative values. Longevity rituals for trance be referred, in practice as those are in vogue among the Tantra-experimentists widely.

## Notes and References

1. St. Augustine (354-430 A.D.) was a bisop of Hippo in North Africa. It was baptized by Ambrose, he left for North Africa. He spent the next thirty-years of his life and died while the Vandals Heppo. His conception regarding God and the person of Jesus had a Neo-platonic tinge to understand God as Real. The physical world holds a derived reality. Those ideas enlightened the British when the Roman Catholic Church adopted the Augustine Theology. His '*Confessions*' and *The City of God* may be regarded important contributions.
2. The Protestant Radicals had geared the Reformation Movement led by Martin Luther and Zwingli. They emphasised on 'reason' than the 'Word of God', A new turn of Anabaptists literally 'rebaptizers' preferred to grasp clearly the meaning of each aspect of the Christian life and practice. The New Testament got priority in understanding the principle how to overcome evil with good, instead of resisting one injury with another. Karl Marx and the Western Humanist Movement leaders preferred to dissolution of religion as a social process. In spreading Materialism a tone of apathy towards 'religion' is to note among a section of Europeans like Karl Marx.
3. Prior to Kautilya who is said to be political Advisor of Chandragupta the Maurya decried the people's governance *gaṇa* which had prevailed in North India during the lifetime of Gautama the Buddha and Mahavira the Jina (c. 6th cent. BCE.).
4. Four culture facets in Indian Sociology have continued among the Hindu since the Vedic age; Vedic distributed in two varieties based on *Shrauta* scriptures, and on *Smṛiti* ethical treatises. 2. *Shrāmaṇa* mendicant facet preferring to the culture of poverty like Buddhist, Jaina, Ajivaka

etc. 3. *Lokayatika* facet belonging to the indigenous groups among the Indian populace with their least scribed materials to identify and the *Tantra* facet. Culture facets of the Muslims, the Jews and the Christians in India may be dealt separately. (Reference: Models of Civic Awareness in Ancient India, pp. 61-72 by the author in *Civil Society in Indian Cultures* eds. Asha Mukherjee et al. Indian Philosophical Studies VI. The Council for Research in Value & Philosophy, Washington D.C. 2001).

5. *Shānti-vashya-stambhanadi vidveṣo ccātane Jaṭhā/māraṇaṁ parameshādi ṣaṭakameva pakīrtitam//yoginitanta Part I, p.4.*
6. In Sanskritic diction *tantra* means 'widening', 'extension'. Any conception extending widely is termed as '*tantra*' in the Indian literatures like Astronomy, *Sankhya* system of Indian Thought etc. Here 'tantra' is used for esoteric practices and accomplishment for extention of the human potentiality. The treatises in the Indian literature are regarded as the tantra scripture distributed in two broad discussions, *agama* and *nigama*. Kamikā-Āgama reads: *tanoti vipulān arthān tantra-mantra samanvitān//trāṇam Kurute yasmat tantram ityabhidhiyate//*

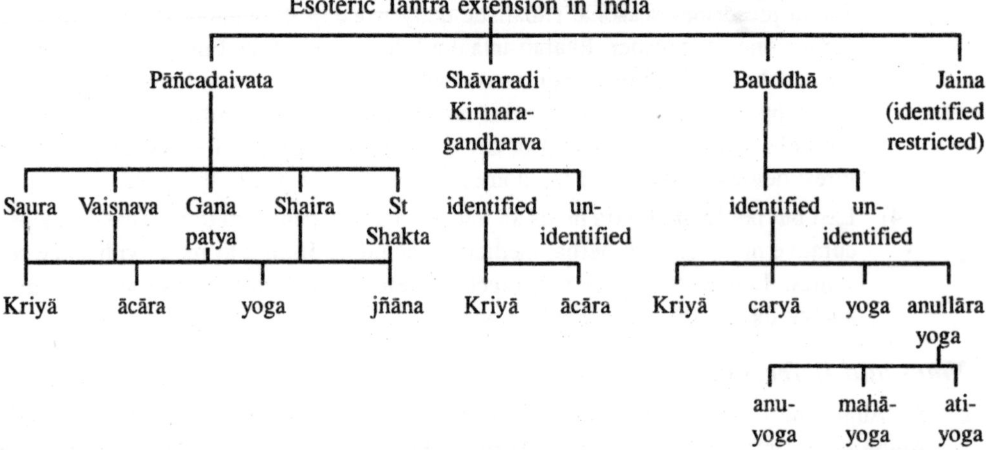


7. The Vedist Aryans *arya* claimed their superiority being elevated by white skin colour in contrast to others like Dravida or Dramila, Kinnara, Shavara, Yaksa, Gandharva, etc. who had been in different topographical regions since hoary olden days. The non-Aryans *anārya* had not been white, rather of twany and dark coloured skin owing to ethnic plurality. They were mostly physiolator for their close association with the Nature around through her alienation and alliance indegene. The Vedic people who had lien to the Shrauta Ashramika forest dwelling up hill the first millennium BCE preferred to accept the physiolatry applied for self preservation and self sustenance as and when required. The Shrauta Ashramika fold among the Vedists explored the Great Potent power *Mahādevi* as the over-all potent power for illuminating the psycho-physical prowess and vigour of the animate being after the Vedicization of Tantra. Thus the Tantra facet of the Indian Culture adapted all communities whether the *ārya*, Aryan or the non-Aryan *anārya*.
8. Among the practitioners of esoteric behaviors *ācāra* two regulations are followed (i) Dakṣina ācāra the pro-Vedic behaviours with social acceptance (ii) Vāma-ācāra, anti-Vedic reverse to the social order. Those are in the Sanskritic diction Five-Ms. Such as 1. *madya* wine; 2. *māmsa* meat; 3. *matsya* fish; 4. *mudra* fried corn/pulse, 5. *maithuna* copulation. A Smārta householder usually repulses against those obnoxious antisocial behaviours of the esateric Tantra practitioners.

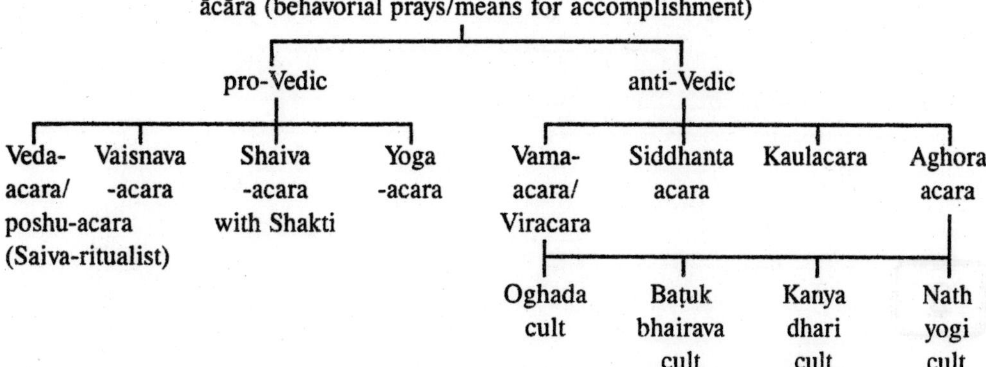


The antivedic Vāmācara has offshooted from the non-Aryan Gandharva tantra and Pishaca tantra practices. Alternatives of the Five-Ms are required for the pro-Vedic practitioners and householder in course of Shakti-worship.

9. For the Buddhist non-dualistic Tantra practice *advaya tantra*, the *Kālacakra Tantra* be referred. *Hevajra Tantra* with its commentary yoga-*ratnamala* and *Guhyasamaja tantra* deal with Yogatantra with duality to proceed in the order of generation *utpannakrama*.
10. The Buddhists contributed in Apubhramsha Tantra Literature by the Siddhas like Saraha, Kanha, Bhusuku, and others. Many of them are available in the Tibetan translations. Caryagiti Kasha edited by Prabodh Chandra Bagchi, Dahakasha edited by Rahula Sankrityayana with Hindi rendering are to mention.
11. Family *Kula* divisions in Tantrā open multi dimensions of literary treatises. Pānch-daivala tantrā,

    *Kaula jnananirnaya* ed. Probodh Ch. Bagchi 1934

    *Kaucavalitantram* ed Rasik Mahan Chattopadhyay

    *Kaulavali-nirnaya* ed. Arthur Avalon. (Tantirk Text Series No.1)

    *Kaula-marga-rahasya* Satish Ch. Siddhanta Bhusan.

    Buddhist texts on families in Tantra and Literature may referred to S.K. Pathak, Kula in the Indo-Tibetan Literature in *Tantric Buddhism Centenary Tribute to Dr. Benaytosh Bhattacharya* ed. N.N. Bhattacharya.

2

# Yoga and the Ancient Indian Method of Stress Management

***Pranabananda Jash***

Stress has a long history, perhaps as old as mankind itself. It is an inseparable ailment of human mind and almost all of us experience stress at some point in our lives, in some form or the other. Of course, there is hardly any specific term for'Stress' in the Āyuraveda, but one gets a concept of stress and its management from the Indian epics, puranas, early Indian classical texts, especially the Sutra-Sastra literature. According to Indian way of thinking, when one gets caught between *kleśas* (stressors), *duhkha* arises. *Duhkha* is the nearest parallel to the concept of stress. Disturbance in the mind breeds physical repercussions and vice versa. The idea of health is not just absence of disease but presence of mental peace and tranquility as well. All this was known to the ancient Indians without the favour of the modern technology.

As far as the scientific thought on the concept of stress is concerned, there is no denying the fact that physics, particularly to Hooke's Law regarding elasticity,has opened a new vista for its approach through scientific perspective. The important point to be derived from this is that whether a particular situation will be stressful for an individual. Stress therefore lies in the mind of a person. In an excellent article on *Neurosciences and philosophy,* G.C.Pande, Chairman of the Indian Institute of Advanced Studies, Shimla, comments that "the ancient science of Yoga formulates a science of the mind which is practical and testable."[1]

The consequences of stress can be various, affecting one physiologically, emotionally, behaviourally or cognitively. Physiologically, stress affects the heart rate, respiration, blood pressure, and digestion, among other things; the emotional consequence leads to anxiety, anger and depression. And Professor Pande thus points out "Although the search for the physical basis of human personality and behaviour has been as old as mankind, the break throughs which have been achieved in recent years through the development of neuro-science have produced a revolution act only in therapy,but also thrown a challenge to philosophical thinking."[2]

The Yoga system which could be translated as 'spiritual meditation' or 'transcendental meditation' is traceable as early as the time of the Harappan civilization. The posture of a 'proto-type' of Śiva-Paśupati or Yogīśvara in one of the famous clay-seals from the Harappan culture bears unquestionable testimony of the oldest popularity of the Yoga model of stress management in India. In fact, this appears to be the most sophisticated model of the ancient Indians to approach the phenomenon of stress. Although scattered and sporadic references to this model are found in the classical literature, particularly in the epics and the puranas. But it is the *Yoga-Sūtra* of Patanjali along with notable commentaries on it that presents the most scientific and coherent system of Yoga.[3]

There are various kinds of Yoga in reference but they are hardly codified in systematic manner. The *Mantra-Yoga* is regarded as the system of the ritualistic, and emphasizes the way of union between the individual and the supreme soul through beauty. The *Bhakti-Yoga* or the meditation through devotion; the *JñānaYoga* or the method of knowledge; and also the *Haṭha-Yoga* which is known for its spectacular asceticism to its followers. It is largely connected with bodily austerities and hardships, and breathing exercises calculated to stimulate the spiritual faculties.

Patañjali while dealing with the Yoga model for spiritual elevation analysed the nature of man in the traps-personal state, and considered all individual attributes to be limitation to which the mind becomes attached. The Yoga psychology of '*citta*', i.e. mental condition, is probably similar to those modern Psycho- analytical theories which ascribe all psycho life to self-motivated impulses, and describe human behaviour to be the result of his animal instincts. But unlike those theories, Yoga offers to one a path of liberation from that state: a way to react a state of full awareness, of being the master of one's motivation. It opens an avenue for transcendening their life for higher goals.[4]

It is stated that "Yoga too like neuroscience seeks to apply its results to curing man of his mental defects but there is a difference in these methods and levels of operation. For Yoga the common individual with his ego-centric desires and aversions and identification with the body suffers from a deep existential malaise rooted in a false notion of the self. Yoga trains the mind to attain one-pointed tranquility which enables pure consciousness to see itself as distinct from the mental states and the body. This also leads to the awakening of the latent powers of the self which are manifested in paranormal experiences. The instrument of Yoga is the sustained and detached one-pointed absorption of the mind which is capabale of revealing the subtle ideal essences of phenomena."[5]

The conventional Indian psychology lays stress on the development of will, and on the individual's potential power of bringing out his inner strength. It explains that tensions arise because of ignorance, which is also termed as *māyā*. The success in the resolution of tensions is related to the understanding of the goal of human life and to the power one possesses for attaining it. To gain this understanding one has to adopt a technique that prescribes certain psycho-physical discipline. With the development of mental power, one gains the perception of reality directly and not through the sense organs.[6] The Yoga psychology also explains that in man there is a basic urge for eternal happiness, and that the destructive tendencies are the result of the perverted application of this basic urge. So there are two main aspects of this psychological technique – one is the realization of the supreme goal of the life and the other is the cultivation of detachment and ceaseless effort to undergo the necessary discipline.

It should be noted in this connection that the supreme aim of life is to realise *Parāmartha*, which implies the manifestation of divinity that is already in man. It stands for the realization of *Ātman* or *Brahman* or *Ātman-jñāna* or the attainment of *Nirvāṇa*. Tensions will prevail as long as the primary end of human life remains materialistic and hedonistic. Moreover "the objects of sense enjoyment change; and man himself, the subject of enjoyment, changes also. If he thinks that in this finite world he can have continuous sense pleasure as he likes, he is bounds to be frustrated and full of tensions."[7] Also, the material objects being limited, the pursuit after them is tempted to lead to competition, to give rise to preferences, to damage the individual's sense of proportion and to warp his understanding.

A close scrutiny of the *Yoga-Sūtra* of Patañjali demonstrate that mind played a vital role in the human anatomy, and he thus emphasies on the role and activities of *citta* (mind) in Yoga: *Yoga-cittavṛtti-nirodhaḥ dṛashtuḥ svarūpe 'vasthānām*,[8] i.e. 'Yoga is the suppression of' the activities of the mind, for then the spectator abides in his own form; and at other times there is identity of form with the activities.' This shows the soul in its true form is only the spectator of the mind's activities. The contact of the soul with the mind creates consciousness and then the soul appears to experience; emotions but when absorbed in deep meditation, the mind ceases to have its activities and the soul remains in its nature. This isolation *(kaivalya)* of the soul is sole object of Yoga.

Patañjali holds that there are five states of *antahkaraṇa*[9] or mind:

*Kshite* - the extreme restless state full of emotional tensions;

*Mudha* - an enert state where low passions prevail;

*Vikshipta* - partly concentrated state;

*Ekāgra* - concentrated state;

*Niruddha* - superconscious state.

According to him, these states of mind are made up of various conscious and unconscious emotions. Consequently, the mind has different and varying tendencies. Tension prevails in the first three states of mind. It results when the mind suffers from indecisiveness in relation to the varying and conflicting emotions. Since mind is regarded as an instrument of perception, one can not realise the ultimate truth if it is unstable. *Paramārtha* as the fundamental principle stabilises the mind.

The *Yoga-darśana*[10] distinctly categories the five *Bhūmis* (stages) of the *citta* (mind):

*Kshipta*-agitated;

*Vikshipta*-distracted;

*Muḍha*- inactive

*Ekagra* - concentrated.

These various categories of mind are very much active in human affairs, and one has to overcome the influence and impact of the activities of mind for the achievement of ultimate reality. It is stated that the *cittc* of a man in the wakeful state (*jāgratāvasthā*) is generally in the *Kshipta* a stage. One gets the fifth stage, i.e. *Niruddha* or super-conscious state in the *Asamprajñāta Samādhi* (*Samādhi* where one is not conscious of any object). The fourth stage, i.e. *Ekāgra* or the concentrated state is the stage of the mind in the *Samprajñāta Samādhi* (*samādhi* where one is conscious of an object). This stage is connected with the wakeful state only. When a man is completely absorbed in an action or concentrates on an object, this stage is called *Samprajñātāvasthā* (*Samyak prakāśena jñāyate yasminnasam Sampra-jñātāvasthāh tadbhinnaḥ Asamprajñātah*).

These two stages,*Ekāgra* and *Niruddha* are connected with the *Samprajñāta-samādhi* and the *Asamprajñāta-samādhi* respectively. The former as explained by Vācaspati Miśra, the *vṛttis* coloured by *rajas* as and *tamas* of the *citta* are suppressed and only the *vṛtti* of the *sattva* remains predominant. But in the *Asamprajñāta-samādhi* the *vṛttis* of all the *guṇas* including the *sattva* are suppressed. Thus when all the *vṛttis* of the *citta* are controlled, *Asamprajñāta-samādhi* results and when the *sattva* remains predominant there would be *Samprajñāta-samādhi*. (*Vyasabhashya-ṭīkā* on *Yoga-sūtra*, I.i.)

The nature of the *Samprajñāta-samādhi* is further explained by the fact that this *samādhi* associated with *vitarka* (argumentation), *vicāra* (deliberation), *ānanda* (joy), and *asmita* (the sense of being)-(*Yoga-sūtra*,1.17). As is described in the *Yoga-bhāshya* the *Samprajñāta-samādhi* is that which makes a *sadbhūta-ārtha* (a beautiful object) illuminated in the concentrated mind, destroys the *klesass*, (hindrances) weakens the bonds of *karma* and takes the mind towards the *Niruddha* or the super-conscious state.

Thus by setting the attainment of the knowledge of God or self-knowledge as the primary aim of life, the conventional Yogic psychologists try to remove the causes of maladjustment which exists due to the varying conditions of life. The idea that all men are the manifestations of God enables the individual to minimise tensions and stress in impersonal relations also. For such an idea tends them to realise that their interests are not basically different. This minimises competition. But this does not mean that sense pleasure is totally abnegated; it is subordinated to *Paramārtha* for the realisation of ultimate Reality.

The aspect of the Yogic psychological technique prescribes the cultivation of the detached outlook and the adoption of disciplines. It regards mind and body interdependent: a change in the mind also brings in the body, and vice versa. Thus certain dietary regulations are prescribed to keep the body in such a state that may helpful for development and enrichment of the mind. It is stated that the practice of Yoga is associated with fasting Sometimes the use of herbs is recommended for producing supernatural powers.[10] Fasting is taken to only to suppress passions and evil thoughts. Similarly, some specific mental training is also prescribed for the physical health. The immediate object of *Kriyā-yoga* which deals with the method of mental discipline is to destroy five evils- viz., ignorance, egoism, desire, aversion and love of life and it consists in asceticism and calm submission to God.

This aspect of the technique is ascribed to Yoga. As mentioned earlier, Patanjali distinctly mentioned that Yoga means full control and unification of *cittavṛittis* or mind stuff; it reveals Truth. Corresponding to four types of human mind or *antaḥkaraṇa*, viz., intellectual, emotional, active and meditative are four main *Yogas*. The intellectual type of seeker adopts the intellectual method of knowing truth. This method implies *jñāna yoga*. In this method, non-essentials and transitory phenomena are clearly distinguished from essential and the permanent, which is Truth. It therefore requires a strong will-power which controls emotions. The individual having the emotional type of mind follows *bhakti-yoga* which implies love and devotion. He directs his emotions towards the ultimate Reality. To achieve the concentration of mind, he adopts the technique of repeating the name of God. Similarly, the *karma-yoga* is related to action. The individual in this aspect engages himself in action with a sense of duty, without any attachment to the results. He realises Truth through action. He sees its manifestation in all living beings and serves them. The meditative individual follows *rāja-yoga*. This process unifies all mental states and integrates the mind. It lays stress on the fact that psycho-physical disciplines are essential for mental development. Hence the emphasis on *haṭha-yoga* practices in the beginning.

In the *rāja-yoga*, there are eight steps to the perfect state of super consciousness[11]:-

*Yama* or mental control;
*Niyama* or physical regulation and mental training;
*Asana* or posture;
*Pranayama* or control of breath;
*Pratyahara* or withdrawal of mind from sense objects;
*Dharana* or concentration;
*Dhyana* or meditation; and
*Samādhi* or super consciousness.

*Yama* signifies ethical observance and mental control. *Niyama* is related to physical cleansing and dietary regulations and some form of mental training. The first two processes of the *rāja-yoga* are generally considered as the purificatory practices for higher mental development. Self-control is prescribed for the tranquilit of the mind.

It is interesting to note that those emotional urges which create tensions and stress are transformed through it. Non-killing truthfulness, non-stealing, continence, internal and external purification, contentment, and self-control constitute the *Yama* and *Niyama* stages. *Āsana*, the practice of posture of relaxation or non-tension and *Prāṇāyāma*, the breathing exercises, aim at releasing the neuro-muscular system and pacifying the restlessness of the mind. *Dhāraṇa*, the practice of concentration and the *Dhyāna*, the practice of meditation, aim at the development of will-power. *Dhyāna* strengthens the conviction that man is basically divine, and develops the perception to realise the self. Tensions and mental stress are resolved when the will is integrated and its power of concentration is manifested on the divine. All these practices primarily aim at the realisation of the Ultimate Reality.

By *dhyānam* there is 'unobstructed illumination'; one visualises oneself like the sun or the moon. Through meditation (*dhyāna*) one becomes enabled to penetrate and assimilate the real essence of things and the mysteries of the infinite; it elevates to the transcendent silent realm of the *aśabdam* or 'soundless'. It is the access to 'holiness'. Where as the mind, when incarnates tee in a human body, is the cause of the driving force of the five senses, continuously in thought-formation activity, its discarnate state is a state of quiescence, comparable to its condition in the highest of *dhyāna* when sit united to a human body. *Dhyāna* is the highest contemplation.

It is the steady endeavour to bring the mind into harmony with all, that is, it is a deliberate effort to eliminate egoism and be lost in the truth.[12]

The Yoga discipline that is, the purification of body, mind, and soul is to prepare the individual for the beautific vision. There is an interesting passage in the *Yoga-sūtra* of Patañjali mentioning-*Siddhadarśanam*[13], i.e. vision of the *Siddhaḥ* (meaning those who have attained their goal, are perfect and 'beautified', endowed with 'preternatural' faculties) the text states that as a result of *pratibhā* -the Yogin can discern. All (the totality): *Pratibhād va sarvam*.

The *Yoga-sūtra*[14] and the commentaries on it clearly explained that when, in virtue of the perpetual sacrifice of the personal man, the spiritual man is realised, there awakes in him those powers the physical counterparts of which we know in the empirical world; there arises an intuitive knowledge of the subtle or concealed or remote, whether past or future; one has-access to supernal sounds, consciousness of supernal colours, flavour etc. The central organ (*manaḥ*) and the organs of hearing, feeling, sight, taste and smell are in each single case in direct causal relation with the supernal sounds etc. and with the intuitive knowledge called *pratibhā*.

In Patañjali's Yoga system of thought *pratibhā* is therefore the supreme faculty of 'omniscience' which is evolved through a continued practice of concentration on the self as appearing in the form of the phenomenal ego. "It is said that as practice continues, and before the glory of the final illumination yet breaks forth, there dawns...., in the fashion of the effulgence of the morning sun before the actual rise of the orb above the horizon, an unspeakable splendour in which the entire universe stands fully revealed. It is a vision in eternity, simultaneous, truthful, all-comprehending; and serene. It is, so to speak the vision of the many as reflect in the mirror of the one, and although there is still predominance of multiplicity it at this stage so thoroughly infused with the unity that it is in a sense identical with it." The authorities on Yoga explained that when one goes beyond the first two stadia of ecstasy and concentrates one's *citta* (mind comprising the sense faculties) on one's phenomenal ego, i.e. the subject of relative consciousness (*asmitā*) as illumined by the light of the spirit, one becomes self-conscious, that is to say one attains to a state of subjective intuition.

At the same time it also integrates will, emotion and thought. Specially, concentration brings out the *saṁskāras* or the hidden unconscious tendencies of the individual into light which strengthen one's mind and provide one with an insight to trace the causes of one's tension. Through *samādhi* or superconscious realisation, the knowledge of the Ultimate Reality is acquired. "Truth is attained in its integral unity of existence."

Mind can express itself most fully when it is totally integrated and illumined. Through the practices of concentration and meditation, it can transcend even the limits of nervous system and can directly reach the superconscious state where it perceives Reality. Due to the Yoga practices, the nerve tissues of the body are transformed. The unification of physical and mental forces results in emotional balance. To experience the superconscious state, that is, *samādhi*, is to possess the whole mind-conscious, subconscious and superconscious. The unified mind becomes the centre of power.

Indian philosophers like Aurobinda, Ramanna Maharishi, R. Radhakrishnan and others have convincingly pointed out that the nature of consciousness as the fundamental reality of the universe can be realised only through Yoga and that such realisation constitutes the evolutionary goal of nature and man. Consciousness is in itself timelessly absolute but in time it freely involves itself in matter and then evolves through life and mind to the supramental Overmind and Supermind.

The traditional Indian psychological technique stresses the realisation of self for the resolution of stress and this realisation necessitates the integration of personality. Personality is integrated by harmonising emotion intellect and will. It is transformed when the individual's outlook is directed towards the higher or spiritual plans. The harmony of emotion, intellect and will essentially needs self-control, and self-control needs a sound philosophy, a supreme objective of life. The emphasis on duty in place of right cultivates cooperation and the emphasis on the understanding of the divinity in every individual and on service accentuates this sense of duty and minimizes competition.

All mental stresses and tensions arising out of anxiety, fear, frustration or aggressions are resolved as the personality is integrated. Anxiety as a cause of stress cannot be uprooted if the individual's desires remain on sensate level; such circumstances only multiply tensions. Anxiety arises when the urges of the individual are pervarted and become disproportionate and out of balance. By elevating the outlook to higher or spiritual level, the individual allots every urge its proper place, and sets the balance right. The practice of concentration develops will power and brings out the hidden powers of the mind. Anxiety vanishes with the development of the will through such practice, and the individual becomes transformed. Similarly, the higher consciousness eliminates fear and thereby stress arising of it. Fear is chiefly caused by ignorance of the real nature of man. The realisation of the divinity of man in the oneness of existence becomes the true solution of the problem of fear. Frustration is caused when the individual desires for more, but is unable to get. The nature of man should be changed so as to prompt him to seek bliss and not pleasure; and bliss is attained only when the individual becomes aware of his true nature. 'When anyone proceeds in a search for bliss, he becomes satisfied. He attains a state of mind which dissolves frustration.'

Sometimes the idea of spiritual development by process of meditation is inextricably bound up with religion and morality. Meditation is regarded as a method of making a personal link with a personal aspect of the deity. Patañjali approaches the subject from an entirely different angle. He regards meditation as a method of training human consciousness in such a way that it can function at levels other than the ordinary range through a wider compass.

To conclude, Yoga is not a training in the tenets of any particular faith or belief, but an exercising of the spiritual faculty of man, an expansion of his capacity to deal with spiritual reality in whatever form. The *Yoga-sūtras* neither set forth a religious dogma nor inculcate any form of morality as such. It is, as analyses by G.C.Pande, "the practical aspect of the science of consciousness. It aims at the direct intuitive knowledge of consciousness in itself and also presents the phenomenology of consciousness in action. The principal means of *Yoga* is the cultivation of a cognitive state of the mind called *samādhi* or putting together, concentration or integration. It is different from the states of sleep and dreaming because it is a state of higher alertness and lucidity. It is also different from the waking state because it is free from the distraction of speech and thoughts, sensations and images, feelings and desires. ...... *Yoga* is a science but it is not a moral or value-free. Knowing the true self requires a firm detachment from one's habitual lower self."[15]

### *Notes and References*


1. Neurosciences and Philosophy, Summerhill: IIAS Review, Shimla, Institute of Advanced Studies, 1999, p.4.
   It is to be noted in this connection that in the *Caraka-Saṁhitā*, *Nidānasthāna*, Chapter VII on the diagnosis of Madness (*unmadanidana*)- "That many functional disorders in human behaviour may be treated by the use of drugs was known to earlier medical practice. The role of prenatal factors of food and drink and of unbalanced and conflicting mental dispositions overt and latent was studied in this context.
2. Pande, G.C., *op.cit.*, p.4 ; cf. also Rita Agrawal, *Stress in Life and at Work*, Saga Publication, Delhi.
3. The Yoga system, of Patañjali or the Ancient Hindu Doctrine of Concentration of Mind by James Haughton Woods, Harvard Oriental Series, Vol.17, Cambridge, First Edition-1914, Second Edition-1927.
4. *Yoga Sūtra*, I.41.
5. Pande, G.C., *op.cit.*, p.6.
6. *Bhagavat Gītā*, VI.18.
7. Dasgupta, S.N., *History of Indian Philosophy*, Vol.I, First Indian Edition-1975, Delhi, pp.271ff.
8. *Vyasabhāshya-ṭīkā on Yoga-sūtra*, I.1.
9. *Yoga-sūtra*, I.17.
10. *Ibid.*, IV.1.
11. Pranabananda Jash, *History of Śaivism*, Calcutta, 1974, pp.64ff.
12. *Sthira-sukham-āsanam - Yoga-sūtra*, II.46.
13. *Yoga-sūtra*, III.33.
14. *Ibid.*, III.36.
15. Pande, G. , *Consciousness, Neuroscience and Philosophy*, Summerhill: IIAS Review, Shimla, Vol.VI, No.1,2000.

3

# Brahmanical Religion and its Literature in Early India

*Bhagirathi Biswas*

If we wanted to speak about the Brahmanas or the Brahmanic religion or the Brahmanic literature then we can not but avoid the Vedic religion and the Vedic literature because the genesis of Brahmanas is in the Vedas. The word 'Veda' is derived from the root "vid". According to "Dhatupath of Panini, there are following five verbs of this form viz., Vida Jnane – to Know; Vida Sattayam – to be; Vida Labhe – to obtain; Vida Vicharane – to consider; Vida Cetanaakhyaananivaaseshu – to feel, to tell, to dwell.

"Vid jnane vid sattayam vid lr lave, vid vicharane, etebhyo halasceti sutrena karanadhikaranakarakayorghan pratyaye krte Vedasabdah sadyate." (Rgvedadi-Bhashya-Bhumika).

Veda is the fountain-head or repository of all knowledge and wisdom; an outline of the whole universe covering all the matters relating to animate and inanimate. The original and the main sources of vedic literature are the four Samhitas (bare-texts). These Samhitas are four in number, viz., Rg. Yajuh, Sam and Atharva. 'Veda' or 'Vedic Literature' consists of three different classes of literary works; and to each of these three classes belongs also a large or small number of individual works. These three classes are: —

***Samhitas*** i.e. 'Collections' namely collections of hymns, prayers,magic, songs, benidictory words, sacrificial formulas and litanies.

***Brahmanas*** i.e. extensive prose texts which contain theological discussions, especially, observations on the sacrifice and the practical or mystical significance of the individual sacrificial rites and ceremonies.

***Aranyakas*** (forest texts) and Upanishads (secret teachings) which are partly included in or appended to the Brahmanas themselves and partly are supposed to be independent works. They contain the meditations of hermits in forests and ascetics on God, world and man. And in them a good amount of Indian philosophy is contained.

The Brahmanic Religion and the Brahmanic literature have occupied a great place in the corpus of knowledge of the ancient Indian Civilization. The Indian civilization can not be examined, interpreted and translated without the help of Brahmanic religion and the Brahmanic literature. The Brahmanic Religion is a philosophy of religion which the Indian has inherited. It is a wide connotative concept. The Brahmanic Religion connotes and denotes various meaning and concepts. It is the traditional philosophical faiths, believes which have been handed down to us from generation to generation. It has become a cultural tradition and heritage. In ancient India religion and literature was inseparable. Literature in strict sense developed very late. It is the religion which constituted literature. It continues up to mediaeval period beginning from Vedic religion to Ramayana and Mahabharata even up to Gaudiya-caryyapada centre around religion. Religion and literature were complementary to each other for the enrichment of culture and tradition in India.

If we wanted to understand whole corpus of the Brahmanic Religion and the Brahmanic Literature first of all we are to make our self clear about the concept of Brahmanic Religion and of the Brahmanic Literature. An operational explanation and of its delimitations are to be made.

What is the significance of the term Brahmana? What do actually we mean by the Brahmana? Many definitions are available in the ancient texts. Jaimini gives the definitions in his book Purva-Mimamsa (2.1.33) "Sese Brahmana-sabdah" which means the remaining bulk of the Vedic literature besides the mantras is called 'Brahmana". Apastamba defines Brahmanas as, - "Karmacodana Brahmanani,' which means Brahmanas are injuctions for the performance of sacrificial rites. The term 'Brahmana' has been variously interpreted. It has come from the word ' Brahman' which means both the Veda and the Brahmana or the priestly class who are versed in the Veda. Satapatha Brahmana says Brahman is verily the Brahmana – " Brahmeti Brahmananam namasti. Atra Pramanam.'Brahma vai: Brahmanah' which means 'Brahman is Brahmana, the priestly class'. Patanjali observed during commenting on Panini (5.1.1) that – "The words 'Brahman' and 'Brahmana' convey the same meaning – 'Samanarthavetau brahmansabdo brahmana – sabdasea (Astadhyayi-5-1-1). Dayananda Saraswati remarks in his introduction to the commentary on the Rgveda – "Brahman is a name of the Brahmanas'. Martin Haug says – "Etymologically the word 'Brahmana' is derived from 'Brahman' which properly signifies the Brahman priest who must know all the Vedas and understand the whole course and meaning of the Sacrifice. He is supposed to be a perfect master of divinity and has in this capacity to direct and superintend the sacrificial ceremonies. The most eminent of this class of priests laid down rules for the proper performance of sacrificial rites, explained them, and defended their own opinions, on such topics against those of their antagonists; - - - the dictum of such a Brahman priest who passed as a great authority, was called a Brahmana" – (Introduction to Aitareya Brahmana translated by Martin Haug). Dayananda Saraswati maintains – "Those works are called Brahmanas, which are explanations of the Vedas (Samhitas) given by Brahman seers versed in all the four Vedas – "Caturvedavidbhirbrahmabhih brahmanaih maharsibhih proktani yani veda-vyakhyanani tani brahmanani"- Rg-Bhasyabhumika.). The Brahmanas contain the accumulated wisdom and speculations of generations of the Vedic divines.

According to Apastamba the Brahmanas deal with the six topics such as – Vidhi, Arthavada, Ninda, Prasamsa, Purakalpa and Parakrti. Vidhi means injuctions for the performance of particular rites. Arthavada comprises the numerous explanatory remarks on the meaning of mantras and particular rites. The speculative parts of Brahmana are these explanations or Arthavadas wherein may be traced the beginnings of Indian philosophy, grammar and philology. Ninda or censure consists in criticism, refutation and denunciation of the opponents views. Prasamsa means eulogy, recommendation. That which is praised is recommended; whenever a rite or a hymn is eulogized, the implication is, one is enjoined to practice that rite or utter that hymn. Purakalpa means the performance of sacrificial rites in former times shrouded in the mists of antiquity. Many legends connected with the performance of sacrifies by the gods are included in purakalpa. Parakrti is the last characteristic feature which means the achievement or feats of others. Above mentioned six topics are often brought under two main heads only viz. Vidhi and Arthavada, Ninda, Prasamsa, Purakalpa and Parakrti come under the general head of Arthavada.

The Brahmana literature can never be over estimated. The Brahmana texts are invaluable records not only of sacrificial paraphernalia but also of ancient Indian thought and civilization which finds expression through legendary lore, metaphysical thought, social and political customs and linguistic speculations.

The Brahmanas form a part and parcel of the vast Vedic literature. These are generally designated as later Vedic literature. The word 'Veda' means supreme knowledge. According to Manu the Veda is the repository or fountain-head of all religious and duties-'Vedo akhiladharmamulam'. Yajnavalkya opines-'it enlightens one on the knowledge of supra-sensible matters which lie beyond the domain of perception and inference, hence it is called the Veda" - "Pratyaksenanumitya va yastupayo na vidyate; Eman vidanti Vedena tasmad vedasya vedata". The word 'Veda' comprises both the Mantra and the Brahmana. 'Veda' is the name given to mantra and brahmana jointly' – "Mantra-brahmanayorvedanamadheyam"- (Apastamba-Srauta-Sutra, 24-1-31). Sayanacarya also opines in the introduction to his commentary on the Rgveda – "The name Veda is given to the vast body of literature made up to Mantra and Brahmana jointly" – "Mantra brahmanatmaka – sabdarasirvedah". Sabara swamin also defines in his commentary on Purva-Mimamsa-System (1-2-33) that "Mantras and Brahmanas together constitute the Veda". Mantrasca Brahmanam ca Vedah". Mantras, Brahmanas, Aranyakas and Upanisads together constitute the huge mass of literature i.e. the 'veda'. 'Mantras' which are collections of hymns, prayers, benidictions, incarnations, sacrificial formulae called Nivids and litanies. 'Brahmanas' are standing for a huge mass of prose texts which contain speculations on the mantras, precepts for the application of mantras in different sacrifices, details of sacrificial paraphernalia and theological, philosophical, grammatical, etymological and metrical speculations, 'Aranyakas' and 'Upanisads' which are partly included in the Brahmansa themselves but partly are also reckoned as independent works. The Brahmanas deals with the huge bulk of sacrificial paraphernalia which represents Karma-Kanda. The Brahmanas are the source of the particular school of Indian philosophy known as Purva-mimamsa or Karma-mimamsa or Dharma-mimamasa.

***Number of the Brahmanas*:-** Vedas have many Brahmanas. To the Rgveda belongs the *Aaitareya Brahmana* and *Kausitaki Brahmana* which is also known as Sankhayana Brahmana. There are eight Brahmanas of the Samaveda. These are the *Tandya Brahmana* or the *Pancavimsa Brahmana*, the *Sadavimsa Brahmana*, the *Chandogya Brahmana*, the *Jaiminiya* or the *Talavakara Brahmana*, the *Samavidhana Brahmana*, the *Arseya Brahmana*, the *Vamsa Brahmana* and the *Devatadhyaya Brahmana*. The last four Brahmanas are nothing but the index of the Samaveda. Black Yajurveda has only one Brahmana *Taittiriya* by name. To the white (Sukla) Yajurveda belongs the famous Satapatha Brahmana, 'The Brahmana of the Hundred paths'. This Brahmana has one hundred Adhyayas or lessons. It has two recensions – one is the Kanvas and another is the Madhyandinas. To the Atharbabeda belongs the Gopatha – Brahmana which is divided into two parts, Purva and Uttara.

***The Aitareya Brahmana*** belongs to the Rgveda. The authorship of this Brahmana is attributed to one Mahidasa the son of Itara and hence Itara's son Mahidasa is called 'Aitareya'. This Brahmana consists of eight books termed Pancikas. Each Pancikas consists of five chapters or Adhyayas making forty chapters in all. Each chapter is divided into many sub-chapters called Kandas. The total numbers of Kandas being two hundred eighty five. This Brahmana is written mostly in prose and partly in verse. The first sixteen chapters deal with the Somayaga known as Agnistoma or Jyotistoma which is the model or Prakrti of all Soma Sacrifices. These chapters treat of the duties of the chief Rgvedic priest Hotr at the Agnistoma Soma sacrifice only. The ceremony generally lasts for five days. The ceremony of the first four days are only introductory consisting of the election of priests (Hotr-varanam), the initiation of the sacrificer or Yajamana called Diksaniya-isti, the Prayaniya or opening isti (Sacrifice), the purchase of Soma (Soma-Kraya), the ceremony of doing hospitality to king Soma (Atithya-isti), the Pravargya, Upasad, Agni-soma-pranayanam, Havirdhana-pranayanam, the animal sacrifice (Pasu), the three pressings and libations of Soma juice called Soma-savana taking place in the morning, mid-day and evening and lastly the concluding or Udayaniya-isti, the ablution known as Avabhrta. The above ceremonies covering the first four days are absolutely necessary and serve as a prelude to the actual sacrifice which takes place on the fifth day. The universal character of the Agnistoma and its significance is treated specially in the fourth chapter of the third book (Pancika) i.e. the fourteenth chapter. In the last chapter of the third book and first two chapters of the fourth book, the principal modifications of Agnistoma are mentioned and briefly described viz. the Ukthya, Sadasi and Atiratra along with Asvina satra. The third chapter of the fourth book embodies the principal rules for the performance of the Hotr priests relating to Sattras or sacrificial sessions which required a long period of time, in some cases a complete year or a century even for their completion. The model or

Prakrti of Sattra type of sacrifice is Gavamayana which covers a whole year consisting of 361 days. The duties of the Rgvedic priests concerning the Gavamayana Sattra are enumerated from the sixth Kanda of the seventeenth chapter till the end of the eighteenth chapter. The last two chapters of the fourth book and the first four chapters of the fifth book describe very minutely the duties of the Hotr- priest during the ten principal days of Dvadasaha, which may be performed as a Sattra, or as a Ahina i.e., a Soma sacrifice lasting for more than one and less than thirteen days. The last chapter of the fifth book i.e. the twenty-fifth chapter deals with various matters such as the penances required of an Agnihotr when he comits mistakes or when some misfortune such as expiry of his wife etc. befalls him. It also enumerates the expitory rites to be performed by the Superintending priest Brahmana for the mistakes committed by any one of the performing priests. The whole of the sixth book treats of the duties of the minor Hotr-priests, at the great soma sacrifice called Sadaha. At the beginning of the sixth book there are some remarks on the two priests Gravastut and Subrahmanya.

The seventh and the eighth books deal mainly with the sacrifices of the Ksatriyas or the ruling class and the relationship in which the princes stand to the priestly class or Brahmanas. The seventh book describes first the vivisection of the sacrificial animal into thirty six single pieces, and their distribution among the officiating priests, the sacrificer, his wife and other persons connected with the performance of the sacrifice.

The thirty-second chapter deals with penances or expiatory rites for neglects on the part of an Agnihotr or mishaps which might befall him. This is a continuation of the fifth chapter of the fifth book. The remains chapters describe the important ceremony known as royal coronation (Abhiseka). The coronation ceremony of ancient India is described in detail in connection- with the Rajasuya ceremony. In chapter thirty-three the interesting story of Sunaha-sepa is narrated. Three kinds of inauguratory sacrifices for the king, called the Rajasuya are described, viz., Abhiseka, Punarabhiseka and Mahabhiseka, inauguration, re-inauguration and great inauguration ceremonies. Aindra-Mahabhiseka or the great coronation ceremony of India is the model for the inauguration of all earthly kings. These ceremonies are called Abhiseka, because one main item of the royal coronation ceremony consists in sprinkling holy-water collected from different sources on the head of the king.

The last chapter is taken up with the appointment by the king of a properly qualified Brahmana to the office of domestic priest called Purohita. There is also a eulogy of the office Purohita (Purohitaprasamsa). The ceremonial part of the last chapter is made interesting by short stories of Kings who were said to have performed the great coronation ceremony, and as a result thereof attained to paramount sovereignty on earth. The last kanda of the eight books, i.e. the concluding kanda of the whole Brahmana enumerates some magical performances called Krtya by means of which a king can secretly destroy his enemies. The complete Aitareya Brahmana beginning with the words "Agnir vai devanamavamsa (1-1-1)" and ending with "Strnute Strnute" (8-5-5)" and then the Aranyaka commencing with "Atha mahavratam" (1-1-1) and closing with the words "Acaryah Acaryah" fleshed in Mahidasa's mind as divine revelations.

***Kausitaki or Sankhyaya Brahmana***: In the closest relationship with the Aitareya Brahmana is the Kausitaki or Sankhyayana Brahmana, also belonging to the Rgveda. It is consisting of thirty Adhyayas. It is named after the great teacher Kausitaka. The first six Adhyayas of this Brahmana deal with the food sacrifice which consists of the culling of fire, fire-sacrifice, new-moon and full-moon sacrifices and the sacrifices of the seasons. The Adhyayas from the seventh to the thirteenth deal with the Soma-sacrifice fairly agreeing with the Aitareya Brahmana. The Kausitaki Brahmana is later than the Aitareya Brahmana. However, while the later is not the work of one hand and of one period, the Kausitaki Brahmana is a uniform work. It is a better organized text and covers more or less the entire sacrificial procedure.

The Samaveda has the largest number of Brahmana texts, but only two or three of them can properly be called Brahmanas. All the others are more or less of the nature of appendices Sadavimsa-Brahmana i.e. the "Twenty-Sixth Brahmanas" is only a completion of the Tandya which consists of Twenty-five books. The last part of the Sadvimsa is the so called "Adbhuta Brahmana" which deals with omens and portents.

***The Tandya-Brahmana or The Tanda-Maha-Brahmana*** belongs to the Samaveda, also called Pancavimsa means "Brahmana consisting of twenty five books". This is one of the oldest Bramana and contains some important old legands of special interests are the Vratyastomas and the description of sacrificial ceremonies by means of which the Vratyas were received into the community of the Brahmanas. The Tandya-Maha-Brahmana is named after its author, Sage Tandi. The speciality of this Brahmana is that it supplies us with the details of innumerable varieties of the Soma Sacrifice that covers a thousand years for its completion.

The Brahmana of the Tandins is divided into forty chapters. The first twenty five chapters form the ***Tandya or Pancavimsa Brahmana***. The ***Sadvimsa Brahmana*** consists of the next five chapters. The following ten chapters go to the compilation of the ***Chandogya Brahmana***. Of these ten chapters, the first two form the Mantras Brahmana and the next eight the Chandogya Upanisad. The ***Jaiminiya or Talavakara Brahmana*** treats of various ceremonials. This work is of special interest for the history both of religion and legend. It contains the Kena-Upnishad. It is divided into two parts, Purva and Uttara. Unfortunately the manuscript material is so fragmentary that it can not be edited. Hitherto only portions of it have been made known. The ***Samavidhana Brahmana*** explains the application of incantations for various superstitions purposes. The ***Devatadhyaya***, ***Arseya*** and ***Vamsa Brahmanas*** furnish us with the names of the deities of the Samavedic hymns and a genealogical table of the teachers of the Samaveda respectively.

***Taittiriya Brahmana*** belongs to the Black Yajurveda. This Brahmana is nothing but a continuation of the Taittiriya Samhita and contains only later additions to the Samhita. In the black Yajurveda the characteristic features of the Samhita and the Brahmana have been mixed up; there is overlapping of boundaries. There are profuse Brahmana passages in the Samhita portion and vice versa. This mixture of the Samhita and Brahmana is a peculiar feature of the Black Yajurveda which is not met with in the other Vedas including the white Yajurveda. For this overlapping of Samhita and brahmana texts the Black Yajurveda is called 'Krishna' which besides its current meaning of 'Black' also means 'mixed' in Sanskrit. The Taittiriya Brahmana contains three Kandas also called Astakas, twenty eight prapathakas and three hundred fifty three Anuvakas.

***Satapatha-Brahmana***, "the Brahmana of the hundred paths" belongs to the Vajasaneyi Samhita or White Yajurveda. The word 'Sata' means a hundred and the name is very significant as this Brahmana consists of one hundred Adhyayas. It is quite remarkable in many respects. This is the most famous, extensive and doubtless also by virtue of its content most insignificant of all the Brahmanas. There are two recensions of this Brahmana that of the Kanvas and that of the Madhyandinas. In the Madhyandina recension of the Satapatha Brahmana the hundred Adhyayas are distributed among fourteen books called Kandas. Each book or Kanda is divided into several adhyayas which are sub-divided into several Prapathakas, the Prapathakas in their turn are sub-divided into several Brahmanas which again are sub-divided into many Kandikas. Thus in all there are fourteen Kandas, sixty-eight Prapathakas, four hundred thirty eight Brahmanas and seven thousand six hundred twenty four Kandikas in the Madhyandina recension of the Satapatha Brahmana. In the usual procedure of references the Prapathaka is not mentioned, the rest four divisions are mentioned; e.g., the reference 10-4-2-22 will mean the 22nd Kandikas of the second Brahmana of the fourth Adhyayas belonging to the tenth Kanda or book. In the Kanva recension there are seventeen Kandas, one hundred four Adhyayas, four hundred thirty five Brahmanas and six thousand eight hundred six Kandikas. The name Satapatha justly applies to the Madhyandina Sakha which actually consists of one hundred Adhyayas whereas the Kanva Sakha consists of four more chapters. One of the important features of the Satapatha Brahmana is the large number of legends it contains. Among them may be mentioned: Manu and the fish; the migration of Videgha Mathava from the region of the Sarasvati to the region of the Sadanira; the rejuvenation of Cyavana; the romantic affair between Pururavas and Urvasi and the contest between Kadru and Vinata. Another important feature is that, while some portions of this Brahmana are intimately connected with Kuru-Pancalas, others have their provenance in Kosala-Videha. This fact clearly indicates that the Satapatha Brahmana is a composite work and that its composition must have extended over a wide range of time and area.

The first kanda of the Satapatha Brahmana treats of the famous sacrifice known as Darsa-purnamasa. The second kandas deals with various sacrifices such as the daily rite of agnihotra, pinda-pitryajna, the daksayana sacrifice, an isti type of sacrifice call navanna and the celebrate caturmasya which consists of various rites and performances such as varuna-praghasa, sakamedha, pitryesti, isti called tryamvaka, sunasiri etc. The third and fourth Kandas give the details of the celebrated Some-sacrifice of Diksa or initiation, the commencing sacrifice or Prayaniya isti, the purchase of soma creeper and the placing of Soma in the cart, rites of hospitality or Atithya-isti done to king Some, Upasad isti creation of the great altar, pressing of Soma juice, rites relating to the slaughter of animal, offering of animal flesh and rice pap, Upayaja and Patni-samyaja (rites concerning the wife of the Yajamana), Soma liberations, receiving of different vessels called Grahas in the Soma sacrifice by the priests, Anubandha and Avabhrta rites etc. The fifth kanda deals with the two important sacrifices known as Rajasuya and Vajapeya connected with the royal coronation and consecration of kings. The status of the king, his cabinet, the representative persons of the kingdom, the status of queens, the relation between the king and his ministers, the relation between the ruler and the ruled, the democratic elements in ancient Indian Kingship, different types of monarchy and territory, the vox populi in matters of administration, the tax-system and the like paraphernalia of the state and politics are met with in the sacrifices having a political end-in-view such as the Rajasuya, Vajapeya, Asvamedha, Sautramani, Purusamedha etc. The kandas from the sixth to the tenth mainly deal with the culling of the sacrificial fire and construction of the fire-altar which is symbolic of Prajapati, Agni, Yajamana and the creation of the universe. The eleventh kanda treats of Pasubandha, the five Mahayajnas, an isti called Mitravinda, Darsapurnamasa-sesa etc. The twelfth kanda deals with the satra or sessional sacrifice called Dvadasaha, the annual or samratsava satra and the expietory rite for excess in drinking etc., known as Sautramani. The thirteenth Kanda gives the details of four important sacrifices Asvamedha, Purusamedha, Sarvamedha and Pitrmedha. In the eighth Adhyaya of the thirteenth Kanda the funeral ceremonies of the Vedic age, the disposal of the dead and construction of burialmounds of different sizes according to different sexes and castes of the dead have been embodied in connection with pitrmedha. This piece merits importance as a record of the then social custom. The last i.e., the fourteenth Kanda or book deals with Pravargya and contains the great metaphysical and theological discourse known as Brhadaranyaka-Upanishad which is worth its weight in gold.

Gopatha-Brahmana is the only Brahmana of the Atharva Veda. This Gopatha-Brahmana is one of the latest works of the whole vedic Literature. It is also limited in content, consisting as it does of only two books with eleven prapathakas. The Caranavyuha, which is one of the parisistas of the Atharvaveda, says, however, that the Gopatha-brahmana originally consisted of one hundred chapters out of which only two have survived. This is quite plausible, since many statements referred to in other texts as being derived from the Brahmana are not traceable in its extant text. A significant point about the Gopatha-Brahmana is that, for the most part, it contains myths, legends and parables which illustrate and explain various ceremonies in the Vedic ritual. The Atharvanic character of this Brahmana becomes evident in several ways. For instance, it glorifies Angiras as the 'sage of sages' and emphasizes that a Vedic sacrifice performed without the help of a priest of the Atharvaveda is bound to fail. In olden days there was evidently no Brahmana to the Atharvaveda. Only a later time which could not imagine a Veda without a Brahmana has then tried to fill this gap.

## Conclusion

The difference between the Brahmanas which belong to the individual Vedas lies mainly in the fact that while describing the ritual, the Brahmanas of the Rgveda stress that which is of importance to the Hotar-priest who has to recite the verses and hymns of the Rgveda, where as the Brahmanas of the Samaveda are concerned with the duties of the Udgatar and those of the Yajurveda are concerned with duties of the Adhvaryu. In their essential contents all the Brahmanas almost concur with one another. Fundamentally they all deal with the same objects, and they all have the same characteristic features.

## *Notes and References*

**Original Sources:**

- Ṛgveda
- Yajurveda
- Samaveda
- Atharvaveda

**Other Sources:**

Basu, Jagiraj, India of the Age of the Brahmana, Sanskrit Pustak Bhandar, Cal-6, 1969.

Chatterjee, Santi Kumar, The Cultural Heritage of India, Volume-V, The Ramkrishna Mission, Institute of Culture, Calcutta, 1991.

Eggeline, The Satapatha Brahmana, Sacred books of the east series.

Haug Martin, The Aitareya Brahmana, Asiatic Society Publication.

Winternitz Maurice, A History of Indian Literature, Volume-1, Motilal Banarsidas Publications Pvt. Ltd., Delhi, 1981.

4

# Śaivism in India: A Historical Study

*Gargi De*

Śaivism had its origin in the pre-Vedic period, the evidence for this is seen in some ancient artifacts and seals discovered during the archaeological excavations at certain sites, like, Mohenjodaro, Harappa, Lothal, Ropar etc. Historians have identified terracotta seals found at these places as that of Paśupati. Phallic icons discovered in these places conclusively prove that the Śaivism prevailed in that area in ancient times as a religious cult.

That Śaivism existed as a popular religious cult is seen in the Vedic period also when it inter-mixed with other cognate religious cults. We have literary evidence in Vedic literature to prove the existence of Śaivism. For instance, some mantras in the *Ṛg-Veda* refer to Śiva as *Rudra* and *Tryambaka*[1].

In the *Śukla-Yajur Veda*, section XVI of the *Vājasaneyī Saṁhitā*, and section IV of the *Taittirīya Saṁhitā* of the *Kṛṣṇa-Yajur Veda*, a list of hundred names of Śiva is given[2]. All these indicate the popularity of Śaivism in the Vedic period. There are evidences of the existence of Śaiva religion in the *Atharva-Veda*[3].

The *Aṣṭādhyāyī* of Pāṇiṇī also mentions the names of Śiva and Rudra[4]. It is said that he was an ardent devotee of Śiva.

Patañjali's *Mahābhāṣya* provides one more evidence for the existence of Śaiva cult. In the *Mahābhāṣya*, the devotees of Śiva are referred to as *Śivabhāgavatas*[5]. Different names of Rudra-Śiva, such as *Girīśa, Mahādeva, Tryambaka, Bhava, Sarva* etc. occurs there[6].

One more important proof of Śaivism existing as a religion in pre-Christian era and early Christian era is seen in the coins and the seals of those days. Some of these numismatic items bear the legend of *Śivarakṣita* in Brāhmī and Kharoṣṭhī scripts[7]. Besides, the most significant emblem *Nandipāda* is seen represented on the North Indian and the South Indian coins[8]. All these archaeological evidences indicate the existence of Śaivism as a religion in ancient time.

Besides archaeological evidence for the existence of Śaivism, there are literary evidences too to prove the existence of Śaivism, e.g., *Śaiva Siddhānta* School, *Kālānala*, also known as *Kāruka Śaiva*, *Pāśupata* with *Lakulīśa Pāśupata* as a sub-sect founded by Lakulīśa and Kāpālika with sub-sect called *Soma* occur in some ancient Sanskrit texts.

For instance, *Suprabhedāgama*[9] mentions four schools namely *Śaiva, Pāśupata, Soma* and *Lakulīśa.*

In the *Āgamaprāmāṇyam*, Yāmunācārya says that followers of *Siddha* tradition are fourfold viz. *Kāpālika*, *Kālānala* or *Kālāmukha*, *Pāśupata, Śaiva*[10].

Vācaspati Miśra in his commentary called *Bhāmatī* on *Śārīrakabhāṣya* on *Brahmasūtra*[11] mentions four prominent schools of Śaivism that prevailed in his time. These are *Śaiva, Pāśupata, Kāruṇika, Kāruka Siddhānta* besides *Kāpālika*. Those *Kāpālikas* are associated with *Soma* cult has been mentioned in the Sanskrit drama *Prabodhacandrodaya*, Act. III[12].

Thus the Śaivism mentioned in different Sanskrit texts can broadly be classified under two heads – one, religious cults that existed only as religious cults having no literature of their own, two, religious cults which have literature of their own, throwing light on their philosophical postulations. *Kāpālika, Kālāmukha* or *Kālānala*, *Soma Siddhāntins* etc. come under the first category, while Śaiva schools possessing some literature of their own form the second category. There were eight distinct schools of Śaivism which not only prescribed their distinctive mode of spiritual practice but also discussed the metaphysics on which their *sādhanā* is based.

We shall begin with giving a brief outline of religious cults which have no literature, nonetheless had good following-

Kāpālika

Kālānala or Kālāmukha

Soma Siddhāntin

## Kāpālika

The earliest reference to Kāpālika is seen in the *Maitrī Upaniṣad*[13], *Śivapurāṇa*[14], *Vāyavīya Saṁhitā*[15], *Mattavilāsa*[16], *Mālatīmādhava*[17], *Karpūramañjarī*[18] etc. The followers of *Mahāvrata* were identical with *Kāpālika*. Kāpālikas were also associated with *Śivaśāsana* and *Soma Siddhānta*. As they do not have any literature of their own, nothing is known about the philosophical base of their beliefs. The *Varāhapurāṇa* mentions that they adopted Pāśupata doctrine as their philosophical base. Kāpālikas worship Śiva wearing a garland of skulls. *Prabodhacandrodaya*[19] describes that Kāpālikas worship Śiva in the form of *Mahābhairava* which is his terrifying representation.

## Kālānala

Śaivas were very much influential in South India but no trace of this sect is seen in North India. Kālānalas were also known as *Kālāmukhas* who have been mentioned by several writers belonging to Śaṁkara School. They had many centers in Southern India under the Chālukya kings whom they served as *Rājaguru*. *Yaśastilak-Campu*[20] gives some description of a Kālāmukha ascetic.

## Soma Siddhāntin

They have been mentioned in a number of texts, like *Prabodhacandradaya*, *Īśānaśivagurupaddhati*[21], *Tantrādhikāranirṇaya*[22], *Vīramitrodaya*[23]. The founder of *Soma* cult was Soma who is said to have constructed a golden temple of Somnātha at Prabhāsapattana at the instance of Lord Śiva. The *Vāyavīya Samhitā* (Ch. V)[24] of the *Śivapurāṇa* states Śiva incarnated himself at Prabhāsa as Somaśarmā who had four disciples – Akṣapāda, Kaṇāda, Uluka, (teacher of Logic) and Vatsa. The *Prabodhacandrodaya* identifies Kāpālikas with the Soma Siddhāntins, but the *Tantrādhikāranirṇaya* mentions them as two distinct schools. Though Soma Siddhānta had its origin in Gujarat and it prevailed also in Nepal.

## Schools of Śaivism

Besides the Śaiva religious cults some Śaiva schools were supported by literature of their own. Śaivism developed as religio-philosophical school in the second phase when as many as eight distinct schools of Śaivism emerged in different parts of the country.

The following are the eight *religio-philosophical schools*:

i) **Pāśupata Śaiva School**: It is mentioned in the *Mahabharata*[25] as one of five principal religious cults which appears to be the earliest school of Śaivism propagating dualistic philosophy. It is said that this school was founded by Śrīkaṇṭha, son of Brahmā and consort of Umā. The name of Śrīkaṇṭha as the founder of Pāśupata School is also mentioned in the *Tantrāloka*[26], the *Śivadṛṣṭi*[27], the *Bṛhadyāmala*[28], the *Piṅgalamata*[29] and the *Śivapurāṇa*[30]. The Tantrāloka mentions (III P. 347) a text called *Māṅgalyaśāstra* in which Śrīkaṇṭha has discussed the nature of Śakti and Śaktism[31]. No literature giving exposition of the metaphysical thoughts of this system has been found, but Śaṁkara has referred to a school of Śaivism which accepted five categories – *Kāraṇa, Kārya, Yoga, Vidhi* and *Duḥkhānta*[32]. Pāśupata Śaivism is very often referred to as intimately associate with the Vaiśeṣika system. Haribhadra Sūri in his *Saḍdarśanasamuccaya* has stated that both the Pāśupatas and the Vaiśeṣikas believed in similar kind of liberation. Mādhavācārya in his *Sarvadarśanasaṁgraha* has summarized the teachings of this school of Śaivism under the Pāśupata. Pāṇinī and Patañjali, the well-known Sanskrit grammarians were Śaivites, and in all probability, they were all adherents of Pāśupata thought.

   It may be mentioned here that K. C. Pandey has spoken of two different Pāśupata schools, the older school i.e. *Pāśupata* and later *Pāśupata* school, i.e. *Lakulīśa Pāśupata* School[33].

ii) **Lakulīśa Pāśupat Śaiva School**: *Sarvadarśanasaṁgraha* mentions Lakulīśa or Nākula Pāśupata as a distinct school of Pāśupata Śaiva which propagated dualistic-cum-non-dualistic philosophy.

The *Vāyupurāṇa*[34], the *Gaṇakārikā*[35], the *Tantrāloka* etc. mention Lakuīlśa, an incarnation of Śiva, and as the founder of Lakulīśa Pāśupata School. The *Pāśupatasūtras* also known as *Pañcādhyāyī* form the basis of this school. R. G. Bhandarkar places the rise of the school in 2nd century B.C. in his book "Vaiṣṇavism, Śaivism and other minor religions"[36]. While D. R. Bhandarkar suggests his date in the second quarter of the 1st century A.D. on the basis of Mathurā Pillar Inscription of Chandragupta II[37]. Purāṇas and other inscriptions mention Kuśika, Gārgeya, Maitreya and Kauruṣa as his disciples. All his disciples were historical persons who are evident from their names occurring in different inscriptions like Udaipur Inscription, Mathurā Inscription, Cintrā Praśasti etc. Haribhadra Sūrī in his *Saḍdarśanasamuccaya* gives a long list of Śaiva teachers who lived at different holy places and were venerated by people. They were Nākulīśa, Kauśika, Gārgeya, Maitreya, Kauruṣa, Īśāṇa, Pāragārgeya, Kapilāṇda, Manuṣyaka, Kuśika, Atri, Piñgala, Puṣpaka, Vrihadārya, Agasti, Santāna, Rāśikara[38].

It may be mentioned here that both the Nyāya and the Vaiśeṣika schools were closely associated with the Pāśupata School which has been mentioned in *Saḍdarśanasamuccaya* by Haribhadra Sūrī[39] and Guṇaratna in his commentary on the same[40]. It is not known whether these schools were associated with the older Pāśupata School or Lakulīśa Pāśupata School. The accounts of the tenets of this school are found in the *Sarvadarśanasaṁgraha* and the *Rāmānujabhāṣya* on the *Brahmasūtra*. The *Pāśupatasūtras* attributed to Lakulīśa and its commentary by Kauṇḍinya is known as *Pañcārthabhāṣya*[41]. This particular kind of Śaivism has a great deal of similarities with the Vedas. They admit five basic tattvas - *Kāraṇa, Kārya, Yoga, Vidhi* and *Duḥkhānta*[42].

iii) **Śaiva Siddhāntin School**: It is a dualistic school of Śaivism which held its sway in the Southern part of India from the 9th Century onwards. It is based on the dualistic interpretation given to twenty-eight *Śaivāgamas*, ten of them belonging to Śaiva group and eighteen belonging to *Rudrāgama*. It developed in two forms the literature of earlier form is in Sanskrit, while that of later form is in Tamil. Sadyojyoti, who flourished towards the close of 9th century, was one of the well-known exponents of this school in Sanskrit[43]. He is said to have written commentaries on the *Rauravāgama* and the *Svyāmbhūāgama* interpreting them from dualistic point of view[44]. He wrote *Tattvatrayanirṇaya, Bhogakārikā* and *Mokṣakārikā* explaining the fundamentals of Dualistic Śaivism[45]. Since he was contemporary of Abhinavagupta (990-1015 A.D.), he is referred to by Abhinavagupta as Kḥetapāla in his refutations of the dualistic Śaivites. Other authorities referred to in the texts belonging to Advaita Śaivism are Bṛhaspati, Śaṅkarānandana, Devabala. Rāmkaṇṭha I (1158 A.D.) is the author of a commentary on the *Spandakārikā* (Advaita Śaiva text). He is referred to by Śrīkaṇṭha as the author of *Sadvṛtti* (a dualist Śaiva text). Śrīkaṇṭha (11th Century A.D.) and Nārāyaṇakaṇṭha (11th Century A.D.) are the other prominent exponents of dualistic Śaivism. Rāmkaṇṭha II[46] is also a prominent exponent of this school. The Śaiva Siddhānta also developed around 11th Century A.D. Umāpati Śivācārya was one of its prominent ācāryas. The *Śivajñānabodha* by Meyakaṇḍar (13th century

A.D.) is most authentic treatise on Śaiva Siddhānta. It admits two ultimate categories viz., *Pati* and *Paśu*.

iv) **Vīra Śaiva School**: Vīra Śaiṿism arose in the middle of the 12th Century as a revolt against the *Varṇāśramadharma*. Basava, the founder of this school started an institution called *Śivānubhavamata* in Karnataka[47]. It was founded in A.D. 1160. The followers of Vīra Śaiva are also known as *Liṅgāyata* since they wear idol of *Śivaliṅga* on their body. The Vīra Śaivites base their philosophical projections on the twenty-eight *Śaivāgamas* admitted by the Siddhānta School, but they give different interpretation to the Śaivāgamas than that given by the Śaiva Siddhāntins. Its main thesis is based on *Aṣṭārṇava* and *Śaṭasthala*. The metaphysical exposition of this Śaiva school can be learnt from its literature, like *Siddhāntaśikhāmaṇi* by Revaṇācārya and *Śrīkarabhāṣya* by Srīpati Paṇḍita[48]. So far as their metaphysical exposition is concerned they admit three primary categories – *Pati, Paśu, Pāśa*. Umāpati Śivācārya was one of its most prominent ācāryas. Śivajñānabodha by Meyakaṇḍar (13th century A.D.) is the most authentic treatise on Śaiva Siddhānta[49]. They hold that creation consists of thirty-six tattvas - *Śiva, Śakti, Sadāśiva, Īśvara* and *Śuddhavidyā* are pure and the rest thirty-one in number are impure ones. The Vīra Śaivites accept three kinds of bondages - *Mala, Kārma* and *Māyā*. Since they advocate realism, so the idea of super-imposition has no place in their philosophical thought, rather it has been refuted in their metaphysical exposition. Being the staunch supporter of dualism-cum-non-dualism, they admit the difference between soul and Brahman, the former limited in form, and the latter, all-pervasive, omniscient all-powerful object of worship and adoration. It thus leans on the side of theism too in its treatment of metaphysics.

v) **Nāndīkeśvara Śaiva School**: Nāndīkeśvara is another ancient school of Śaivism which also had its origin in the pre-Christian era although, it was not as popular as its contemporary Pāśupata. It is a monistic school founded by Nāndīkeśvara who is said to be a contemporary of Pāṇinī, the author of *Aṣṭādhyāyī*. According to ancient tradition mentioned by Nāgeśa Bhaṭṭa in his *Uddyota* on the *Mahābhāṣya*, the fourteen *Māheśvarasūtras*[50] on which the entire system of Pāṇinian grammar rests, were discovered by Nāndīkeśvara from the sound of *Damaru* (hand-drum) struck by Lord Śiva. Patañjali too refers to this in his *Mahābhāṣya* calling Nāndīkeśvara as *Brahmarṣi*[51]. There is only one text available that expounds the philosophical principles of this school, namely *Nāndīkeśvarakārikā* which was commented upon and elaborated by Upamanyu in his *Tattva-Vimarśinī*[52].

Nāndīkeśvara Śaivism admits thirty-six tattvas[53] constituting the world out of which *Parama Śiva* is the highest *tattva*. In course of his interpretation the *Māheśvarasūtras*, Nāndīkeśvara observes the first letter '**a**' in the first sūtra symbolically represents *anuttara* the highest metaphysical reality. It is present in everything that exists and in all form of speech. The Supreme Reality becomes the world voluntarily exercising its power called *Citkalā* or *Cit Śakti*. The letters 'i' and 'u' represent its power and the Lord (*Īśvara*) respectively.

vi) **Qualified Monistic Śaiva School**: Śrīkaṇṭha who lived in 11th Century A.D., is the sole exponent of Qualified Monistic school which is based on the authority of twenty-eight *Śaivāgamas*. It has affinity with Siddhānta Śaivites but it does not support them, on account of their projecting dualistic Philosophy and Śrīkaṇṭha projecting Qualified Monistic Philosophy[54]. Śrīkaṇṭha has attempted to show that the Vedic and

Āgama tradition are not divergent ones but they have much in common. This school holds that the relation between the *Brahman* i.e. *Śiva* and the objective world is one of soul and body. The ultimate reality *Brahman* is free from all kinds of limitation like that of space-time etc. He possesses infinite *Śakti* whereby He manifests the world which is real as it lies within him in potential form. But He is different from multiplicity. He is the cause of *creation*, *maintenance*, *annihilation*, *absorption* and *grace*. The *jīva* or *paśu* is the limited being, and not pervasive. Ignorant of his true nature, the limited being exists in physical body according to his *karma*. The relation between Śiva and Jīva is similar to one between king and his subject.

vii) **Raseśvara Śaiva School**: *Raseśvaradarśana* is yet another distinct school of *Śaivism* which has alchemy as the base[55]. The probable time when Raseśvara Śaiva philosophy emerged is about the commencement of the Christian era. Mādhavācārya's *Sarvadarśanasaṁgraha* expounds its metaphysical principles. Though it appears more as an empirical science, but it has laid stress on emancipation, and according to it *Maheśvara* is the Highest Lord and the Ultimate metaphysical principle. It does not follow the footsteps of the Vaiśeṣika, the Sāṁkhya and the Vedānta. This tradition of philosophy was dominated by the alchemy. According to it, *pārada* or mercury, which literally means that which takes one beyond the series of transmigratory states, is called *rasa*. The *rasa* helps the practice of Yoga to obtain perfect body[56].

viii) **Trika Śaiva School:** The Advaita Śaiva Philosophy of Kashmir, popularly known as Kashmir Śaivism is said to be based on ninety-two *Śaivāgamas* which comprise sixty-four *Bhairavāgamas*[57]. Of these, the most important ones from which Advaita Śaivites draw their support are the *Mālinīvijaya* or *Mālinīvijayottaratantra*, *Netra* or *Mṛtyujitbhaṭṭārakatantra*, *Svacchandatantra*, *Vijñānabhairavatantra*, *Mṛgendratantra* and *Rudrayāmalatantra* which have been frequently quoted in the Advaita Śaiva texts.

It may be mentioned here that some Advaita Śaiva writers like Abhinavagupta have called Advaita Śaiva Philosophy of Kashmir as *Ṣaḍārdhaśāsana* or *Trika* to distinguish it from other Śaiva schools which existed in Kashmir before the rise of Śaivism here.

He has interpreted the word *Trika* in the following way to justify its use as most appropriate:

i) The word *Trika* denotes three principal Āgamas, namely, *Mālinī*, *Siddha* and *Nāmaka* or *Vāmaka*. These three revealed texts form the foundation of the Advaita Śaiva Philosophy.

ii) Another reason given by Abhinavagupta is that *Trika* means
   a) *Śiva-Śakti* and their union,
   b) *Śiva, Śakti* and *Nara*,
   c) *Parā* (benevolent), *Aparā* and *Parāpara* (wild and terrifying)[58]

iii) The metaphysical thought of the school owes its origin to a variety of Sanskrit texts which can be classified under three heads, viz., *Āgama śāstra*, *Spandaśāstra* and *Pratyabhijñāśāstra*. Incidentally, it may be mentioned here that Mādhavācārya in his *Sarvadarśanasaṁgraha*[59] summarizes the philosophy of this school under the heading *Pratyabhijñādarśana*. This represents only one phase in the development of philosophy of this school.

## Religio-philosophical scenario before the advent of Advaita Śaiva Philosophy

Kashmir is traditionally called *Sāradādeśa*, the land of Goddess of learning on account of the unique contribution it made in the past to enrich the various branches of Sanskrit studies ranging from literature, literary criticism, aesthetics, grammar, dramaturgy, music etc. to philosophy, religion and spirituality. The peaceful atmosphere, salubrious climate and natural surrounding prevailing there, provided ideal setting for all creative literary activities on the part of ācāryas.

Long before the rise of the Advaita Śaiva Philosophy in the 8th century A.D., Kashmir was a place of Buddhist thought. Some historian reveals that Buddhism and Śaivism flourished here side by side as it is received royal patronage from the Emperor Ashoka in equal measure. It is stated that before the advent of Buddhism, the valley was dominated by the Vedic religion. Besides, some local practice like *Nāga* worship was another popular tradition there. The success of Buddhism was essentially a revolt against Brāhmaṇism. Yet, the Catholic Brāhmaṇas with their proverbial forbearance did not adopt the same attitude as the Buddhists had employed in respect to Brāhmaṇism. Some of the scholars are of the opinion that Buddhism was introduced in Kashmir as early as 3rd century B.C. during the reign of the Emperor Ashoka. He deputed Madyāntika as an emissary for the propagation of Buddhism in Kashmir. In course of time when the Kuṣhāṇa King Kaṇiṣhaka became the Emperor of North India the Buddhism occupied a predominant position. Kaṇiṣhka chose Kashmir as a venue of the 4th Buddhist council which was attended by about 500 Buddhist monks and scholars from different places. The Canon of Abhidharma was codified and the *Tripiṭakas* were revised[60]. A school of Sarvāstivāda and also the idealist school of Yogācāra flourished there. Kumārajīva (334-413 A.D.) came from Central Asia to Kashmir to study scriptures of Mahāyāna Yoga. Kashmir produced many Buddhist Logicians like Dharmakīrti, Vinītadeva and Dharmottarācārya in the 7th century A.D. Teachers like Dharmabhikṣu attracted a large number of students from China and Kashmir. It is from Kashmir that Buddhism entered into Tibet during the reign of Dūrlabhavardhana 7th century A.D. G. Tucci observes that Kashmir was one of the places where Buddhism prospered most even though it had no state patronage[61]. The Valley was best suited for meditation and exegetes Buddhism of the time. According to Kalhana's *Rājataraṅgiṇī*[62], Buddhism could not achieve much success because of the Greek powers. Although, *Milindapañho*[63], the most authentic Buddhist text extracts that the Indo-Greek King Menendara adhered to Buddhism. During the period of Kalhana, there was hardly any antagonism between the different religious sects and the Buddhists. Even, the 6th-7th century classical Sanskrit source *Nīlamatapurāṇa*[64], a text of the worshippers of Nīla Nāga, also corroborated the facts of Kalhana. It mentions that the prevalence of Buddhist worship was a common practice in Kashmir.

Kashmir was a home of great scholars from time immemorial. The Valley of Kashmir had been a meeting ground of many cultures. The Tāntric Buddhism also developed in Kashmir. Many Tāntric teachers, eg Nāropa and Padmasambhava who hailed from Uddyāna[65] (Swāt Valley), settled in Kashmir. Of all schools of Buddhism, Yogācāra flourished most and it is here that Buddhasena translated the major work of Yogācāra school – *Yogācāra Bhūmi* into Chinese which shows that Buddhism held sway there in the 5th century A.D. The famous Chinese Buddhist pilgrim Hein Tsang came to Kashmir in 631 A.D. and stayed for two years. He has reported that Buddhism was popular during his days and it influenced the minds of the Kashmiri Philosophers especially the Advaita Śaivites of Kashmir. Even, the philosophic literature of Mahāyāna Buddhism bears a deep impress of Kashmir Śaivism. Even the *Nīlamatapurāṇa* does not make any clear-cut mention of monism, though it has just paved the way for the monistic Śaiva Philosophy of Kashmir.

Most of the authorities agree that such a well developed system of thought propounded by the Buddhist prevailed in the Kashmir Valley for one thousand years. Buddhism became an important part of the classical Kashmiri culture under the influence of their erudite scholars. Moreover, Kashmir witnessed the great resurgence of this particular religious thought in response to the Śaṅkar Vedāntins' futile effort to wipe out Buddhism from the Valley in the 8th century A.D.

Besides Buddhism, Pāñcarātra Vaiṣṇavism was also popular in Kashmir prior to the rise of the Advaita Śaiva thought. Its roots in Kashmir can be traced right to the time of the *Māhābhārata* where it has been seen as an off-shoot of *Sātattva* tradition. Utpala was familiar with this particular school of thought as he had referred to it as *Śruti* in his commentary on the *Spandakārikā*. As a matter of fact the *bhakti* element percolated into the Advaita Śaiva thought from the *Pāñcarātra* tradition. Utpala was the first *Śaivācārya* who introduced *bhakti* as *dāsya* type by composing *Śivastotrāvalī*. He was followed by his disciple, Abhinavagupta, who composed short *stotras* incorporating *bhakti* in the non-dualistic thought of Śaivism in Kashmir. The *Stavacintāmani* by Nārāyaṇabhaṭṭa is another example of the influence of Pāñcarātra on the Śaiva thought.

When Abhinavagupta came to the scene in the 10th century A.D., he found *Ādhārkārikā* by Śeṣamuni to be very popular among the masses. It is a Vaiṣṇava text in which *bhakti* dominates. He decided to transform the *Ādhārkārikā* into *Paramārthsāra* by giving it the form of Advaita Śaiva text[66]. Though no work of Utpala Vaiṣṇava comes down to us except *Spandapradīpikā*, Dr. Barnett is inclined to believe that Utpala Vaiṣṇava was a Vaiṣṇavite as the name suggests. There is no doubt about the fact that he is a different person from the famous Utpalācārya of *Īśvarapratyabhijñākārikā*.

It is a historical fact that Śaiva Siddhānta prevailed in Kashmir before the rise of the Advaita Śaiva Philosophy. According to the Advaita Śaiva tradition, the founder of Dualist Śaivism in Kashmir was Āmardaka, *mind born* son of Durvāsā. His name is mentioned by Somānanda in the colophon of *Śivadṛṣṭi*. K. C. Paṇḍey in his introduction to *Bhāskarī* has given an account of Kashmirī Śaiva Siddhāntins whom the non-dualistic Śaiva authors referred to with great reverence[67]. There is no doubt that Śaiva Siddhānta greatly influenced the Advaita thought. In this connection, mention must be made of one Khetpāla, whom Abhinavagupta has referred to as his contemporary. He has refuted the Śaiva Siddhāntins view about *malas*. Abhinavagupta was also responsible for incorporating the philosophy of *Krama* and *Kula* in the philosophy of Advaita Śaivism. These schools belonging to the *Śākta* stream were popular in Kashmir.

## Development of Advaita Śaiva School in Kashmir

When we survey the origin and growth of the religio-philosophical thought of Trika School in historical perspective we come across the following three phases:

i) *The Āgamaśāstra*

ii) *The Spandaśāstra*

iii) *The Pratyabhijñāśāstra*.

i) **The Āgamaśāstra Phase**: The phase of Āgama is the earliest one which, according to tradition, has no beginning (*anādi*) and no end. It is eternally present. It has no founder. It is revelation of eternal wisdom to the seekers of truth. The revelations are collected in ancient texts, called Āgamas. According to the tradition, Trika School is said to have emanated from sixty-four *Bhairavāgamas*, but most of them are not available in a written form. Besides this, different texts give their own list of sixty-four *Bhairavāgamas*, majority of them is not available. However, some of the important tantras are available even at present. They include *Mālinīvijayatantra*[68], *Svacchandatantra*[69], *Netratantra*, also called *Mṛtyujitbhaṭṭārakatantra*[70], *Vijñānabhairava*[71], *Ānandabhairava* (lost), *Ucchuṣmabhairava* etc.

Some commentaries on the abovementioned Tāntric texts are available. The chief ones are the *Uddyota* on the *Svacchandatantra*, the *Uddyota* on the *Netratantra* and also on the *Vijñānabhairava*. From these commentaries, we get an idea of the teachings of Advaita Śaivism. It may be mentioned here that the Śaivatantras were interpreted by the dualist Śaiva writers as propagating dualist Śaiva thought. In order to put an end to misinterpretation, it is traditionally held that Śiva himself appeared in dream to Vasugupta and implored him to give correct interpretation of the Āgamas. Śiva revealed the essence of Śaiva thought in the form of *Śivasūtras* to him[72]. Hence, the *Śivasūtras* can also be included under the phase called Āgama along with other Āgama texts.

Vasugupta is regarded as the founder of the non-dualistic school of Śaivism in Kashmir as he made the *Sūtras*, revealed by Śiva, available to people. He was a historical person who lived in Harvahan near Srinagar. There are stories mentioned in different texts about the origin of *Śivasūtras* compiled by Vasugupta. These are as follows:

i) Kallaṭa in his *Spanda-Vṛtti* says that Vasugupta who was living in the valley of Harvahana stream near Srinagar discovered the *Śivasūtras* inscribed on a stone slab as told by Śiva himself.

ii) The *Vārttika*, a commentary on *Śivasūtras* by Bhāskara describes that the *Śivasūtras* were revealed to Vasugupta by a semi-perfect being appeared in his dream.

iii) *Vimarśinī*, another commentary by Kṣemarāja on the *Śivasūtras*, declares that Śiva appeared in a dream to Vasugupta and advised him to go to the Mahādeva Mountain. There he saw the *Śivasūtras* inscribed on the *Saṅkarapala* rock and asked him to teach non-dualistic Śaiva thought to those who possessed the fitness to receive this knowledge[73].

An attempt has been made in these different versions of the story to show that the *Śivasūtras* were not written by Vasugupta himself but they were revealed to him through a divine source. Hence it is included under Āgama. He must have elaborated the inner meaning of these *sūtras* only to his disciple Kallaṭa while teaching him the philosophy of the *Śivasūtras*. Therefore, Vasugupta may be regarded as the founder of this school.

The text of the *Śivasūtras* consists of seventy-seven *sūtras*[74] divided under three heads called *Sāmbhavopāya*, *Śāktopāya* and *Ānavopāya*. These are meant as spiritual paths prescribed for the *sādhakas* having varying capacity and inclination. The first section *Sāmbhavopāya* contains twenty *sūtras*. The *Śāktopāya* has ten *sūtras* and the *Ānavopāya* consists of forty-five *sūtras*.

A number of commentaries is available on the *Śivasūtras*, the oldest one being a *Vārttika*[75] commentary in verse form by Bhaṭṭabhāskar (10th century A.D.). Kṣemarāja (11th century A.D.) a disciple of Abhinavagupta, wrote an elaborate and scholarly commentary called *Vimarśinī*. A *Vṛtti* on the *Śivasūtras* by an unknown author is available. One more commentary on the *Śivasūtras* is the *Śivasūtravārttikam* by Varadārāja alias Kṛṣṇadāsa (end of the 15th century A.D.)

ii) **The Spandaśāstra Phase:** The *Spanda School* derives its name from one of its root texts viz. the *Spandakārikā*[76], *the stanzas on vibration*. The *Spandaśāstra* elaborates purely the *advaitic* principles as enunciated in the *Śivasūtras*, without giving logical arguments in support of the principles. The *Spandasūtras*[77], popularly known as the *Spandakārikā* containing 52 verses are based on the *Śivasūtras*. Authorship of the *sūtras* is ascribed to Vasugupta by Kṣemarāja but others hold that it was written by Kallaṭa (2nd and 3rd quarter of 9th century A.D.), a disciple of Vasugupta. The controversy over the authorship of *Spandasūtras* has been created by Kallaṭa, in his concluding remark occurring in the *Vètti* on the text. He says that he received the nectar like *Upadeśa* on the *Spandaśāstras* (*Spandāmṛtam*) from Vasugupta. The text is divided under four sections called *niḥsyānda*. The first *niḥsyānda* called *Svarūpaspanda* contains 25 kārikās in which the essential nature of *Spanda* has been explained. The second *niḥsyānda* named *Sahajavidyodaya* has only 7 kārikās and the third section called *Vibhūtispanda* has 20 verses mentioning supernormal powers a yogin acquires through *Spanda* while the concluding section contains 21 verses called *Abhedapala*. Kallaṭa is said to have written a brief commentary called *Spandasarvasva* or *Spanda-Vṛtti* but unfortunately this is not available. Rāmakaṇṭha (875 A.D.) has written a commentary called *Spanda-Vivṛtti* in which he has explained briefly the purport of the text. Kṣemarāja (11th century) has written two commentaries, one called *Spandanirṇaya*[78] which is wellknown for its scholarly exposition of the philosophy of Spanda. The other *Spandasandoha*[79], also a commentary by Kṣemarāja, is written on one verse, explains the purport of the whole work. Another elaborate commentary by UtpalaVaiṣṇava (2nd & 3rd quarter of the 10th century A.D.) on *Spandakārikā* is known as *Spandapradīpikā*[80]. This Spanda literature comprises of commentaries on the *Spandakārikā*, the basic text is said to be the summary of philosophical tenets found in the *Śivasūtras*.

iii) **Pratyabhijñāśāstra Phase:** The Siddha Somānanda, probably a disciple of Vasugupta, is said to be the founder of the *Pratyabhijñāśāstra*. He is known as the Originator of reasoning[81] (*Tarkasya kartā*) in the tradition. Somānanda was the first Śaivācārya who established the philosophical texts of Kashmir Śaivism on sound logical argument, refuting the views of other rival schools. His sole work *Śivadṛṣṭi*[82] which is the same as Śivadarśana is the philosophy of Kashmir Śaivism par excellence. It became so famous that Kashmir.s Advaita Śaiva School came to be known as *Pratyabhijñādarśana*. Mādhavācārya has devoted a section in his book *Sarvadarśanasaṁgraha* to describing the main thesis of Advaita Śaivas. Somānanda has traced the origin to this school of thought to *Siddhadarśana*, to Sage Durvāsā who lived in epic age. Somānanda has given an interesting account how Śaivism originated in Kashmir and developed in different forms in course of time in the colophon of text.

According to him, Lord Śiva while roaming on the mountain of Kailāsa found that the knowledge of Śaivism had disappeared under the influence of *Kālī* era. He appeared before the sage Durvāsā assuming the form of Śrīkaṇṭha and asked him to revive the Śaiva tradition in an authentic way. Durvāsā produced his three *mind-born* sons Tryambakāditya, Āmardaka and Śrīkaṇṭha and taught them the secrets of Śaiva philosophy. They propagated the Śaiva Philosophy in three different forms viz, in non-dualistic (*abheda*), dualistic-cum-non-dualistic (*bhedābheda*) and dualistic (*bheda*) respectively. Besides these three schools, another school of Śaivism was started by a descendant of Tryambaka on the daughter's side which was called the *Ardha Tryambaka* School. This school however was later given the name of *Siddha School*. Some scholars identify this with the *Kaula School*. All these schools prevailed in Kashmir at different times. Next appears Utpaladeva, a noted disciple of teacher Somānanda. He offers a valuable commentary on *Śivadṛṣṭi*, containing seven chapters. Unfortunately only four *āhnikas* or chapters (the fourth in fragments) of this book along with a commentary are available and the rest have been lost. It is also to be noted that this book is not further commented upon.

Rājānaka Utpaladeva was one of the most prolific writers of the Advaita Śaiva Philosophy of Kashmir. He was not only a philosopher but also an ardent devotee of Lord Śiva. He was a disciple of Siddha Somānanda and lived in c. 875-925 A.D. in Srinagar. Some of the most important Śaiva texts which give him outstanding position as an ācārya of Trika Philosophy are *Siddhitrayī* (*Ajaḍapramātṛsiddhi*, *Īśvarasiddhi*, *Sambandhasiddhi*), *Śivastotrāvalī* etc.

Utpaladeva's fame rests on the *īśvarapratyabhijñākārikā*[83] that means *verses on the Recognition of God*. It became so famous that Advaita Śaiva Philosophy came to be known after his work. He stresses the doctrine of recognition (*Pratyabhijñā*) as a means for achieving highest goal, i.e. realization of one's Śiva nature *sine qua non*. He therefore has named this text as *Īśvarapratyabhijñākārikā*. It contains 92 verses, divided into four books technically called *Adhikāras*. These are *Jñānādhikāra*, *Kriyādhikāra*, *Āgamādhikāra*, *Tattvādhikāra*. He also wrote two auto-commentaries on his *Kārikā*: *Vṛtti*[84] and *Vivṛtti*[85]. But no complete manuscript of either of these commentaries has yet been discovered. The *Vṛtti* on *Śivadṛṣṭi* by Utpaladeva was most probably written after *Āśvarapratyabhijñākārikā*, since the name of this very text is mentioned in the *Śivadṛṣṭi*, a text by Utpala's teacher Siddha Somānanda.

Utpala's *Śivastotrāvalī*[86] made its first appearance in 1902 in Varanasi under the Sanskrit series of Chowkhamba. The second edition came in 1964 along with the commentary of Rājānak Lakṣmaṇ Joo. This is a devotional poem in which *bhakti* is mentioned as an additional means for realization of one's Śiva nature. Here *bhakti* is of *dāsya* variety.

The *Siddhitrayī*[87] gives the metaphysical exposition of Advaita Śaiva Philosophy. Among the three Siddhis, the *Ajaḍapramātṛsiddhi* contains 27 verses in which Utpala advocates the non-insentient nature of the subject. Next in the *Īśvarasiddhi*, Utpala focuses his attention on the Sāṁkhya thought and gives a number of arguments against them along with 56 verses to admit *Īśvara* as one of the causes. Last the *Sambandhasiddhi* offers on the concept of relation through 21 verses. Besides these, there are two more *Vṛttis* on the *Īśvarasiddhi* and the *Sambandhasiddhi* which are authored by Utpaladeva. We can obtain knowledge of some tenets of Advaita Śaiva Philosophy from them.

Abhinavagupta, the Kashmirian Śaiva theologician, and also considered to be the most versatile author of the Advaita Śaiva Philosophy of Kashmir, wrote a number of pioneer works both original texts and commentaries on old texts projecting the philosophy of this system. Some of his significant works are *Paramārthasāra*[88], *Tantrāloka* and a number of smaller works such as *Parātriśikā-Vivaraṇa*, *Bodhapañcadaśikā, Tantra-Vaṭadhānika, Paramārtha-Carcā* and a few stotra texts. The *Tantrāloka*[89] is a voluminous text, his *magnum opus* containing 27 Āhnikas or chapters in 12 volumes. This monumental work forms a class by itself and expounds all aspects of Śaivism comprehensively. As regards the *Tantrāloka*, K.C. Pandey observes that it is mainly based upon the authority of the *Mālinīvijayatantra*. The *Tantrasāra*[90], a prose work in which he has summarized his own work *Tantrāloka*, is written in the form of verse. His unique contribution to the Advaita Śaiva thought lies in his attempt to synthesize diverse thought currents prevailing in Kashmir within the ambit of Śaiva thought. He blends it with the philosophical thoughts from the *Śākta* tradition, especially the *Yoginī Kaula* tradition. Among the commentaries mention may be made of *Vimarśinī*[91] commentary on *Īśvarapratyabhijñākārikā, Vivṛtti-Vimarśinī*[92] on the same text, *Vārttika* commentary on *Mālinīvijayottaratantra, Gītārthasaṁgraha* on the *Bhagavadgītā, Vivaraṇa* commentary on *Parātṛṁśikā, Laghuvṛtti*, another commentary on the same text and many others. According to K.C. Pandey, Abhinavagupta flourished in the 10th century A.D. who elevated the Pratyabhijñā phase of Trika philosophy to its highest feat.

Kṣemarāja, the brilliant pupil of Abhinavagupta, must have flourished and written in the 11th century A.D. His outstanding contributions to the system are *Pratyabhijñāhṛdayam*, *Spandasandoha*, *Śivasūtra-Vimarśinī*, *Parāpraveśikā*, *Spandasandoha* etc. The book *Pratyabhijñāhṛdayam* considers to be the digest of the Pratyabhijñā system. After Abhinavagupta and his disciple Kṣemarāja, the third phase of the Trika spread to the Tamil country.

## Notes and References

1. *imār rūdrāya tapase; imā rūdrāya śatadhanve; tryambaka yajāmahe*. Quoted by K. C. Pandey in History of Saiva Philosophy, p 2 Y. V.

2. Op. Cit cf. *veda'sti saṁhitā raudrivācyā rūdraśca devatā.* Mṛgendrāgama. Quoted by K.C. Pandey in Hist. of Saiva Phil. p 2.
3. A.V. Kānda VI, An 2 Prapāthaka 20; Anuvāka 4, Prapa.
4. Op. Cit I, 49; III 53; IV, 10
5. *śivasya bhagavatahitśivabhāgavataÿ.* Patanjali's Mahābhāsya, Keilhorn trans. Vol. II pp. 387-80
6. Keilhorn, *Vyākaraṇa Mahābhāsya*, p.19
7. Comprehensive History of India Vol. II p.401
8. Catalogue of Coins of Anc. India in Br. Museum, pp.130-32
9. *śaivam pāśupatam somaṁ lākulaṁ ca caturvidhām.* Suprabhedāgama, Kriyāpāda, p.19
10. Op. Cit
    *yathā māheśvare tantre viruddhāṁ bahujalpitam /*
    *caturvidyāhi tatsiddhacaryāmārgānusāriṇah //*
    *yathā kāpālikāḥ kālāmūkhāḥ pāśupatāstathā /*
    *Śaivastantraca kāpālamatamevaṁ pracakṣate //*
11. Op. Cit, Ch. II, 2, 35
12. Op. Cit, Act. III
13. *atha ye cānye ha vrithā kasāyakuṇdalinaḥ kāpālinaḥ.*
    Maitr. Prap.VI, Verse 8
14. Cf. Handiqui: Yaśaṣtilakacampu and Indian Culture, pp.348
15. *śaivāḥ siddhāntamārgasthā śaśaivāḥ paśupatāstathā /*
16. *śaivāḥ mahāvratadharāśśaivāḥ kāpālikāpare //* Vāy. Sam. XXIX
    It is a prahasana (farcical play) by Mahendra Vikram Verma in which an incident has been described. A young lady and a Kāpālika were drinking wine from kapāla. The kapāla was taken away by a dog.
17. Aghoranātha and Kapāla-Kuṇdalā are the Kāpālika characters in the play by Bhavabhūti. The play (a *prakaraṇa*) in ten acts depicts love of princess Mālatī for Madhava.
18. Op. Cit IV, 23
19. Act III, Verse 13
20. Handiqui: Yaśaṣtilak Campu and Indian Culture, pp 348 ff
21. *vā (lā) kulaṁ somatantraṁ ca jagād parameśvaraḥ* / ISG, III, p. 6.
22. Tantrādhikāranirṇaya p.2 (Benaras ed.) attributes the following verse to Vaśiṣtha and Liṇgapurāṇa:
    *kecillokāyataṁ brahmān kecit somaṁ mahāmune /*
    *nākulaṁ kecidicchanti tathā kecitu bhairavam //*
23. *vāmaṁ pāśupataṁ somaṁ lāmgalam caiva bhairavam.*
    *na saivyametat kathitam vedavadyam tathetaram.*
24. Op. Cit
25. *sāṁkhyaṁ yogaṁ pāñcarātraṁ vedāh pāśupataṁ tathā /*
    *jñānāni etāni rājarṣe viddhi nānāmatāni vai //*
    *umāpatiḥ bhūtapatiḥ śrīkaṇṭho brahmaṇaḥ sūtaḥ /*
    *uktavanidamvyagro jñānaṁ pāśu pataṁ śivaḥ//*
    Mahābhārata Śāntiparva Ch. 347
26. Kashmir Saivism, pp 5-6, Tantrāloka,1, p. 27

27. *kalau pravṛtte yāteṣu dūrgamgocaram /*
*kalāpigrāmapramukhacchinne śivaśāsane //*
*kailāsādrau bhramandevo mūrtyā śrīkaṇṭharūpayā /*
*anugrāhāya avatīrṇaścodayāmāsa bhūtale //*
Op. Cit, pp. 22-23
28. *jñānaudhena samākhyātaḥ padabandhajanena tu /*
*śrīkaṇṭhasya prasādena sarvo'yam pariṇato mama //*
Quotes in Studies of Ṭantras, p.102
29. *asya tantrasya kā saṁjñā, piṅgalamata saṁjñā ........ ka kartā, bhagavan śrīkaṇṭhanātha kartā*
Quoted in Studies in Tantra p.106
30. *anugrahāya avatīrṇaścadayamasa bhūtale,* pp.22-23
31. Op.Cit III, 347
32. *atha vaiśeṣika vrumaḥ pāśupatānyanāmakam.*
Saḍdarśanasamuccaya, pp. 11-12
33. An Outline of Hist. of Saiva Philo. p. 65
34. Vijñānabhairava with commentary by Kṣemarāja and Śiva
35. Op.Cit Gaek. Oriental Series Appendix p. 25
36. Op.Cit p.116
37. Epigraphica Indica Vol. XXI, pp. 1f.
38. *iha kuśika gārgya kauruṣa maitreya iti tadaṁtahsadaḥ /*
Udaipur Ins. of Naravahan. Epig. Inq. I, p. 281
39. *nakulīśo'tha kauśikah gārgyah maitreyah kauruṣah īśānah pāragārgya kapilāṇda manuṣyakah kuśikah atrih piṅgalah* .............. / Saḍdarśanadsamuccaya
40. *paraṁ śāstreṣu naiyāyikāḥ sadā śivabhaktatvāt śaivā ityueyante vaiśeṣikāstu pāśupatā.* Gunaratna on Saódarśanasamuccaya, p. 30
41. Pāśupatasūtras, also known as Pañcādyāyī by Lākulīśa has a comm. by Kauṇḍinya known as Pañcārthikābhāṣya
42. Cf. Pandey K.C. Outlines of Hist. of Saiva. Philo. p. 15
43. Ibid p.16
44. Ibid
45. Ibid p.15 ff
46. Ibid p.16
47. Cf. Sinha, J. N. Hist. of Indian Philo. Vol. III, p. 176
48. Ibid
49. Pandey K. C. Outlines of Hist. of Śaiva Philo. p. 47
50. Ibid p. 49
51. Ibid
52. Ibid
53. Ibid p.51
54. Ibid
55. Ibid p. 52

56. Ibid
57. Cultural Heritage of India, Vol. IV, pp. 79-97
58. The Encyclopedia of Religion, Vol.13, pp.15-18
59. Chp.8, pp.190-201
60. Dyczkowski, Mark S. G. Doctrine of Vibration, p.2
61. Tucci, G. La Via dello Svat. p16. Quoted by Dyczkowski p.3
62. Translated by Pandit, Ranjit Sitaram. Invitation, p. xxv
63. The Sacred Books of the East. Vol. 35 Introduction p. xxxviii & Vol. 36 Introduction p. xxiii
64. i) *viṣṇudevo jagannātho brahman prāpte kalau yuge /*
    *aṣṭāviṁśattame bhāvo buddho nāma jagadguruḥ // 709 //*
    ii) *buddhārcāsnāpanaṁ kāryaṁ śākyovatai rvacanaistathā /*
    *sudhāsitāśca kartavyā śākyāvāsāḥ prayatnataḥ // 712*
    iii) *śākyānāṁ pūjanaṁ kāryaṁ cīvarāhārapustakai /*
    *sarvametad bhavetkārya yāvatprāpta bhavenmaghā // 714*
65. Ibid.
66. Dwivedi, Kamala, Paramārthasāra (trans.) Intro.
67. Op. Cit p. 15 ff
68. It is one of the foundational texts of Trika School. Abhinavagupta's Tantrāloka is based on this text. It was published in Kashmir Series of Texts and Studies, No. 37 Srinagar 1922
69. Uddyota by Kṣemarāja. 7 Vols. K.S.T.S., no. 21, 1921; 38, 1923; 44, 1925; 48, 1927; 51, 1930; 53, 1933; 56, 1955 All edited by M.S. Kaul
70. Published in K.S.T.S. in 2 Vols. No. 46, 61, 1922
71. Published in K.S.T.S. No 8 Srinagar, 1913
72. Chatterjee, J.C. Kashmir Śaivism, p. 8 ff published in K.S.T.S. No. 4 Srinagar, 1913
73. Ibid
74. Published in K.S.T.S. No. 1 Srinagar 1911
75. Published in K.S.T.S. No. 4 Srinagar 1916; it is comparatively of a later date, probably 11th century since there is confusion about the date of Bhaṭṭabhāskara.
76. Published in K.S.T.S. No. 5 Srinagar 1916
77. The Sūtras, generally called the Spandakārikā. Verses were also designated as Sūtras, eg. Pratyabhijñāsūtra
78. Published in K.S.T.S. No. 43 Srinagar 1925. It is doubtful whether any complete Ms. of this comm. is available.
79. Published in K.S.T.S. No.16 Srinagar 1917. This comm. explains the purport of the whole work.
80. Published in Tantrasaṁgraha Vol.1 Varanasi 1970. But the author of this commentary is not the same author of the āśvarapratyabhijñākārikā since Utpala Viṣṇava's date was later than Utpaladeva but earlier than Abhinavagupta.
81. Chatterjee, J.C. Kashmir Saivism, p. 17
82. Published in K.S.T.S. No 54 Srinagar 1934
83. Published in K.S.T.S. No. 34 Srinagar 1921
84. Published in K.S.T.S. No. 34 Srinagar 1921, Edited by M.S. Kaul, 161 verses are only available.

85. It is almost lost, some fragment only available at the personal disposal of Dr. K.C. Pandey.
86. Sanskrit text with Intro; Eng. Trans., Glossary by N.K. Kotru, Delhi: Motilal Banarsidass, 1985
87. Published in K.S.T.S. No. 34 Srinagar 1921
88. This particular text is later adaptation of Ādhārkārikā attributed to Śeṣhanāga in which Abhinavagupta suited something to his own purpose as to make it into Śaiva text. Published in K.S.T.S. No. 7, 1916. Edited by J.C. Chatterjee. English translation titled Paramārthasāra of Abhinavagupta by L.D. Bernett. Journal of Royal Asiatic Society of Great Britain and Ireland, London, 1910
89. Published in 12 Vols. with Viveka by Jayaratha. Part 1 edited by M.R. Sastri; Part 2-12 edited by M.S.Kaul in K.S.T.S. No. 23, 1918; 28, 1921; 29, 1921; 30, 1921; 36, 1922; 41, 1924; 47, 1026; 52, 1933; 57, 1936; 59. 1938
90. Edited by M.S. Kaul. Published in K.S.T.S. No. 17, 1918
91. Vol. 1 K.S.T.S. No. 22, 1918. Edited by M.R. Sastri. Vol. 2 K.S.T.S. No. 33, 1921. Edited by M.S. Kaul. English translation of the Vimarśinī by K.C. Pandey in 3 Vols. with Bhāskarī. Comm. Saraswati Bhawan Texts, No. 84, Benaras, 1954
92. 3 Vols. Published in K.S.T.S. No. 60, 1938; 62, 1941 and 66, 1934 respectively. All edited by M.S. Kaul

5

# Śiva Literàture and Religion: An Overview of Śivapurāna

*Lalita Chakraborty*

The long history of Indian literature reflects Indian culture and civilization consisting of beliefs and superstitions. The word 'religion' connotes an idea propounded by man which varies from environ to environ, from community to community even from person to person. But in India religion in the broader connotation of the term is the way of life. Though in Indian language the word '*dharma*' is substituted with the word 'religion' the word '*dharma*' expresses something more than religion. Dharma represents the intrinsic potential of life in its totality. Apart from this we can not conceive any Indian thought. So literature in general, whether sartras or otherwise is not only a way of thought but also is reflective of a particular way of life inspite of the great diversity in Indian thought and lifestyle.

चतुर्वर्ग or the fourfold goals of human life i.e. *dharma, artha, kāma*, *moksa* are the common aims of literary compositions that are enlightened by spiritual thought. The चतुर्वर्ग with the primary focus on *moksa* is attained through the execution of *kāma* and *artha* bound by *dharma*. Here *dharma* means religion, *kama* means requirements for life and *artha* is that which mobilizes the requirements and *moksa* means emancipation from mental hindrances.

Indian mind has never denied the natural instinct of human beings. But the aim is to sublimate them by challenging them through *dharma*. No work whether the religious or secular can be conceived without *dharma*. Every literature therefore has a spiritual touch in it which otherwise may be difficult to be accepted by the Indian mind.

The concept of चतुर्वर्ग is a later development. Leaving the Vedic literature all the streams of thought have aspired to attain these aims of life otherwise known as पुरूषार्थ with the ultimate goal of attaining मोक्ष or liberation. The way to attain this पुरूषार्थ may be diverse but the goal is same.

Diversity is a characteristic of Indian thought whether in religion or in common life. Diverse religious thoughts have given rise to numerous sects of worship of particular such as *Śaiva*, *tantric, vaisnavite, gānapatya* and so on.

The essence of Indian spiritualistic thought is the three visible forms of the deity or the trinity consisting of *Brahmā*, *Visnu* and *Śiva*. *Brahmā* is regarded as the creator, *Visnu* the preserver and *Śiva*, the destroyer. In course of time the social ecology got a new approach due to influx of multiethnicity in the Indian peninsula. Though *Brahmā*, *Visnu* and *Śiva* are the important functional divinities, the relative emphasis often varies from one text to another in different periods of time. *Śiva* became the most important and popular deity in the Indian religious thought. This importance have a long history which may be traced to a remote past even before the Vedic literature or the Vedic culture. Gradually *Śiva*-worship was established as a cult it goes back to pre-Vedic times. It is very difficult to ascertain any particular date of *Śiva*-worship which had spread in a long tract of land from Mesopotamia to India may not be in the same form but as the fountainhead of the creation of the universe.

In course of time the Rgvedic Rudra became *Śiva* of the later period. In Rgveda Rudra is raised to supreme power. In ancient time whenever a man came to anything which are terrible and destructive then Rudra was the god thought of and prayed to protect. Some of the phenomena of external nature which are dreadful and inspired awe and terror are attributed to the wrath of god. The ancient Indians saw the god Rudra in it. In the Vedic literature Rudra was a common epithet for any god in their terrible and destructive aspect. By prayer praise and offerings Rudra becomes propitiated. Subsequently this belief rendered him in the omnipresent supreme lord of the universe. In course of time Rudra was no more an epithet but an independent god. He became the auspicious *Śiva* who pervades the universe. Hence the god that is feared is Rudra *Śiva*. Gradually the idea developed Rudra the god of wild became the beneficent *Sankara*.

Rudra was the common epithet for any Vedic deity because they were fearful as they were to be propitiated for the welfare of human beings. Later on Rudra were conceived in a group of eleven. Where in the Yajurveda *Śiva* has been given as the epithet of Rudras. There was a gradual evolution of thought and with the nuances of Rudra in the Vedas no exact time of the development of the concept of *Śiva* can be assigned.

## Rudra vis-à-vis Śiva

Etymology of the word '*Rudra*' according to *Sayana* is thus: रुद् दुःखम् दुःखहेतुर्वा पापादि तस्य द्रावयिता देवोऽसि[1] Hence *Rudra* means one who drives away the suffering. Again it leaves a room to hold that the word Śiva means the one who removes sin. The word Śiva is derived from the root '*so*'[2] means 'to make thin'. Then both *Rudra* and Śiva are identical in removing the sufferings of the animate beings. That concept is justified by the epithet of

Śiva as *Pasupati*. Here पशु refers to the animate beings of the world and पशुपति is the guide to lead and liberate them from their worldly sufferings by removing ignorance.

## Etymology of the term Śiva

It may not be irrelevant to focus on the problem of genderisation of the words in Sanskrit language in this context. The formation of शिवम् and शिव in neuter and masculine gender respectively suggest different connotations with reference to the context of the expression. In Sabda Kalpadruma the word Śiva is explained in two ways, firstly:

> शिवं कल्याणं विद्यत्येऽस्य शिवः। श्यति अशुभमिमि वा। शेरतेऽवतिष्ठन्ते अणिमादयोष्टौ गुणा अस्मिन् इति वा शिवः।

Secondly the word शिवम् is explained in the sense of मङ्गलम or सुखम्। In Vedic literature the term शिव is used mostly in the sense of auspiciousness.

In *Śivapurana* the term Śiva is explained as:

> शं नित्यं सुखमानन्दमिकारः पुरुषः स्मृतः।
> वकारः शक्तिरमृतं मेलनं शिव उच्यते।।[3]

श denotes eternal bliss, इ is *purusa* and व means amrita *sakti*, then the whole word means the creator of eternal bliss.

## Śivapurana

In Indian traditional literature numerous works are available in multiple Indian languages. In order to be critical in studying *Śaiva* religion the literary resource is restricted to the *Śivapurana*. It requires a separate treatment elsewhere to survey the Śiva literature oral and scriptural in Indian languages (Sanskrit, Prakrit and Tamil).

Because the field and time of *Śiva* studies is very vast and may need thorough and separate research. In this study particularly reflects the thought contained in the *Śivapurana*.

The purana in general is a class of literature that contains materials on religion, philosophy, sociology, politics as well as different aspects of ancient Indian culture. The puranas are divided into two classes - the Mahapuranas[4] and the Upapuranas *Śiva*purana the fourth one of the Mahapuranas[5] belongs to *Śiva*, created by *Śiva* and all sacred rites are mentioned therein. This excellent purana is prescribed for a devotee of *Śiva* and a follower of the *Śaiva* cult. The Mahapuranas are classified in three names also i.e. Sattvika Rajasika & Tamasika. Among these three the *Śiva*purana is known as Tamasikapurana, which deals with a lot to norms and rituals. However, this purana conceives *Śiva* as the eternal principle, the cosmic soul and the support of all existence. Moreover the greatness of this purana lies in stating that the *Śiva* himself is the narrator of this purana.[6] The purana alone grants the salvation to him who reads the entire text and it removes the three types of distress (*ādhyātmika, ādhibhautika, ādhidaivika*). Thus the glory of this purana has a deep and sustaining influence on the mind of the *sādhakas* as well as on the general *Śiva* worshippers.

Shivapurana[7] as it is available to us is distributed into seven samhitas designated as *Vidyesvara, Rudra, Satarudra, Kotirudra, Uma, Kailasa* and *Vayaviya*. *Rudrasamhita* is divided into five sections viz. सृष्टिखण्ड, सतीखण्ड, पार्वतीखण्ड, कुमारखण्ड and युद्धखण्ड। The seventh संहिता i.e. *vayaviya samhita* has two parts पूर्वभाग and उत्तरभाग। The Bengali edition consists of six *samhitas* (section) – *jnana, vidyesvara, kailasa, sanatkumara, vayaviya* (divided into two parts: पूर्वभाग and उत्तरभाग) and *dharma samhita*. Each section of this Purana covers the magnanimity of Śiva separately and that makes the Purana interesting to the listeners as well as the practitioners.

According to *Śivapurana*[8] that is the *Śaivadharma* where in *Śiva* the bestower of salvation is directly perceived and this is the excellent practice of the *sadhakas*. This practice of dharma is divided into five sections i.e. *kriya, tapah, japa, dhyana* and *jnana*. Here *kriya* means the rite of *candrayana*, '*tapah*', is the worship of *Śiva*s phallic image, '*japa*' is the repetition of the names of *Śaiva*, dhyana is pondering over *Śiva* and 'knowledge' means the perfect knowledge which is explained in *Śaiva* Agamas. These five constitute the greatest *Śivadharma* which is elaborately explained in *Śiva* Agamas.

The *Śiva* Agamas are of two varieties – *Srauta* and *Asrauta* or independent texts.[9] This *Asrauta* Agramas are called as *Śiva Siddhanta*. In this literature the *Pasupata* Yoga is also discussed through which direct perception of *Śiva* can be possible. In this context *Namastakayoga* also prescribed by *Śiva* himself. These eight names are *Śiva, Maheswara, Rudra, Visnu, Pitamaha, Samsaravaidya, Sarvajna* and *Paramatmana*.[10] By means of this yoga the supreme knowledge of *Śiva* is generated. Through this knowledge the devotee can perceive *Śiva* and is being liberated becomes identical with *Śiva*. *Śiva* is the perfect knowledge. The five great *saktis* of *Śiva* are activity, knowledge, completeness, eternality and pervasiveness.[11]

In this context *Śivapurana* holds the following points: *Śiva* has also been designated with several names: *Śiva, Maheswara, Rudra, Vishnu, Pitamaha, Samsaravaidya, Sarvajna*, and *Paramatmana*. Without the contact of the *avidya Śiva* the *puresouled* is endowed with good attributes and called as *Śiva*. He is *Maheswara*, beyond the *Purusa*, who is the enjoyer and becomes merged in *Prakriti*.

He is rightly termed as *Rudra*, who dispels the misery or the cause of misery. He is called as Vishnu for his all pervasiveness. Being the cause of the universe he is regarded as *Pitamaha*. Shiva dissolute the cause of the संसार or भागयन्त्रणा like a physician so he is संसारवैद्य, he is सर्वज्ञ who knows every objects of the world and there is no greater atma than him being attributed with the great qualities.

The universe consists of eight forms of lord *Śiva* i.e. *Sarva, Bhava, Rudra, Ugra, Bhima, Pasupati, Isana* and *Mahadeva*. These eight forms constitute the gross material elements, they are respectively earth, water, fire, wind, ether, soul, sun and the moon. These eight forms of *Śiva* is regarded as Atman. In *Isa upanaisad* the same idea has been explained in the mantra:

ईशावास्यमिदं सर्वं यत्किञ्च जगत्यां जगत् (1/1)

*Śiva* is characterized by equanimity of soul every where. He is the ultimate principle of the world.

The five supreme ethical qualities namely क्षमा, सत्य, धृति, तपो and वैराग्य have been attributed to *Śiva*.[12] He is at the same time विधातृ and *Visnu* and hence achieved the epithet of *Maheswara*. He creates the universe, protects it and preserves also. He is the generator of the *dyavabhumi* i.e. heaven and earth and from him are created all the deities. As the ultimate principle of the world he gave intense spiritual satisfaction to the thinkers of the upanisadschool. To them *Śiva* is regarded as the *purusam mahantam*. So the Rsi of the *Svetasvatara upanisad* could pray to him in the mantra:

अजात इत्येवम कश्चित भीरु प्रापद्यते[13]

He is uncreated and unborn. Likewise *Śaivapurana*[14] states:

अशरीरो महादेवो अनुत्पत्तिरयोनिजः ।।

*Śiva* presides over all by means of this murtis, which are known as – *Brahma, Visnu, Rudra, Mahesa* and *Sada Śiva*. There is nothing which is not pervaded by these five murtis these are famous as *pancabrahmanas* or the five embodiment as *Isana, Purusa, Aghora, Vamadeva* and *Sadyojata*. These murtis are the presiding deities of the sense organs and the sole cause of the prosperity.

*Śiva* is often described as *ardha nārisvarah*. *Śiva* and the *parasakti* are the inseparable tattvas. At the will of *Śiva, Sakti* is united with Him and manifests at the first creation, like the oil from the seed. This corresponds to the idea of *ardha nārisvara*, long ago formulated in the Indian mind. This form of *Śiva* is symbolical of the process of creation. This concept is comparable to the *Samkhya* doctrine of *Purusa* and *Prakriti*. The *paramasakti* united with the *kriyasakti* of *Śiva* originated the primordial sound or Nāda, from this Nāda comes out Bindu and then Sadā *Śiva*, *Mahesvara* and from *Mahesvara Suddhavidyā* is originated. This vidya is called a *Vagisa*.[15] Thus this vidya is recognized as *Sarvavallava* (beloved of *Śaiva*) holds all the words and *Śiva* the moon crested lord holds all their meanings.

शब्दजातमशेषस्तु धत्ते शर्व्वस्य वल्लभा।
अर्थरूपं यदखिलं धत्ते मुग्धेन्दुशेखरः।।[16]

This verse might be referring to the *ardha-narisvara* Tantrasadbhava[17] has elucidated this idea in detail. As has been said there the letters are a form of *sakti* or *matrika* which is known as the very form of *Śiva*.

As the cause of all types of the miseries ignorance can be removed by the comprehensive knowledge of the object. Object is twofold: sentient and non-sentient and there is a controller of these two. These three are called as पशु, पाश and पति। They are also called as अक्षर, क्षर and क्षराक्षरपर respectively. Pasus are bound with the पाश, पति is the releaser of the पशु. Siva is regarded as पशुपति। Here पशु suggests the animate beings of numerous kinds who are under the veil of ignorance. In other words those veils become the limitation or bondage to reach the state of सदाशिव 'The Ever Good One'.[18]

Siva is said to be '*Bhagavan*'. Here the word *Bhaga* denotes prakriti out of which every enjoyable objects are evolved and *bhagavan* is Lord Shiva Himself, because he is the alone bestower of enjoyment.[19] The *Svetasvatara*[20] upanisad states that the omnipotent *paramatman* is also designated as Bhagavan. But there *Śiva*, the pervader of the entire phenomenal existence is regarded as auspicious and Bhagavan is attributed with great six ethical qualities namely, ऐश्वर्य्य, वीर्य, यश, श्री, पूर्णज्ञान and वैराग्य Here भग means these six types of qualities. Therefore the prevedic terrible Rudra gradually evolved to the auspicious lord the omnipresent *Śiva* hidden in all beings, ultimately responsible for creation, preservation as well as the destruction. *Śivasutra*[21] describes the main powers of *Śiva*. As the fundamental Reality from which arises everything and to which every thing is withdrawn. There *Śiva* is regarded as Bhairava-'bha' indicating maintainance of the of the world 'ra' ravana or the withdrawal and 'va' vamana or projection of the world.

For the average animate beings Shiva is regarded as an emanation of opposite virtues. The Purana in narrative style of composition describes the white embodiment has blue - azur colour in neck i.e. नीलकण्ठ. Puranic legends refers to the occasion of swallowing poisons coming out of the king of the serpent while the great ocean was churned by two competitive groups namely सुर and असुर and that bespeaks the two opposite nature of *Śiva* complaisant and sheer destroyer.

*Śiva* is also Iswara for holding opposite characteristics enumerated broadly to be eight in number.

At the time of creation he creates the universe and at the time of dissolution he withdraws everything. Śivapurana states :

स सर्गकाले च करोति सर्वं।
संहारकाले पुनराददाति।।[22]

This opposite nature makes Him more auspicious. He has neither happiness, nor unhappiness, neither karmas nor akarmas, neither birth, nor death. He is regarded as terrible and gentle, passionate and passionless, stable as well as not stable, expressible and in expressible. He is *sabdātmāka* and *sabdātīta*.[23] Many of the episodes in the *Śaiva* myth cycle revolve around the dynamic character of *Śiva* as the god equally as ascetic and erotic, a master of both yogic restraint and creative prowess. Thus the sages unable to determine the true nature of their Lord *Śiva*, express their feeling by saying :

तव तत्वं न जानामि की कीदृशोऽसि महेश्वेर।
यादृशोऽसि महादेव तादृशाय नमो नमः।।[24]

To his devotee *Śiva* is the light of the lights, fruit of all holy things, the knower of the knowledge, the self controller of the self controlled and the wisdom of the wise. He is the promoter of the universe, who always enjoys the act of creating, absorbed in protecting and bent upon destroying. He is vibrating in His own nature.

*Śiva* tradition has emerged with indigenousness since the hoary past. Several emanations of *Śiva* founding visual and performing arts all over the peninsula claim the glory of *Śiva* through ages in multiple forms and presentations. The present study is restricted to only the literature but the aesthetic items beginning from Harappa culture upto the South-East Asia beseech a wide panorama which is not restricted to the sophisticated elite group but also to the average peoples who may not be always literate. The spirituality behind the *Siva* worship is simple - *Let me submit to Śiva that is I am Śiva and Śiva is myself.* The ultimate goal of the invoker, praiser and devotee of *Śiva* is a final merging in *Śiva* Himself –

न मे द्वेषरागौ न मे लोभमोहो
मदो नैव मे नैव मात्सर्य्यभावः।
न धर्म्मो न चार्थो न कामो न मोक्ष -
श्चिदानन्दरूपः शिवोऽहं शिवोऽहम्॥[25]

### Notes and References

1. Rgveda II. 1. 6.
2. Unadi Sutra 1. 153.
3. Vide – Pracin Bharater Devabhavana – Mita Chattopadhyay Sanskrita Pustak Bhandar, Kolkata, 1980, p. 179.
4. Śivapurāna, Vayaviyasamhita, Purvabhaga, 1.37 Ed. Panchanan Tarkaratna, Kolkata, 1314.
5. Ibid., 1. 41- 42.
6. Śivapurāna, Sivapurnamahatmyam – 8, Ed. Pt. Sriramji Sharma Acharya, Samskriti Samasthan, Bareli, 1966.
7. Several recenssions of this purana exist. Two printed editions have been used and those are of different manuscripts. To avoid anomaly references are given on the printed date and the sloka no. Two separate versions opens a new dialogue regarding the understanding of the text.
8. Śivapurāna, Vayaviyasamhita, Purvabhaga, 28. 2-8, Ed. Panchanan Tarkaratna, Kolkata, 1314.
9. Śivapurāna, Vayaviyasamhita, Uttarabhaga, 8. 36-38, Ed. Panchanan Tarkaratna, Kolkata, 1314.
10. Śivapurāna kotirudrasamhita, p. 797, Ed. Pt. Sriramji Sharma Acharya, Samskriti Samasthan, Bareli, 1966.
11. Śivapurāna kailasa samhita, 10. 158-159, Ed. Panchanan Tarkaratna, Kolkata, 1314.
12. Śivapurāna sanatkumar samhita, 59. 7-8, Ed. Panchanan Tarkaratna, Kolkata, 1314.
13. Svetasvatara upanisad, 4. 21.
14. Śivapurāna sanatkumar samhita, 2. 33, Ed. Panchanan Tarkaratna, Kolkata, 1314.
15. Śivapurāna, Vayaviyasamhita, Uttarabhaga, 5. 18-21, Ed. Panchanan Tarkaratna, Kolkata, 1314.
16. Śivapurāna, Vayaviyasamhita, Uttarabhaga, 5. 66, Ed. Panchanan Tarkaratna, Kolkata, 1314.
17. सर्वे वर्णात्मका मन्त्रास्ते च शक्त्यात्मका प्रिये।
    शक्तिस्तु मातृका ज्ञेया सा च ज्ञेया शिवात्मिका - तन्त्रसद्भाव, vide Śivasutra. II. 3. Ed. Jaideva Singh, MLBD, Delhi, 1979, p. 89.
18. Śivapurāna, Vayaviyasamhita, Purvabhaga, 5. 13, Ed. Panchanan Tarkaratna, Kolkata, 1314.
19. Śivapurāna, Vidyeswara Samhita, 14 101-102.

20. Svetasvatara upanisad, 3. 11.
21. Śivasutra, 1.5.
22. Śivapurāna, Vayaviyasamhita, Purvabhaga, 4. 141, Ed. Panchanan Tarkaratna, Kolkata, 1314.
23. Śivapurāna, Vayaviyasamhita, Uttarabhaga, 6. 28-38, Ed. Panchanan Tarkaratna, Kolkata, 1314.
24. Śivamahimna Stotra, 29.
25. Nirvana Shatkam Stotram, Sankaracharya.

6

# 'Rama-katha' as Heroic Theme in Ramayana: A New Interpretation

*Debashree Dattaray*

Raymond Trousson (1964) has suggested that dividing Theme into two subspecialities may help in making their examination more focused. First of these two subspecialities is Heroic Themes. Heroic themes are those, which lend dignity to the Stoff or subject matter. For example, Faust or Rama could be taken as instances of Heroic themes. The heroes of heroic themes outgrow their original frame of reference; and their memory is kept alive by a body of texts, by works produced by various authors across the ages.

For the past two thousand years *The Ramayana* has been among the most important literary and oral texts of South Asia. This epic poem provides insights into many aspects of Indian culture and continues to influence the politics, religion and art of modern India. The heroic deeds of Rama have been a source of inspiration to poets for centuries. In this context, we would examine the Rama-katha as a theme found in the works of three poets, Valmiki (original author, 500 B.C.) in Sanskrit, Kamban in Tamil (9th Century A.D), and Tulsidas in Hindi (16th Century A.D).

Universally acclaimed and accepted as the 'adi kavi' (first poet) among Sanskrit poets, Valmiki is credited with discovering a metrical expression containing such dimensions, visions and ideas that his verses remain unparalleled to this date. Valmiki's *Ramayana* in classical Sanskrit consists of 24,000 verses and is divided into seven sections.

Kavi Kamban was born in the culturally rich Thanjavur district in the modern state of Tamil Nadu, India. His version of *The Ramayana* in Tamil called '*Iramavataram*' is an epic of 10,000 verses of 4-lines each. *Kamba Ramayana* is not a translated version of the Sanskrit epic by Valmiki, but an original retelling of the story of Rama, as the incarnation of Lord Tirumal (Vishnu). His poetry, which includes brilliant use of rhyme and simile, earned him the title — Kavichakravarti (emperor among poets).

Tulsidas, a great scholar, was well versed in Vedic lore, philosophy and mythology. Probably the most marvellous thing about the life of Tulsi, apart from, his devotion to Rama, is his capacity of assimilating different tenets, Vaisnava, Saiva, advaita, Sankhya, etc. His *Ramcharitmanas* in Hindi, widely popular in northern part of India, lays a strong emphasis on Rama as an incarnation of Lord Vishnu. In addition to his great work, Tulsidas composed at least six other poems, all of them having the one object of popularizing the cultus of his tutelary divinity. They are the *Ramagitavali*, the *Dohavali*, the *Kabit-sambandha*, the *Vinay-Patrika*, the *Satsai*, and the *Ramagya*. The basic religious principles of Tulsidas, so far as they can be known, are contained in the dialogue between Bhusundi and Garur in the Epilogue (Uttara Kanda). His religion is a religion of being wholeheartedly devoted to Rama whose name itself he says is like a sun to dispel the darkness of ignorance.

The focus of my discussion would be Book II or the ***Ayodhya Kanda*** in the *Ramayana* one of the most dramatic chapters in the Rama legend, dealing with the story of Rama's exile from Ayodhya.

With an in-depth study of the ***Ayodhya Kanda*** in Valmiki, Tulsidas and Kamban, I will focus on the assemblage of 'oral' and literary' narratives, plot structure, the constraints placed on language and topoi, and the strategies employed to enrich the narrative, under the tutelage of a common heroic theme, namely, Rama. The thematic element structures a work in a perceptible manner. A theme is the result of a passage from the general to the particular. The thematologist deploys a tactical move by highlighting content and thus re-routes questions of form and meaning via that of content. Theme relates to *characters*. Most importantly, theme initiates a relationship between author-reader based on convergences and divergences of socio-political realities.

A specialist in folklore who was familiar with the creativity, scope and diversity in oral tellings in India, A.K. Ramanujan argued that we should abandon the binary notion of 'the Ramayana' and 'its variants.' Instead Ramanujan likened the Ramayana tradition to a pool of signifiers, arguing that each author (or performer) 'dips into it and brings out a unique crystallization, a new text with a unique texture and a fresh context.' Ramanujan concluded: 'In this sense, no text is original, yet no telling is a mere retelling.[1]

His perspective pushes us to view each text as a telling rather than a variant, since 'variant' implies divergence from the 'real' one. This view is called the 'Many Ramayanas' approach. The 'Many Ramayanas' model fosters appreciation of multiple tellings of their own, instead of in relation to Valmiki. Each of these tellings therefore provides interesting readings in relation to analytical tools of narratology (especially discourse analysis). Further, through these tellings, another important aspect of a narrative, that is, its syntagmatic structure or the mode of time-awareness in which listeners are placed is highlighted.

According to Paula Richman, a telling of Rama's story always carries political messages, whether they are explicitly stated or not, and whether listeners perceive *Rama-katha* as a political text or not. She observes:

> Rama's story is inherently political for at least three reasons. First, the Ramayana tradition elevates the ideal of 'Ramraj', a polity whose king practices absolute justice, maintains order, preserves stability, and ensures the prosperity of the kingdom, as these functions are set out in *dharmasastras*.... Second, because devotees praise Rama as *maryada purusottama* (exemplar of social propriety), Rama's story presents ideal behaviour not only for ruler and citizen, but in relation to family, caste and gender hierarchy as well. ...Third, the vision of Rama is utopian; utopian visions tend to encourage people to achieve perfect society here on earth, a project that often mobilizes elite, courtly, state, and/or electoral institutions to do so.[2]

These controversies about power, propriety and kingship within the Ramayana tradition results in various narrative conflicts, viz., Man vs. Himself, Man vs. Man, Man vs. Society, Man vs. Nature, Man vs. Supernatural, Man vs. God. Such conflicts comprise epic themes and incidents.

The narrative preface or *upodgatha* of the Valmiki *Ramayana* opens with one of the culture's most elaborate and well-known celebrations of the idealized South Asian male. Here Valmiki, a forest sage, but not yet the 'first poet', questions the divine seer Narada as to the existence in the world of their time of an ideal man in terms of his moral, physical and intellectual qualities. Valmiki, the *tapasvi*, meditating on the nature of things asks Narada, 'Who is the perfect hero?' Narada is best qualified to answer the question as he has the freedom of the three worlds: he knows the past and the future as well as the present. And he answers the question without a moment's hesitation:

> 'Many and rare are the *qualities* that you have mentioned, O sage; but listen.
> I will tell you of a man I know who unites in himself all these qualities.'[3]

Narada responds with ten verses in which he identifies the Kosalan king Rama as such a person, elaborating on Valmiki's terms. The seer follows his dense desctription of Rama's qualities with a terse account of his tragic career, a brief description of his utopian reign, and an account of the differing benefits that accrue to the members of the four great 'varnas' of Aryan social classes from hearing his story. All this takes him less than sixty verses. The accent is on the 'nara'. There is no hint in the *Samkshepa Ramayana* of the avatar, though long before the poem is done the receptive reader feels that even if mere men could have done many things, which Rama did, they could never be what Rama was. But the Rama of Narada is even for the Devarshi a unique phenomenon and a transforming experience. His reply is not improvised on the spur of the moment. He has known Rama by his *tapas* just as Valmiki is prompted by his tapas to ask the question to which the answer his Rama.

Valmiki's desire to know about the 'best of men' is noteworthy because what the oral poet sings out is final in style of construction. One remembers that it is on none other but Brahma's promptings which inspire Valmiki to tell Rama's story, — a story that runs in the world of gods to a hundred crore verses—in the same metrical form but in a version condensed to the capacity of human understanding and retention. The dissemination of the Rama-katha is by word of mouth, completely as far as Valmiki is concerned.

Immediately after hearing the edifying tale of Rama and its soothing conclusion, Valmiki makes his way through the beautiful forest to a pleasant ford on the banks of the nearby Tamasa river for his ritual bath. The natural beauty of the place enraptures him until his attention becomes focused on a charming pair of mating cranes. But his delight turns to horror as a tribal hunter or *Nisada* emerges from the woods to kill the male bird. Witnessing this violent disruption of the quiet sylvan scene and and hearing the piteous wailing of the hen-crane the sage is filled with a mixture of pity and rage. Denouncing this transgression (*adharmo 'yam*) of the norms of civilized conduct, Valmiki utters his famous curse (*ma nisada*) through which his grief (soka) is transmuted into a new medium of expression, sloka or poetry. Through the intercession of Lord Brahma, this new form born of a moment of rupture and violation, will serve as the poetic rendering of Narada's tale, even as it foreshadows its underlying theme of separation and its central aesthetic-emotive tenor, of pity, *karunarasa*.

Valmiki's *ma nisada* strikes him in retrospect as rather important. Even with Brahma sitting before him, Valmiki's mind goes back again and again like the weaver's shuttle to the cruelty of the *Nisada* and the marvel of the *anushtubh metre* emerging from his mouth like Minerva in panoply. This was undoubtedly due to his conviction that the chemistry that had transformed soka into sloka had given him the ideal vehicle for his poem. The *anushtubh,* which is the predominant metre of the epic, is eminently fitted for it. It is the equivalent to rhythmic prose, — not Bana's but that of the Brahmanas. Though the *anushtubh cchandas* is as old as the Veda, its introduction into non-Vedic literature was probably the contribution of Valmiki. It has infinite flexibility; and it goes harmoniously with the more gorgeous style that Valmiki occasionally brings in to suit the context. Moreover, it lends itself more easily to the absorption of the epic stock phrase, which has its own place in a long work. This is also where his manner differs from the literary poet's. The literary poet is not bound by the tyrannous time limits of the oral poet, so it is not difficult for him to supply new themes and new forms of expression. While the listening audience is satisfied with the established stories told in the established style, the reading public demands novelty. The writer has time to review what he has written, then to polish it and twist it at will to suit the taste of his reader.

Therefore, while Valmiki has the same metrical structure throughout (except for the ending of individual kandas), Kamban on the other hand, has around ninety variations of three kinds of Tamil poetic metres, namely, *kali*, *viruttam,* and *turai*. Tradition makes Kamban the son of a temple drummer with exceptional opportunities for self-education in Tamil and Sanskrit classics. There is more solid evidence for the fact that he was a friend and protégé of one Sadayappan of Vennainallur in the Thanjavur district of Tamil Nadu, considered with good reason the cradle of Tamil art and culture from immemorial times. Sadayappan was a member of the upper caste of the Vellallas, whose main vocation was agriculture. Apart from about ten references in *Kamba Ramayana* itself, there is independent evidence of wealth, influence at the Chola court, scholarly interests, and above all, his munificence, particularly for artistic endeavours, which earned for him the honorific of Vallal (bestower).

There is ample internal evidence of Kamban's wide learning and total assimilation of all the classics in Sanskrit and Tamil available in his time and his complete mastery of the philosophical and aesthetic theories, both Sanskrit and Tamil, of his time. Of the Ramayana lore, he was a total master, having, as he himself puts in his exordium, 'lapped up like a cat the milky ocean of Rama's lay.' He mentions three earlier works as extant in his time, of which he specifically chooses for his source Valmiki, 'the earliest master'. But Valmiki was only his source, not a text for translation. Kamban delights in verbal wit, elaborate Homeric similes and involved poetic conceits. His is the grand manner of leisurely narration, lovingly lingering over particular episodes. These are marked by a certain descriptive panache and allusiveness and by a conscious recall of other legends and stories— all of which add to the reading pleasure of the cognoscenti. Kamban's fertility of invention and exuberance and gusto in narration are in sharp contrast to Valmiki's austere verbal economy. Consequently, in sharp contrast to Valmiki's simplicity and austerity, Kamban's portraitures are on a grand scale. This is partly because of the changes in poetical fashions, the conventions of heroic epic having become well established by the time Kamban came to the scene. More importantly—and this is a basic distinction between him and Valmiki from which all else flows—Rama was no longer, as he was in Valmiki, just a man, though the best among the species—Purushotama. He has, in fact, become God. The difference between Valmiki and either Kamban or Tulsidas is that, with the later poets, Rama is God at every turn.

Tulsidas' *Ramcharitmanas* is written in Hindi, in stanzas called 'chaupais', broken by 'dohas' or couplets, with an occasional 'sortha' and 'chhand' – the latter a hurrying metre of many rhymes and alliterations. Tulsidas speaks of his aim as follows:

> 'In accord with all the Puranas and the different sacred texts and with what has been recorded in the *Ramayana* (of Valmiki) and elsewhere, I, Tulsi, to gratify my own heart's desire, have composed these lays of Raghunatha in most choice and elegant modern speech.'[4]

Tulsidas' aim is to 'narrate the great deeds of Raghupati'[5] and make them live again for his countrymen in his homely speech.

> 'I declare and record it on a fair white sheet,' says Tulsidas, 'that thought my style has not a single charm of its own, it has a charm known throughout the world, which men of discernment will ponder as they read — the gracious name of Raghupati; all purifying essence of the Puranas and the Vedas, abode of all that is auspicious, destroyer of all that is inauspicious, ever murmured in prayer by Uma and the great Tripurari.'[6]

Yet, he states:

'My language is that in vulgar use, but my subject is the highest, the story of Rama, enrapturing the world.'[7]

Even the constant repetitions of certain stereotyped phrases in the *Ramacharitmanasa* — such as 'lotus feet', 'streaming eyes', 'quivering frame' etc— and prayers and invocations appear to be a heritage from the ancient epics such as Valmiki's *Ramayana*, or minstrel poetry. The technique of the oral epic is largely that of improvisation with constant epithets, repeated lines, copious store of synonyms and alternative word-forms. *Ramacharitmanasa,* as a written epic is more closely woven and less wordy and diffuse. Allthough Tulsi uses stock phrases and is master of a tradition language which has little relation to the vernacular of his home, it is because he is consciously following Valmiki in the conscious conviction that he ought to do so, no because his condition compels him to use devices which are indispensable to oral poetry and make it what it is.

The Valmiki *Ramayana* is also known as *itihasa,* a text perceived as history that is ideologically influential, in forming a set of new values, its institutions, and new ideals of good behaviour. But in Valmiki, though Rama is undoubtedly recognized as an incarnation of Vishnu, yet the treatment of character and incident, on the whole, is that of a devout and valiant prince. By the time Kamban and Tulsidas came to sing *The Ramayana*, Rama had already been completely deified for generations with temples and rituals dedicated to His worship as an *Avatar*. Thus, it would have been wholly artificial for Kamban or Tulsidas to portray Rama as was done by Valmiki. The oral tradition of *The Ramayana* is spread over territories far apart and the enormous epic material shows thematic and linguistic differences due to local usage. However, the men, women and children who were to hear Kamban or Tulsidas knew Rama only as God incarnate. Even today to try to undo the work of ages and to un-deify Rama or Krishna in India would be as futile as positively blasphemous. In them is rooted India's living culture. India cannot be India without Rama and Krishna.

Tulsidas begins the *Ayodhya Kanda* with an invocation in Sanskrit to Siva, Visnu and Rama, and then elaborates with a Doha,

> 'Cleansing the mirror of my soul with the dust of the lotus feet of the holy guru, I sing Rama's spotless fame; the giver of the four rewards.'[8]

One of the most impressive kandas in the *Ramayana,* the *Ayodhya Kanda* is replete with dramatic episodes and a series of actions determining the narrative movement.

These episodes and actions may be enumerated as follows:

1. Dasaratha's desire and the meeting of the Court
2. Counsel to Rama
3. Manthara's reaction
4. Kaikeyi's Conversion
5. The Two Boons
6. Dasaratha's and Kaikeyi's Command to Rama
7. Kaushalya's reaction
8. Lakshmana's reaction
9. Sita and the exile
10. Dasaratha and the Departure
11. Sumantra and the Departure
12. Death of Dasaratha

13. Rama and Guha crossing the Ganges: Arrival at Chitrakoota
14. Bharata's arrival at Ayodhya
15. Censure of Kaikeyi and departure of Bharata from Ayodhya
16. Guha and Bharata
17. Lakshmana's anger
18. Bharata reaches Rama's abode
19. King Janaka reaches Rama's abode (only in Tulsidas)
20. Bharata and Rama: The Sandals

C.M. Bowra points out the reason for the series of actions and episodic quality of a longer epic as

> 'When it is a short lay or a short epic, one single crises is enough. But for a longer epic, a series of crises are necessary, hence the technique becomes episodic. But the art of the poet is to see to it that the episodes hang together and ultimately produce a single result.'[9]

In her essay on "Thematic Structure of Epic, Poems in the East and in the West: A Comparative Study"[10], Nabaneeta Dev Sen collects and discusses on the presence of 14 themes in the former group and 24 for the latter. The narrative themes are vital to the structural integrity of the kanda. The physical space in which the various episodes of the *Ayodhya Kanda* are set is systematically marked with the thematic attributes. This marking is systematic, intentional and necessary for the internal logic of the text. In the introduction to his translation of *Ayodhya Kanda*, Sheldon Pollock opines that the Ramayana's integral problem is kingship itself and its attendant problems: the acquisition, maintenance, and execution of royal power, the legitimacy of succession, the predicament of transferring hereditary power within a royal dynasty.[11]

The *Ayodhya Kanda* is in many ways the starting point of the tragedy of the Ramayana. King Dasaratha, feeling his advancing years, decides to abdicate. He designates his first-born son Rama to succeed him as King of Ayodhya. Astrologers are consulted and a date is set for the coronation. Just before the fateful day, Kaikeyi, one of Dasaratha's three wives, falls under the influence of a servant, Manthara, who awakens Kaikeyi's jealousy toward her co-wife, the mother of Rama. Kaikeyi goes before the king and demands to redeem the two boons he had granted her long ago after she saved his life in war by her expert charioteering. Exploiting this promise, which the helpless Dasaratha is honor-bound to fulfill, she asks for the two boons as follow:

1. Her own son, Bharata, should be crowned instead of Rama;
2. Rama should be exiled from the Kingdom for 14 years.

Rama, being an obedient son, leaves for the jungle with Sita and Lakshmana, who in spite of repeated requests, decides to shun the kingdom and follow his older brother devoutly in his time of crisis. Dasaratha dies of sorrow from having to be separated from his son. Meanwhile, Bharata returns to Ayodhya and, being also devoted to Rama, becomes furious with Kaikeyi for her malicious deeds committed in his absence. He travels to the forest and tries to persuade Rama to return to the kingdom and assume the throne. Rama politely refuses, saying that he is duty-bound to see that his father's promise is fulfilled. Reluctantly Bharata agrees to return to the kingdom, requesting Rama to present to him his sandals. He formally treats Rama's sandals as the reigning entity, and ascribes himself as the representative ruler of the rightful king Rama in his absence. Bharata also vows to end his life, if Rama did not return after the fourteen years in exile. The Kanda is also the catalyst for the fulfilment of the promise made by Visnu to the gods to destroy the demon-king Ravana and the eventual victory of good over evil.

The *Ayodhya Kanda* in Valmiki *Ramayana* begins with Dasaratha's desire to crown Rama as heir apparent. The poet's voice is heard whereby he says of Rama:

> 'Was he not the Eternal Vishnu Himself, born into the world of men in answer to the earnest prayer of the gods, who longed for the destruction of Ravana because of his overweening pride?'[12]

This forms a link between the Balakanda and the *Ayodhya Kanda*. The poet then describes Rama as the 'best of men', an epithet that is repeated over and over again in relation to Rama in the Valmiki *Ramayana*.

> 'He knows Dharma and is a man of his word, he is upright and wholly free from malice'[13]

The council of ministers, the sage Vasishta, the king himself and the poet repeat the qualities of Rama, the best of men. This is the oral poet reiterating traditional phrases and incidents involved in the rapidity of composition.

Again, Vasishta gives elaboate instructions of worship and similar instructions are offered to Kausalya, Rama and Sita. The celebration of the people of Ayodhya and their joy at Rama's coronation is expressed with the help of similar stock phrases.

Kamban, on the other hand, improvises upon Dasaratha's desire to coronate Rama with an elegant metaphor:

> 'It was as if Rama's sins had taken the form of a lock of Dasaratha's hair and whispered into his ears: 'The time has come for you to yield this land to your son and depart for the forest.'[14]

Unlike in Valmiki, Kamban's Rama is the 'stithapragnya' or the steadfast one. He is not elated when he is offered the crown by Dasaratha or depressed when Kaikeyi tells him the bad news about the cancelled coronation and his exile. In Valmiki, Rama rejoices at the king's offer of the crown and shares his joy ecstatically with Lakshmana. In fact, when the King sends the charioteer Sumantra to summon Rama to counsel him after the announcement of the Coronation, Rama is 'filled with misgivings' upon seeing Sumantra. One notes the irony in Rama's apprehensions about the coronation when there was no cause for alarm, and his usually exuberant welcome to Sumantra when (later, in Sarga XV) he comes to take Rama to the King to hear the verdict of exile. Dasaratha too desires to do the 'Crowning' of Rama as quietly as possible, and does not invite the King of the Kekayas and Janaka. He reasons that though Bharata might have felt the strivings of ambition before the Coronation, he would thrust such ambitions aside once the thing that was so reasonable and good for the people was done.

In the *Ramcharitmanas,* Dasaratha is reminded of his old age by the grey hairs near his ear and immediately decides to make Rama regent. What is of the utmost important in Tulsidas is to 'sing of Rama's spotless fame'. Rama upon hearing of his coronation remarks:

> This is the one flaw in a spotless line that the eldest only should be enthroned without his younger brothers.[15]

Moreover, Bharata who is on vacation at his Grandparents place along with his brother Shatrughna, is fondly remembered and missed by Rama, Sita and the people of Ayodhya as the dearest friend. Tulsidas offers a simile:

> Everyday Rama was as lovingly anxious about his brother as a turtle for its eggs in the sand far away.[16]

Tulsidas also vindicates scheming Manthara and Kaikeyi as victims of 'divine delusion' and 'overmastered by Fate'. Unlike Valmiki or Kamban, Tulsidas also introduces a conversation between Lakshmana and his mother, the third queen of Dasaratha, Sumitra:

Sumitra, upon hearing of Laksmana's decision to accompany Rama to the forest, declares:

> You have become the receptacle of the highest good fortune, and I too — ah, woe is me! —if from an unfeigned heart you have made Rama's feet your home.[17]

The episodes involving Manthara's reaction and Kaikeyi's conversion exploit the archetypal themes of 'jealousy, treachery and revenge'. The 'lamentations' of Dasaratha, the women in Dasaratha's palace and the courtiers and people of Ayodhya are also part of epic tradition.

Valmiki offers no reason for Manthara's act. What is interesting is how the latter poets, especially Kamban deals with Manthara. Kamban states that upon hearing the news of the coronation of Rama, the hunchback Manthara recalls Rama as a young boy shooting mud balls on her hump and wants to take revenge. He also remarks:

> 'But for her fate-driven heartlessness, would we have been given a taste of the nectar of Rama's legendary fame?'[18]

In Tulsidas, Saraswati, the Goddess of Learning is forced by the gods, much against her wishes to corrupt the minds of Manthara and Kaikeyi. Saraswati agrees, since:

> Reflecting on the future, she became cheerful of heart and flew to the city of Dasaratha, as if she were some intolerably inauspicious aspect of the planets.[19]

The Goddess is heartened by the prospect because if Rama goes to exile, his adventures will form an inexhaustible theme for poets of all time, who will therefore be always invoking her aid and propitiating her good will.

R. Antoine opines that Rama's exile is inevitable because:

> In the Ramayana, the theme of the power of the word is omnipresent. In fact it is so central that it provides a completely unified understanding of the whole epic. All the important incidents happening in the treat-yuga are the outcome of words uttered in the krta-yuga. The Ramayana could be called the Epic of the Word.[20]

Sumantra is the suta, the charioteer. But he is also the bard, for the word *suta* has both meaning. He epitomizes the epic theme of 'singer of tales'. He is responsible for informing Rama of his coronation, the command of Kaikeyi and Dasaratha to call Rama and inform him of his exile, to take Rama from Ayodhya, to return to Ayodhya and inform the King of Rama's journey to the forest and also to enlighten Bharata about the boatman Guha as Rama's friend and devotee. In Valmiki Ramayana, he is also the first one to rail against Kaikeyi. All of these actions are carried on by word of mouth.

On the human plane, the efficacy of the divine word is reflected in the irreversibility of curses and promises. Once uttered, the word cannot be recalled: it operates infallibly. This is one of the most familiar themes of the ancient epic and one of the most pertinent debates that Rama himself engages in. Surely the most complex and revealing debate around the issue of the potential conflict between personal loyalties and adherence to the abstract principles of truth and dharma is embodied in the series of emotionally wrought conversations involving Rama, his brother Lakshmana, his mother Kausalya and his wife, Sita concerning whether Rama should obey his father's order that he be banished and if so, who should accompany him in exile. In his essay on resistance to the idolization of Rama, Robert Goldman examines the relationship of the Valmiki *Ramayana* with the narrative and ideological tradition it initiated, especially in the context of the implication of its design. Noting the formative influence of the great epics of India on the construction of the South Asian ethos, especially on the formulations of gender and power, Goldman shows how the authority of Valmiki's text is modulated by its rhetorical strategies. In his study of episodes from Valmiki's original narrative that are built upon debates, and of the symbiosis of their rhetorical and conceptual texture, Goldman uncovers the narrative process by which ideologies of gender and power are formed. The 'forensic encounters' between the major characters of the *Ramayana*, Goldman argues, work toward enforcing adherence to the ethical and political ideals that emerge as dominant directives. However since the narrative falters whenever the opposition embodied in these encounters become irreconcilable, Goldman views this as Valmiki's own problematizing of women's subordination to the patriarchy, and raises the possibility that Valmiki himself accommodates within his narrative a degree of resistance to hegemony.[21]

Kamban and Tulsidas on the other hand are more intent on idealizing Rama and on showing the path of emancipation through Bhakti. Kausalya in Kamban and Tulsidas is shown as the 'Mother of all' and is devoid of all petty feelings in spite of her intense grief on being separated from Rama. Sita's anxiety on being separated from Rama is given expression but not her disdain (as in Valmiki) at what she feels to be Rama's cowardice on disallowing her to accompany him to the forest. Laksmana's anger is also assuaged similarly. Lakshmana's faithful and loving obedience to Rama is a concrete example of man's unseeing submission to a transcendent order, which he cannot fathom. Again, Rama is the avatar of Vishnu, the Preserver of the Universe. His seeming lack of sensitivity to ordinary human standards and his blind adherence to the WORD are the human reflection of the mythic and timeless function of the Lord Vishnu. His interest lies in the greater good of humanity, 'lokanam hitakamyaya'.[22]

Thus the redeeming design of Vishnu finds its realization in the human context of sin and retribution and the human story of Dasaratha is the vehicle of the divine plan. The curse of the blind hermit, the blessing of fatherhood long foretold by Sanatkumara, the promise of the boons to Kaikeyi, everything moves in the realm of the Word pursuing its fulfilment. Therefore, In Kamba Ramayana, the gods frightened at Bharata's determination to take back Rama to Ayodhya or to remain in the forest, intervene with the words:

> 'Worthy Rama has the right to obey his father and go into the forest; and it is your duty to rule the land for fourteen years. Both must be done.'[23]

In *Ramacharitmanas*, Indra gets puzzled at the determination of Bharata and Brihaspati gives him necessary advice.

The epic is also marked by the theme of journeys and stopovers. The *Ayodhya Kanda* has a number of these, which mark the turning points in the book:

1. Departure of Rama, Sita and Lakshmana from Ayodhya
2. Departure of Sumantra to Ayodhya
3. Arrival at Valmiki's hermitage and Bharadwaj's hermitage.
4. Rama and Guha crossing the Ganges: Arrival at Chitrakoota Messengers departure from Ayodhya to Kekaya to fetch Bharata and Shatrughna
5. Bharata's arrival at Ayodhya
6. Bharata's departure from Ayodhya
7. Bharata reaches Rama's abode
8. King Janaka reaches Rama's abode (only in Tulsidas)
9. Bharata returns to Nandigram

Sita's father, King Janaka's visit to the forest and the long discussions on Rama and Bharata's virtues, which occupy almost all the remainder of this book, are the invention of Tulsidas and find no counterpart in the Sanskrit poems. Devoting itself largely to the eulogy of Bharata, Tulsidas shows Bharata as the ideal devotee of Rama in *Ramacharitmanas*.

> 'if Bharata had never been born, imbued with the ambrosia of devotion, to Rama and Sita, then who would have practiced such self-restraint and penance, such composure, patience and rigorous fasting, transcending every imagination of the sages? Who in legendary disguise would have removed our burning sorrows and poverty, our arrogance and sin? What poor wretch like Tulasi now in this iron age would have ventured to set Rama before you?'[24]

The *Ayodhya Kanda* in Tulsidas ends with a 'soratha':

> 'All, says, Tulasi, who makes a vow and listen with reverence to Bharatha's acts shall assuredly acquire a great devotion to the feet of Sita and Rama and a distaste for worldly pleasures.'[25]

Kamban, on the other hand, stages a dramatic meeting of two Rama-bhaktas with great elaboration: Bharata and Guha. In Kamba Ramayana, Rama is unknown to Guha, an ordinary chieftain of boatmen, who even mistakes Lakshmana for Rama at first. In Kamba Ramayana, Guha offers Rama honey and fish but in *Ramacharitmanas* and in Valmiki

Ramayana, Guha offers fruits, honey and roots. Kamaban apparently models Guha on the Tamil Shaiva saint, kannappa Nayanar who offered similar things to his deity. In Kamba Ramayana, prompted by Guha's sincere devotion, Rama considers him as his own brother. Bharata and Kaushalya bear similar feelings later. In *Ramcharitmanas,* Guha is only a friend and never reaches the status of a brother. Kamban seems to have got this spirit of brotherhood from the Tamil Vaishnava saint, Tirumangai Alwar. Tulsidas addresses Guha as one who is gifted with 'unclouded faith.'

In the words of Tulsidas:

> 'Even a Candala, a savara, a Khasiya, a stupid foreigner, an outcaste, a Kol or a Kerata, by repeating the name of Rama becomes wholly pure and renowned throughout the world.'[26]

The emphasis, yet again, is on the efficacy of the word.

> "The belief in the power of the word seems to reflect a pre-literary culture in which there were no written records to preserve the spoken word. Yet the word has permanence, especially when it reaches from the present into the future, as it does in promises, threats, wishes, commands. Here the word posits the reality which it signifies and endures in the process which it initiates."[27]

In primitive and ancient cultures, there are no 'empty words', but every uttered word is not only significative, but also operative. In the *Ramayana*, the theme of the power of the word is omnipresent. In fact, the whole epic has been tightly knitted based on this only. *The Ramayana* is the epic of fidelity to truth and the human world appears in it as the symbolic reflection of a divine order to which all other values are subordinate. Both in terms of the 'time-series' and 'spatial locus', the 'quality of dharma' in the legend of Rama has a mass appeal. To be and to act according to present situation is 'dharma' or 'religion'. And the supreme dharma is **word** given to one. And by remaining faithful to this dharma, man contributes in some unknown mysterious way to the maintenance of the cosmic order. Like most of the ancient epics, the Indian epic, too, attaches to this uttered word a power. Such power operates on both the human and divine levels.

The epic in the Indian tradition has a human level on which human motivations and decisions are real. The human sphere is limited, no doubt, and encompassed by the divine will. The epic does not deny human freedom and initiative, but it has the wisdom to recognize that the human sphere of activity is not self-sufficient. Consequently, what *The Ramayana* insists on is not that Rama is faithful to his word, but that he is bound by it. If he were untrue, then the three cosmic worlds would be untrue.

## Notes and References

1. Ramanujan, A.K., "Three Hundred Ramayanas: Five Examples and Three Thoughts on Translation" in *Many Ramayanas: The Diversity of a Narrative Tradition in South Asia*, ed. Paula Richman (Berkeley: University of California Press, Delhi: Oxford University Press, 1991), 46
2. Lord, A. B. *The Singer of Tales*, (Cambridge, Mass.: 1960), 4

3. Richman, Paula. "Questioning and Multiplicity Within the Ramayana Tradition" in *Questioning Ramayanas: A South Asian Tradition* ed. Paula Richman (Delhi: Oxford University Press, 2000), 6
4. Tulsidas, *The Ramayana of Tulasi Dasa*, translated by F.S. Growse (Delhi: Motilal Banarasidass, 1978), 3
5. Ibid. 12
6. Ibid. 12
7. Ibid. 12
8. Ibid. 12
9. Bowra, C.M., *From Virgil to Milton* (London: Macmillan & Co. Ltd., 1963), 1
10. Dev Sen, Nabaneeta. "Thematic Structure of Epic, Poems in the East and in the West: A Comparative Study" in *Jadavpur Journal of Comparative Literature*, (Calcutta: Jadavpur University, 1974), Vol. 12, 30-73
11. Pollock, Sheldon I. *The Ramayana of Valmiki: An Epic of Ancient India,* vol. 2., *Ayodhya Kanda* (Princeton, NJ: Princeton University Press, 1986), 10
12. Valmiki, *Srimad Valmiki Ramayana*, translated from the Sanskrit by N. Raghunathan, (Madras: Vighneswara Publishing House, 1981), Vol. I, 150
13. Ibid, 150
14. Kamban, *Kamba Ramayana*, translated by S. Sundaram, (New Delhi: Penguin Books, 2002), 51
15. Tulsidas, *The Ramayana of Tulasi Dasa*, translated by F.S. Growse (Delhi: Motilal Banarasidass, 1978), 233
16. Ibid, 231
17. Ibid, 270
18. Kamban, *Kamba Ramayana*, translated by S. Sundaram, (New Delhi: Penguin Books, 2002), p 54
19. Tulsidas, *The Ramayana of Tulasi Dasa*, translated by F.S. Growse (Delhi: Motilal Banarasidass, 1978), 234
20. Antoine, Robert. *Rama & the Bards: Epic Memory in the Ramayana* (Calcutta: Writers Workshop, 1975), 78
21. Goldman, Robert "Resisting Rama: Dharmic Debates on Gender and Hierarchy and the Work of the *Valmiki Ramayana*" in *The Ramayana Revisited* ed. Mandakranta Bose (New York: Oxford University Press, 2004)
22. Antoine, Robert. *Rama & the Bards: Epic Memory in the Ramayana* (Calcutta: Writers Workshop, 1975), 81
23. Kamban, *Kamba Ramayana*, translated by S. Sundaram, (New Delhi: Penguin Books, 2002), p 103
24. Tulsidas, *The Ramayana of Tulasi Dasa*, translated by F.S. Growse (Delhi: Motilal Banarasidass, 1978), 417
25. Ibid 418
26. Ibid 337
27. McKenzie, John L. *Myths and Realities* (London: 1963), 41

7

# The Term of '*Dharma*' in Indian Perspective with Special Reference to the Mahābhārata

***Shiuli Ghosh***

'*Dharma*' is one of the comprehensive terms in the whole Sanskrit literature. The word '*dharma*' is derived from the root '*dhṛ*'. It is an eastern term whose western equivalents might include morality, ethics, virtue, righteousness, and purity. Most of those terms are distinctly unfashionable in our modern culture. The word 'religion' can hardly be rendered into English. The root meaning of *dharma* is 'to bind' in Indian tradition. The word '*dharma*' has a multiple meaning and it does not mean only religion in its narrow sense. *Dharma* which sustains the universe, signifies the 'law of being' and the 'fulfillment of that law'. The manifestation of everything of the world depends on *dharma* viz. sweet murmur of birds, flowing of river, inflammation of fire etc. According to influence of *dharma*, every animate and inanimate things dwells in a fixed way.

Rabindranath says *"ai yāhā kichu jagat, samasta prāṇer(a) madhye kaṁpita haiteche e kathā mone uday(a) haivā mātra tatkṣaṇāt tṛṇagulmalatā, puṣpapallava, paśupakṣi, manuṣya, candra-sūrya-graha-nakṣatra jagater(a) pratyek(a) kampamān aṇu paramāṇu ek(a) mahāprāṇer(a) aikyasamudre hillolita dekhite pāi, ek(a) mahāprāṇer(a) ananta kaṁpita vīṇātaṇtrī haite ai vipul(a) vicitra viśva saṇgīt(a) saṃkṛta śunite pāi. ananta prāṇer(a) sai anirdeśyatā anirvacanīyatāi āmāder(a) cittake prasārita kariyā thāke."*[1]

Then universal law may be defined as *dharma* which conceives everything of this universe. In vedic literature the term '*ṛta*' is almost identical with this *dharma*. Here we are discussing '*ṛta*' elaborately.

Thus the word '*dharma*' has a multiple meaning and does not mean only religion in its narrow sense. It permeates the entire life of man. The words like *dharmāsana* (throne), *dharmāraṇya* (*tapovana*), *dharmādhikaraṇa* (court of justice) and so on show that the connotation of *dharma* is much wider than the practice of religious rites only. In the

*Mahābhārata 'dharmāsana'* has been identified with *vicārāsana*. Being seated in the *dharmāsana*, the king should protect righteousness, otherwise he must sustain or undergo forever.

The *Mahābhārata* is second epic of India. Byāsadeva, author of the epic has compared *Mahābhārata* with northern Himālaya, named as *devatātma* and southern ocean.

> *"yathā samudra bhagavān yathā hi himavān giriḥ /*
> *khyātāvubhau ratnanidhī tathā bhāratamucyate //"*2

In the *Mahābhārata*, the four puruṣārthas i.e. *dharma*, *artha*, *kāma* and *mokṣa* have been explained elaborately:

> *"dharme cārthe ca kāme ca mokṣe ca bharatarṣabha /*
> *yadihāsti tadanyatra yannehāsti na kutracit //"*3

In ancient India the goal of human life is known as the '*puruṣārthas*', viz. *dharma*, *artha*, *kāma* and *mokṣa*. Among them *dharma* comes first. This is the righteous path which controls the other two *puruṣārthas* viz. '*kāma*' (desire) and '*artha*' lead a man towards *mokṣa* which is the ultimate goal of man. While going through the ancient matter it becomes evident that 'the conception of *dharma* was a far reaching one, how it embraced the whole life of man'.[4] It is a way of life and the codes of conduct by which the entire life of an individual and then of a society is regulated and directed towards a gradual development which enables man to realize the meaning of life. *Dharma* plays important role in Indian two epics i.e. *Rāmāyaṇa* and *Mahābhārata*. Among these two epics, *Mahābhārata* is the vast and it is not one poetic production at all, but rather a whole literature. It means "the great narrative of the battle of the *Bhārata*. The *Bhārata*s are already mentioned in *Ṛgveda* as a warlike tribe".[5]

This book comprises eighteen *parvas*, where complete teaching for the human being has been preserved nicely. The teaching of *Mahābhārata* is based on *dharma* which is closely and inseparably attached in the thinking of India. There are various or miscellaneous connotation of this word. The *Mahābhārata* has shown the two types of derivative or etymological meaning of the word '*dharma*' viz. धन - √ऋ + मक् and धृञ् + मन्.

Firstly धन - ऋ + मक् = धर्म :- *Dharma* is something from which extramundane wealth must be obtained or achieved.[6] Secondly *dharma* (धृञ् + मन्) refers something which conceives everything, by which everyone can progress in a proper way.* '*Lokasaṁgraha*' is utmost dependant on *dharma*. Thus *Mahābhārata* says:

> *"lokayātrāmihaike tu dharmam prāhurmaṇīṣiṇa /"*[7]

Although *Mahābhārata* upholds the ancient history, yet it is one of the best books, based on *dharma*. The war between *kauravas* and *paṇdavas* is the main theme of it, but description of war is not ultimate aim of *Mahābhārata*. Rabindranath says in '*Kālāntara*' *"Mahābhārater(a) ākhyān(a) bhāger(a) adhikaṅgśa yuddha varṇanār(a) dvārā adhikṛta; kintu yuddhei tār(a) pariṇām(a) nay(a). Naṣta aiśvaryake raktasamudra theke uddhār(a) kare pāṇḍaver(a) hiṁsra ullās(a) ete varṇita hay(a) ni. ete dekhā yāy(a) jita sampadke kurukṣetrer(a) citābhaṣmer(a) kāche parityāg(a) kare vijayī pāṇḍava vipul(a) vairāgyer(a) pathe śāntiloker(a) abhimukhe prayāṇ(a) karlen(a) – e kāvyer(a) ai caram(a) nirdeś(a). ai nirdeś(a) sakal(a) kāle sakal(a) mānaver(a) prati*".[8] Majority of stories of the *Mahābhārata* are occupied by the description of war, but war is not its conclusion. Cruel joys of *pāṇḍavas* after rescuing lost supremacy from ocean of blood are not described here absolutely. We see here that victorious *pāṇḍavas* leave conquered wealth near ashes of funeral pyre of *kurukṣetra* and they start for abode of peace on the path of vast apathy towards worldly interests - this is the absolute direction of this epic and that direction is for all ages and for all persons.

In the *Prācīnasāhitya* Tagore also says that "*mahābhārate karmei karmer(a) caram(a) samāpti nahe, tāhār(a) samasta śaurya, vīrya, rāgadveṣa, hiṁsā – pratihiṁsā prayās(a) o siddhir(a) mājkhāne śmaśān(a) haite mahāprasthāner(a) bhairava saṅgitā bājiyā uthiteche*".[9] In the *Mahābhārata* absolute end of action does not occur in action only. In the midst of its all strength, courage, anger malice, enmity killing revenge effort and success the song of voluntary journey to infinite is being sung. This is the main characteristic of *dharma* which reveals utmost dignity of renunciation.

Thus '*dharma*' cannot be explained in one sentence. Self complacency, purification of mind and salvation etc. are very closely related to *dharma*. All these are extramundane wealth which is originated from *dharma*. In the whole *Mahābhārata*, various types of *dharma* are found, such as *samājadharma*, *varṇāśramadharma*, *āpad-dharma*, *dāna-dharma*, *rājadharma*. The *Mahābhārata* has given importance '*veda*' while explaining about '*dharma*'. Not only *veda*, the *Mahābhārata* has given importance on *dharmaśāstra* also.

> "*vedaktaḥ paramo dharmo dharmaśāstreṣu cāparaḥ /*
> *sadācāraḥ smṛtirvedastrividam dharmalakṣaṇam //*"[10]

If *Śruti* is unable to give answer, *dharmaśāstra* will be authority to show the right way. *Dharmaśāstra*, the last authority to show the real path must be courteous people. Thus *Mahābhārata* says:

> "*tarkōpratiṣṭhah śrutayo vibhinnā, naiko ṛṣiryasya matam pramāṇam /*
> *dharmasya tattvam nihitam guhāyam mahājano yena gata saḥ panthāḥ //*"[11]

The *Mahābhārata* is an Epic of different nature. Once the *Mahābhārata* has pronounced: '*yato dharmastato jayaḥ*'. This is keynote of whole *Mahābhārata*. The *Mahābhārata* has searched '*dharma*' which holds man in pleasure and pain, in all difficulties, in moral suspicion, and illuminates the real path in the conflict of *śreya* and *preya* and man is able to protect this *dharma*. Human being can only preserve *dharma*. So the *Mahābhārata* has proclaimed that man is the superior most of the creatures in the universe.

> "*na manuṣācchreṣthataram hi kiṁcit /*"[12]

They can achieve their goals completely by their own power because having of six organs in their physical structure. Any other animals apart from human being have lack of this ability. Man has huge responsibility in the progress of civilization. Man is endowed with all divine qualities and he manifests such human qualities i.e. *dāna*, *adhyayana*, *tapasyā*, *satya*, *kṣamā*, *ahiṁsā* etc. All these are universal ethical concepts and extramundane wealth of human being also. It has been mentioned in the *Mahābhārata*:

> *"adattasyānupādānam dānamadhyayanam tapaḥ /*
> *ahiṁsā satyamakrodha ijyā dharmasya lakṣaṇam //*
> *akrodhaḥ satyavacanam saṁvibhāgaḥ kṣama tathā /*
> *prajānaḥ sveṣu dāreṣu śaucamadhoha eva ca //"*[13]

All these human qualities should be assimilated not only for one's own self but for the whole creation. At the first stage these may be practised for the upliftment of an individual but ultimately they become significant with reference to all creatures of the universe who are embraced within the fold of human consciousness. According to the *Mahābhārata* '*dharma*' has a universal approach. The large extension of *dharma* brings social welfare.

Thus unblamable behaviour is *dharma*. This practice is not necessary outwardly but internally also. Good thinking is also the outcome of religious practice. Generally *dharma* has manifold meaning and it may also be interpreted with reference to time, space and situation. It depends on social custom. So the *Mahābhārata* says:

> *"sa eva dharmaḥ sō dharmo deṣakale pratiṣthitaḥ /"*[14]

Although ceremonial *dharma* differs accordingly to *jati* and *varṇa*, but the inner nature and aim of *dharma* is equal to all.

Mental peace and well being of all are the primary of *dharma*. The conduct of virtuous man is the source of *dharma*. According to *Mahābhārata* the interaction of the individual pain and pleasure with the world is the real definition of Supreme *dharma*. Hence the *Mahābhārata* says:

> *"mānasam sarvabhūtānām dharmāhurmaṇīṣiṇaḥ /*
> *tasmātsarveṣu bhūteṣu manasā śivamācaret //"*[15]

In this context the *Mahābhārata* upholds '*ānṛsaṁsa dharma*'. The *anuśānaparva* also says:

> *"ahiṁsā paramo dharmastatha'hiṁsā parama tapaḥ /*
> *ahiṁsā paramang satyam yato dharmaḥ pravartate //"*[16]

*Ahiṁsā* is the greatest *dharma*, *ahiṁsā* is the greatest *tapas*, *ahiṁsā* is greatest *satya*, *ahiṁsā* is the basic support of all *dharma*.

> *"ahiṁsā sakalo dharmo hiṁsā dharmastathāhitaḥ /"*[17]

It is said in the *Mahābhārata* that *ahiṁsā* can be considered as a complete and self-sufficient *dharma*. Not only the virtue '*ahiṁsā*' is glorified but the glorification of '*ānṛsaṁsa*' occurs repeatedly in the *Mahābhārata*. The most effective instances are to be found in the context of the tests of Yudhisthira conducted by *dharmarāja*. Here may be recalled the relevant parts of the whole dialogue.

> *"anṛśaṁsam paro dharmaḥ /"*[18]

In reply to the Yakṣa, Yudhisthira says '*ānṛsaṁsa*' (absence of cruelty) is highest *dharma* and he has been praised by Yak.a as he (Yudhisthira) has demonstrated his highest devotion to *ānṛsaṁsa*. Therefore, he grants him a boon by which all of his brothers may come back to life.

> *"tasya térthācca kāmācca ānṛsaṁsam param mataṁ /*
> *tasmātte bhrātaraḥ sarve jīvantu bharatarṣabhaḥ //"*[19]

There is large number of verses which glorify *ahiṁsā* in the whole of the *Mahābhārata*.

Although *Mahābhārata* praises *ahiṁsā* yet this *Mahābhārata* never denies the real worth of self-defency. Actually malevolence for the sake of self-defency is not harmful at all. There is no genuine friend of human beings than *ahiṁsā*.

Yet there happen war extending over eighteen days. As a consequence extensive damage, loses of relatives friends have been occurred, Lord Śrikrishna has made to understand Arjuna as well as all people who are depressed and morose, that this inevitable war is not for any personal interest, but for the establishment of '*dharma*'.

In the first verse of *Śrīmadbhagavadgītā Kurukṣetra* has been entitled as *dharmakṣ etra*.

> *"dharmakṣetre kurukṣetre samavetā yuyutsavaḥ /*
> *māmakaḥ pāṇḍavāścaiva kimakurvata Sañjayaḥ //"*[20]

According to S. Radhakrishnan "this *Kurukṣetra* may well become a *dharmakṣetra*. The end may be long in coming. It may take many years of decades or even centuries. It may be a hard birth, the birth of the new world, but any permanent breakdown of human values is unthinkable. There is in each of us a hidden knowledge, a spiritual perception of the unity of life, which holds the human heart to a belief in a better order."[21]

Śrīkṛṣṇa upholds the importance of '*svadharma*' which is for more important than '*kuladharma*'. Lord Kṛṣṇa has focused on the duty of an individual. Every individual has to work according to the law of nature.

> *"sradharmamapi cāvekṣya vikampitum arhasi /*
> *dharmyād hi yuddhacchreyó nyat kṣatriyasya na vidyate //"*[22]
>
> *"atha cet tvam imam dharmyam saṁgramam na karisyasi /*
> *tataḥ svadharnam kīrtim ca hitvā pāpamavāpsasi //"*[23]

Arjuna becomes totally disbalanced in search of personal happiness. At this moment he stresses more on his pleasure and sorrow. This is a great error of all human beings. It must be remembered that the personal sorrow and pleasure have no value at all for the welfare for all. The ultimate aim of this war was to establish righteousness. On the contrary to establish '*dharma*' and to remove '*adharma*' the war is required. Duryodhana and his brothers totally deprive *pāṇḍavas* of their lawful possession and he rules his subjects in an unjust way. So at that moment war is essential for maintenance of social and national life and protection of '*dharma*'. Here *dharma* refers law and rule which conceive everything. Śrīkṛṣṇa says in the '*jñāna-yoga*' 'He' appears in human form when the world is vitiated by vice:

> *"yadā yadā hi dharmasya glanirbhavati bhārata /*
> *abhyutthāmadharmasya tadātmāṇam sṛjāmyaham //"*[24]

Here '*dharma*' can also be defined as the law of the being as a social and moral rule. '*Dharma*' is the law of being and the principle of man's existence. There is the famous saying:

"*dharma rakṣati rakṣitaḥ* /"[25]

To save '*dharma*' from '*adharma*' the *avatāra* in the form of human beings have appeared in this world age after age and save the human beings from utter destruction. Rāmacandra established '*dharma*' by killing Rāvaṇa. Paraśurāma established '*dharma*' by subduing the *kṣatriyas* etc. Vāmana avatāra established justice by destroying Valirāja. The Buddha and Jesus Christ catered the message of '*dharma*' as the ultimate aim of life - a message of new law of religious and spiritual life.

As a fighter, Arjuna must fight with the opponent in the battle field. Though they were his relatives, brothers and his family members, yet he must ignore all the personal relationship for the sake of *svadharma*. Swami Tapasyananda is of opinion that "such work as accures to one according to one's nature and is done with a spirit of dedication is called *svadharma*, one's natural duty ... It will secure the social good as also bring about the individual's spiritual evolution."[26]

As a *kṣatriya* his *svadharma* is to fight for the right, he must protect justice and must beat down injustice and lawlessness. In this way he would protect his subjects who are weak and who could not protect themselves. Every man has some *svadharma*. If each does his duties, the world becomes prosperous. S. Radhakrishnan says "Our *svadharma*, outward life, and *svabhāva*, inner being, must answer to each other. Only then will action be free, easy and spontaneous".[27]

The *Mahābhārata* upholds the '*Rājadharma*'. This epic shows that *Rājadharma* has also universal approach. For the unjust attitude of the *Kauruvas* the whole world is under the calamity. So war becomes very essential for the establishment of *dharma*. As the aim of war of *kurukṣetra* is for protesting to the unjust, it is called '*dharma yuddha*'. At the end of the war *Pāṇḍavas* leave everything and proceed towards *mahāprasthāna*. Then the question may arise why such a war? Certainly it is not for gaining the kingdom or to satisfy any pretty self interest, but for the greater interest of well being of world and to protect *dharma*.

From the ancient period it may be observed that the strong oppresses the weak and as a result the greater interest of mankind is restrained. It is clearly expressed in the *Mahābhārata*.

"*rājā cenna bhavelloke pṛthivyām daṇḍadhārakaḥ* /
*jale matsānivabhakṣyandurvalam balavattaraḥ* //
*arājakaḥ prajāḥ purvam vineṣuriti naḥ śrutam* /
*parasparam bhakṣayanto matsā iva jale kṛśān* //"[28]

The duties of the king are the ultimate resort for the whole world. They contain all the four *puruṣārthas* and control the whole world. They can dispel all evil.

Bhiṣma expounds Yuddhiṣthira the duties of the king very briefly. According to Pitāmaha Bhiṣma, the first and foremost duty of the king is that he should conduct himself properly towards the deities and the *Brāhmaṇas*. Thus Bhiṣma says:

> *"namo dharmāya mahate namaḥ kṛṣṇāya vedhase /*
> *brāhmaṇebhyo namaskṛtya dharmān vakṣāmi śāśvatān //*
> *ādāveva kuruśreṣtha! rājñā rañjanakāmayā /*
> *devatānām dvijānāmca vartitavyam yathāvidhi //*
> *daivatānyarccayitvā hi brāhmanāngśca kurūdvaha*
> *a nṛṇyam yāti dharmasya lokena ca samarccyate //"*[29]

Bhiṣma tells Yuddhisthira that king's success lies down in truth, which can bring delight in the world.

> *"ṛṣīṇāmapi rājendra! satyameva param dhanam /*
> *tathā rājñām param satyānnānyadviśvāsakāraṇam //"*[30]

Bhiṣma advises him that the king should forever bear in mind the interest of the people. The king should be courageous and strong to achieve respect by the people. But he should not loose his personality to his servants, as they can not misuse him. After that Bhiṣma points out that the science of polity or *rājadharma* was promulgated by Lord Bṛhaspati. Thus the science of *rājadharma* or *daṇḍanīti* belongs to mythical past and possesses a very long respectable tradition.

Bhiṣma glorifies *daṇḍanīti* and he points out that when a king applies it properly, the people are endowed with welfare and absence of fear. If *daṇḍanīti* is properly employed, it sustains the world like the mother or the father. Thus the greatest *dharma* of the king is the knowledge and practice of *daṇḍanīti* which ensures the wellbeing of the king as well as the state.

> *"saptaprakrti caṣtaṅgam śarīramiha yadviduḥ /*
> *rājyasya daṇdamevaṅgam daṇḍa prabhavah eva ca //*
> *isvareṇa prayatnena kāranāt kṣatriyasya ca /*
> *daṇḍo dattaḥ samānātmā daṇḍo hīdam sanātanam //*
> *rajñam pūjyatamo nānyo yathā dharmaḥ pradarśitaḥ /*
> *brahmaṇā lokarakṣārtham svadharmasthāpanāya ca //"*[31]

This *daṇḍanīti* is essentially based on the proper use of *daṇḍa*. The proper use of *daṇḍa* by king leads to the realization of *dharma*, *artha*, *kāma*. It is *dharma* or *vyavahara* which protects the people by employing the *daṇḍa* properly.

In the *Manusaṁhita*, Manu also has shown the real importance of *daṇḍa*. Manu like *Mahābhārata*, states that it is *daṇḍa* which governs all people and protects them. *Daṇḍa* is wide awake when others are asleep, and hence it is equated with *dharma* itself. All people honour rules because of the fear of *daṇḍa*. If there were no *daṇḍa* in the world, people would simply perish.

Manu has identified '*daṇḍa*' with king. *Daṇḍa* control subjects and being awakened *daṇḍa* protect all in every moment. If there is *daṇḍa*, everyone will be peaceful, otherwise there may be great disaster due to lack of *daṇḍa*. Thus wise people think that *daṇḍa* and *dharma* are same to each other.

*"daṇḍa śasti prajāḥ sarva daṇḍa evābhirakṣati /*
*daṇḍa supteṣu jāgarti daṇḍam dharmam vidurbudhāḥ //"*[32]

For the well-being of all mankind *rājadharma* is essential. This view has been elaborated in the *rājadharma*. The *pāṇḍavas* and *kauravas* have been ruling from generation to generation. But there is such example that one with numerous qualities is selected as king be replacing wicked and incapable king. The first and principal duty of the king is to protect the society from disharmony. Harmony is essential in the human physique, in human mind, in nature and in universe and it is also essential between the macro and the micro cosmic world. To restrain the society or to create a harmonized world it is essential to purify himself through observing some rules, such as the act of non-violence, moral behaviour, giving up anger and ego which are already mentioned here. In this context the *Mahābhārata* says:

*"arājakesu rāsteṣu dharmo na byatitiṣthate /*
*parasparam ca khādanti sarvathā dhigarājakam //"*[33]

The *Mahābhārata* says that a wicked should be dethroned by a righteous and capable person. It shows that the subject has the power to select a king and also that a king must remain on the right path to conduct his people. Citizens under a religious king may be prosperous by performing their own duties easily. The king's prosperity depends on the prosperity of the *loka*.

*"prajānām pālanam dharmo rājñam rājīvalocana /*
*dharmaḥ pramāṇam lokasya nitya dharmānuvartiṇaḥ //"*[34]

Not only self-sacrifice for the benefit of others there exists in the *rājadharma* i.e. kindness towards creatures, the knowledge of human nature, power to rescue the distressed people.

*"ātmatyāgaḥ sarvabhūtānukampyā lokajñānam mokṣaṇam pālanam ca /*
*viṣaṇanānām mokṣaṇam pīḍitanām kṣātre dharma vidyate parthivānām //"*[35]

The *Mahābhārata* shows or establishes the ideal of *rājadharma* which says all religious practice, all renunciation, all learning or sill.

*"sarve tyāgā rājadharmeṣu dṛṣtāḥ /*
*sārva dīkṣā rājadharmeṣu coktāḥ //*
*sarvā vidyā rājadharmeṣu yuktāḥ /*
*sarve lokā rājadharme praviṣtāḥ //"*[36]

As the king is the pioneer of *dharma*, the unlimited consumption is not desirable for him, it is sure that one can attain godliness by observing religious practices and condemnation to hell by sinful practice. Thus he who is able to project *dharma* is worthy of being a king. Thus '*Rājadharma*' upholds/indicates full-dedication to the subjects and supervision of them which is closely related with the protection of *dharma* or the protection of himself. Fostering or maintaining of subjects is the main part of *rājadharma*. If king is indifferent to this matter, he should be dethroned and *rājadharma* may be mortified. The king should protect his own *dharma* i.e. *rājadharma* which leads to '*lokasaṁgraha*'. *Mahābhārata* repeatedly shows that *lokasaṁgraha* is ultimate purpose of *rājadharma*.

The '*rājadharma*' as depicted in the *Mahābhārata* is not politics at all. The duties of king has identified with *dharma*, here *rājadharma* is very close to *moksadharma*. The *Kṣatriya* king used to maintain discipline in the society. The main purpose of king is to be beneficial to the public.

> "*rañjitāśca prajāḥ sarvāstena rājeti śabdyate /*"[37]

According to *Mahābhārata* the animal kingdom has been abolished due to non-existence of king. Being favoured or graced by king the human beings dwell in peace. Thus *Mahābhārata* says:

> "*yasyābhāvena bhūtānāmabhāvaḥ syāt samantataḥ /*
> *bhave ca bhavo niyam syāt vastam na pratipuyayet //*"[38]

Being represented the worth saying of *prajā* or subject, the ideal kind never make them averse. The ideal king should be generous to live his subject and treat them like own son.**

The relationship of both i.e. king and his subject is not merely apparent, but very cordial.

As king is expected to think his kingdom, subjects also are expected to give proper respect to king, that means mutual understanding of them is very essential to achieve or to govern a balanced state.

But unreasonable act of subjects never be supported and it is obviously restrainable by applying *daṇḍa*. Proper application of *daṇḍa* leads to proper protection of subjects as well as establishment of '*lokasthiti*'. So *daṇḍa* may be identified with *dharma*.

> "*supraṇīteṇa daṇḍena priyāpriya sanātmanā /*
> *prajā rakṣati saḥ samyag, dharmaḥ eva sa kevalḥ //*"[39]

The king must inspire his subjects to be a person with righteous practice and religious rites. Non-malevolence atmosphere of human society is fully dependant on king. Thus *rājadharma* is the root of all *dharma*. A loftiest place may be achieved by king in the mind of human society. The king himself is the epithet of *dharma*. Thus it is said:

> "*dharma rāja bhavati na kāmakaraṇāya tu /*
> *atha yeṣām punaḥ prājño rāja bhavati dhārmikaḥ //*"[40]

According to the *Mahābhārata*, the king is the guardian of the social order. Hence he is expected to possess qualifications and cultivate necessary virtue. As he is the pioneer of society king's sin may be effective in the society.

Thus the *Mahābhārata* requires that a king to be with a noble family and to be himself a noble personality. The king should be a completely dedicated soul, he must be an ideal to be imitated by the society. The king is advised to destroy enemies and protect distressed people. The destiny of the whole nation depends upon the conduct of the king. Any violation of king's *dharma* causes destruction of the king as well as of the whole society. The great poet Kalidasa once upholds the nature of ideal king in the drama '*Abhijñanaśakuntalam*'.

> "*ārtatrāṇāya vaḥ śastram na pratihartumanāgasi /*"

A king is named as '*rāja*' only because he sincerely discharges duties and pleases all.

The *Kurukṣetra* war was indispensable due to laxity of *rājadharma*. *Rājadharma* may be related with the meaning of the second type of *dharma* as said before. Hence this war has been defined as '*Dharmayuddha*'. In this *dharmayuddha dharma* have been tried to establish wholeheartedly.

One can maintain proper *dharma* through unblamable behaviour; but it should not be outward rather noble thinking from the core of heart is the highest *dharma*. The twofold etymological meaning of *dharma*, mentioned before, extends in all types of *dharma*. The *Mahābhārata* shows extensive concept of *dharma* which not only deals temporal world, but the world beyond death. Liberation from worldly bondage is the ultimate purpose of practising *dharma* rather to say universal welfare is main purpose of *dharma*. Outward nature may be different, but inner nature of *dharma* should be same. Thus '*dharma*' which is inner thing, helps the upliftment of living beings. Therefore that which ensures welfare of beings is surely *dharma*. Rather to say, universal welfare can be possible in practicing of all these *dharma*.

### *Notes and References*

* *"dhanat sravati dharmo hi dharanadveti niscayaḥ /*
*dharanaddharma nityahudharmo dharayate prajaḥ //*
*yat syaddharanasamyuktam sa dharma iti niscayah //"*
Santiparva 90/17, Karnaparva 69/59, Santiparva 109/11

** *"āt manaśca pareṣañca vṛttim sa ṁrakṣa bhārata,*
*putravaccāpi bhṛtyān s vān prajāśca paripalaya /"*

1. Rabindra Racanavali, 14th Khaṇḍa, P. 575
2. *Mahābhārata* 18/5/66
3. *Mahābhārata* 1/2/390
4. Kane, P. V., History of Dharmasastra, Vol-II, Part-I, P. 2
5. Maurice Winternitz, A History of Indian Literature, Vol-1, P. 317
6. Sukhomay Sharma, Mahābhārater Samaj, P. 276, 1389 vaṅgābda
7. *Mahābhārata* 12/142/19
8. Rabindra Racanāvalī, 13th Khaṇḍa, P. 405
9. *Op cit.* 10th Khaṇḍa, P. 662
10. *Mahābhārata* 12/258/3
11. *Mahābhārata* 3/312/117
12. *Mahābhārata* 12/299/20
13. *Mahābhārata* 12/36/10, 12/60/7
14. *Mahābhārata* 12/36/11
15. *Mahābhārata* 12/193/31
16. *Mahābhārata* 13/115/23
17. *Mahābhārata* 12/272/20
18. *Mahābhārata* 3/313/76

19. *Mahābhārata* 3/313/133
20. *Śrīmadbhagavadgītā* 1/1
21. Radhakrishnan, S., Religion and Society, P. 20
22. *Śrīmadbhagavadgītā* 1/31
23. *Śrīmadbhagavadgītā* 1/33
24. *Śrīmadbhagavadgītā* 4/7
25. Pathikonda Viswambara, Tattvam Asi, P. 164
26. Swami Tapasyananda, *Śrīmad Bhagavad Gītā*, P. 467
27. Radhakrishnan, S. , *The Bhagavadgītā*, P. 73
28. *Mahābhārata* 12/67/15
29. *Mahābhārata* 12/55/10,12,13
30. *Mahābhārata* 12/55/18
31. *Mahābhārata* 12/118/47,48,49
32. *Manusa.hita* 7/18
33. *Mahābhārata* 12/63/3
34. *Mahābhārata* 12/32/2
35. *Mahābhārata* 12/64/27
36. *Mahābhārata* 12/63/29
37. *Mahābhārata* 12/59/125
38. *Mahābhārata* 12/68/37
39. *Mahābhārata* 12/121/11
40. *Anuśāsanaparva* 62/43,44

8

# Lakshmi Purana: An Analysis

*B.N.Patnaik*

*Lakshmi Purana* is an immensely popular religious text in Odia language, next in popularity in Odisha to *Srimad Bhagavata* alone. This short narrative in verse, too short indeed to be called a purana - so short that it makes it unnecessary for us to go further and see whether it really has any of the distinguishing features of a purana, in any tradition, classical or local - is widely believed to have been composed by the sixteenth century Odia poet, Balarama Dasa. It is not one of his best works, but certainly his most frequently read work. It is more like a, *katha* ("tale"), *brata katha*, somewhat more specifically, than a purana, although unlike in a typical *brata katha*, here the conflict involves gods and goddesses alone. If it was called a purana at all, it might have been due to the fact that Bhagavan Jagannatha Himself, who has generally been regarded as a form of Vishnu, and has been the most revered deity in Odisha for centuries, is a major character in this narrative.

Successful protest against authority can be said to be the central theme of this narrative. And successful protest entails power. Rather uncharacteristically, again, for a *brata katha*, *Lakshmi Purana* is an emphatic statement of the power of the victim of injustice. It is ritually read out as part of the worship of goddess Lakshmi. This worship is strictly family centred; it is performed at home, by the married women. It is a women's puja: *narinkara lakshmi brata*, as the poet says (p.17). There is no role for a priest in the performance of this ritual, and there are no mantras. These are among the typical features of a *brata puja*. The story of *Lakshmi Purana* celebrates the power and the glory of goddess Lakshmi: if she is displeased, one suffers great misery and humiliation. If she is pleased, one enjoys every happiness and prosperity on earth and in heaven.

From one point of view, as already mentioned, *Lakshmi Purana* is a protest against the then prevailing practice of caste-based pollution, and from another, it is a protest against the denial of any space to the married woman in the male dominated society. The narrative nicely integrates these two protests. The goddess Lakshmi protested against her totally unfair dismissal by her spouse Bhagavan Jagannatha, from the Great Temple at his elder brother Bhagavan Balarama's behest. She had visited the house of a low-caste woman, who was the only one in that locality who had cleaned her house and was worshipping her with great devotion. Balarama happened to see her in the house of the low-caste woman, and was very upset. He told his brother that Lakshmi should be thrown out of the Great Temple because the food cooked by her for them would be ritually polluted, as she had herself got polluted by visiting the low-caste woman. Jagannatha tried to calm Balarama, but failed; Balarama told his younger brother that if he wanted to live with his wife, he should leave the temple. The obedient brother then asked his wife, Lakshmi, to leave.

The goddess was taken aback. Deeply hurt and humiliated, she left, but cursed the brothers before she did: they would not get any food for twelve years and would have food only when she cooked it for them. Leaving aside details, this was precisely what happened: finally Balarama and Jagannatha begged food at her palatial abode. Just as they did not suspect that it was Lakshmi who was behind their suffering, they did not know that it was her palace; all they knew was that it was the house of a low-caste woman, but were far too hungry to feel concerned about having food cooked by her. When Jagannatha at his elder brother's wish requested her to return to the temple, she did, but only after extracting two promises from her husband: caste distinctions must be ignored while partaking of *mahaprasad* (food cooked by her in the Great Temple, and offered to Jagannatha), and she would not be forbidden to visit the house of any devotee of hers, irrespective of his or her caste. This is how the poet Balarama Dasa explained the tradition associated with the partaking of *mahaprasad*. It continues to be the most popular explanation, but by no means the most satisfactory, from a scholarly point of view. The origins of this great tradition, which in practice today is only barely reminiscent of the recommended manner of partaking of *mahaprasad*, are unknown, but this is a matter that is of no concern for us here. Today one might consider the resolution of the issues of caste and of the married woman's space in Balarama Dasa's work unsatisfactory on the ground that it is limited to a restricted domain, but it must have looked nothing short of revolutionary in the sixteenth century social context in Odisha.

One of the basic concerns of *Lakshmi Purana*, like other *brata kathas*, *mahatmyas*, etc. is dharma, in its sense of moral conduct, which is only one of its senses in which it is used in the language. In the style of the literature of this genre, it informs people about the great benefits of following the prescribed code of conduct, and also warns people of the terrible consequences of violating the same. Now sanction from "divine" authority is what it gives the code its legitimacy. The goddess Lakshmi herself spells out the code for the most part, as do goddesses in the *brata kathas*. In this sense it appears to be in the "revelation" mode, but if it is not given the status of *Srimad Bhagavat Gita*, often considered to be a "revealed" text, it is because it does not contain the words of Bhagavan Himself. Now the code is not spelt out by the goddess Lakshmi alone in *Lakshmi Purana*, but by the great sage Parashara as well, who was informing another great sage, namely Narada, about the worship of the goddess. The words of such great sages have been assigned nearly the same status as those of a god or a goddess in the tradition.

In *brata kathas* in general, *Lakshmi Purana* being no exception, the moral code is concerned primarily with woman's life in her husband's family. Performance of religious rituals is part of it. Thus it specifies in what form and how to install the deity to be worshipped on some specific occasion, when and what to offer to the deity, etc. Of particular interest in the context of *Lakshmi Purana* is the prescription about the partaking of the *prasad* (food offered to the deity). The *prasad* must not be offered to anyone outside the family, not even to the daughter, if she is married: *sri mahalakshmi prasada paraku nadeba / bibha hoithiba jhia suddha na khaiba* ("Do not give Sri Mahalakshmi's prasad to the outsider / Even the married daughter must not partake of it.") (p.16). This restriction seems to be local, restricted to Odisha. As Aditi Ghosh observes, this not sharing of Lakshmi's *prasad* with people outside the family is not a practice among the Bengalis (personal communication). This restriction is an expression of the attitude that the property of the family must not be shared with an outsider, irrespective of the closeness of him or her to the family. After her wedding, the daughter becomes a *para gotri* ("belongs to a different gotra" – a different family), as it is said; she ritualistically loses her identity with respect to her father's family.

A woman must not do certain things on a Thursday, the day of the goddess Lakshmi. She must not fry rice, must not eat food that is burnt, and non-vegetarian food too. She must not eat left over food, neither should she eat too much. She must not leave her hair unwashed, must not use oil, and must not leave her house dirty. She must not sleep on carelessly made bed, and not sleep on the shadow of a cot. She must not delay to light the sacred evening lamp, neither must she beat her children. Although it is specifically mentioned that a woman must not do these things on a Thursday, it does not mean that she should feel encouraged to do the same on the other days of the week. The *vyanjana* (roughly, "logic" here) is the same as in the following: When the mother, who is going to the river to have her bath, tells her child to protect the butter from the crow during her absence, she does expect the child to feed the butter to a cat or a squirrel.

A woman must be clean and pleasant. One who does not wash her face on waking up, does not use an *asana* ("seat") while eating, does not wash her mouth after eating, and eats in the dark, invites the goddess's displeasure. A woman must obey her parents-in-law and must be completely devoted to her husband. This is not just her most important family duty, it is her most important religious duty as well: *sadhaba narira pati bina nahin gati / japa tapa deba puja tahara aniti* ("For the woman whose husband is alive, there is no other recourse than her husband / For her, religious activities such as the chanting of the names of god, meditation, worship of the gods, etc. constitute irreligious acts") (p.20). A woman who has extramarital relationships, who does not perform religious duties, and has no respect for the brahmins and the guests, and who has no consideration for the poor and the needy, does not receive the grace of the goddess. Similarly, a woman who is quarrelsome, lazy, unclean, unpleasant, fearless and daring, is not dear to the goddess. The basic idea is that in the narrative woman is conceived as the uniting force in the family. It would fall apart if she was inconsiderate, headstrong and not fully committed to the family. So she has to be pleasant in her words and action, respectful to the elders, and be fair in her dealings with everyone in the family.

Interestingly, the goddess herself did not follow the moral code she had articulated in her family domain. She cursed her husband, resorted to manipulations to ensure that her husband, and his elder brother underwent great suffering and humiliation, almost upbraided her husband at the moment of her victory over him, insisted on her freedom as a condition to return to the family, and overall, behaved in a way the woman of the house is not supposed to, in terms of the very moral code she had spelt out. It is unclear why the goddess who was so uncompromisingly insistent on physical cleanliness (what a virtuous woman does is clean herself: *nija anga pariskara kari suci hue*, (p.20), demanded that one must not wash one's hands after partaking of *mahaprasad*, but wipe one's fingers on one's head: *samaste khaina hata jale na dhoibe / ... anna khai sabre munde pochuthibe hasta* ("Eating (*mahaprasad*) no one would wash their hand in water / ... after eating rice (*mahaprasad* they would wipe their hand on the head.") (p.62). It is again difficult to understand why she explicitly asked her devotees not to share her *prasad* ("food offered to her") with anyone outside the family, but insisted that no social difference must stand on the way for people to partake of *mahaprasad*, which implied the absence of any restriction whatsoever in the matter of *mahaprasad*.

What message would this send to the people? Are there two moral codes, one for the humans and another for the gods? If so, then why tell gods' stories to the humans in the context of instructing them about what qualities to be called moral behaviour? Her story is the demonstration of her power; as for the moral code, it means that one could violate a norm if one had the power.

However there could be another way of looking at things. Balarama Dasa, the humanist, was aware that the moral code for the married woman could lead to a situation where she would be denied her individuality and space, and exploited most cynically. Consider that on the matter of choosing between one's brother and wife, Balabhadra told Jagannatha that a crore of wives would be available, but not a brother (p.26). So the wife could be discarded. The code specifies how the woman must behave with her husband and the elders of the family, but says nothing about how they in turn must ensure that she has her space, and is not humiliated. The poet was of the view that the woman did have a right to protest when she was unjustly treated. But then did the woman have any hope to get justice in that kind of society? She had almost none.

In order to save the protest from being devoid of meaning, the poet had a related message: the men of the family must realize and appreciate the invaluable contribution of the woman to the family, and must willingly and happily give her space and respect. The tribulations of Jagannatha and Balabhadra can be viewed as a warning in the typical *brata katha* tradition: the one who disregards from the code, no matter how mighty, must undergo suffering. The warning is of particular significance in that if this could happen to Jagannatha and Balabhadra, then ordinary celestials and humans would never escape from the consequences of their act of injustice to the woman. By stating that the woman in the family must be accorded dignity of treatment and consideration, the poet, in effect, adds to, and thereby modifies, the moral code governing the family.

As for the victim's, i.e., goddess Lakshmi's power, as she fought her family, an important source of it was the implicit support for her cause by the celestials. The gods who cooperated with her included the fire god, Agni, Sun god, Surya, and goddess of learning, Saraswati. They realized that if Balabhadra and Jagannatha did not suffer, men would have no need for women, and would turn them out of home at will. The poet was indirectly advocating that it would be ethical on the part of the people to stand up for a victim of injustice. All in all, there is indeed a message for the humans here: those who treat others unjustly must remember that there will always be people to help a victim of injustice, and such collective power of the people can be really strong.

In a way, *Lakshmi Purana* is a victim's story, but at the same time it is the story of a family, where there was happiness and harmony until that single act of injustice took place. It brought suffering to all concerned, both the victim and those who caused it. But it was completely without bitterness and ill will. So at the end forgiving was easy. Apart from the simplicity of its diction and design, and the lyrical quality of the verse, it is this positive note that has made this work so popular and so memorable.

## Notes and References

Manasingh, Mayadhara (1981). *Odia Sahityara Itihasa*. Cuttack: Grantha Mandira. (3rd Edn.)

Mishra, Jayakrushna (ed.) *Balarama Dasa kruta Manabasa Lakshmi Purana*. Srimandira, Puri: Sadgrantha Niketana.

Sarangi, Nrusingha (1999). *Odia Purana Sahitya*.Cuttack: Bidya Prakashana.

9

# Śākta Cult in Dance of Bengal

*Mahua Mukherjee*

Worshipping *Śakti* or the female principle of creation has been an age-old tradition in the history of Indian austere practices. Whether inspired by the non-Aryan or by the Aryan religious beliefs, the worship of *Śakti* was taken up by the Vedic saints and got spread throughout India, it got compounded with *Tāntrik* rituals and transformed into a religion itself. With the passage of time, *Śakti* – worship with its typical austere practices and principles blossomed into a matured replete religion. In *Devi Upaniṣad*, *Mātrikā Śakti* has been referred to as an everlasting eternal power. The term *Śakti* feminine in gender, has long been associated with the various male deities as their energy but *Śaktism* as the energy of each god became personified as his consort, and thus if a god was separated from his consort, he was powerless and inert. The triadic division of primordial nature into three *Śaktis* according to the *guṇas*, identifies each with one another form of *Sarasvati*, *Lakṣmī*, and *Durgā* for the sake of creation, preservation, and destruction of the Universe.

From ancient times, three religions — *Śaiva*, *Vaiṣaṇava* and *Śākta*, were pre-dominant in Bengal. Extensive influence of *Śaiva* cult can be witnessed in '*Gājan*' festival; iconographic and architectural evidences also give us the same idea. The influence of *Vaiṣṇava* cult is also pre-dominant. Its consequence is *Gauḍiya Vaiṣaṇava* religion propounded by *Śrī Caitanyadeva*. Both these religions have dance playing an important role in them. However, the *Śākta* cult is also no less important. The profound impact of Śākta cult in Bengal can easily be understood from the stories of *Purāṇas*. The *Śākta – pīṭha* is a general name given to certain sacred places in the Indian subcontinent associated with the *Śakti* – cult, the cult of the mother – goddess. The places are usually called the *pīṭha – sthāna* or *mahā – pīṭha* in Bengali. the word '*pīṭha*' means '*alṭār*' or 'seat' where the body parts of the goddess *Satī* (goddess *Durgā*) fell to earth after she had been cut to pieces by the discuss (*Cakra*) of *Viṣṇu*, the origin of the *Śākta – pīṭha* has been told in a popular myth called *Dakṣa – jajña*, which is a part of the magnificient epic

*Mahābhārata*. It tells of the time when the god *Dakṣa* held the ritual ceremony of the sacred fire and invited all the gods, except, *Śiva*, the husband of her daughter *Satī*. At the altar of the sacred fire, the furious goddess *Satī*, as a protest against the insult to her husband, threw herself into the fire and burnt to death. Hearing the death of his wife, the bereaved *Śiva* came and carried her body on his shoulder. He went nearly mad with grief and wandered the world stamping the ground with his feet and danced *Samhāra Tāṇḍava*. The world could not endure this earth – tremours, and finally the gods asked *Viṣṇu* to put an end to the wandering of *Śiva*. *Viṣṇu* annihilated her body into fifty pieces by discuss (*Cakra*), according to scholars among which thirty one / twenty one pieces had landed on Greater Bengal. Wherever one landed, the believers enshrined an altar to worship the goddess. Each *pītha* having mythological origin regarding the goddess *Satī*, has its own separate name as a *pīṭha – sthāna*, but also bears the names of the goddess (*devi*) and her husband (*Bhairava*). From this heresay, the strong impact of *Śākta* cult in Bengal can be understood. *Satī* is the wife of *Śiva*, but she is better known in Bengal as *Durgā* and *Kālī* being merged with the various other folk goddesses. *Śaktism* is a direct offshoot of the primitive Mother Goddess cult, so prominent a feature of the religion of agricultural people with each village or tribe having their number own particular name for the goddess, their has increased even more. Included among the goddess worshipped in villages and by tribes in Bengal are, for example – *Māheśvarī, Netā Dhobānī* — the caste goddess of the *Dhobās*, the washermen, *Mahālaxmī, Kālisundarī, Caṇḍī, Ghanṭeśvarī, Basumātā, Sāt bon, Hāḍi – Jhi, Śyāmā, Kālikā – Caṇḍī, Ugra – Caṇḍī, Dhāi – Caṇḍī, Jagadambā, Jagat – Tāriṇī, Bipad – Tāriṇī, Sankaṭā, Bargabhīmā, Bāsuli Sītalā, Cāmuṇḍā, Ambikā* etc. According to the scholars, the Bengalee race is a conglomeration of mainly Austric, Dravida and Aryans.

The erudite persons opine that from ancient time worship of Mother deity was in vogue over here, and this opinion has been substantiated by various archaeological and practical evidences. The goddesses have appeared, be it directly or indirectly, in the various inscriptions obtained from Bengal. In the inscriptions we get the goddesses either as a spouse or as an independent identity regardless of their husbands. The names of the places also give such ideas, like — *Ātbāicaṇḍī, Ambikānagar, Debipur, Ādyāpīṭh, Kālighāt, Sītāhāṭi, Kālikāpur, Tārāpīṭh,* and so many. Most of the goddesses whose names can be found from the analysis of the inscriptions, have been introduced in the *Purāṇas* as the better – half of Lord *Śiva*. Of course, the wives of Lord *Viṣṇu, Brahmā, Indra, Agni, Candra, Kubera, Madana etc.* with their different names have also found places as goddesses in inscriptions and *Purāṇas*. Moreover, from inscriptions we get the reference of a few goddesses who have not been introduced as a consort deity, instead, they are some natural or supernatural power or consciousness, which has emerged as a goddess. Contextually it can be mentioned that the word '*Śakti*' is mainly applicable to *Śiva – Śakti*.[1] In the *Devi Bhāgavata Purāṇa, Śakti* alone is present in cause and effect:

The highest *Ādyā Śakti* by her mere will create and preserve this Universe and it is she who again destroys in time the whole *Brahmāṇḍa,* moving and non-moving; no one is capable to do his respective work be he *Brahmā, Viṣṇu, Maheśvara, Indra,* Fire, Sun,

*Varuṇa* or any other person whatsover; verily all the *Devas* performed the respective actions by the use of this *Ādyā Śakti*. That she alone is present in cause and effect in doing every action, can be witnessed vividly.[2]

The term *Śakti,* feminine in gender, had long been associated with the various male deities as their energy but in *Śaktism* the energy of each god become personified as his consort, and thus if a god was separated from his consort, he was powerless and inert.

In the inscriptions of Bengal, the goddess as an embodiment of *Śiva – Śakti* has a number of names which are equally diverse and significant with regard to their meanings. Sometimes she is the daughter of the mountain — *Śailasutā, Śailatmajā, Girijā, Himaśailajā, Girisutā, Adritanayā.* Again sometimes she is the offspring of *Dakṣa – Satī, Umā, Gaurī,* then again as the wife of *Śiva* she is – *Śivaṇī, Sarvānī, Rudrānī, Bhavānī*. *Devī* Durgā as a distinct entity, as the Supreme Mother of entire Universe has names like – *Sarvamaṅgalā, Śyāmāmcanḍī, Carcikā, Mahagāurī, Mahālaxmī, Jagadeśvarī* etc.

*Devī* — as *Viṣṇu – Śakti – Śrī Laxmī, Padmā, Padmālayā, Kamalā.*

*Devī* – as the wife of *Brahmā.*

*Devī* – as the wife of *Agni.*

*Devī* – as the wife of *Indra.*

*Devī* – as the wife of *Candra.*

*Devī* – as the wife of *Madana.*

*Devī* – as the wife of *Kuvera.*

*Devī* – as *Bageśvarī, Mahāneel, Sarasvati,* Mother *Catuhsasṭhī.*

*Devī* – as the Mother River *(Nadī)*

*Devī* as the earth (*Prithivī*)

*Devī* – as *Sarpadhiṣthātrī* (sitting on the serpant). The impact of *Tāntrik* cult is predominant in all — *Vaiṣṇava, Śaiva, Śākta* religion. But it is so influential in case of *Śākta* religion, that many take *Śākta* and *Tāntrik* cult synonymously. During the PĀLA regime in Bengal *Tāntrik Buddhism* started developing. *Śākta / Tantra* cult has played a major role in the religion and culture of Bengal. Archaeological and historical evidences, likewise, suggest that Bengal must have played a major role in the development and dissemination of *Tāntrik / Buddhist* doctrine, concept and imagery. The contribution of Bengal to *Mahāyāna, Vajrayāna,* and its offshoot, *Kālacakrayāna,* and their varied iconography is overwhelming, Sarasikumar Sarasvati points out.

Among *Śākta* goddesses, *Durgā* and *Kālī* are specially worshipped in Bengal. Though the story of Autumnal worship of *Devī Durgā* by *Śri Rāmacandra* has not been mentioned in *Valmikī's Rāmāyana*, still it has been found its place in the *Rāmāyana* by *Krittibāsa* of Bengal, *Devī Bhāgavata, Brihaddharmapurāṇa* and in *Kashmikāpurāṇa,* in a bit different style. It is quite difficult to specify the time when *Durgā Pujā* came into vogue, but from the books like *'Durgābhakti Taranginī'* by *Vidyāpati, 'Kalvivek'* (15th cent. A.D.) by *Jimutbāhana*, *'Durgotsavavivek'*, *'Basantavivek'* and *'Durgotsava Prayoga'* ($15^{th}$-$16^{th}$ cent. A.D) by *Śūlapāṇi,* moreover, from the writings like *Śrināth Govindapura, Raghunandan* etc. of 16th century, we get to know a lot about the *Durgāpuja*. From many other books similar to these, weget the information about various rituals of *Durgā pujā*.[3]

Krishnananda Agambagish, the writer of *'Tantrasāra'*, had played a vital role in making the worship of *Kālī* popular in Bengal. He was a post Caitanyaite. There is a heresay that, the image in which *Devi Kālī* is worshipped today, was first imagined by him. There is a mention of *Dakṣinākālī, Mahākālī, Śmaśānakālī, Cāmuṇḍākālī, Siddhakālī, Hamsakālī* and *Kamakalākālī* in *'Tantrasāra'* and *'Āgamatatvabilāsa'* of Raghunath. Gopinath, Srinath and Vacaspati issued a ruling as to worship *Devī Kālī* on the fourteenth lunar night. We could not find any reference to *Kālī* worship on *Dipābalī* night in ancient books. The first reference of inter-relationship between *Kālīpujā* and *Dipāvalī* could be found in *'Sayamasaparyay '* by Kashinath of 1669 Scythian era (*Sakabda*). In Bengal, *Kālī* is also special as the first *Vidyā* of *Daśamahāvidyā*.[4]

There is a tradition of animal sacrifice in the worship of *Śākta* goddesses like *Kālī, Durgā, Manasā,* etc. in Bengal.[5] Blood sacrificies play a major role in mother Goddess cults of India — it is only *Śaktism* and its offshoots, which are developments of the primitive Mother Goddess cults that require sacrifices — both human and animal.[6] Ritual involving human sacrifice to the mother Goddess in Bengal continued well upto nineteenth century. The ceremony of immersion of the image of *Durgā* into water has been defined by Jimutabahana as the auspicious ceremony perfomed on the concluding day of *Durgāpujā*, in which the people —

> Clothe themselves like the Savaras with leaves, besmear their body with mud and indulge in sporadic dance, play, music, fun and frolic to the extent that the free exchange of slang even the act of intercourse in public becomes sanctified by the grace of the god Durgā.[7]

In Bengal, as elsewhere, animal sacrifice is especially associated with *Kālī* and the number of animals sacrificed on certain occasions is staggering. In the sixteenth – century *Tantrasāra*, we are informed of the various benefits that will act to the devotee if different animals are sacrificed. Quoting the *Muṇḍamālā–tantra*, it is stated that a goat increases one's power of oratory; a ram increases one's poetic skills by sacrificing a buffalo, one gains wealth and prosperity; moksa or liberation if a deer is sacrificed; prosperity with a bird; great result, though not specified, when a iguana (godha) is sacrificed; and great prosperity as well as the eight *siddhas*, by sacrificing a man. There are elaborate rites for the act of sacrifice as well as for the offering of flesh and blood.[8] The above mentioned example clearly proves that alongwith *Śaiva, Vaishṇava* etc. religion, there has been a strong seat of *Śākta* cult in Bengal. In *Caitanya* era also *Śākta* cult and *Tantric* rituals spread throughtout Bengal. Many scholars are of the opinion that *Tāntric* cult originated in Bengal and gained acceptance in Assam, Nepal — even in far–off Tibet and China. Tantra developed in Eastern India particularly in Bengal many many years ago. During pre-Caitanya and Caitanya era the main identity of Brahmanya culture laid in — *Nyāya* (Logic), *Smriti* (Law) and *Tantra*. The evidences obtained till date suggest that, *Tāntric* rites (known as the traditional usage of family or ancestral ritual) were in vogue in Bengal from 10th-12th century. Most probably, the ancient *Tantrakāra* (one versed in *Tāntrik* rites) Mahamahopadhyay Paribrajakacarya, was alive during the 14th century. Penned in Bengali letters, the manuscript of his writing '*Kāmyo Yantroddhāro*' was transcripted in c. 1375 A.D.[9]

The above mentioned evidences prove that, *Śākta* cult was extensively practiced in Bengal from far-off times, whose impact can be witnessed in different songs–dances–dramas and sculptures of later period. A brief example is being presented below. Bengal has a number of dance forms. For example—dance in religious rites, ritual dance (*Gājan*), dance in folk-drama. We can classify dances into four categories –

i) Dance in religious rites.

ii) Ritual dance.

iii) Dance in folk – drama.

iv) Gauḍiya Nritya or Classical dance of Bengal.

(1) Dance as Religious Rites — *Dhāicanḍī Nritya.* In this dance we get a hint of meditating *Bhadrakālī* as mentioned in *Tantras*. The gestures of the dance suggest as if *Devī Canḍī* is going to devour the entire creation. The body – movements and speed of the dance have tremendous impact and endless enthusiasm and is accompanied by indomitable energetic beat of *Dhāk* (a percussion instrument). It symbolizes the furious awakening of the violent goddess *Kālī*. Different *caris* (graceful movement) viz. *Vidyutbhranta cari*, different *gatis* (gait) like *Manduki, Vira ;* different *utplavanas* — *Kurmalaga* etc. and various types of *bhramari* i.e., whirling movements are used in this dance.

Instrument – only *Dhāk* (percussion instrument) is used in this dance.

Āharya or Costume–make-up—*Ghagra* (long skirt), and the entire body is painted in black.

Area – Dinhata area of Coochbehar.[10]

(2) Ritual Dance – The *Bhaktyās* (Devotees) of *Gājan* guise themselves as deities and perform different entertaining dances — (a) *Haragaurī* dance, (b) *Kālīkāch Kālī-nach–Kālipātāri,* (c) *Jhānṭākālī, Camunḍā, Ugracanḍā, Bāsulī* dance of *Gambhirā,* (d) *Kālīnritya, Mahiṣāsuramardinī* of *Chhau* dance, *Mahiṣāsura vadh* of *Gājan.*

*(a) Hara-Gaurī Nritya* - In this dance, a boy plays the role of *Śiva* ; beside him another boy of 8-10 years, put on a veil and dance as *Gaurī* with the rhythm of *Dhāk*. Generally, it is a duet dance but the accompanying instrumentalist, i.e., *Dhāki* (the *Dhāk* player) and other devotees also dance along with *Hara – Gaurī*. There is a trident in one hand of *Hara* and '*Ḍambaru*' (a kind of small tabour) on the other with matted hair. After completing dance in one house, *Hara Gaurī,* go to others being accompanied by all the devotees. They are also accompanied by the ghosts and ghouls.

(b) *Kālī Kāch – Kālī Nāch – Kālikā Pātāri – Jhānṭa Kālī Nritya of Gambhirā – Dhāi Chanḍī Nritya* etc.

All these above mentioned dances are found on the concept and philosophy of the '*Kālī*- cult' and has been popular in various names in area basis and there are also differences in its application and artistic approach. *Kālī-Kāch* can be seen in Dhaka region on the occasion of *Gājan* festival. According to erudite scholars, the connotation of the word '*Kāch*' is the participation of the artistes to acting.In the *Kālī-Kāch* dance, the artistes participate with the costume and make-up of the deity '*Kālī*', so it is named after *Kālīkāch*. Along with the *Kālīkāch* of Dhaka, almost every region of Bengal have *Kālī Nritya* or *Kālī Nāch*. The dance is performed with the mask of *Kālī*, painted with black of course with the beat of *Dhāk*. This is a kind of war dance. Mask is not used in the *Kālīnāch* of Dhaka. *Kālīnāch* can also be seen in *Bahurupī* dance of South-24 Parganas, where the performer does not wear mask; his face is painted as like as *Kālī*. While performing vigorous dance with the rhythm of *Dhāk, Kālī* stands up on the chest of prostrate *Śiva*. Somewhere, *Śiva* lays down on dust and ripe banana is placed on his chest, thereafter *Kālī* comes dancing with a sword in her hand and bisects the banana by striking the sword while leaving *Śiva* untouched, unhurt. At present days, showing of such dexterities has got the major importance. Heresay goes that, earlier *Kālīkāpātāri* dance was performed carrying human-skull in hand. Now, *Kālīkāpātari Nritya* is performed to introduce repulsive *(Bibhatsa rasa)* and fearful *(Bhayānaka rasa)* sentiment.[11]

(c) *Gambhirā* – Various forms of *Kālīkāch* is found in *Gambhirā*, like, *Jhānṭākālī, Ugracaṇḍā, Cāmunḍā, Basuli* dance of Maldaha and adjacent regions of Maldaha of Bangladesh. But typical form of *Kālīnāch* of *Gambhira,* where *Kālī* used to perform wearing garland of human skulls and with 'falchion' in one hand being accompanied by *Jaidhak* (big Drum) and a dish of bell – metal (*Kansar)*. With beat of *Dhāk* is create a variety of vigorous dance-gestures (*Tānḍava*), aeriel movements (*Ākasha Carī*), surface movements (*Bhoomi Cārī*), revolving movements (*Bhramari*), jumping movement *(Utplavana)* expressing the sentiment of fear *(Bhayānaka*) and anger (*Raudra)*. In *Jhānṭākālī* dance, *Kālī* carries a broom made out of canes. Only in the *Gājan* festival of Bengal, this tradition of dance carrying cane-sticks in hand could be found. (It is noteworthy that, references regarding dance with cane-sticks in hand surrounding the sacrificial altar in *Vedic* era can be found). The masks of *Gambhīrā* are made out of wood. In the *Kālīnāch* of other regions, *Kālī* dressed with trousers making the two legs distinct and cut hands stick out from waist. But the costume of *Kālī nāch* of *Gambhīrā* is different. It comprises of *ghāgra* (long skirt) – blouse and a wooden mask of face; the dance gestures are a bit slower. The mask of *Dakṣinā – Kālī* is prepared imitating the image of the *Kālī* of *Kalighat*. After putting the mask on the face of the dancer, he is made to smell burnt incense. Immediately he gets possessed by the *Devī* and lie down. With the accompaniment of the rhythm of *Dhāk* goes on *Kālīnāch* with different gestures and postures. it starts at a slow pace and gradually gets faster and fastest. The above mentioned vigorous movements, surface and aeriel movements, jumping movements revolving movements are applied in *Cāmunḍā, Ugracanḍā* and *Bāsulī* dance.[12] In all of these the musical accompaniments used are *Dhāk* and *Kānsi*.

(d) *Kālī Nritya* and *Mahiṣāsura Vadh* in *Chhow* dance – Like *Gambhīrā, Chhow* dance also has masked *Kālīnāch*. Currently the masks are made up of paper – pulp and clay. here the rhythmic instruments are *Dhāmsā* (a large surfaced Kettle drum) and *Baṅgla Dhōl* (a kind of percussion instrument made up of wood and played on by a small stick in one hand while the other remains free, same as found in *Kavi Gaan*). Moreover, the rustic melody of *Shehnāi* (wind instrument) makes the terrific image of *Kālī* come alive with the fearful vigorous gestures.

*Mahiṣāsuramardinī* – The Opera dance can be seen in the *Chhow* of Purulia, specially in *Gājan* festival expanded from far east Tripura to the West Seraikella of Jharkhand. In this opera, artists guised as *Hara – Pārvatī* enter the stage. Thereafter, *Ganeśa, Kārtika, Mahiṣāsura* etc. characters come on to the stage one by one. Finally comes *Durgā* and her mount lion. After her heroic brandishing dance starts her battle with *Mahiṣāsura*. After the defeat of *Mahiṣāsura*, in war, emerges on stage one by one – *Laxmī, Sarasvatī, Kārtika, Ganeśa, Śiva* and *Durgā. Durgā*, finishes her dance with her family.

(3) Dance in Folk-drama – Right from the ancient time Drama was very popular. The text on dance and music — *'Nāṭya Śāstra'*, is supporting this comment. The role of dance or *nritya* in the aforesaid folk playlet is very significant and its reference is also available in *'Nāṭya Śāstra'*. The spread of *Mangal Kāvya* was quite evident in Bengal during 11th to 18th century. It become more influential on music, drama, and dance especially between 15th century A.D. to the 7th decade of 18th century A.D. Still it exists in Bengal. Though in *Śivāyan, Dharmamangal, Rāymangal* etc. male deities are important, and play a major role, however, *Manasāmangal, Ṣaṣthīmangal, Abhoymangal Annadāmangal, Annapurnāmangal, Ambikāmangal, Śītalāmangal* all are female deity-centric. From 600 -700 years, these *Mangal – Kāvyas* are being presented in dramatized forms in different areas of Bengal. For example – *Manasāmangal. Manasāmangal* is famous as *'Ojhā Nritya'*, in Srihatta and Mymensingh of Bangladesh and in Bengalee inhabited part of Barak valley which was actually a part of Srihatta that has been attached to Assam after independence; as *'Biṣahari'* or *'Biṣaharā'* in Jalpaiguri and Coochbehar region of North Bengal, as *'Manasā Kīrtan'* in Maldah, as *'Manasā Jātrā'* or *'Manasā bhāsān'* or *'Manasā Jāgoran'* in some places. The style of dramatized presentation of these *Śākta Mangal Kāvyas* vary in different areas as there is difference in melody, instruments used, presentation, literature and dancing postures. For example, in *Manasāmangal performance,* somewhere they used *Śrīkhol* or *Mridanga,* somewhere *Mahāmridanga,* somewhere *Pākāja*. The main artist carry a flywhisk (*cāmara)* in hand.

Earlier the *Manasā mangal* drama used to be throughout the month of *Śrāvaṇa* (July – August). To keep pace with the modern age or due to economic condition, now the span of performance has been reduced to seven or somewhere three days. '*Ojha Nritya'* is an age-old, *guru-mukhi* (mentor-disciple succession) dance tradition, where the training follows a mentor – disciple lineage. To become a complete '*Ojhā'* artist one has to be (i) Literate, (ii) Undertake voice training, (iii) Elocution training, (iv) learn acting and meditation, (v) memorizing, (vi) Dance, (vii) Have conception about rhythm and speed, (viii) Should be versed in composing songs and poems, (ix) Have a good memory. Learning *Yoga* is compulsory — as it helps in keeping one's body light, flexible and swift. In this dance one has to –

dance on a clay – plate (*sarā*) without breaking it.

- move with the clay – plate under the feet, with the accompaniment of the rhythm of instruments ;
- dance on sand, flour or husk – like material and make designs of flower, lotus, bird etc;

- dance on brass and bell – metal plate;
- dance on '*batasa*' (cube sugar / molasses – cube) without breaking it;
- exhibit various types of *gati* (gaits) like – *Hamsi* or *Marali* (duck like), *Mrigi* (like deer), *Gaja* (like elephant) etc. and different revolving movements.[13]

In the Maldah district, there is 500 years old, traditional *Manākaṣā Manasākīrtana Sampradāya* (group). The mentor or guru is Haranath Trivedi. Generation after generation they have been performing *Manasā – kīrtan* by singing melodious notes and with bold, upright steps carrying flywhisk in hand. Earlier all the female characted the male members only perform the female characters.

(4) *Gauḍiya Nṛtya* (A classical dance of Bengal) – As *Śākta* cult is quite influential in Bengal, *Gauḍiya Nṛtya* has a number of dance items based upon *Śākta* religion (Mother cult). For example – *Ambikā stuti, Caṇḍī Vandanā, Daśamahāvidyā, Krisnakālīkīrtan, Mahiṣāsuramardinī, Kālī–nāmamāla, Kālī – Tārā stuti, Ṣodaśī – Bhubaneśvarī stuti* age old traditional dance numbers. Moreover, *Gauḍiya Nṛtya* has been found its application in *Śākta – Padavalis* composed by Ramprasad Sen and other poets. In this connections Iwish to draw the attention of the readers to state that in the year 1936, the classical dance of South India, re-constructed by Rukmini Devi Arundale, was introduced with the name of *Bharatanātyam*. It was Rukmini Devi herself who first choreographed dance items with compositions of *Tyagarājā, Dikshitar, Śyāma Śāstrī* of South India, which are now mandatory in the repertoire of *Bharatanātyam*.[14] *Tyagarājā* is an arduous singer of South India, and not a dancer. His approximate time was 1767 – 1847. Again the period of arduous artist *Ramprasad Sen* ranged from 1718 to 1781; i.e., almost 50 years before *Tyagrājā*. If after 1936 the verses of *Tyagrājā* could be applied to perform *Bharatanātyam*, then application of *Gauḍiya Nṛtya* on the compositions of *Ramprasad Sen* is also quite justified.

Beside the art of dance, there are ennumerous sculptures of *Śākta* deities spread all over Bengal. In them we can observe different dancing postures. Like standing postures, hand gestures, adornments etc. These *Śākta sculptures* are preserved in Maldah Museum, Rajsahi Varendra Research Museum, Museum of Burdwan University, Behala State Museum, Asutosh Museum of Calcutta University, Gurusaday Dutta Museum, Aksoy Kumar Moitra Museum of North Bengal University, Dhaka Museum etc. Moreover, many *Śākta* sculptures can be seen in the different temple – wall carvings of Bengal.

Long before Turkish invasion worship of *Śākta* cult was in vogue in Bengal. It has found its expression in manifold ways over the next thousand years. Contemporary to Sri Caitanya, Krishnananda Agambagish wrote a great book '*Brihata Tantrasāra*', which is revered as the standard book of *Tantra* practices throughout India. A noteworthy point of *Gauḍiya Vaiṣṇava* philosophy is '*Rādhā Vina Kṛṣṇa Asiddha*' (without *Rādha Kṛṣṇa* is incomplete). The power of *Śākta* cult lies in *Rādhikā*. Though these are quite different apparently, but *Gauḍiya Vaiṣṇavism* could not imagine of *Kṛṣṇa* devoid of the power of *Rādhikā*. This conception proves that, in Bengali culture and religion there was no scope of ignoring *Śākta* cult and *Tāntrik* philosophy. In the *Rāmāyaṇa* of *Krittibasa, Sri Rāma* himself is an incarnation of Lord *Viṣṇu*. He was made to worship *Devī Durgā* or *Śakti*. *Krittibasa Ojha* was the poet of 15$^{th}$ century. This again suggests that tremendous *Vaiṣṇava* influence also, could not wipe out the inclination towards *Śākta* from the Bengali

*Rāmāyaṇa*. Bringing any such context in *Rāmāyaṇa* is almost unthinkable outside Bengal, atleast before *Krittibasa*.[15]

The tradition of *Devī Śakti* is very old in Bengal. Among them *Durgā pujā* the best festival in the national life of the Bengalees is popular from many centuries. Due to this special intellectual aptitude of the Bengalees, the impact of *Śākta* cult is deep rooted and boundless in the field of music – dance – painting – sculpture – literature.

According to *Vaiṣṇava* philosophy – the sentiment of devotion can be classified into 5 kinds – *Śānta* (Serene), *Dāsya* (sentiment of Servant), *Sakhya* (friendly), *Vātsalya* (parently), and *Madhura* (lovely).

In *Śākta* literature also, sentiments are of 5 types — *Vātsalya* (parentyly), *Veera* (bold or brave), *Adbhuta* (strange), *Divya (godly)* and *Santa* (serene). *Vātsalya* or parently feeling overflow the rest.[16] *Gauḍiya Nṛtya* of Bengal comprise of all these sentiments.

**Acknowledgement :** Late Manindra Nath Roy former Jela Sabhadhipati of Coochbehar, Sri Amitava Mukherjee (Gaudiya Music researcher), my guru Padmasree Gambhir Singh Mudha, my students Satabdee Banerjee for assisting me in this article and Basanti Chowdhuri, Dr. Gautam Sengupta [Director-General of Archeology, Govt. of India], Malda Museum.Late Dr. Niranjan Goswami [Former curator of Asutosh Museum C.U.], National Museum, Delhi and Behala State Museum.

**Mahiṣāsura-Mardinī**
c.11th cent. Maldah-Museum

**Sculpture of Śākta Devī Gaudiya Nritya has many repertoires about her**

## *Notes and References*

1. Kundu, Shambhunath, Prachin Vange Pouranik Dharma O Devabhabana, Bardhaman University, 1996, Pg. 263 – 264.
2. Vijnanananda alias Chatterjee, Prasanna Hari, Srimad Devi bhagavatam, SBH 26, 1974, reprint, Pg. 28.
3. Bhattacharyya, Narendranath, Madhyeyuge Bangler Samaj O Samakriti, ed. by Aniruddha Roy and Ratnaboli Chattopadhyay, K.P.Bagchi & Co.,1992, Pg.171 -172.
4. Bhattaccharyya, Narendranath, Madyayuge Bangler Samaj O Sanskriti, ed. by Aniruddha Roy and Ratnabali Chattopadhyay, K.P. Bagchi & Co. 1992, Pg. 171 -174.
5. Dasgupta, Tamonash, Prachin Bangla Sahityer Itihas, Cal. Univ. 1951, Pg. 22.
6. Bhattacharyya, N.N. The India Mother Goddess, Pg. 75 -76.

7. Donaldson, Thomas Eugene, Tantra and Śākta Art of Orissa, Vol. 1, D. K. Printworld, 2002. Pg. 20 -26.
8. Pal, P. Tantrasara, Pg. 14 -15.
9. Bandyopadhyay, Asit Kr. Bangla Sahityer Itibritto (2nd part), Modern Book Agency Pvt. Ltd. 1983 (3rd ed) Pg. 42 – 43.
10. Vardhan, Sri Mani, Bangler Lokonritya O Gitibaichitra, Publisher – Prachar Adhikarta, Govt. of W.B. 1961, Pg – 84
11. Mukhopadhyay, Mahua, Bangler Loukik Nritya ....chapter - Kālīnāch, Pg. 6.
12. Mukhopadhyay, Mahua, Bangler Laukik Nritya, Published by Bidhubhushan Saha, 2001, Pg. 33 -34.
13. Bhattacharyya, Mukundadasa, Barak Upotyaker Lokonritya, Silchar Sangeet Vidyalaya, 1996, topic – Ojha Nritya
14. Sarada, S., Kalakshetra Rukmini Devi, Kalamandir Trust, 1985, Pg. 45.
15. Gangopadhyay, Sambhunath, Śāktatantrik Sadhana O Sahitya, Punthi Prakashani, 1407 (Bengali year) Pg. 11 -14.
16. Basu, Arun Kumar, Śākta Padavali, Pustak Bipani, 1408, Pg. 54 – 55.

10

# Epigraphical Glimpses of Brahmanical Cults in Early Bengal

*Krishnendu Ray*

Humans in search of their necessaries of life find out a space on the earth and branch out there like a tree. In due course they relate their activities to different physical segments of the earth such as the hilly area or the agricultural area or the coastal area or the riverine area etc[1]. Thus they actively interact with or utilize the landmass they settle in for the purpose of living. In doing so they develop various forms of behaviour by which they become conditioned gradually.This conditioning develops in them a kind of feeling for their land. They try to exist with this feeling. In doing so they develop some beliefs which they embrace.The aim is to mentally secure their physical existence on the earth. In connection with this they also develop some rituals in course of practicing their beliefs in real life situations. These beliefs and rituals gradually make them feel emotionally integrated or attached with their habitat and thus a kind of territorial belongingness. In other words, they feel themselves a part of the territory they live in. They develop a kind of social belongingness[2]. The matter may be attempted to understand in the light of recent archaeological discoveries in the Vanga region. The region during the period under study included the north and south 24 Parganas, the Midnapur, Hooghly, Howrah districts, parts of Burdwan, West Bengal and coastal Bangladesh upto the joint streams of the Padma, Meghna, and Brahmaputra in the east (21° N—24° S. Latitude, 85° E—90° W Longitude)[3].

This vast expanse of land has recently yielded many artefacts. Different Black and Red Ware (BRW) objects, traces of house-building activities, religious activities have been noticed at different sites in the Midnapur, Birbhum, Burdwan, Bankura and Purulia districts[4]. Hence it appears that the people who used these BRW articles adopted themselves to the areas abounding in rivers. Naturally this vast area was conducive to 'agricultural and commercial pursuits'[5]. The artefacts like jars, potteries etc may drive home the fact that the people utilized the natural resources of this rivery and fertile region. The objective was obviously to cater to their needs of life. At this point their 'overseas connection'[6] through the Ganges, as have been inferred, acquires meaning. Their real life situations probably led them to develop and empower their belief as ' the mental state of conviction, the attitude of mind towards its own experiences in which it accepts and endorses them referring to reality, as having real significance or value'[7]. Probably with this kind of belief the people of Vanga developed certain ritual formalities. These constituted the essence of their religious culture. These non-physical phenomena probably involved them in culturally conceptualizing the territory they lived in. Thus they regarded their territory also as a cultural entity apart from its geographical entity[8]. It is in the sense of cultural entity that the people integrated themselves with the territory. Thus their ethnic name Vangas became coterminous with the territory they culturally conceived. Hence it is in their cultural perspectives of the region of Vanga that the study of a few inscribed terracotta objects[9], for an understanding of their Brahmanical religious bearings may be contextual; because the culture of humans also includes their religious activities.

In this connection the religious conditions of so-called ancient Bengal have been discussed at length.R.C.Majumdar, N.R.Roy, Rama Chatterjee, to mention a few, to suit the statement. Long back R.C. Majumdar rightly observed that the people of ancient Bengal had also religious ideas, although those ideas could hardly be traced certainly in detail before the Gupta period (c.fourth century C.E. to the sixth century). Majumdar has brought to light the Brahmanical religious ideas of the people of ancient Bengal as a whole from fourth / fifth century onwards[10]. Niharranjan Roy has discussed different aspects of the religious life of the Bengali people. In that connection he has clearly said that there was hardly any foundation and spread of Vedic religion and culture or more significant Puranic religion and culture in pre-Gupta Benga[11]. According to Rama Chatterjee, Bengal before the Gupta period was culturally neglected because of her association with Jain culture as well as with 'the Mlecchas around the Bay of Bengal'[12]. At best a small section of the people of ancient Bengal might have had a little knowledge of letters. This may be corroborated by a third century B.C.E inscription from Mahasthan (Bogra district, Bangladesh)[13] written in Prakrit in Brahmi characters. Now, it is well known that ancient Bengal represented a number of culturally different subregions such as Pundravardhana (North Bengal), Radha (the Burdwan division of West Bengal), Vanga (the area between the Bhagirathi and the Padma and beyond) and Vangala (the lower portion of the Bhagirathi-Padma tract), Samatata (south-eastern Bangladesh), Harikela (Chattagram area) etc. But the religious activities of the people of a particular subregion of ancient Bengal is hardly available before the Gupta period. In this context the discovery and decipherment by B.N.Mukherjee of a good number of Kharosti and Kharosti-Brahmi inscriptions in lower West Bengal in 1989 may be proposed. It is only N.N.Bhattacharyya who has first dished out to the reader a general introduction to the religious aspects of the Kharosti and Kharosti-Brahmi inscriptions found in lower West Bengal or Vanga[14]. Taking cue from him certain Brahmanical characteristics of the inscribed objects found in the region may be attended to in the context of tracing the religious activities of the people of pre-Gupta Vanga. This is how the present essay acquires relevance from the point of religious historiography of so-called ancient Bengal as a whole.

## II

Humans have been living in Nature admittedly through hazards and uncertainties from immemorial time. In due course of their interactions with Nature they have developed and embraced certain spiritual beliefs in order to mentally qualify and strengthen themselves to cope with the uncertainties of life. They have been manifesting their spiritual beliefs through rituals and religious practices to live their lives. The people of Vanga were no exception. The discussion may be initiated with a reference to an inscribed terracotta potsherd of the late first or early second century C.E. from Chandraketugarh. The inscription points out the name of probably a Maga brahmana called Vastra. He is described in the record as a victorious Maga (*Maka*) brahmana (*jayanto Makatah eko Vastrah dvijah*)[15]. Another inscribed terracotta seal of the late first century C.E. may lead one to think that as a brahmana he became victorious because of his being as wise as Brahma, or the creator or as Brahmana the most learned of the principal priests (*dhiyasi Brahmadhvaja*)[16]. According to an inscribed seal from Chandraketugarh (c. first century C.E.), the brahmana was a Brahmavid who knew Brahma or had knowledge in Vedic philosophy and Saiva by his banners (*dhajaih Sivah Brahmavidah*)[17]. The point may interestingly be corroborated by the *Mahabharata* (c.fourth century B.C.E to c.fourth century C.E.). The text mentions that Siva as philosophical god is the highest Brahman[18]. With this philosophical knowledge about Brahma or Siva he became victorious in some religious debates or discussions. It might have developed a philosophical / religious tenet of 'self-restraint / self-sacrificing' (*tyajatah yah damah dharmah*)[19]. Although there is no direct evidence as to such philosophical debates, yet an indication may be given towards its probable holding in an institution. The indication is provided by an inscribed terracotta pot of c.second century C.E. from Gajitala (North 24 Parganas). The inscription points to the chief or best religious institution where oblation was probably to be given / offered (*jyestha mathe ejyam deyam*)[20]. Along with this the monastic institution might have been considered the venue for philosophical debates or discussions. These discussions might have followers gradually. The matter may be corroborated by a third century C.E. inscribed terracotta seal from Chandraketugarh. The obverse of the seal bears one Priti, the son of Senatimitra (*Senatimitraputrah Pritih*)[21]. The reverse of the object shows that there was an asylum of disciples (*sisyatraka*) for whom (*auddesikayai*) probably the seal was prepared. The disciples included probably some people of the region under study. And Priti in some capacity seems to have been in connection with the asylum[22]. It therefore may lead one to assume that a monastic organization had come into being in Vanga by the second century C.E. and philosophical discussions (probably Saiva) were held there. Gradually it grew with a sister organization for housing disciples (Saiva?) under the care of one Priti.

It may be assumed that the Brahmin scholars (of knowledge about Siva?) became the ordinary people's last and final trust so much so that they were accepted as a charm in real life situations. The assumption is interestingly supported by an inscribed terracotta seal of c.second century C.E.The seal carries the interesting line *bhajatha dvijesu udadhau*. It has been meant as 'you take resort unto the Brahmins (while) at sea'[23]. In other words, it may be assumed that they became worthy of worship in daily life.

In this connection two terracotta objects showing three figures representing either deities or deified personalities may be proposed. The objects with the inscription *dha(r)magras(r)ala* meaning 'in chief enclosure of religion' have been dated to the last part of the first or early second century C.E. It has been interpreted that these objects represent two open air shrines of worship in the late first or early second century C.E. Vanga[24]. In this context it may be pertinent to assume that those trustworthy Brahmin scholars had become personalities worthy of worship in Vanga by the early second century C.E.

It seems that brahmanas, gods and religious persons had support from the well-to-do section of the then society of Vanga. This is indicated by an inscribed terracotta seal (c.third century C.E.) from Chandraketugarh. The seal bears the inscription as Karaphagma ('who had crore of ploughmen working under him'). It may bring home that there were some people who could be put into agricultural works. The person who employed them was supposedly an influential (rich?) man in the society of Vanga. Now this inscription occurs in the context of another such inscription as *karrisajita-jyestha-natasya (natasya)-dvija-de(va)risitane*[25]; one of its meaning has been made thus 'for (issued praying for) the continuation (or propagation) of the Brahmins, gods and ascetics'[26]. It may therefore appear that the activities of the spiritual persons were supported by a certain section (that may be influential or rich) of the people of the region in the early Christian era.

Certain Brahmanical deities are also known from inscribed objects found in the region under study. A third century inscribed terracotta seal from Chandraketugarh bears the inscription *Surijikah* meaning "excellent Indra"[27]. Indra, the god of rain[28], seems to have been worshipped by people for agricultural prosperity. The terracotta objects (c.first-second centuries C.E.) representing Agni, the god of Fire from Chandraketugarh may allude to its worship with ritualistic sacrifices[29]. In this connection it is to be noted that *yupa*-like devices are known from inscribed terracotta objects (c.first, second and fifth centuries C.E.) from the region under review. These indicate the popularity of the cult of sacrifices. Gradually proper rules were followed up for the successful performance of sacrifices (*vidhisamena medah atra yajne dattah*)[30].

A section of the people of the region also practiced the cult of Yaksa. A c.first century C.E. inscribed terracotta rouletted dish bears the line *sasye Yaksasya Yasasya* meaning 'of Yasa, the Yaksa in grain'. Probably the dish was used for the god Yaksa who presided over the production of / possessed, grain[31]. In connection with the production of another agricultural crop people worshipped the goddess Yaksi. It is interesting to note that people worshipped the goddess Yaksi-Jirambi (*Trisnadirnaprana cudake Yaksi-Jirambi*).Probably the goddess was considered as the spirit who protected (the production of) the grain *jira* or cumin-seed[32].

From the above discussion it therefore appears that the people of Vanga had also a culture, particularly religious culture, of their own from the pre-literate days onwards. They had also their own understanding of life. They also gathered experiences in their own way in life. Their real life experiences have to be understood through their material traces they have left behind.They were hardly culturally so inferior as to be kept away[33].

### *Notes and References*

1. Chattopadhyaya B.D, *Studying Early India Archaeology,Texts and Historical Issues,* Delhi,2003, p.50
2. Borgatta Edger F and Montgomery J.V. Rohnda (eds.), *Encyclopedia of Sociology*, Vol.5, Second Edn., USA, 2000, pp.3128-29.
3. Mukherjee B.N, 'Kharosti and Kharosti-Brahmi Inscriptions in West Bengal (India)', in *Indian Museum Bulletin* (Hereinafter *IMB*), Calcutta, 1990, p.66, plt.I; cf.*The TTK Atlas of Indian States*, pp.30-31.
4. The BRW artifacts occur practically all over India from Harappan Gujarat to Megalithic south. It is said that the BRW migrated through two routes one from Gujarat to western *doab* and eastern Punjab and the other through central India, eastern Uttar Pradesh, Bihar to West Bengal. It is also said that the BRW culture spread in the train of rice cultivation. In West Bengal the BRW artefacts have been found from four major excavated sites. These are: Mahisadal (Birbhum district), Baneswardanga (Burdwan district), Mangalkot (Burdwan district), Pandu Rajar Dhivi (Burdwan district). Different objects like jars, bowls,tumblers of use have been found from the sites. Traces of house-building activities, religious activities (a terracotta phallus, Mahisadal), rice cultivation / consumption (Mangalkot) from different sites have been reported. Even it is assumed that the people of Mangalkot might have an overseas connection through the Ganges. It is said that the sites show a long period of occupation from about 1619 B.C.E onwards through our period (Chattopadhyaya B.D et.al (eds.), *An Annotated Archaeological Atlas of West Bengal, Prehistory and Proto-history*, (Hereinafter *An Archaeological Atlas)* Kolkata, 2005, pp.93-95; Ghosh A (ed.), *An Encyclopaedia of Indian Archaeology*, Vol. I, New Delhi,1989, p.94.).
5. Mukherjee B.N, *Indian Museum Bulletin*, p.24.
6. Chattopadhyaya B.D et.al (eds.), *An Archaeological Atlas*, p.94.
7. Hastings James (ed), *Encyclopaedia of Religion and Ethics*, Vol. X, New York, 1974, p. 662, coll. II.
8. Cohn Bernard S, *An Anthropologist among the Historians and Other Essays*, Delhi, 1987, p. 102.
9. Mukherjee B.N, *IMB*, pp.44-62.
10. Majumdar R.C, *History of Ancient Bengal* (Hereinafter *HAB*), Calcutta, pp.506-519.
11. Roy N. R, *Bangalir Itihas Adi Parva*, Bengali, Calcutta, 1400 B.S. (1993), pp.477-565, particularly,497-98.
12. Chatterjee Rama, *Religion in Bengal during the Pala and the Sena Times*, Calcutta, 1985, pp.35-84, particularly pp.38-39.
13. Majumdar R.C, *HAB*, p.350.
14. Bhattacharyya N.N, 'Prak-Gupta Amaler Nimna Paschimbanger Dharmavyvastha', in Kamal Kumar Kundu (ed), *Prabandha Sankalan: Prasanga Tamralipta*, Midnapur, 1993, pp.53-62.
15. Mukherjee B.N, *IMB*, p.44, Item No.4.

16. Mukherjee B.N, *IMB*, pp.50-51, Item No.20.
17. Mukherjee B.N, *IMB*, p.51, Item No.21.
18. *Mahabharata,* XIII *Parvan*, ch.22, *sloka* 144-45 quoted in Ishwar Chandra Tyagi, *Saivism in Ancient India from the Earliest Times to A.D.300,* New Delhi, 1982, p.113.
19. Mukherjee B.N, *IMB*, pp.57-58, Item No.52.
20. Mukherjee B.N, *IMB*, p.58, Item No.54.
21. Mukherjee B.N, *IMB*, p.53, Item No.29.
22. Mukherjee B.N, *IMB*, p.53, Item No.29.
23. Mukherjee B.N, *IMB*, p.57, Item No.51.
24. Mukherjee B.N, 'Two Representations of Open Air Shrines in Ancient Vanga', *Journal of Bengal Art*, Vol.5, 2000, pp.41-42.
25. Mukherjee B.N, *IMB*, p.46, Item No.9.
26. Mukherjee B.N, *IMB*, p.46, Item No.9.
27. Mukherjee B.N, *IMB*, p.47, Item No.9.
28. Datta Ramesh Chandra (tr.), *Rgveda-Samhita*, Bengali, Vol. I, Second edn, Second reprnt, Calcutta, 1993, p.147, *Mantra*1-52-15.
29. Biswas S.S, *Terracotta Art of Bengal*, Delhi, 1981, pp.159-80, plts. XIII & XIV; Mukherjee B.N, *IMB*, p.28, Section C.
30. Mukherjee B.N, *IMB*, p.28, 46, 49-50.
31. Mukherjee B.N, *IMB*, p.54, Item No.35.
32. Mukherjee B.N, *IMB*, pp.55-56, Item No.39
33. Max Muller F (ed.), *The Sacred Books of the East, The Sacred Laws of the Aryas*, Vol. XIV, Part II, First Reprnt, Delhi, 1995, p.148, I.1.2.13-15; cf. Datta Ray Rajatbaran, *Vedicism in Ancient Bengal*, Calcutta, 1974, pp.9-10.

11

# Vaishnavism and Vaishnava Literature in Coastal Karnataka

*Nagendra Rao*

Study of religions in coastal Karnataka did not receive special treatment, till recently, by the historians of the region. Like in other parts of India, religion was studied as a part of political history that included dynastic history pertaining to Alupas, Hoysalas, Vijayanagara, and the Keladi kingdom. The traditional scholars such as Ganapati Rao Aigal[1] and Sheenappa Heggade[2] analyzed historical traditions of the region. In a way, Ganapati Rao can be considered as a pioneer of the study of history of South Kanara, even though his methodology may not be considered as scientific. B.A. Saletore is one of the first historians who studied society of coastal Karnataka in a systematic manner.[3] However, he has not analyzed the growth of religions in the region. K.V. Ramesh[4] and P. Gururaja Bhatt[5] are other historians who have contributed immensely to coastal Karnataka historiography, but they did not consider religion as a distinct entity and studied them as a part of their general project. At the same time, one can obtain valuable information from these works. K.G. Vasanthamadhava, in his work – Religions in Coastal Karnataka-has studied growth of religions in this region.[6] Above analysis shows that not many works have concentrated on the study of religion, even though there are works, which have studied philosophical content of teachings of Sankara and Madhwa. The main aim of the present study to analyze the progress of Vaishnavism in coastal Karnataka as revealed in Madhwa literature. The study becomes all the more important due to lack of previous works on this topic. Madhwa Vijaya or Sumadhwa Vijaya is major primary source, which will be used in this paper, while there are inscriptions, Gramapaddhati, and secondary sources. Madhwa Vijaya shows the ideology and methodology used by Madhwacharya in expanding Vaishnavism is coastal Karnataka. Gramapaddhati, a traditional brahmanical work, deals with issues concerning brahmanas, who played an important role in the spread of Madhwa traditions in the study region.[7] Gramapaddhati refers to regions such as Rajatapithapura or Sivalli, which became centre of Vaishnavism. Inscriptions of the region show that gradually there was shift from Shaivism to Vaishnavism, particularly with the emergence of the Vijayanagara Empire, which gave large numbers of grants to Vaishnava institutions. There is a need to corroborate data from literature and inscriptions in order to arrive at a reasonable conclusion with reference to the present topic.

## Origin and Growth of Vaishnavism in Coastal Karnataka

It appears that prior to the emergence of Vaishnavism in the region, majority of people had accepted Shaivism as their religion. Even today, a section of brahmanas called Kota brahmanas have remained Shaivas, even though they maintain social interaction with Vaishnavas. The emergence of Sankara was an important event, which resulted in the rise of Shaiva religious institutions in the regions such as Sringeri in Karnataka. Balekudru matha, near Kota, maintained close relationship with the Sringeri matha. In the post $10^{th}$ century AD, there were Vaishnava saints in Karnataka who played an important role in conversion process, leading to the popularity of this religion. For example, Ramanuja who migrated from the Tamil region to Karnataka converted Hoysala king Bittideva into Vaishnavism. This was an important event, as it indicated the beginning of vaishnavization process of Karnataka. Scholars in coastal Karnataka seem to have taken a cue from emergence of Vaishnavism in other parts of Karnataka. Consequently, Madhwacharya is credited with establishment of eight mathas in Udupi, the place, which comprises both Shiva and Vishnu temples. The continuation of Shaiva tradition is proved by the existence of Ananteshwara and Chandramoulishwara temples. The mathas' priests were expected to worship Krishna daily in their respective structures. During this period, in other parts of Karnataka, Vaishnavism was emerging as a major religion, as proved by the construction of Vaishnava temples by the Vijayanagara kings including Krishnadeva Raya. The Vijayanagara inscriptions found in Udupi show that Vaishnavism was patronized by the state.

## Religion and literature

Religion in pre-modern India depended on conscious and not so conscious creation of literary texts. For example, brahmanas could strengthen their influence by authoring works such as Manu Smriti, a law code text, which prescribed that people belonging to different varnas needed to adhere to their respective functions. Puranic literature is an example of use of literature to legitimize particular religious group. Shiva Purana, Skanda Purana, Vishnu Purana belong to this category. Two kinds of literatures were composed: one at pan India level, which could act as guide for people belonging to different regions. They comprised general rules, which commanded the respect of people of different regions. Second category of texts is purely regional in nature. Their composition was necessary in order to appeal to the masses. Both at national and regional levels, there was composition of two categories of works. One category of texts dealt with pure philosophy, which revealed philosophical traditions of saints. Second category of texts dealt with religious as well as secular aspects. It is the second category of texts, which were important as they conveyed the message of a religion to the people, who were not able to read and digest complex philosophical aspects. For example, Upanishads, even though challenged a few preconceived notions that was current in Vedic religion, could not reach masses due to their complex philosophy. Puranas, on the other hand, became more effective as they narrated philosophy which could be easily understood by common people. Biographical works become important in this context. Regional level texts become all the more important due to their obvious advantages when compared with complex philosophical works. Madhwa Vijaya and Gramapaddhati are two important regional level texts that narrate the process of origin and growth of Vaishnavism in coastal Karnataka.

## Vaishnavism and Gramapaddhati

Gramapaddhati is a text, which reveals the traditional history of South Kanara, as it is a combination of myths and historical events. It is written in Kannada language and found in traditional brahmanical houses. Curiously, I was able to find this text in Vaishnava mathas of Udupi, and B.A. Saletore quotes Puttige version, implying that Vaishnava mathas took interest in composition and preservation of this text. Vaishnava religious leaders had a compulsion to know different brahmanical sects. For example, there is reference to conflict between Kota brahmanas and Koteshwara brahmanas, concerning land ownership.[8] It is possible that both Kota and Koteshwara brahmanas originally practiced Shaivism. Due to conflict, Koteshwara brahmanas had to look for an alternative religious ideology, which was offered by Vaishnavas of Udupi. Tradition claims that Koteshwara brahmanas, in distress, were protected by the Vaishnava saint Vadiraja, who was the leader of Sode matha. Today, Koteshwara brahmanas claim allegiance to Sode matha. Historical research shows that Koteshwara brahmanas originally belonged to an outside region called Shimoga and they might have migrated to the coastal region and ultimately settled in Kota.[9] The conflict between Kota and Koteshwara brahmanas provided an opportunity to Vaishnava saints to convert non-Vaishnavas into Vaishnava faith. It will be showed later that Madhwacharya was also interested in converting large numbers of people in different parts of India, proved by his religious dialogue with leaders belonging to other religions. An important theme of Gramapaddhati is the fallen brahmanical villages. Sahyadri Khanda, another brahmanical text, refers to similar development, as there are various brahmanical groups that become part of mixed castes, thereby showing Varna Sankara in western coastal India. It is possible that stories concerning fallen brahmanas were inspired by similar myths present in pan-Indian texts such as Manu Smriti, which refers to proliferation of jatis.

Similarities persist between Gramapaddhati and Sumadhwa Vijaya. Both works mention sanskrtised version of places and personalities such as Odipu, Shivalli, Mudillaya, Kudavuru, Talekude, Neyampalli, Madinaya, Totantillaya, Karyuru, Kutyadi, Maraditaya, Pashupe, Padmatirtha, Kavu, Kodipadi, Kabenadu, Mudembadi, Idetude, Kokkada, Kabesimha or Jayasimha, Nidillaya and Pejittaya. At the same time, there are differences between these two texts.[10] The function of Gramapaddhati, a brahmanical tradition was to strengthen the position of a particular brahmanical community in the region. The function of Sumadhwa Vijaya, on the other hand, was to exhibit the power of Madhwacharya. To achieve this motive, various Madhwacharya's achievements were listed. Whereas Gramapaddhati mentions 32 villages in south coastal Karnataka, Sumadhwa Vijaya refers to 63 brahmanical villages.[11] This number is mentioned in the context of argumentation between Madhwacharya and another scholar. The brahmanas of 63 villages were exposed as they exhibited their lack of knowledge.

## Vaishnavism, Literature, and Sumadhwa Vijaya

As mentioned earlier, Madhwacharya played an important role in popularizing Vaishnavism. The Udupi version of Vaishnavism is also called Madhwaism. This is due to the leadership provided by Madhwacharya to the people of the region. Sumadhwa Vijaya is biography of Madhwacharya. The work also reveals the saint's ideas, ideology, struggles, and philosophy. The main function of the work is to exhibit the power of Madhwacharya, who is expected to possess divine might, due to direct relationship with Anjaneya and Vayu. The work comprises various incidents, the miracles performed by Madhwacharya.

Madhwacharya and his successors indulged in the process of knowledge production, though various writings. The saint himself was a great writer as he is credited with the composition of more than thirty works, which presented the views of Madhwa school of thought. In these works, one can find a critique of Advaita philosophy and exposition of new philosophy of Madhwa saints. The time was ripe to write a critique of Sankara's works. The scholars in eight mathas of Udupi are expected to study various works such as Brahma Sutra, Bhagavadgita, and Bhagavata written by Vedavyasa ; Brahma Sutra Bhashya, Anu Bhashya, Anu Vyakarana, Upanishad Bhashyas, Gita Bhashya, and Bhagavat Tatparya Nirnaya composed by Madhwacharya ; and various works written by Jayatirtha, Vyasatirtha and Raghavendra Tirtha.[12] The collection of works available in libraries of eight mathas of Udupi shows that importance of given to the creation of a body of knowledge, which could be used to justify Madhwa philosophy. Recitation and interpretation of such works were necessary to popularize the religion. An important function of religious texts seems to give divine status to saints such as Madhwacharya.[13] This is because based on the religious literature today Madhwa disciples claim that Madhwacharya was the divine part of God Vayu, proved by excellent energy that was present in this saint. Miracles become important to show the prowess of Madhwacharya.

Sumadhwa Vijaya comprises incidents that relate to intellectual and physical prowess of the saint. The work, written by Narayana Panditacharya, the disciple of the saint, refers to his intellectual campaign. In the process, the saint has to exhibit his superior knowledge. Ultimately, he was able to emerge victorious in the debates.

Sumadhwa Vijaya narrates establishment and consolidation of brahmana settlements of south coastal Karnataka, which ultimately became the basis for popularization of Madhwa traditions in the regions like Udupi. Madhwa tradition is linked with the places like Sivalli, Kokkada, Ramakunja, Padi, Kudalu, Ujire, and Kodipadi, the regions located in south coastal Karnataka and north Kerala. During the Madhwa and post Madhwa period, the regions such as Sivalli, Kota, Brahmavara, Niravara, and Kandavara emerged as major brahmana settlements of the region. It was important for Madhwa saints to attract attention of brahmanas who had settled in these regions. Interestingly, one finds large numbers of Vijayanagara inscriptions in this region. Even though Madhwacharya did not maintain direct link with Vijayanagara, there are evidences to suggest that his disciples were able to emerge as influential religious group in Vijayanagara court.[14] It is true that Vijayanagara did not differentiate between various religions in the empire. Despite this, one can suggest that Madhwa saints were able to emerge as a dominant religious group, affecting the popularity of other sects. This achievement was made possible through the composition of several works of prominence by Madhwacharya and his successors. Obviously, they understood the importance of knowledge as *shastra* could be used to win over even hostile groups.

The superior knowledge of Madhwacharya is revealed by the fact that he was able to give hundred meanings of Vishna Sahasra Nama that praised the glory of Lord Vishnu. In this way, the book attempts to differentiate between this saint and other scholars of the period. Sumadhwa Vijaya comprises chapters that include greatness of Hanumanta, Bhima, and logic of Madhwa incarnation, his early life and childhood, education, and asceticism. It is mentioned that Madhwacharya visited regions such as Badari in North India where the saint was able to obtain information concerning God. He also went to Goa and exhibited his religious and spiritual authority. It is mentioned that in Goa a brahmana called Sankara offered him 4000 bananas, which were easily consumed by the saint. When he was not allowed to leave the place, Madhwacharya was able to disappear by using mystical power. He performed various other miracles in Goa.[15] Today Vaishnavism has emerged as a major religious sect among Hindus of Goa.[16] The last section of the book consists of various miracles performed by this saint. He seems to have considered the region between Goa and Kerala as his main area of operation. Consequently, this region today comprises people who respect Madhwa sect.

In the context of coastal Karnataka, it becomes important to study relationship between religion and literature as this topic is ignored in the existing literature. Literature can influence growth of a religion. This is found at pan Indian level and this thesis can be extended to the regional level also. Gramapaddhati, a traditional literature of coastal Karnataka exhibits features of a literary work that represented interest of brahmanical groups of the region. One can note similarities and differences between Gramapaddhati and Sumadhwa Vijaya. They are the brahmanical works, but the function of Sumadhwa Vijaya is to glorify the achievements of Madhwacharya. Composition of this work enhanced the prestige of this saint. This is proved by the fact that Udupi has emerged as the center of Madhwa religion and literature.

### Notes and References

1. Ganapati Rao Aigal, *Dakshina Kannada Jilleya Prachina Itihasa,* Mangalore, 1923.
2. Balakrishna Shetty (ed), *Sheenappa Heggade Samagra Sahitya,* Udupi, 1991.
3. Saletore, B.A., *Ancient Karnataka History of Tuluva*, Poona, 1936.

4. Ramesh,K.V., *A History of South Kanara from earliest times to the fall of Vijayanagara*, Dharwar, 1970.
5. Bhatt, P. Gururaja, *Studies in Tuluva History and Culture*, Kallianpur, 1975.
6. Vasanthamadhava, K.G., *Religions in Coastal Karnataka*, New Delhi, 1985.
7. Saletore, B.A., *Ancient Karnataka*; Nagendra Rao, *Brahmanas of South India*, New Delhi, 2005.
8. Nagendra Rao, *Brahmanas*, p. 59.
9. Bhatt, P. Gururaja, *Studies in Tuluva*, p. 288.
10. Vyasanakere Prabhanjanacharya (ed), *Sumadhwa Vijayaha* (in Kannada), Aitareya Prakashana, 2000, pp. 576-577.
11. Vyasanakere Prabhanjanacharya(ed), *Sumadhwa*, p. 173.
12. Vasudeva Rao, *Living Traditions in Contemporary Contexts: the Madhwa Mathas of Udupi*. Orient Blackswan, 2002, p. 86.
13. Vadudeva Rao, *Living Traditions*, p. 100.
14. Nagendra Rao, *Brahmanas*, p. 95.
15. Vyasanakere Prabhanjanacharya(ed), *Sumadhwa*, pp. 317-318.
16. Chavan,V.P., *Vaishnavism of the Gowd Saraswat Brahmins and a few Konkani Folk Tales*. New Delhi, 1991.

12

# Devadasis in Early Medieval Tamil Society:
## A Socio-Religious Study

*K. Mavali Rajan*

The temple is the focus for all aspects of everyday life in the Hindu community- religious, cultural, educational and social. The temple is also the place where one can transcend the world of man. The temples in the medieval Tamil society were maintained through donations from royal patrons and private individuals. They were given money, gold, silver, livestock, and income from grants of lands including whole villages. Such gifts would provide religious merit (*punya*) which would increase the possibility of ultimate liberation for the donor. Some temple became wealthy often invested in land and hired tenants to provide income. The important temples hired priests garland makers, suppliers of ghee, milk, oil, rice, fruits, sandal-paste and incense. A famous detailed account made in 1011 of the people supported by the Rajarajeswaram temple at Tanjore listed dancing girls, dancing masters, singers, drummers, conch-blowers, accountants, parasol bearers, lamp-lighters, sprinklers of water, potters, carpenters, astrologers, tailors, and jewel-stitchers. There were 600 people in total. In return for their temple work, they were given land which they cultivate and could live off. By providing livelihoods for such large numbers of people, the temple not surprisingly could exert influence on the economic life of the community.

Among the important temple servants the dancing girls were very popular and their services respected by the whole society. A large number of dancing girls engaged in singing and dancing before the deities mornings and evenings. They were expected to perform the services also on special occasion such as festivals, at the time of offering poojas, or at the time of the king's visit to the temple[1]. These dancing girls were popularly called as *devadasi* and who were dedicated their life to the service of the temple deity and there was no escape for them. Even if they wanted to escape, the society would not accept them.

They are known by different names in different areas. In Andhra these Devadasis are called *Jōginis*, in Maharashtra they called as *Muralis*. Jogan Shankar gives names by which they are known in various parts of India such as *dēvaradiyāl* in Tamil Nadu, *Maharis* in Kerala, *Nātis* in Assam, *Basavis* in Karnataka, and in Goa they are called *Bhavanis* and *Kudikar*[2]. They were also known by different names in Tamil Nadu as *Dēvakannis*[3], *Padiyilār*[4], *Talichchērippendugal*[5], *Kōilpendugal*[6], *Tiruppadiyar*[7] and *Rudrakannikas*. Two Chola inscriptions[8] of medieval period mentioned them as *dēvanar magal* (the daughter of *dēvanar)*. The term *dēvanar* stands for *dēva* or Siva. The *dēvanar magal* considered themselves to be the daughter of the deity and dedicated their life to *dēva*. It would be interesting to note that in the inscription of Parantaka I (the Chola ruler ruled Tamil country from 907-955 A.D.) these women were called *dēvaradiyal,* but later monarchs call them both *dēvaradiyal* and *padiyilar.* But it is only Rajaraja I (985-1014 A.D.) who refers to these temple women as *talichcherippendugal.*[9] Their names suggest that most of them were drawn from Siva temples.

The Devadasis literally means gods (*dēv*) female servant (*dāsi*) where according to the ancient Indian practice, young pre-pubertal girls were 'married off', 'given away' in matrimony to god or local religious deity of the temple. This matrimonial ceremony is called '*pottu-kattuthal*' or *tāli*-tying dedication ceremony, was a widely advertised community event requiring the full co-operation of the local religious authorities. During the marriage *tāli* was tied round their neck by the temple priest and flower patterns in Sandal wood paste were imprinted on his shoulders[10]. It initiates the young girl into the Dēvadasi profession. In the Brahmanical tradition marriages is viewed as the only religious initiation (*diksha*) permissible to women. Thus the dedication is a symbolic marriage of the pubescent girl to the temple's deity. After dedication of a girl to the temple, she had to take bath everyday early in the morning and should present herself at the temple during morning worship. In addition to taking care of the temple and performing rituals, they learned and practiced *Bharatanātyam* and other classical Indian arts traditions and enjoyed high social status. She is not allowed to enter the *sanctum sanctorum*. But she would bow to the deity from outside.

The Devadasis, the female slave of god were found in the Hindu temple. These women surrendered themselves in the service of god in the temples, dancing, singing and playing music, where the idol was kept. The Devadasi system was a recognised institution of the Hindu society. In this institution of dancing girls, they were connected to the spiritual world and sensual world. As they were in the service of the temples and dedicated their lives to the service of god they obtained training from the 5$^{th}$ year till the age of fourteen. In case if they are married they loose their profession of serving in temples. The girls took an examination in the temple compound, if successful were appointed as *sānis* or Devadasis[11].

There are many opinions about the origin and growth of Devadasi system. For a comprehensive understanding of the dominant schools of thoughts, many factors have to be taken into consideration while trying to trace its origin and development. Factors like religious beliefs, caste system, male domination and economic stress have been recognized as the stimulants behind the perpetuation of this phenomenon. Another school of thought discuss that the origin of this socio-religious institution was assigned to the age of the popularisation of the Tantric cult on the 8th century A.D. to the age of the emergence of the structural temples. M.Srinivasa Iyengar, K.K.Pillay and H.D.Sankalia are of the view that the emergence of structural temples was the age of origin of the Devadasi system in India[12]. M.Srinivasa Iyengar says that the aesthetic arts were given a religious tone from about the 7th century A.D. when dancing and playing dramas were encouraged to draw large crowds of devotees to the temples. Thus hundred of dancing girls were attached to every important temple[13]. According to K.K.Pillay the system became common in South Indian temples only after the 7th century A.D. when we hear of women dancers called *Adigalmār*, otherwise known as *Manikkāttar* and *Kanikaiyar* in the inscription of 8th century A.D.[14] But he thinks that these women attendants and dancers must have arisen probably with emergence of structural temple[15].

In North India the custom of the association of dancing girls with temples is unknown to *Jataka* literature. It is not mentioned by the Greek writers; the *Arthasastra* which describes in details the life and duties of dancing girls, is silent about it[16]. The custom, however, had come into vogue by about the 3rd century A.D. for Kalidasa refers to dancing girls present in Mahakala temple of Uijjayini at the time of evening worship (*Meghaduta*, I, 35). Several *Puranas* also recommend for that arrangements should be made to enlist the services of singing girls to provide vocal and instrumental music at the time of divine services[17]. A.L.Basham views that the earliest record of Devadasis is found in the Ramgarh cave inscription of Vindhya hills, some 160 miles to the south of Varanasi[18]. Further he articulates that in later years the institution did not find much favour in the north but continued to flourish in the south[19].

This custom probably became quite common in the 6th century A.D, when most of the *Puranas*, containing a reference to it, seem to have been composed. In the 7th century A.D. Hiuen-Tsang saw numerous singing girls in the temple of the sun at Multan. The *Rajatarangini* (IV 31) attests to the existence of this custom in Kashmir from about the 7th century A.D. The famous temple of Somanath is said to have employed 500 dancing girls in order to provide music before the deity continuously throughout day and night[20].

The Devadasi system was prevalent in the medieval Tamil Nadu particularly in the Chola times. The Devadasi formed a separate caste, having its own laws of inheritance, customs and rules of etiquette and its own panchayats[21]. They mostly belonged to the *Kaikkōla* (weaver) caste of South India[22]. The temple had a hundred or more women of good family; some unmarried women became Devadasis on their own free will, and some time they were forced to play and sing before the idols for certain hours every day[23].

Sometimes they were presented to the temple by rich men on certain occasions and they were transferred from one place to another by a royal decree[24]. An inscription dated 1479 A.D. mentions that Ettappa Nayak, who gave 29 Devadasis to the temple of Periya Nachiyar at Devikapuram in memory of King Esuranganayaka[25].

The lands were allotted to them and the king also granted hereditary *inams* to them. Their children were considered legitimate and had social status. The daughters of the Devadasis usually were offered to the temple to carry on their traditional profession, while their sons became court and temple musicians[26].

The Devadasis sold themselves to the temple as a slave of god[27]. A record from Tiruppullani, refers to some shepherds, who became slaves to the temple by branding upon their person the insignia of the temple[28]. A record of the reign of Rajaraja I from Tiruvadandai, dated in the seventeenth regnal year 1002 A.D. states that twelve families of fishermen (*Pattinavar*) were dedicated to the temple of Srivaraha Deva[29]. Marco Polo observes that parents themselves gave away their daughters to the temple as slaves[30]. Sometimes they were also purchased [31]. Families dedicated their daughters to the temple service or they were gifted[32]. Epigraphical references also support the fact that temples had a large number of slaves attached to them. An inscription of 1235 A.D. gives a list of slaves both male and female, numbering more than 100 persons owned by the temple of Virattaneswara having been made over to it by an order of the king, by purchase from several people and by gifts from private individuals in the 9th and 10th years of the reign of Kulottunga III[33]. Another Chola inscription (1187-1188 A.D.) mentions that gift of five women and their descendants for husking paddy in the temple[34]. A Vijayanagar inscription refers that a number of maid servants (*deva adimai*) were provided for temple[35].

Devadasis were employed in temples to performed different services. They were to dance and sing in front of the idols during worship, procession and festivals[36]. According to an inscription[37], they performed different kinds of dances such as *sokkam* (pure dance), *sandikkunippam* (dance during worship), *agamaragam* (dance performed to the pleasure of mind) and *varikkolam* (one of the fourteen limps). A record[38] from Nellaipper temple, Tirunelveli, says that a Devadasi, brought flower for daily morning *pujas*. An inscription[39] of Kulasekhara Pandya records the great services of Devadasis. In festival days, they enacted even dramas[40]. In some other temples, they were directed to look after the temple garden and its servants[41]. They were also engaged in smearing the temple premises with cow-dung paste and sweeping it[42]. On certain occasions, the Devadasis were called for rendering personal services to the king[43]. The interest evinced by the priestly class in maintaining the Devadasi is revealed by a record of Kulasekhara Pandya[44].

They also performed various kinds of works in the temples. Looking after the lamps, conduct the festivals, husking paddy and washing clothes were some kinds of works allotted to them[45]. The nature of service done by the Devadasis in the Hindu temples is described by Marco-Polo as;

"They have certain abbeys in which are gods and goddesses to whom many young girls are consecrated; their fathers and mothers presenting them to that idol for which they entertain the greatest devotion. And when the (monks) of a convent desire to make a feast to their god, they send for all those consecrated damsels and make them sing and dance before the idol with great festivity. They also bring meats to feed their idol withal;

that is to say, the damsels prepare dishes to meat and other good things and put the food before the idol, and leave it there a good while, and then the damsels all go to their dancing and singing and festivity for about as long as a great. Baron might require to eat his dinner. By that time they say the spirit of the idols has consumed the substance of the food, so they remove the viands to be eaten by themselves with great jollity. This is performed by these damsels several times a year until they are married"[46].

Temple slaves were often branded with a *sūla* (trident) or some symbol to mark them off [47] from other slaves e.g., of the king who had some other distinguishing mark e.g. *illaiccinai*[48]. A Chola inscription states that Kulottuna I ordered in 1088 A.D. that some *Dēvaradiyāl* of the temple of Kalahasti who had been wrongly appropriated to the Palace service should be restored to the temple; these persons had been stamped with the kings seal which was erased and the trident stamped on their bodies in token of their servitude to the temple[49]. At Tiruvallam, in 1119 A.D., one of the *villikal* (bowmen) of Banapuram, dedicated some women of his family as *Devaradiyal* after stamping them with trident[50]. In the reign of Rajadhiraja II sale of four women to the temple of Tiruvalangadu for a sum of seven hundred *kasu* in 1175 A.D. was recorded[51]. The Devadasis lived in the quarters around the temple streets[52]. Inscriptions refer these quarters as *tirumadaivilāgam*[53]. As the servants of god and as concubines of kings, priests and chiefs, they enjoyed a high social status. In appreciation of the service, rendered by a *Dēvaradiyāl*, she was conferred the hereditary honour of sounding the conch and the drum at the time of her entry into the temple[54]. It is an instance to point out their privileged position.

Temple slaves got paddy field for dancing in the temple. An inscription records that, 400 dancing girls, who had been transferred to the establishment of the Rajaraseswara temple from that of other temples of the Chola country. Each person received one or more share, each of which consisted of the produce of one *vēli* of land, which was calculated at 100 *kalam* of Paddy[55]. Kings and wealthy men gave gifts of lands in favour of dancing women[56]. Ragunatha Nayak of Tanjore also gave a gift of certain lands to the dancing girls of Thiruvanjiyur[57]. Nedungunam inscription of 1614 A.D. says that Sonadri Ayyan gave gift of 3 *kāni* of land to a Devadasi and conferred the title of Vijayaraghava Manickam on her during the festival in the Periyannan – Mandapa of the temple[58]. It clearly shows that the Devadasi were honoured by donations of lands and awards of titles. Another inscription states that the land was granted to the *pujaris* and dancing women attached to the temple[59].

The economic position of the temple servants (Devadasis) must be considered as one of utter dependence. They were not free, the work to be done by them in the temple was allotted to them and they were expected to do it well. They were no doubt maintained; sometimes even when they were dedicated to the temple, land also provided for their maintenance[60], and in a few instance houses were also provided to them[61]. Such a provision was made in general, when persons from well to do families dedicated themselves to the service of the god. In other instances, the temple supported the slaves. In return, however, they were expected to perform the different kinds of work allotted to them[62].

The Devadasis enjoyed high social status in the society and they were also very rich. Apart from the donations of lands, wealth, etc, by the rich people to the temple they also gave the endowments to the temple. They granted gift of money for offerings to the image of Tirunavukkaraudeva located in the temple of Kailasamudaiyan by a dancing girl[63]. Another inscription states that a dancing girl gave some money as an endowment for the provision of food offerings in the temple[64]. Gold jewels were also given by some as gift to the Siddharatheswara temple at Uttattur[65]. Sometimes lands too, were donated to the temple[66]. In addition to donation of land, sheep also were gifted to the temple for the maintenance of *nandavilakku* (perpetual lamps) in the temple[67]. A record[68] of the time of Maravarman Sundara Pandya registers that a *padiyilar* donated some sheep for the purpose of burning four twilight lamps before the deity. They did constructions works too. A record of the time of Jatavarman Kulasekara Pandya from Thirumalai registers the construction of the *prakara* of a temple by a *dēvaradiyal*[69]. The *kundam* and *pattigai* (parts of temple architecture) of a temple at Pullur in Periyakulam were the constructions of Marakatapperumal, a *Dēvaradiyāl*[70]. Fees were also paid to them for their maintenance in the temple. A record of the Saluva king Dharmaraya, son of Saluva Narasingaraya, records that a certain Ammana Nayak gave to the temple of Karivaradaperumal at Aragalur the fee called, *adimai kāsu* collected from the *Kaikkōlās* and a female servant (*adiyāl*) providing for her maintenance[71].

The Devadasis were generally skilled in music, singing and dance. Their accomplishments were well developed. They had an outstanding proficiency in dance and they were expected to dance on ceremonial occasions at palaces and also at temples[72]. These Devadasis acquired proper education and gained good knowledge in music, dance and singing and other fine arts. N.Venkataramanayya states that education which was imparted to them was such, developed in them sex-instinct at a very early age. Love stories were painted on the walls of the rooms, where they played and moved about. The Kamasastra principles were also explained to them[73].

Apart from Devadasis, the temple also engaged other types of servants in cleaning and temple decoration, drawing water, washing the clothes of gods and goddesses[74] looking after the burning of perpetual lamp[75] and husking the paddy[76]. They were also *matha adimaigal* who cultivated lands, which belonged to the *mathas*. Both male and female slaves tended cattle, did carpentry, maintained the flower gardens and cultivated lands attached to the temples[77]. An inscription states that a stone-mason named Mulaittan alais Chandesurap, his wife and their four sons were the servants of the *matha*, which had bought them[78]. They were enjoying the patronage of the state as well as the temple. Epigraphic evidences indicate that these *mathas* also practiced slavery (*matha adimai*). An inscription of Kulottunga III found at the Vetaranyeswara temple at Tiruvalangadu also records the sale of men and women as *matha adimaigal* for the cultivation of lands owned by the *matha*. Thus it becomes evident that slavery was not confined only to the temple but it was extended to the *mathas* also[79].

During the medieval period, the women servants of the temple seem to have enjoyed a considerable social status and position. They were allowed to meet the wife of the kings and were even allowed to stay with them[80]. They led a life of ease and pleasure and provided amusement and intellectual companionship to those who could afford the luxury[81].

After the break up of the Vijayanagar Empire they lost their social position and influence due to lack of patronage and support without which they became victims of pleasure and self in the succeeding centuries. Though they lost their social position and importance, they continued their profession due to necessity, economic and religious. In the 19th century, A.D. in Tanjore, Pudukkottai and other places, they continued to enjoy royal patronage. In other places, they were supported and eagerly sought after by Muslim and other native officers.

### Notes and References


1. Mahalingam, T.V., 1975, *Administration and Social life under Vijayanagar,* Part-II, University of Madras, Madras, p.227.
2. Jogan Shankar, *Devadasi Cult – A Sociological Analysis*, Second Revised Edition, Ashish Publishing House, New Delhi, 1994.
3. *Inscription of Pudukkottai State (I.P.S.),* Part-I, No.136, p.114.
4. *Annual Report on Epigraphy (A.R.E.),* No.208 of 1912; *South Indian Inscriptions* (S.I.I.), Vol. VIII, No.170.
5. Manickam, S., 1993, *Slavery in the Tamil Country – A Historical Overview,* The Christian Literature Society, Madras, p.44.
6. *S.I.I.*, Vol. IV, No.254.
7. *S.I.I.*, Vol.VII, No.769.
8. *S.I.I.*, Vol. XIII, No.88 ; A.R.E., No.122 of 1931 ; cf. S. Swaminathan, *The Early Cholas History, Art and Culture*, Sharada Publishing House, Delhi, 1998, p.126.
9. *S.I.I.*, Vol. II, No. 66.
10. Lakshmanan Chettiar, S.M.L., 1973, *Folklore of Tamilnadu*, National Book Trust, NewDelhi, p.173.
11. Jayaseela Stephen, S. (ed.), 2006, *Literature, Caste and Society: The Masks and Veils,* Kalpaz Publications, Delhi, p.32.
12. Sadasivan, K., 1982, "Origin of the Devadasi System", *Proceedings of the South Indian History Congress*, Third Annual Conference, p.139.
13. Srinivasa Iyengar, M., 1982, *Tamil Studies – Essays on the History of the Tamil People, Language, Religion and Literature*, New Delhi, pp.189-190.
14. Pillay, K.K., 1982, *A Social History of the Tamils*, Vol.I, Second Edition, University of Madras, Madras, p.378.
15. Pillay, K.K., 1979, *Studies in Indian History (with Special Reference to Tamilnadu)* Madras, pp.321-322.
16. Altekar, A.S., 2005, *The Position of Women in Hindu Civilization*, Reprint, Motilal Banarsidass Publishers Pvt. Ltd., Delhi, p.182.
17. Ibid.
18. Basham, A.L., *The Wonder that was India*, Third Revised Edition, London, 2004, pp.185-187.
19. Ibid.
20. Altekar,A.S., *op.cit.*, p.183.
21. Subramanian,P., *Social History of Tamils (1707-1947),* New Delhi., 1996, p.45.

22. Simon Casie Chetty, *Caste, Customs, Manners and Literature of the Tamils,* New Delhi, 1992, p.46.
23. Appadurai,A., *Economic Conditions of South India(1000-1500 A.D.)*,Vol.I, Reprint, University of Madras, Madras,1990, p.319.
24. Manickam,S., *op.cit.,* p.45.
25. *S.I.I.,* Vol.VII, No.470, pp.290-292.
26. Jagdish Sharan Sharma, *Encyclopaedia Indica*, Vol.I, Second Revised Edition, New Delhi, 1981, pp.307-308; cf. S.M.L. Lakshmanan Chettiar, *op.cit.,* p.173.
27. *A.R.E.,* No.86 of 1911.
28. *S.I.I.,* Vol.VIII, No.396.
29. *A.R.E.,* No.274 of 1910.
30. Sastri,K.A.Nilakanta, *Foreign Notices of South India from Megasthenes to Mahuan*, University of Madras, Madars, 2001 p.117.
31. *A.R.E.*, No.499 of 1904.
32. *A.R.E.*, No.289 of 1910.
33. *A.R.E.*, No. 223 of 1917.
34. *Annual Report on South Indian Epigraphy (A.R.S.I.E.),* No.122 of 1912.
35. *A.R.E.,* No.401 of 1912.
36. *S.I.I.,* Vol.VIII., No.333.
37. *A.R.E.,* No.212 of 1912.
38. *S.I.I.,* Vol. XIV.No.132.
39. *I.P.S.,* Part II, No.561.
40. *A.R.E.,* No.577 of 1916-17.
41. *A.R.E.,* No.253 of 1927-28.
42. *A.R.E.,* No.212 of 1912.
43. Charya,V.P.Krishna, *The Place of Devadasis in Society*, Madras 1934, p.10.
44. Nagaswamy, R. and Ramasamy, N.S., *Ramanathapuram*, Madras, 1979, p.122.
45. *A.R.E.,* No.248 of 1906, 274 of 1910, 122 of 1912 and 578 of 1916.
46. Sastri,K.A.Nilakanta, *op.cit.,* p.171; cf. A.Appadurai, *op.cit.,* p.320.
47. *A.R.E.,* No.230 of 1921.
48. *A.R.E.,* No.141 of 1922.
49. *A.R.E.,* N.141 of 1922.
50. *A.R.E.,* No.230 of 1921.
51. *A.R.E.,* No.80 of 1913.
52. Rina Singha and Reginald Massey, *Indian Dances their History and Growth*, London, 1967, p.55.
53. *S.I.I.,* Vol.XXIII, No.121.
54. *A.R.E.,* No.124, Part.II, Para 26.
55. *S.I.I.,* Vol.II, No.66, p.259.
56. *A.R.E.,* No.195 of 1910.
57. *A.R.E.,* No.79 of 1911.
58. *A.R.E.,* No.401 of 1912.

59. *A.R.E.*, No.445 of 1913.
60. *A.R.E.*, Nos. 59 of 1923, 95 of 1926.
61. *A.R.E.*, No.289 of 1910.
62. Iyengar, M.Srinivasa, *op.cit.*, p.190.
63. *A.R.E.*, No.117 of 1908.
64. *I.P.S.*, Part II, No.152, p.126.
65. *A.R.E.*, No.522 of 1912.
66. *A.R.E.*, Nos.347 of 1911, 352 of 1961-62.
67. *S.I.I.*, Vol.XIV, No.222.
68. *A.R.E.*, No.240 of 1932-33.
69. *A.R.E.*, No.33 of 1924.
70. *S.I.I.*, Vol.XXIII, No.423.
71. *A.R.E.*, No.445 of 1913.
72. Devaraj, G. "Devaradiyar", *Proceedings of the Indian History Congress,* 66th Session, Visva-Bharati, Santiniketan, 2005, p.400.
73. Venkataramanyya, N., *Studies in the History of the Third Dynasty of Vijayanagar,* Gian Publishing House, Delhi, 1986, p.402.
74. A.R.E., No.570 of 1916.
75. *A.R.E.*, No.248 of 1906.
76. *A.R.E.*, No.122 of 1912.
77. Manickam, S., *op.cit.*, p.46.
78. *A.R.S.I.E.*, No.409 of 1925.
79. Manickam, S., *op.cit.*, p.47.
80. Subramanian, P., *op.cit.*, p.67.
81. *Ibid.*

13

# Imaging Feminine Religiosity Through Rajasthani Folk Literature

*Preeti Sharma*

> Women's sense of religious self seems more continuous with their sense of social and biological self; women's images are most profoundly deepenings, not inversions of what "woman" is; women's symbols express less contradiction and opposition than synthesis and paradox.
>
> (Bynum 1987: 289)

The paucity of interest towards women and their lives has been archaic and constituted an ontological sub-structure of all civilizations. However, since the twentieth century on, there has been a massive surge in imparting significance to gender studies/women related discourses. Although constrained by the lacuna of an inability to contextualise women's history in terms of larger processes and structures, yet the endeavour has proved to be a success in so far as according greater academic space to women, especially of the marginalized categories. As highlighted by Kumkum Roy (2009: 213-14) the histories of women can be located under two broad frameworks: (i) a grand dominant narrative with a majestic sweep from the Vedic to contemporary times. Assumptions under this narrative are based on an understanding of progress and regress in terms of marriage age, education, access to resources, and presence/absence of social evils. They present the women's history as following a neat, linear trajectory of steady decline. (ii) This framework addresses a range of issues like gendering of productive/reproductive processes; politics; religions; sexuality, etc., hitherto prevailing under normative Brahmanical traditions.

The new approach has manifested itself in folkloric studies too. The consequent growing body of folkloristic literature on women may be classified into three broad areas of concern: the images of women that are projected in verbal folklore; women's oral genres and performance and female use of folklore, which may be different from male use; and female folk performers and artists. Although there has been little folklorist work directly addressing feminist theoretical issues, all three of these areas may be connected with general feminist concerns, gaining grounds in the wake of greater realisations of patriarchic constructions of the society.

## Universality of Patriarchic Socialisations

Almost all the religions of the world practice misogyny in one way or the other and most of world's traditions and cultures are distinctly patriarchal in character. (Okin 1999: 14-17) So, the spirit of disdain against womenfolk and assertion of feminine subservience underlies almost all major religious faiths of the world, at all times. Religious strictures have proved to be discriminatory with respect to women. Beliefs of the spiritual inferiority of women remained commonplace in all early theologies. Ancient Indian lawgiver Manu had recommended a woman to be controlled by her father in childhood; her husband in youth; and her sons after the husband's death. Even Buddha, the founder of so-called egalitarian Buddhism, could not rise above and forego the gender bias in closing doors of the *samgha*, the Buddhist congregation, for women followers. When the first woman joined the sect he prophesied to Ananda that the *samgha* would now perish within thousand years.

The orthodox Jewish prayer, to be recited by a male daily, echoes the sentiment: 'I thank Thee, O Lord, that thou hast not created me a woman!' The New Testament instructs the women thus: 'Wives, submit yourselves unto your own husbands, as unto the Lord. For the husband is the head of the wife, even as Christ is the head of the church... Therefore as the church is subject unto Christ, so let the wives be to their own husbands in everything' (Ephesians 5: 22-24). The Quran admonishes: 'Men are in charge of women, because Allah hath made the one of them to excel the other...' (Sura 4, ayah 34). Under Hinduism while observance of *vratas*, and household/domestic worship is exclusively a womanly affair, *puja* as a 'temple worship of a single religion' is assigned to men. These injunctions vividly illustrate that major religious doctrines invariably sanctified the unequal status of women in society and rather succumbed to the patriarchic norms. Hence the paraphrase of Virginia Woolf's statement - 'religion, it would seem, is not sexless; it is a man', - (cited by Gelpy) seems to be quite appropriate. The original assertion reads: 'Science it would seem is not sexless; she is a man, a father and infected too' (Signs 1983).

As already indicated religion has its own rewards and ways of empowerment. However, when prejudices against girls and women are 'within the very fibre of the religious establishment,' it is genuinely difficult to imagine how women could be empowered through participation in religious activities. In Engels' opinion the holy scriptures pertinently reflect 'the world historical defeat of the fair sex' (1948: 60) which led to the overthrow of maternity rights and the dismissal of women from social production, predetermined in its turn by crucial socio-economic transformations. It is an established fact that 'the most important clue to woman's status anywhere is her degree of participation in economic life and her control over property and that which she produces, with both factors related to the kinship system of a society' (Levitt 1971: 396). Over many centuries the patriarchal character of social relations went virtually unquestioned universally. The religious rules and institutions acted as the inexorable guardians and guarantors of the patriarchal world organization.

It was in the sixteenth century with the Reformation that radical changes were brought forth in Christianity and the 'feminist Renaissance' given a fresh impetus. A brief moment of freedom was enjoyed by women in the years between Luther and Calvin. However, by the end of the century this brief interlude of liberation also came to a close. The advent of Puritanism in the Protestant world led to the re-consolidation of the unequal status of women. Moreover, the 'witch-hunt' initiated by the Protestant church resulted in the deaths of thousands of women (Davis 1971: 287). The Calvinist doctrine concerning divine predestination left no hope for any changes in the status of Eve's progeny, cursed for the sin of the mother of the human race (Stepaniants 1992: 238).

Twentieth century witnessed the movement to counter discrimination against women assuming an irreversible character. In India, number of unfair religious precepts were revoked and had to be curtailed by legislative bans. Articles 14 and 15 on Fundamental Rights granted under the Constitution of the Indian Republic 1950, proclaimed the equality of citizens irrespective of their sex. Nonetheless, most of these overt legislative acts failed to ensure actual equality between the sexes. There are numerous appalling evidences of discrimination against women, among them the still prevailing practices of sati; enforced widowhood; instances of 'witchcraft'; restrictions on women reading and interpreting scriptures on their own; the mounting dowry for bridegrooms, and so on. It is noteworthy that majority of the customs involving the disparagement of women are grounded in religious dogmas.

In most religious cultures, women remain under greater pressure than men to observe customs and practise rituals and suffer greater punishment, if they do not observe them. Even when men turn religious zealots, they exhibit their zealotry by forcing women to follow religious strictures in the strictest imaginable way, i.e. observing fasts, wearing veil, etc. To make the matters worse, under male-domination the apparent feminine religiosity faces denial and obscurity, despite females' indispensable involvement with all routine/specific rituals and spiritual pursuits. While women's experiences in theological and liturgical language remain largely excluded or unrecorded, they face segregation even in the delineation of the divine principle.

## Sexism in Divinity

In the West sexism pervades even in the demarcation of divinity. Despite the earliest beliefs in the cult of Mother Goddess, the divine force/energy has been perceived as a powerful male, a father with absolute power. Such a theology with overtly patriarchal God has established a patriarchic hierarchy in a patriarchal church. Under such a church, women have lost their position of equality with men and remain devalued and marginalized.

Contrarily in the East although both male and female representations of divinity are ubiquitous unlike the androcentric images of God, however, the nature of divinity wherein male and female deities are accorded distinct attributes bespeaks the gender bias. That male deities may be closely equated with rulers is easily established. They are frequently designated by honorific titles, such as *annadata*, *thakurji*, *maharaj* - all terms used to address kings, lords and overlords. Deities are enshrined with thrones - *gaddi* - and offered umbrellas - *chatari* – the two prime symbols of kingship. The royal model is not the only one within which to interpret the phenomenon of divine conservation. The female *devis*, rarely addressed as queens, are more frequently called Mothers - *Mataji*. Their protection and the shelter they offer - as well as the authority their 'proofs' demonstrate - reflect kinship rather than political patterns. Instead of the hierarchical, dualistic and patriarchal notion of God they are endowed with a non-intrusive, inclusive and sustaining aspect and offer a model that is ecological, feminine and organic.

## Femininity and Religiosity - the Correlation

Femininity, also called womanliness, has been explained variously. It is the attribute of behaving in ways considered typical for women and refers to qualities and behaviours judged by a particular culture to be ideally associated with or especially appropriate to women and girls. In brief, it may be defined as the sum of all attributes that convey, or are perceived to convey, womanhood. While biological femininity refers to the female gender, psychological femininity refers to the submissive character type.

Whether this submissiveness has any bearings on their religious behaviour or not make the issue of feminine religiosity a contentious one, more so when instinctively females are believed to be deeply religious. The array and significance of their religious ideas, practises and discourses necessitates critical scrutiny considering that their religiosity was never assigned its due place in historical, sociological or anthropological analyses.

To define and discuss religiosity it is imperative to comprehend what religion is. August Comte, in his famous Cours de philosophie positive had defined his theory of the 'Law of Three Stages' with the theological as the 'lowest' state of development. 'Positivism', the creed of Comte, tended to regard religion as 'merely a survival from Man's primitive past and doomed to disappear in an era of science and general enlightenment.' However, even a synoptic survey of the growth of the science of religion in the last one hundred and fifty years is sufficient to show how wrong both these savants were. Religion is with us all even in the most scientifically advanced societies (Shrimali 1988:14-15). It is a complex phenomenon that potentially comprises 'ritual, doctrinal, mythic, experiential, ethical/legal, organizational/social, material and political/economic dimensions' (Smart 2000: 24). Even in the present world novel patterns of social stratification, identity construction, economic polarization, and the impact of the alleged postmodern 'crisis' on the modern paradigm of science provide the context to the manifold contemporary resurgence of religion. It may be argued that the social and psychological consequences of globalization have heightened the appeal and relevance of religions: As discourses of political resistance, as anxiety-coping mechanisms, and as networks of solidarity and community.

There are many potential rewards for religious faith: comfort, security, a sense of belonging, and/or personal growth. The positive feelings associated with each of these gains would likely help the religious individual to feel somewhat better about her/him or to feel empowered through divine grace.

Religiosity, or how religious an individual is, is a key variable in social psychological research on religion. In the late 1950s the problem of how to conceptualize religiosity became a major issue in the sociological study of religion. Some researchers questioned the assumption that religiosity was a single, monolithic phenomenon (Glock 1959; Lenski 1963). During the 1960s and 1970s, the concept of multidimensional religiosity became widely accepted. The contributions of Charles Glock, assisted later by Rodney Stark, were especially crucial to this development (Glock and Stark 1965; Stark and Glock 1968).

Glock and Stark's multidimensional conceptualization of religiosity reflects an attempt to measure how religious individuals are, given that one can be religious in a variety of ways and that these different dimensions are empirically distinct. The final version of this approach proposes five dimensions of 'religious commitment' and offers operational definitions for each: (1) belief orthodoxy, adherence to a set of beliefs associated with one's religious tradition; (2) ritual involvement, the performance of public religious practices; (3) devotionalism, the performance of private religious practices; (4) experience, perceptions of rather direct contact with the divine; and (5) religious knowledge, the extent of one's knowledge about one's religion. The sphere of religiosity has also been an authentication of the general gender biases prevalent in human societies against women. Most of the religions are patriarchal in their beliefs, images, language, and practices. This fact applies not only in context of the lay followers but also in the delineation of the deities.

## Feminine Religiosity

Toward late nineteenth century, a male French philosopher announced a significant modern discovery about gender: 'Different in mind and heart, different in imagination and character, intimately and essentially different woman brings us a new spiritual world and not only a more or less watered down re-edition of the spiritual world of man'(Izoulet 1946: 176). This man of wisdom proclaimed the widely accepted truth that women possess unique, spiritually potent feminine souls. A woman is 'more sympathetic, more moral, more religious than the rougher, often hard-hearted man.' As emphasised by Meyer her virtue is no longer obedience but 'innocence of spirit and purity of heart' (cited in Hausen: 54-55).

Thus, it is quite evident that even in the Western societies, women were believed to be more religious and spiritually finer than men on every measure of religiosity. Why this should be so has attracted the sporadic attention of clerics, sociologists and psychologists, but it has never been a major interest of either the sociologists of religion or Christian feminists. The sociology of religion has only recently included gender on its agenda

(Robbins and Anthony 1990: 345-407, Robbins and Robertson 1991: 327). Feminists, on the other hand, have been more concerned with why there are so few women in the chancel than with why there are so many in the pews. They have also been concerned to document in history the anti-women stance of Christianity, the pre-Christian spirituality of women, and the spirituality of hitherto ignored but highly gifted individuals, rather than document the ordinary religiosity of millions of churchgoing women (Walter and Davie 1998: 640).

> Feminist research on women in religion has tended to focus either on exploitation or on innovation, rather than on routine practice; feminist theory seems to have difficulty in integrating the idea that women found fulfilment in what appears to feminists as second-class citizenship. (Swatos 1997: 31)

The question, however, cannot be ignored. If the Christian churches - along with most other formal religions - are patriarchal, why should more females than males choose to join? Why have women been particularly prone to join precisely those establishments that offer them least equality? While feminists have explored why women choose to submit themselves to the patriarchal institution of the family, equivalent analyses for religion hardly exist; studies undertaken by Jacobs (1984), Davidman (1991), and Ozorak (1996) being exceptions. The gender imbalance by no means is just a twentieth century phenomenon. McLeod (1996: 65-70) provides comparable data for the nineteenth century, documenting the particular types of churches that appealed most to women. Thus, the variation between masculine and feminine religiosities has proved to be too apparent.

Independent of the degree of belief, what men and women believe religiously also differs. If asked to describe the God in whom they believe, women, concentrate rather more on a God of love, comfort and forgiveness, while men tend to refer to a God of power, planning and control. The prime dimension of religious life where the difference between women and men is quite implicit is private devotion - prayer and ritual offerings.

This, as argued by Argyle (1996: 140), raises the question whether men engage in religious practices when they are publicly acceptable or even required, but tend not to bother with private devotions when there is no social pressure. Islam and Judaism, in which religion is still part of public life, involve men more than women in public worship. As researched by McLeod (1981) in pre-industrial Britain, when church going was more of a public duty, men went as the representative of the household; now that faith is more a private choice, an optional leisure activity, the men seem to have dropped away. Hence, the motive between public and private behaviour regarding religious affiliations by men may be traced to exhibitionism.

## Theories of Feminine Religiosity

Religious beliefs and behaviour-centric studies have demonstrated consistently the predominant religious nature of females. They are more likely to express a greater interest in religion (Yinger 1970; Sasaki 1979), and have a stronger personal religious commitment (Bensen, Donohue, and Erickson 1989). This appears to hold true over their life course

(Cornwall 1989; Glock et al.1967) and regardless of the type of religious organization or belief system such as cult, sect, or church affiliation; belief in astrology, magic, spirits, and so on (Stark and Bainbridge 1985).

Several theories have emerged in the course of time that explains this facet of women's personalities. The initial focus was on differential socialization. It was argued that females are taught to be more submissive, passive, obedient, and nurturing than are males, and that these traits are associated with higher levels of religiosity (Mol 1985; Suziedelis and Potvin 1981). It has also been opined that these characteristics are predictors of religiosity not only between the sexes but also within each sex (Thompson 1991). In other words, men who exhibit these personality traits tend to be more religious than men who do not exhibit these traits and the same holds true for women. Thus, it is contended that the apparent gender difference is related to the fact that more females than males possess these personality traits.

Another explanation related the implicitly more religious nature of females to their structural location in society. The development of a gender-based division of labour, which feminises family duties for women and masculinises workplace duties for men, produces higher levels of female religiousness since religion falls under the general sphere of family matters (Douglas 1977). Luckmann (1967) contended that lower participation in the labour force leaves women with more time for church-related activities and also a greater need for a source of personal identity and commitment. In a similar vein, Iannaccone (1990) believed that females are socialized into the role of the religious consumer and therefore, not only allocate more time to religious activities than do men, but are also more skilled at obtaining 'religious rewards' for their families. Some scholars suggest that women's prominent role in raising children increases their religiosity because it correlates with concern for a family's well-being (Glock et al.1967). Thompson (1991), using a femininity-masculinity scale, found a strong relationship between religiousness and feminine personality characteristics. The perspective of gender differences in social power expounded by Turner (1991) focused on the relative lack of social power experienced by women in society to redeem which they tend to be more religious. In a recent study Sherkat (2002) detected a strong relationship between gender orientation and religiousness. He concluded that heterosexual females and homosexual males are far more religious than heterosexual males or homosexual females.

Yet another theory of gender differences in religiosity was put forth as risk preference by Alan S. Miller and John P. Hoffmann (1995). They reconceptualised the question and instead of asking why women are more religious than men, asked why men are less religious than women. This led them to focus on men rather than women, and to recognize that men are more 'irresponsible', short-sighted and risk taking than women. Accordingly they suggested that gender differences in religiosity are related to differences in risk preferences - that to be irreligious is to risk divine punishment. Religious acceptance may be conceived as risk-averse behaviour and the rejection of religious beliefs as risk-taking behaviour. A risk-averse person is more likely than a risk taker to deal with uncertainties and fears in a culturally appropriate way, i.e. through participation in religion. Several studies have shown that, in general, risk-averse people prefer traditional ways of handling stressful and uncertain situations while risk takers are more likely to look for innovative responses (Holloway 1979: 391-414).

This type of conceptualization is similar to the classic apologetic argument known as Pascal's wager: Religious beliefs are desirable because one has nothing to lose by believing in God but potentially much to gain. Long back Malinowski (1925) had claimed that religiosity is related to a desire to control those things that cannot be controlled given the level of technological sophistication of a society (e.g., weather and disease), and is also a way of dealing with the fear of death. Scholars like Homans (1941) have made similar claims. These arguments are consistent with the risk analysis approach wherein risk taking is seen as a masculine characteristic that emphasizes courage and adventurousness, while females are socialized to be more passive and gentle (Veevers and Gee 1986; Graney 1979).

Marx saw religious suffering as 'an expression of real suffering and a protest against real suffering, suffering which is socially induced. Religion is the sigh of the oppressed creature, the feeling of a heartless world, and the soul of soulless circumstances. It is the opium of the people'(Marx 1964: 43-44). For him the most vulnerable ones to social, economic and political oppression may seek emotional and practical solace through religion. This thought inspired Glock (1964) and fellow American sociologists like Stark and Bainbridge (1987) to develop deprivation-compensation theories of religion. Though Marx saw religion largely as a response to class inequality, the deprivation-compensation theorists have extended his approach to see it as a response to other forms of deprivation, including gender inequality; material; social and sexual deprivations. While tracing roots of religion in economic vulnerability the religiosity of women needs to be explained by economic or social circumstances.

If religion is rooted in social and economic vulnerability, it is to be expected, surely, that modernity - despite its possible origins in Calvinism (Weber 1976) - is inherently secularizing. Modernity may be seen as catering at root to the vulnerability for which religion was a prime compensator. This point of view provided a theoretical context for the claim of Luckmann (1967) that the more people are immersed in the institutions of modernity, notably by working for bureaucratic and/or capitalist organizations, the more secular they are likely to become. Women who stay at home are, therefore, secluded from the modernising influence of the marketplace and may remain religious.

Further marking the shift from modernity to postmodernity, a complex set of cultural and historical phenomena, factors which are conducive to enhance feminine religiosity may be reckoned with. While modernity was for universality/monolithic imaging, postmodernity roots for diversities/local autonomies. The postmodern characterizations may be comprehended variously as the end of metanarratives; decanonization; hybridization; multiculturalism; pluralism, etc. If postmodernism entails the freedom to play with nature, it also entails the undermining of traditional authorities, leaving the individual as his/her own ultimate authority (Heelas et al. 1996). Hence religion, hitherto controlled by the church authority or mainstream religious/sectarian organizations, may be replaced by spirituality, which the individual discovers for him/herself. Since women have been particularly subject to the patriarchic authority of religious structures, it is not implausible that women are at the forefront of developing postmodern discourses of 'spirituality' and they also experience these new discourses as quite liberating.

Whether or not religion is/has been a response to socially-induced vulnerability, it is / always has been a response to the physical vulnerability of the body that has been the human condition. Birth and death are not only mere physical events that frame human life; for many people they entail some encounter with the sacred (King 1989: 73-81). Such reflections continue despite enormous strides in technology and the contemporary likelihood that both birth and death will occur in an institutional setting, under the supervision of medical personnel. Even given the professionalization of medical care two facts are obvious: first that child birth remains one of the most profound experiences of a woman's life; second that the institutional setting has little effect on traditional divisions of labour, for even in the medical environment women are disproportionately present in their role as carers. Consequently, they are the most likely witnesses of a new life beginning, or a completed life coming to an end. The disparate exposure of women to the sacred is one consequence of these performances. What remains unnoticed is the expectation that childbirth may lead to death. Houlbrooke (1998: chap. 3) shows how in the early modern period, as part of their preparation for the birth women made spiritual preparations for their own death. In the women's stories of giving birth recorded by Sheila Kitzinger (1987) a sense of spiritual connection is evidenced in little things done or said by her partner or other carers. For instance, one woman in Oakley's study (1981: 95) thus described her experience: 'It was just amazing. It was like a miracle. It could be a religious experience. Now I know it's superior to be a woman.'

With this context, can women be considered to be more aware - because of their acquaintance with birth, sickness and death - about the physical frailty of human existence and thereby, more prone to religious leanings? And whether an 'Ethical Connection' with the sublime may be developed around this awareness? Gray (1971) pointed out that women generally have higher levels of fear than do men. Men have comparable familiarity with sickness and death only on active service in wartime - a time when they too are more likely to turn to religion (Argyle and Beit-Hallahmi 1975: 52-7; Wilkinson 1978).

Seen in the context of communal manifestations, observance of religious rites may be visualized as an alternative strategy. Otherwise confined to the four walls and domestic chores, the religious occasions do provide easy pretext for outings and social gatherings and thereby an escape bid from the fetters of patriarchy.

## Actual Religious Participation Scenario

Women's participation in religion represents a paradox. Although women may be more religious men are always put at the forefront even in religious practices, performance of *yajna* and *puja*. In adherence to the normative beliefs, even the burden of concretising male religiosity fall upon the women. Preparations for the *puja*, with all elaborations, have to be invariably undertaken by them. These may involve taking up early bath; cleaning utensils and the deity images; preparing the *thali* with lamp, grinding sandal paste; working in the kitchen for *prasad* preparation, and so on ... Ironically through their religious practices and convictions, aspiring longevity and prosperity of their kith and kin, women act as saviours of the very patriarchic / hegemonistic constructions that relegate them to subservient or almost non-identical entity status.

It is again an incongruity of fate that the same womenfolk, under guise of notions of auspicious/inauspicious, also bear the brunt of social taboos and disentitlement related with their natural cycle, widowhood, or childlessness, while a man is seldom singled out for exclusion from religious expressions/ proceedings for an identical raison d'ëtre. Again it is often women who are branded and outcaste as witch/evil spirits. Such indiscriminate biases and taboos, entailing their sporadic debarment have resulted in their second class membership in the faith community. Thus, it is apparent that religion, though incessantly lived by women, scarcely gets exteriorized by them. They are both subject to restrictions and deliberately dis-empowered, at the behest of men who control access, amongst other things, to culturally significant experiences and resources.

Against this background an analysis of Rajasthani folklore/literature offers interesting revelations. It presents the women as active agency – performing, sustaining and rather institutionalising religious traditions. The folk literature is imbued with uninhibited energy and unrestrained motivations. In a way, it gives vent to the expectations, aspirations and identity to the womenfolk, otherwise denied to them in mainstream life and may be interpreted as putting forth a claim for rightful place in the male-dominated religious domain.

## Feminine Folklore Expressions

Folk includes all persons – residents of either villages, towns, cities or all of them within a given area – who are conscious of a common cultural heritage and have some constant traits; whose behavioural knowledge is based on the word of the mouth instead of written scriptures; and whose way of life is more traditional, more simple, more natural, less sympathetic and less specialised in comparison to the so-called civilized people (The Standard Dictionary of Folklore cited in Srivastava 1974: 9-10).

Folklore is a body of materials, a cultural process, and a method of research applied to those materials and that process; more specifically, it may be termed as 'literature transmitted orally'. The folkloric traditions, pulsating with rich historical insights, transcend cultural authority and transforms into an image of feminine religiosity. They may be held as countering the usual gendered representations, both Western and Eastern, of feminine passivity and submissiveness in the face of masculine dominance, and uncovers a specific female agency gauged through folk performances. The variety of women's expressive genres: songs sung at social ceremonies; festive gatherings; religious rituals; and informal personal narratives show how women compose poignant responses to Indian gender and kinship ideology and validate their existence in the otherwise male-headed landscape of faith.

The folklore theologies acquire different forms as prayers, liturgies poetry, songs and personal reflections/narratives. They generally do not focus on the abstract nature of Godhood but rather conceive God as the source of life and sustaining power of the universe catering to their mundane requirements and empowering them to face life's adversities as a compassionate entity. In this sense, in a religiously pluralistic world, they represent realities that are primarily different from the monotheistic notions of God as testified by the folklore.

For the folks religion is embedded in all spheres of life, rather than in some precepts or beliefs. From the beginning of life till end each day of their worldly existence; advent of seasons; challenges of survival; wealth or poverty; sickness and death; pregnancy; childbirth; marriage; agricultural operations; protection of crops and cattle; curing snake bites; fertility and barrenness of women, etc. - all are embroiled within the fabric of religion encompassing all strands of human relationships within its fold. Folk religious images are excellent insights into cultural, social, and religious interpretations of village life. Lack of status within the mainstream religion may be one reason for women getting drawn towards by folk deities.

Consequently, idea promulgated especially by Franz Boas, that folklore reflects in some way the culture in which it circulates appears acceptable. The view of the society is that what folklore provides is not necessarily a simple mirror image of real situations or attitudes. In any given culture, folklore may change over a period of time, or different genres or performance contexts may project quite different viewpoints. The question of how society affects folklore is one side of a coin, the other of which is the question of how folklore as a means of communication influences a society and the perceptions of its individual members and how it presents images from the real world.

## The Feminine Folk Religious Images

Village women practice a variety of religious observances that reflect upon their multiple images. Feminine image construction is an inseparable part of the various domestic/communal rituals performed in the countryside. The observance of *vratas*; story narration; singing songs and organising *jagranas*, are some modes of expressing this image of religiosity. There is no village, wherein there is no abode, *thaan*, or platform of folk deities. The rich collection of Rajasthani folkloric traditions testify that a great majority of the venerated ones is comprised of female deities, *mataji*, the embodiment of *shakti* or the cosmic life force bestowing wisdom, wealth, victory and peace upon their devotees. Rajasthan abounds in such representations: *Amba*, *Shila*, *Jwala*, *Jamwahi*, *Harshat*, *Nakti*, *Narayani*, *Chavanda*, *Chamunda*, *Sachiya*, *Nagnenchiya*, *Latiyaal*, *Karani*, *Kaila*, *Chauth*, *Ashapura*, *Oon*, *Arbuda*, *Dadhi*, *Bedla*, and *Mansa mata*, to name few. A special place is accorded to the *Charani* goddesses like *Hinglaj*, believed to have incarnated in the bard community. The eightfold delineation of female *shakti* is worshipped as *ashta matrakas*.

The most significant aspect of these deities is that they epitomize vivid strands of human relationships. This has been possible through a rich array of folk songs, myths and ritualistic patterns. The worship derives a utilitarian influence upon the devotees.

The purposes for which women invoke divine forces provide valuable overview of the feminine religiosity in the folk regions. As stated earlier they specifically pray for the well being, strengthening and fastening the bonds of various relationships within their family as well as enhancing its overall affluence and progress. Quite interestingly upon them lies the onus for familial well being. The range of implorations extend from seeking of husbands by aspiring girls, to longevity and marital bliss by married ones, and ensuring general welfare of their progeny. The popular images emerge as those of the wives, mothers and sisters as carriers of religious traditions. For seeking their wishes they may be seen propitiating both benevolent and malevolent manifestations of divinity.

Amongst the deities invoked in the folklores *Sanjhi* is primarily approached by unmarried girls to obtain a good husband, many children and prosperity. Various *teej devis* such as *Gavar*, *Akha*, *Savan*, and *Kajalya teej* are celebrated by unmarried girls for good husband while married girls for longevity of their husbands. One of the most popular deities, *Gangaur* is worshipped for sixteen days, by virgins in anticipation of a suitable companion whereas married females wish to be blessed with conjugal bliss in marital life. *Chauth* deities like *Karva*, *Tilva*, *Sankat*, and *Baisakh* are worshipped for the well being of their husband or sons. The censors of female morals, *Saat Behna*, act as guards against any incestuous behaviour on part of the married woman. The tradition of *sati* worship, influential in Rajasthan since long, offers another aspect of feminine religiosity. The family *sati* is especially propitiated at the time of child birth, marriage, etc. and offered *jaat*, i.e. obligatory obeisance at child birth and *jadula*, i.e. tonsure.

Amongst images of mother worshippers *Bachha Baras* is celebrated by worshipping cow with a calf. *Gaaj mata* and *Shashthi* (*Ubchhatta*) are invoked for well being of sons. *Ahoi* is another deity sought for long life of sons. The Indian custom of giving euphemistic names to dreaded tendencies to conciliate them and ward off their evil effects is typically manifested by the smallpox deity *Sheetala*. She has to be propitiated regularly by the women to save the children against the disease.

Goddesses like *Jeena* and *Dooj* are invoked for long and smooth life of brothers. Hence, through these Goddesses the womenfolk not only personalize various aspects of their familial life but also express their religiosity. As indicated earlier since most of the prayers and invocations are intended for males than their own self, they are rather substantiating the patriarchic establishments.

## Images of Harmony with Nature

Be it the worship of cow and calf on baccha baras; *tulsi*; *khejadli*; *bad*; and *pipal* trees; *amla* on *amla navmi*; snake on *nagapanchami*; sugarcane offerings to Lakshmi on Diwali, etc., the environmental conservation gets due veneration by the Rajasthani womenfolk. They circumambulate *tulsi* for 108 times and donate 108 items on *somvati amavasya*.

Banana is worshipped on Thursdays and women also refrain from eating it on that day. Sowing *javare* and grains during *Gangaur* and *Navaratras* respectively, is symbolic of their sacred association with cultivation activities. The jubilant welcome to various seasons accorded in form of celebration of fairs and festivals furthers their involvement with natural processes in a religious mode. Another aspect of their concern towards nature may be seen in the sacrifice of Amritadevi with 363 members of Vishnoi community to preserve green trees on the 9th of September, 1730, when the Maharaja of Jodhpur sent his agents into the jungle to cut wood in the village of Khejarli, twenty-four miles from Jodhpur. Protesting against the royal orders the Vishnois, renowned for their veneration towards nature and Kherjarli trees, under Amritadevi's leadership clinged to the Kherjarli trees and were eventually chopped off by the woodcutters. Thus, harmony with nature remains the highest ideal of spiritual quest of folk followers, more so when women in urban areas get little opportunity for such expressions of their religiosity. Such instances aptly epitomises the ultimate of this harmonious relationship between women and ecological components. In the current times of frenetic modernisation and globalisation this empathy assumes particular significance.

The dichotomous world view of patriarchal religions is counter-posed against the integrity and holism inherent in women's perception of the world. Charlene Spretnak characterizes women's spirituality as 'the inner unity of all forms of being' (1982: xvi). This holism implies a harmony between body and reason, flesh and spirit, theory and practice, word and deed (Starret: 187). Holism means also the unity of nature and the human being, which is experienced by women fully and with particular intensity.

Against the radical feminist notion of single sex and homosexuality, the eco-feminists extol and glorify the feminine reproductive powers. They draw an analogy between Mother Earth and the feminine fertility and equate the latter to nature's bounty providing potential. Speaking about women, Susan Griffin points out: 'And we are nature. We are nature seeing nature'(1978: 226). Hence, it may be surmised that in contrast to the patriarchal mentality, which comes into conflict with nature and 'rapes' it with its thoughtless interference, the feminist mentality brings harmony into the world and hopes of salvation from our ecological crisis. In this context the folk awareness exemplified through feminine religious practices assumes utmost importance and also exhibit the range of powers of womenfolk, who are not just capable of creating human race but also of sustaining the human existence.

## Women in Renunciant Traditions

Throughout Indian subcontinent women's oral traditions, whether story, song or *vrat katha*, describe the inner powers of women, which often are similarly attributed to their devotional practices and which provide alternative images of femininity to dominant Brahmanical textual understandings. In this context Rajasthan has had a rich tradition of female devotional asceticism spearheaded by Mira. A study of female *sadhus* in Rajasthan (Udaipur region) undertaken by DeNapoli (2009: 81-109) illustrates how they construct renunciant identity through life story performances in form of devotional *bhajans*; popular religious stories; and sacred text recitation – all constituting their 'rhetoric of renunciation'. Through the themes of duty (*kartavya*), destiny (*bhagya*), and devotion (*bhakti*) they communicate a gendered discourse on female agency in the tradition of renunciation while validating and legitimatizing their own ascetic identity. Thus, they articulate their spiritual authority and agency in a male-dominated domain in which they are clearly minorities.

The personal narrative performances enable them to express devotion towards God. They attribute their life trajectories to God/Goddess. They rather understood religion as an existential personal experience of faith. The subsequent narratives not only allow these *sadhus* to connect with God but also serve as a *bhakti* testimonial to God's power and presence in their lives. They present themselves as exceptions to gender norms and also as ones who experience agency and authority in a gendered way. They usually assign their renunciation to actualization of divine directive or emphasize destiny as original source of their asceticism, thereby conjoin the notions of *bhagya* and *karma*. This strategy permits them to work within the normative androcentric frameworks of femininity. It also enables them to convey that their asceticism is neither a personal choice to break away from normative gender roles nor an escape from domestic hardships, rather a destined path of devotional and dutiful action by following divine commands. They believe that their Godly connection endows them with ability and authority to control their own lives.

The large tradition of folklore is available with the womenfolk of Rajasthan. Through them facets of female lives - celebrating vitality, resisting devaluation, contesting subordination and asserting identities may be visualised. This stands in contrast to a dominant mode in both academic and journalistic accounts depicting rural women as submissive/decorative; kept in their subordinate place by a patriarchal economy and a religious tradition that devalues them; as ashamed of their bodies and their sexuality. The folkloric expressions offer impressions of these women's identities as exuberant, resilient, and often refusing degradations imposed by male ideologies or structures of authority. As a group, they manifest a sense of their own power, dignity, and worth as proved by the instances of female *sadhus*. This worth is not something nourished secretly in defiance of a degraded existence. Rather, it remains integral to their daily lives, labours, relationships, and to the religious and cultural performances that imbues their lives with meaning. In the past decade, many Indian feminists have turned from a blanket rejection of Hindu traditions to re-examine them as possible sources of empowerment. Traditions such as fasts for sons, brothers or husbands, rather than being looked as agents of feminine subjectivity are now being contemplated as instruments facilitating the creation of wider spaces for women to imprint a distinct identity for themselves. Besides through these communal practices they also actualise integration and social cohesion of womenfolk of various families and castes.

Thus, adjudging from the fivefold criteria of religiosity: belief orthodoxy; ritual involvement; devotionalism; experience; and religious knowledge; the feminine religiosity, whether ritualistic or renunciant, as revealed by Rajasthani folk literature stands fully vindicated. Whether adhering to established beliefs and institutionalising them; consistently performing rituals, publicly or privately, with full fanfare; experiencing/visualising communion with the ultimate; or preserving knowledge of theistic dogmas by passing them on through oral transmissions of *vrat kathas* and *bhajan* genre - they act as a vehicle for all through their persona. The survival and perpetuation of folk culture and civilization has been largely been possible through their interventions. In this we may also observe that the folk women exhibit outstanding images even as compared to women in mainstream/ elite religious circles/sections. Elizabeth Davis writes:

> Today... women are in the vanguard of the aborning civilization; and it is to the women that we look for salvation in the healing and restorative waters of Aquarius.... The ages of masculism are now drawing to a close.... Only the overthrow of the three-thousand-year old beast of masculist materialism will save the race. In the new science of the twenty-first century not physical force but spiritual force will lead the way... Extrasensory perception will take precedence over sensory perception, and in this sphere woman will again predominate (1971: 337-339).

Thus, it is apparent that women have a crucial role to play in the current times. There are grounds to believe that one of the constituent elements of the new world perception will be a religious consciousness prevailing not only over the confessional but also over sex differences. In this regard the Rajasthani folk literature renders a valuable service in preserving vignettes of feminine religious aspirations and experiences realised through the centuries. It has been acting as sort of a mouthpiece for delving upon the ultimate and seeking boons for the family. Most importantly, it establishes the selfless feminine religiosity as explicitly supporting male community on a firm footing, and thereby facilitating their possible empowerment in a patriarchal setup.

## *Notes and References*


1. Argyle, M. and Beit-Hallahmi, B. (1975): The Social Psychology of Religion, Routledge, London.
2. Bachofen, Johann J. (1967): Myth, Religion and Mother Right, trans. Ralph Manheim, Princeton University Press, Princeton, N.J.
3. Beit-Hallahmi, B. and Argyle, M. (1996): The Psychology of Religious Behaviour, Belief and Experience, Routledge, London.
4. Bensen, Peter L., Donahue, Michael J. and Erickson, Joseph A. (1989): Adolescence and Religion: A Review of the Literature from 1970-1986. Research in the Social Scientific Study of Religion 1: pp. 153-181.
5. Bynum, Caroline Walker (1987): Holy Feast and Holy Fast: The Religious Significance of Food to Medieval Women. University of California Press, Berkeley, CA.
6. Cornwall, Marie (1989), "Faith Development of Men and Women over the Life Span" in Aging and the Family, pp. 115-139. (Eds. Stephen J. Bahr and Evan T. Peterson, Lexington Books, Lexington, MA)
7. Davidman, L. (1991): Tradition in a Rootless World: Women turn to Orthodox Judaism, University of California Press, Berkeley.
8. Davis, Elizabeth Gould (1971): The First Sex, Penguin Books Inc., Baltimore.
9. Davis, James A. and Smith, Tom W. (1991): The General Social Survey Cumulative Codebook, NORC, Chicago.

10. DeNapoli, Antoinette E. (2009): "By the Sweetness of the Tongue": Duty, Destiny and Devotion in the Oral Life Narratives of Female Sadhus in Rajasthan. In Asian Ethnology. Issue Vol. 68. No.1: pp. 81-109.
11. Douglas, Ann (1977): The Feminization of American Culture, Knopf, New York.
12. Engles, Freidrich (1948): The Origin of the Family, Private Property and the State, Progress Publishers, Moscow.
13. Gelpy, Barbara (1983): Signs 9, No. 1. Special issue on 'Women and Religion'.
14. Glock, Charles Y. (1959), "The Religious Revival in America?" in Religion and the Face of America, pp. 25-42. (Eds. Jane C. Zahn, University of California Press, Berkeley.)
15. Glock, C. (1964), "The Role of Deprivation in the Origin and Evolution of Religious Groups", in Religion and Social Conflict. (Eds. R. Lee and M. Marty, Oxford University Press, New York.)
16. Glock, Charles Y. and Stark, Rodney (1965): Religion and Society in Tension, Rand McNally, Chicago.
17. Glock, Charles, Ringer, Benjamin and Babbie, Earl (1967): To Comfort and to Challenge, University of California Press, Berkeley, California.
18. Graney, Marshall J. (1979): An Exploration of Social Factors influencing the Sex Differential in Mortality. Sociological Symposium 28: pp. 1-26.
19. Gray, J. (1971): Sex Differences in Emotional Behaviour in Mammals Including Man: Endocrine Basis. Acta Psychologica 35: pp. 29-46.
20. Griffin, Susan (1978): Woman and Nature, Harper Colophon Books, New York.
21. Hausen, Karin (1981), "Family and Role-Division: The Polarisation of Sexual Stereotypes in the Nineteenth Century-An Aspect of the Dissociation of Work and Family," in The German Family, pp. 51-61 (Eds. Richard J. Evans and W. R. Lee, Groom Helm, London.)
22. Heelas, P., Lash, S. and Morris, P. (1996): Detraditionalization: Critical Reflections on Authority and Identity, Blackwell, Oxford.
23. Holloway, Charles A. (1979): Decision Making under Uncertainty: Models and Choices, Prentice-Hall, Englewood Cliffs, NJ.
24. Homans, George C. (1941): Anxiety and Ritual: The Theories of Malinowski and Radcliffe-Brown. American Anthropologist 43: pp. 164-172.
25. Houlbrooke, R. (1998): Death, Religion and Family 1480-1750, Oxford University Press, Oxford.
26. Iannaccone, Laurence R. (1990): Religious Practice: A Human Capital Approach. Journal for the Scientific Study of Religion 29: pp. 297-314.
27. Izoulet, Jean (1946): La cite Modern, Metaphyisique de la Sociologie (Quoted in Viola Klein, The Feminine Character: History of an Ideology, Kegan Paul, Trench, Trubner & Co, London.)
28. Jacobs, J. (1984): The Economy of Love in Religious Commitment. Journal for the Scientific Study of Religion 23 (2): pp. 155-71.
29. Kitzinger, S. (1987): Giving Birth, How It Really Feels, Victor Gollancz, London.
30. Lenski, Gerhard (1963): The Religious Factor, Anchor, Garden City, NY.
31. Levitt, Ruby R. (1971), "Women in Other Cultures," in Woman in Sexist Society: A Study in Power and Powerlessness. (Eds. V. Gornick and B. K. Moran, New American Library, New York.)
32. Luckmann, Thomas (1967): The Invisible Religion, Macmillan, New York.

33. Malinowski, Bronislaw (1925), "Magic, Science, and Religion" In Science, Religion and Reality, pp. 18-94. (Ed. Joseph Needham, Macmillan, New York.)
34. Marx, K. (1964): Early Writings, McGraw Hill, New York.
35. McDonnell, C. (1986): The Christian Home in Victorian America, 1840-1900, Indiana University Press, Bloomington.
36. McLeod, H. (1996): Religion and Society in England, 1850-1914, Macmillan, Basingstoke.
37. Meyer, J. (1848): Das Grosse Conversations-Lexicon.
38. Miller, Alan S. and Hoffmann, John P. (1995): Risk and Religion: An Explanation of Gender Differences in Religiosity. In Journal for the Scientific Study of Religion, 34 (1): pp. 63-75.
39. Mol, Hans (1985): The Faith of Australians, George, Allen and Unwin, Sydney.
40. Oakley, A. (1981): From Here to Maternity: Becoming a Mother, Pelican, Harmondsworth.
41. Okin, Suzan Moiler (1999): cited in Is Multiculturalism Bad for Women? (Eds., Joshua Cohen, Matthew Howard and Martha C. Nussbaum, Princeton University Press, Princeton NJ.)
42. Ozorak, E. W. (1996): The Power but not the Glory: How Women Empower Themselves through Religion. Journal for the Scientific Study of Religion 35 (1): pp. 17-29.
43. Robbins, T. and Anthony, D. (Eds.) (1990): In Gods We Trust: New Patterns of Religious Pluralism in America, Transaction. 2nd edition, New Brunswick, NJ.
44. Robbins, T. and Robertson, R. (1991): Studying Religion Today. Religion 21: pp. 319-37.
45. Roy, Kumkum (2009), "Gender Relations During the First Millennium: An Overview", in A Social History of Early India. History of Science, Philosophy and Culture in Indian Civilization Series, pp. 213-31. (Gen. Ed., D.P. Chattopadhyaya, Vol. II, Part 5, Pearson Longman, Delhi.)
46. Sasaki, Masamichi (1979), "Status Inconsistency and Religious Commitment" in The Religious Dimension: New Directions in Quantitative Research, pp. 35-156. (Ed. Robert Wuthnow, Academic Press, New York.)
47. Sherkat, Darren E. (2002): Sexuality and Religious Commitment in the United States: An Empirical Examination. Journal for the Scientific Study of Religion 41: pp. 313-23.
48. Shrimali, Krishna Mohan (1988): Religion, Ideology and Society. Social Scientist, Vol. 16, No. 12. Dec: pp. 14-60.
49. Smart, Ninian (2000) quoted in Fiona Bowie, The Anthropology of Religion. Blackwell, Oxford.
50. Spretnak, Charlene (1982): Introduction, in The Politics of Women's Spirituality. (Ed. C. Spretnak, Anchor Press (Doubleday), Garden City, New York.)
51. Stark, Rodney and Glock, Charles Y. (1968): American Piety, University of California Press, Berkeley.
52. Stark, Rodney and Bainbridge, William (1985): The Future of Religions, University of California Press, Berkeley.
53. Stark, Rodney and Bainbridge, William (1987): A Theory of Religion, Peter Lang, New York.
54. Starret, Barbara, The Metaphors of Power, in The Politics of Women's Spirituality.
55. Stepaniants, M. T. (1992): The Image of Woman in Religious Consciousness: Past, Present, and Future. Philosophy East and West, Vol. 42, No. 2, Moscow Regional East-West Philosophers' Conference on Feminist Issues East and West: pp. 239-247.

56. Suziedelis, Antanas and Potvin, Raymond H. (1981): Sex Differences in Factors Affecting Religiousness among Catholic Adolescents. Journal for Scientific Study of Religion 20: pp. 38-50.
57. Swatos, W. H. (1997): The Politics of Gender and the Two-Party Thesis in American Protestantism. Social Compass 44 (1): pp. 23-37.
58. The Standard Dictionary of Folklore. Mythology and Legend. (Cited in S. L. Srivastava (1974): Folk Culture and Oral Traditions, Abhinav Publication, Delhi.)
59. Thompson, Edward H. (1991): Beneath the Status Characteristic: Gender Variations in Religiousness. Journal for the Scientific Study of Religion 30: pp. 381-394.
60. Turner, Bryan S. (1991): Religion and Social Theory, Sage Publications, London.
61. Veevers, Jean E. and Ellen, M. Gee (1986): Playing it Safe: Accident Mortality and Gender Roles. Sociological Focus 19: pp. 349-360.
62. Walter, Tony and Grace Davie (1998): The Religiosity of Women in the Modern West. The British Journal of Sociology, Vol. 49, No. 4 (Dec.): pp. 640-660.
63. Weber, M. (1976): The Protestant Ethic and the Spirit of Capitalism, Unwin, London.
64. Wilkinson, A. (1978): The Church of England and the First World War, SPCK, London.
65. Yinger, J. Milton (1970): The Scientific Study of Religion, Macmillan, London.

14

# Literature of Theravada Abhidhamma:
## A Timeline of Evolution

*Ankur Barua*

*Abhidhamma* Pitaka is a philosophical collection that forms the third great section of the Buddhist Pali Canon (Tipitaka). It is a system of classifications, analytical enumerations and definitions, with no elaborate explanations on the subject matter. These are huge collections of systematically arranged tabulations, accompanied by definitions of the terms used in the tables. The *Abhidhamma Pitaka*, primarily deals with the philosophy and psychology of the Theravada school of Buddhism (Jayawardhana, 1994). The "*theravada*", however, refers to that school of Buddhism which, supposedly adhere to the most original and purest form of the Buddhist teachings, advocated by those *theras* (monks) who obtained the erudition directly through the Buddha. They used the *bhasa Magadhika* or the *mula bhasa* (the original language) to record the original text or the *pariyaya*, (the text of the canons). The term *pariyaya*, however, when abbreviated became 'pari' or 'pali'; and in course of time was applied to denote the language of the entire canons and other compositions having the same language (Jayawardhana, 1994), (Bodhi, 1993).

### Meaning of the term "Abhidhamma"

The word "Abhidhamma" may be analyzed etymologically, as the compound of *abhi* ("to"; "toward"; "into") and *dhamma* (root: *dhr*, which means "to hold" or "bear"). However, in textual context, it is interpreted as "leading to that which contains the advanced or specialized teachings (of the Buddha)". The renowned Pali commentator Buddhaghosa had interpreted the term 'Abhidhamma' as the *most advanced (atireka) or specialised (visesa) doctrine* to differentiate it from the doctrine of the *Sutta-Pitaka*. It should be noted that every term of the Abhidhamma has a specific connotation or well-defined meaning for the advanced monks or trainees (Bodhi, 1993), (Thera, 1998).

Vasubandhu, in his Sanskrit version of the *Abhidharmakosa*, had stated that the Abhidharma is the undefiled wisdom and it is concomitant. Asanga's interpretation of Abhidharma also extends to the understanding of the above meaning. Prefixing "*abhi*" in four ways with the *dhamma,* he interpreted "Abhidhamma" as (a)The dhamma which is Nibbana-*encountering*, (b)The dhamma which is *analytical*, (c)The dhamma which is *devoid* of the converse views and (d)The dhamma which is *progressive*. It may be reiterated that every term of Abhidhamma is assigned a definite connotation; and is often interpreted by way of its characteristic (*lakkhana*), function (*rasa*), manifestation (*paccupatthana*) and proximate cause (*padatthan*). So, the linguistic interpretation of the term has often been misleading; and its variant renditions create more complications to a reader rather than to extend his understanding. It is believed that Abhidhamma is a way of life; and is meant for the chosen few, particularly for the erudite monks or scholars with specialized training. Scholars interested in Abhidhamma should also refer to the commentaries on cănonical Abhidhammic literature or living Burmese (or Myanmari) traditions for its purest comprehension (Jayawardhana, 1994), (Bodhi, 1993), (Thera, 1998).

The term Abhidharma (a-p'i-ta-mo) in the Chinese records interpret it as *ta-fa* (great dhamma - because of the greatness of the knowledge to the realization of Four Noble Truths etc.); *wu-pi-fa* (peerless dhamma - because of the eight forms of intelligence etc); sheng-fa (excellent dhamma - as it is wisdom-realising); *tuei-fa* (facing dhamma) and *hsiang-fa* (proceeding dhamma - as the cause-effect theory that proceeds from cause to effect) (Jayawardhana, 1994), (Bodhi, 1993).

## Origin of Theravada Abhidhamma

According to the Theravada tradition the Abhidhamma is the proper domain of the Buddhas (Buddha-visaya). According to the Atthasalini, the initial conception of it in the Master's mind (manasa desana) took place immediately after his Enlightenment. It is believed that the Abhidhamma was conceived during the fourth of the seven weeks spent by the Buddha under the Bodhi tree. These seven days were known as 'The Week of the House of Gems (ratana-ghara-sattaha), but one must remember that the Buddha did not preach this to the lay community apprehending their difficulty in interpretation of its true meaning. It is perceived that the Buddha dwelt in the celestial domain of the thirty-three divine beings (Tavatimsa-loka) to teach the doctrine of the Abhidhamma to his mother and an assembly of gods for three months. Then he descended to the lake Anottata; where he instructed the same to his disciple Sāriputta in the form of numerical verses, who in turn taught it to the five hundred distinguished *Arahants*. Following the oral transmission route through *acharya*-disciple tradition, the Abhidhamma was thus transmitted from generation to generation (Jayawardhana, 1994), (Thera, 1998), (Thera and Hecker, 1997).

## Pre-Abhidhammika Abhidhamma

There is historical continuity between the early Buddhist Suttas and the Abhidhamma. The antecedent trends that led to the development of the Abhidhamma can be traced from a number of Suttas and Sutta-passages which were composed according to the expository methodology of the Abhidhamma. These are as follows:

(1) A group of eight suttas with the appellation, *"Vibhanga"* are found in the Vibhanga Vagga of the Majjhima Nikaya. The term *Vibhanga* means distribution, division or classification which is represented as Culakamma-Vibhanga, Mahakamma-Vibhanga, Salayatana-Vibhanga, Uddesa-Vibhanga, Arana-Vibhanga, Dhatu-Vibhanga, Sacca-Vibhanga and Dakkhina-Vibhanga. These suttas present the doctrinal categories in technical terms devoid of literary embellishments such as use of similes or metaphors to illustrate the doctrinal points.

(2) Some suttas in the Samyutta Nikaya specifically deal with one particular doctrinal category. These are Nidhana Samyutta (on Dependent Origination), Dhatu Samyutta (on Eighteen Elements involved in sense-cognition), Khandha Samyutta (on Five Aggregates into which the empiric individuality is analyzed).

(3) In the Anguttara Nikaya, the doctrines are arranged in numerically ascending order which forms a transitory stage between the Sutta-Pitaka and the Abhidhamma-Pitaka.

(4) The Patisambhida Magga, which belongs to the Khuddaka Nikayas of the fifth collection of Sutta-Pitaka, was composed by Venerable Sariputta and could be considered as a work belonging to the expository methodology of the Abhidhamma tradition.

(5) Sangiti Sutta and Dasuttara Sutta of the Digha Nikaya, composed by Venerable Sariputta, show the beginning of the Abhidhamma systematization. The Sangiti Sutta contains a long list of 903 dhammas in 227 different types arranged in numerical order of ones, pairs, triads and up to tens. In the Dasuttara Sutta the enumeration of the doctrinal categories is made not only on their numerical order, but also in consideration of their specific nature.

(6) The term "Abhivinaya", synonymous with the term "Abhidhamma", also occur in the Vinaya Pitaka. It is proclaimed that a monk who is incapable of instructing on "Abhidhamma" and "Abhivinaya" must not take part in ordaining any disciple.

(7) The term *matika-dhara*, meaning specialist in *matikas* that also occurs in the Sutta-Pitaka, is considered to be early Buddhist specialists who were skilful in tabulations of doctrinal topics and paved the way for the emergence of the Abhidhamma.

(Bodhi, 1993), (Thera, 1998), (Thera and Hecker, 1997), (Karunadasa, 2009).

## The Matikas and Seven Original Text Books of Theravada Abhidhamma

The nucleus of the Abhidhamma can be traced back from *matikas,* which are doctrinal tabulations found in the Suttas that form a foundation for the whole superstructure of the Abhidhamma systematization. The *matika* is a matrix or schedule of categories consisting of 122 modes of classification comprised of 100 dyads and 22 triads, which are special to the expository methodology of the Abhidhamma. There are 100 modes of classification called *dyads (duka)* which are individual sets of two terms used as a basis of classifying the fundamental dhammas. There are 22 *triads (tika)* which are individual sets of three terms into which the fundamental dhammas are distributed. The Theravada Abhidhamma has seven original text books. These are *(1) Dhammasangani (enumeration of Phenomena), (2) Vibhanga (book of Analysis), (3) Dhatukatha (discourse on Elements), (4) Puggalapannatti (concepts of individuals or Human Typologies), (5) Kathavatthu (points of Controversy), (6) Yamaka (book of pairs)* and *(7) Patthana (book on Conditional Relations)*. These books do not contain records of discourses and discussions, but are treaties which present the fundamental doctrines of the Buddha in a purely impersonal and technical terminology, free from any kind of historical background or literary embellishment. The Sarvastivadin tradition of Buddhism however, does not accept this list of texts as original composition (Bodhi, 1993), (Thera, 1998), (Karunadasa, 2009), (Dhammajoti, 2003).

## Post-Canonical and Pre-Commentarial Treatises related to the Abhidhamma

Nettippakarana and Petakopadesa are the two treatises which serve as a guide to the interpretation and understanding of the teachings contained in the Pali Canon similar to the Abhidhamma texts (Karunadasa, 2009).

## Post-Canonical Commentaries and Sub-commentaries on the Abhidhamma

(1) Atthasalini – Expositor and Dhammasangini Atthakatha – commentary on Dhammasangini.

(2) Sammohavinodini – dispeller of Delusion and Vibhanga Atthakatha – commentary to the Vibhanga.

(3) Pancappakaranatthakatha – commentary on the remaining five books of the Abhidhamma Pitaka.

(4) Visuddhimagga – Path of Purification, which gives a full expression of Theravada Abhidhamma.

(5) Abhidhamma Mulatika – sub-commentary to the commentaries of the Abhidhamma.

(6) Anutika – sub-commentaries to the sub-commentaries.

(Thera, 1998), Karunadasa, 2009)

## Compendiums on the Abhidhamma

The compendiums compiled in Sri Lanka are Abhidhammatthasangaha, Namarupapariccheda (analysis of mind and matter), Parmatthavinicchaya (an enquiry into what is ultimate), Abhidhammavatara (a descent into the introduction of Abhidhamma), Ruparupavi bhaga (analysis into mind and matter), Saccasamkhepa (an outline/ synopsis/ summary of Truth), Mohavicchedani (that which dispels delusion) and Khemappakarana (the treat is by Khema). The last one is Namacaradipak (movement of mind) which was compiled in Burma. Some of these compendiums also have their own sub-commentaries. The most popular among them is Abhidhammattha Vibhavinitika, a sub-commentary on the Abhidhammatthasangaha (Thera, 1998), Karunadasa, 2009).

## Official Inclusion of the Abhidhamma Pitaka during Third Buddhist Council

The *Mahavamsa* is considered as one of the most reliable sources of the Buddhist history and a principal source for the construction of the history of ancient India. Though many scholars believe that the Tipitaka was compiled in the third Buddhist council, but it is explicitly stated in the *Mahavamsa* that even before the convention of the third Buddhist council, one thousand erudite monks, who were well versed in the Tipitaka, were selected for the re-compilation of the original and purest teachings of the Buddha in order to eliminate the interpolations crept in the original corpuses. This corroborates to the fact that the Tipitaka definitely existed before the third Buddhist council. However, its form might have been different from what was compiled in the third council (Jayawardhana, 1994), (Thera, 1998).

During the 3rd Century B.C., with the initiative of Emperor Asoka, the Third Buddhist Council was held to discuss the differences of opinion among the bhikkhus of various sects regarding some portions of the *Vinaya* and also the *Dhamma. The Abhidhamma Pitaka* was officially included as the third Pali Cannon in this Council. At the end of this Council, the President of the Council, Moggaliputta Tissa, compiled a book called the *Kathavatthu* refuting the heretical, false views and theories held by some sects. The teaching approved and accepted by this Council was known as *Theravada*. After the Third Council, Asoka's son, Ven. Mahinda, brought the *Tripitaka* to Sri Lanka, along with the commentaries that were recited at the Third Council. The texts were written in Pali which was based on the Magadhi language spoken by the Buddha (Jayawardhana, 1994), Bodhi, 1993).

## The High Esteem of Abhidhamma in Buddhist Tradition

Since the time of its inception, the Abhidhamma was highly esteemed and even venerated in the countries of Theravada Buddhism. In the 10th century A.C. on the order of king Kassapa V of Ceylon, the whole Abhidhamma Pitaka was inscribed on gold plates, and the first of these books, the Dhammasangani, was set with jewels. When the work was completed, the precious manuscripts were taken in a huge procession to a beautiful monastery and deposited there. Another king of Ceylon, Vijaya Bahu (11th century) used to study the Dhammasangani in the early morning before he took up his royal duties, and he prepared a translation of it into Sinhalese, which however has not been preserved (Jayawardhana, 1994).

## Evaluation of the Authenticity of Abhidhamma

Even in olden days there were doubts about the authenticity of the Abhidhamma Pitaka as genuine Buddha word. The early sect of the Sautrantikas regarded, as their name indicates, only Sutta and Vinaya as canonical, but not the Abhidhamma. However, the Theravadins urged the authenticity of the Abhidhamma by citing the fact that according to Atthasalini, the Buddha had already penetrated the Abhidhamma when sitting under the Bodhi tree after attaining Enlightenment. They also considered the profound teachings of the Abhidhamma as the ultimate doctrine which is in the exclusive domain of the omniscient Buddhas and not others (Jayawardhana, 1994), (Bodhi, 1993), (Thera, 1998).

A comparative evaluation of the Abhidhamma and Sutta texts revealed that the Sutta Pitaka too contains a considerable amount of pure Abhidhamma. This comprises all those numerous Suttas and passages where ultimate (paramattha) terms are used, expressing the impersonal (anatta) or functional way of thinking, that is, dealing with the khandhas, dhatus, ayatanas, etc. (Karunadasa, 1989), Karunadasa, 1996).

Even the non-Buddhists, who do not regard the Buddha as an omniscient Enlightened One but recognize him as a great and profound thinker, consider that the Buddha was always aware of the philosophical and psychological implications of his teachings. Though he had the knowledge, but he did not speak of them at the very start and to all his followers apprehending that many would not be able to perceive the inner meanings. The basic teachings of Abhidhamma derive from that highest intuition that the Buddha calls Samma-sambodhi or the Perfect Enlightenment. So, it appears quite credible as well as a reasonable when the old Theravada tradition ascribes the fundamental intuitions and framework of Abhidhamma to the Buddha himself. If one wishes to give a psychological interpretation to that traditional account, one might say that the sojourn in the world of gods may refer to periods of intense contemplation transcending the reaches of an earth-bound mentality; and that from the heights of that contemplation its fundamental teachings were brought back to the world of normal human consciousness and handed over to philosophically gifted disciples like the Venerable Sariputta. However, the exact period of origin of the codified Abhidhamma literature, as we have it at present, is still a matter of speculation due to the unavailability of documentation, sources and facts which fail to provide any definite proof of authentication (Jayawardhana, 1994), (Karunadasa, 1989), (Karunadasa, 1996).

The Abhidhamma teachings, which are extremely condensed in parts, are not merely accepted and transmitted verbally, but that they are carefully examined and contemplated in their philosophical and practical implications. But the most important question is that whether the Abhidhamma is necessary for complete understanding of the Dhamma or for final liberation. Similar to the Sutta Pitaka, where many different methods of practice to the understanding of the same four Truths and to achieve the final goal Nibbana are mentioned, but not all of them are necessary or suitable for every person. It depends on an individual to make a personal choice among these various methods of approach judging the circumstances, inclination and growing maturity. The same holds true for the Abhidhamma both as a whole and in its single aspects and teachings.

One must keep in mind that the Abhidhammic parts of the Sutta Pitaka, namely the teachings given there in ultimate (paramattha) terms, are certainly indispensable for the understanding and practice of the Dhamma. The additional explanations of these teachings given in the Abhidhamma proper may also prove very helpful and necessary in some cases. Though the familiarity with all details of the codified Abhidhamma Pitaka is certainly not a general necessity, but if it is studied then it would surely richly enhance a true understanding of actuality and aid the work of liberation. If suitably presented, the Abhidhamma can also provide a stimulating approach to the Dhamma for philosophical minds. It would prove helpful if it is compensated adequately with the practical aspects of the Dhamma (Jayawardhana, 1994), (Bodhi, 1993), (Thera, 1998). The study of the

Abhidhamma should therefore not be restricted to the mere collecting, counting and arranging of conceptual labels, but should be assimilated deep inside mind to understand essence of truth and see things as truly as they are.

### *Notes and References*


1. Jayawardhana, S. (1994): Handbook of Pali Literature, Karunaratne, Colombo, Sri Lanka.
2. Bodhi, B., ed. (1993): "A Comprehensive Manual of Abhidhamma" in the annotated translation of Abhidhammatthasangaha of Acariya Anuruddha (Buddhist Publication Society, Kandy, Sri Lanka).
3. Thera, N. (1998): "Abhidhamma Studies" in Buddhist Publication Society and Boston (Wisdom Publications, Kandy, Sri Lanka).
4. Thera, N., Hecker, H. (1997): From the Atthasalini, as described in Great Disciples of the Buddha, Wisdom Publications, Somerville.
5. Karunadasa, Y. (2009): The Literature of the Theravada Abhidhamma as a guide to the history of the Abhidhamma Systematization, The Centre of Buddhist Studies, The University of Hong Kong, Hong Kong.
6. Dhammajoti, K.L. (2003): Sarvastivada Abhidhamma, The Centre for Buddhist Studies, Colombo, Sri Lanka.
7. Karunadasa, Y. (1989): Buddhist Analysis of Matter (Second Edition), Buddhist Research Society, Singapore.
8. Karunadasa, Y. (1996): The Dhamma Theory: Philosophical Cornerstone of the Abhidhamma, Buddhist Publication Society, Kandy, Sri Lanka.

15

# A Study of Course of Cognition in Early Buddhist Philosophy

*Bimalendra Kumar*

A *citta-vīthi* is a course of cognition in which a number of consciousness appear.[1] It is broadly of two types, namely, *pañcadvāravīthi* and *manodvāravīthi*. The *pañcadvāravīthi* is a course of cognition which takes place at five doors of senses. Accordingly, it is divided into five types as *cakkhudvāravīthi*, *sotadvāravīthi*, *ghānadvāravīthi*, *jivhādvāravīthi, kāyadvāravīthi*. For functioning of each type of course of cognition, there is a process, which is named after particular door as above. These five types of *vīthis* cognise five types of external objects. The *Manodvāravīthi* is generally of one type so far as the door of its appearance is concerned. The internal or ideational objects are cognised by it.[2]

It can be seen that the full course of cognition at five doors of senses has ten stages, beginning from *Bhavanga* to the *Tadalambana*. The first three stages, namely, *Bhavanga*, *Bhavanga-calana*, *Bhavanga-viccheda* are the preliminaries. Further there are seven types of consciousness which happen to be in this process. Since, the *Javana* is repeated for seven times and the *Tadālambana* twice, there is arising of consciousness (*cittuppāda*) for fourteen times. The three preliminaries involve three thought moments and the fourteen times arising of consciousness (*cittuppāda)* contain fourteen thought-moments, making altogether seventeen thoughts moments to complete the full course of cognitions at five door of senses.[3] In detail, there is the possibility of arising of fifty-four types of *kamāvācara* consciousness with above *vīthis*. It is said:

*vīthi cittāni satteva cittuppāda catuddasa/*
*catupaññāsa vitthārā pañcadvāre yathāraham//*[4]

It is to be noted that the speed of the matter is seventeen times less than that of the mind. The duration of life of a unit of matter is seventeen thought moments. A unit of matter appears as an object in the range of a sense organ and the course of cognition starts. By the time, the mind undergoes changes for seventeen times through different stages, the object remains in the same stage. At the end of seventeen thought moments, the full course of cognition is complete and the duration of the life of the matter also expires. Because, such difference in the speed of the two, there is the possibility of taking place of a course of cognition and thereby understanding of an object.[5] Each small unit of time is called one thought moment (*citta-khana*) having three successive states like arising (*uppāda*), staying (*thiti*), and cessation (*bhanga*). When an object enters in the range of sense organ only one thought moment after its rise, there starts a course of cognition on it. It survives up to the *Tadālambana* stage and completes itself in further sixteen thought moments making seventeen in all. The life-moment of the object also expires at this stage. It is a full course of cognition technically known as *Tadālambana-vāra*. The object is fully cognised. It is called as 'very distinct object' or '*ati mahanta-ālambana*'.[6] Sometimes, the object appears in the range of a sense organ a bit late after it has taken its existence. It happens so because the impression of the object is not very clear. As such it does not survive up to the *tadālambana* stage. It dies out in the middle of he course of cognition immediately after the end of *Javana*-consciousness. The course of cognition is named as *Javana-vāra*.[7] Sometimes, the nature of he object is no doubt determined but neither it is utilized nor the experiences are recorded. In this circumstance, the cognition of the object is feeble. Such an object is called *Paritta ālambana* or slight object. The course of cognition is called *votthapana-vāra*.[8] In this way, the cognition of the object as very distinct, distinct, slight and very slight depends on the variation in survival of the course of cognition.

When any one of the six ideational objects enters into the range of mind, there starts the course of cognition at mind door (*manodvāravīthi*). One cannot harbour in his mind any such object, which is not known. Therefore the stages prior determination does not occur in this course of cognition. Thus, on appearance of the object, there occur four stages like *Bhavanga-calana*, *Manodvāravajjana*, *Javana* and *Tadālambana*. The *Manodvāravajjana* is another name of *votthapana* at five doors of senses. It is at this stage the object is determined. On appearance of an object, the smooth flow of the mind is vibrated and thereafter there arise *manodvāravajjana, Javana* and *Tadālambana cittas* successively. The *Bhavanga-calana* lasts for one thought moment, *manodvāravajjana* for one thought-moment, *Javana* for seven thoughts moments and *Tadālambana* for two thought-moments. The full course of cognition takes eleven thought moments to complete itself. The *Bhavanga-calana* is the preliminary. Since the *javana* repeats itself for seven times, the *tadālambana* twice therefore, there are ten times of arising of consciousness (*cittupādas*). After *Tadālamabana* there is the end of (*bhavangapāta*) of the *vīthi*. With this the object is fully known.[9]

There is the possibility of arising of forty-one types of consciousness in it.[10] There is also variation in understanding of the object at mind-door. When the course of cognition survives up to *Tadālambana*, there is the full course of cognition and thereby, there is the perfect understanding of the object. Sometimes, it survives only upto *Javana*-stage and there is no *Tadālambana*. In such case, the course of cognition is not complete and the understanding of the object is not clear. This sort of variation is due to the type of objects appearing in the course of cognition.

There are two forms of individual objects, which appear at mind-door. They are the 'clear' (*vibhūta*) and 'obscure' (*avibhūta*).[11] If a clear ideational object enters into the range of mind, the cognition starts to know it. It begins with the *Bhavanga-calana* and continues up to the *Talālambana* stage, completing the full course of cognition. In these circumstances, there is the clear understanding. On the other hand, when an obscure ideational object is revived through mind-door, the course of cognition survives upto *Javana* stage. There is no arising of the *Tadālambana*. In this case, the understanding remains completely hazy.

The reason for this difference between sense door and mind door process is apparent. Sense door process is aroused by the stimulus of a sense object and exists only in dependence upon such object. It must then lapse if the object ceases to exist. The same is not the case for mind door process, whose object need not be of the present. The different forms of sense door process are due to variation in the 'duration' of particular stimuli even if we experience this as varying vividness of perception. The two kinds of mind-door process differ because of variation in the clarity of the object, the impulse as it were coming from within. In practice, however, the process, which terminates with the *javana*-stage must be experienced as a lack of perceptual clarity in either case.[12]

The theory of mental processes was well established in the older Sinhalese commentaries prior to ācārya Buddhaghosa and ācārya Buddhadutta. It is mentioned in the *Vipākuddhāra-Kathā* of *Atthasālini*,[13] the commentary of *Dhammasangani*, the first book of *Abhidhamma-Pitaka*. Bhikkhu ñānamoli writes: "An already-formed nucleus of the cognitive series, based on such *Sutta Pitaka* material, appears in the *Abhidhamma-Pitaka*." In support of this statement he cites passages from the *Vibhanga* and the *Patthāna-pakarana*.[14]

In fact, almost all the stages of the course of cognition are precisely specified in the *Patthāna-pakarana*, the last text of *Abhidhamma-pitaka*. The *Patthāna-pakarana* introduces twenty-four types of relation (*paccaya*), which have been illustrated by applying them to the twenty-two *tika-mātikā*, and one hundred *duka-mātikā*. *Citta-vīthi* has been discussed in the *Anantara-paccaya*, which has been defined as a type of relation in which the *paccayadhamma* is the preceding factor and the *paccayuppannadhamma* is the succeeding factor. It has been said in the *Patthana-pakarana*—"*yesnm yesam dhammānam antarā ye ye dhammā uppajjanti citta-cetasikā dhammā te te dhammā tesam tesam dhammānam anantarapaccayena paccayo*".[15] In its commentary, it is said that—a phenomenon which conditions another phenomenon by virtue of its immediate antecedence to the latter is an *Anantarapaccaya*—"*antara-bhāvena upakārako dhammo anantarapaccayo*."[16] For instance, the example of *sampaticchanacitta* and *santīranacitta* may be taken. When *sampaticchanacitta* disappears, just after *santīranacitta* arises. The *cakkhuviññāna*, which is immediately followed by the *manodhātu* also stands to the *manoviññānadhātu*, which immediately follows the former in the same relation—"*cakkhuviññanadhātu tam sampayuttakā ca dhammā manodhātuyā tam sampayuttakānam ca dhammānam anantarapaccayena paccayo. Manodhātu tam sampayuttakā ca dhammā manoviññāṇadhātuyā tam sampayuttakānam ca dhammānam anantarapaccayena paccayo*".[17]

It is said in the *Abhidhammatthavibhāvanī* that the preceding consciousness is able to cause such states of consciousness, as are similar to its own, to succeed in the immediately following instant (*attano anurūpacittuppādajananasamatthā*).[18] In the *Patthāna-pakarana*, the distinction between *manodvāravīthi* and *pañcadvāravīthi* has been made, although those terms are not used. Each of the separate functions is shown. This is best illustrated from the sense door process. *Bhavanga* is known by name, but that name is only used where it is needed to avoid ambiguity. In cases where the same statement can be accurately applied both to *javana*, and to *bhavanga* the two stages are subsumed as 'aggregates' or they may be distinguished as 'skilful aggregates' and 'resultant aggregates'. The theory of *bhavanga* is however fully developed. The *ahetuka kiriya citta* with *upekkha are termed as pañcadvāravajjana*. The succeeding sense consciousness are termed the five consciousnesses and succeeded by resultant wind element (*vipāka manodhātu*), which in turn followed by resultant mind consciousness element with either neutral or pleasant feeling. After this comes *kiriyā* mind consciousness element with neutral feeling. Apart from the last each of these lasts for only one moment.

The *Patthāna-pakarana* itself envisages only that *karmically* active stage arise and persist for a while. It does not specify seven moments as the maximum duration. It certainly envisages a return to a resultant consciousness. This may be one under the influence of the active aggregates, which have just subsided or it may be one of a more long lasting kind.

Thus, it can be presumed that the theory of course of cognition was well established in the *Patthāna-pakarana* the last text of *Abhidhamma-Pitaka* and it was not the outcome of the commentaries (*atthakathās)* written by Buddhaghosa and Buddhadutta. It is a unique contribution of Abhidhamma philosophy. By this theory of course of cognition (*citta-vīthi*), movement and action of the mind may be understood or variation in the understanding of the object may be known.

## Notes and References

1. Kosambi '*Vīthi iti citta paramparā*'—*Abhidhammatthasangaho Navanīta tīkā* (Ed.) Dharmananda, Varanasi, 1964, p. 68.
2. '*Cakkhudvāre pavatta vīthicitta paramparā cakkhudvāravīthi-tyādinā dvāravasena, cakkhuviññānasambandhinīi vīthi tena saha ekarammana—ekadvarikattāya sahacaranabhāvato cakkhuviññānatyādinā viññānavasena vā vīthinam nāmayojanā kātabbā ti dassetum cakkhudvāravīthityādi vuttam*'—*Abhidhammatthavibhāvanī tīkā* (Ed.) Ram Shankar Tripathi, Varanasi, p. 105.
3. *Ibid.*, p. 95.
4. *Abhidhimmatthasangaho Navanītatīkā*, op. cit., p. 81.

5. *'Uppādatthitibhangavasena khanattayam eka-cittakhanam nāma. Tāni pana sattarasa citta-khanāni rūpadhammānam āyu'*—Ibid., p. 88
6. *Abhidhimmatthasangaho*, p. 316
7. *Ibid.*, p. 318.
8. *Ibid.*, p. 321.
9. *'manodvāre pana yadi vibhūtamārammanam apāthamāgacchati, tatoparam bhavangalatmana manodvārāvajjanajavanāvasāne tadārammanapākāni pavattanti, tatoparam bhavangapāto. Avibhūte panārammane javanavasane bhavangapato va hoti, natthi tadārammanuppādo ti'*, *—Abhidhammatthasangaho Navanītatīkā, op. cit.*, p. 72
10. *'vīthi cittanitīneva cittuppada daseritā, vitthārena panetthekacattālisam vibhāvaye'* – *Ibid.*, p. 62.
11. *'Atimahantam, mahantam, parittam, atiparittañceti pañcadvāre manodvāre pana vibhūta avibhūtañceti chadhā visayappavati veditabbā'—Abhidhammatthasangaho, op. cit.*, p. 289.
12. *Cf.* L.S. Cousins, "The Patthāna and the Development of the Theravadin Abhidhamma", *Journal of Pali Text Society*, vol. IX, 1981, pp. 22-46.
13. *Atthasālini* (Ed.) Ram Shankara Tripathy, Varanasi, 1989, pp. 380-391.
14. *Cf.* ñānamoli Bhikkhu, *The Path of Purification* (*Visuddhimagga*), Reprinted. The Corporate Body of the Buddha Educational Foundation, Taipei, Taiwan, pp. 131-132.
15. *Patthāna-pakarana*, vol. I (Ed.) Bhikshu J. Kashyap, Nalanda, 1961, p. 5.
16. *Pathāna-atthakathā*, (Ed.) Mahesh Tiwary, Nalanda, 1972, p. 72.
17. *Patthāna-pakarana*, vol. I, *op. cit.*, p. 4.

16

# Buddhist Stotra Tradition

*Anirban Dash*

न गतं नागतं स्तुत्वा सुगतं गतिवर्जितम्।
तेन पुण्येन लोकोऽयं व्रजतां सौगतीं गतीम्॥[1]

(Having praised the Sugata who has neither gone nor come and who is without any movement, may all the sentient beings attain the state of the Sugata)

The term 'stotra' is derived from the root *stuñ* by adding the suffix *stran*. In the *Amarakośa*, we come across three synonyms of stotra: *stava*, *stuti* and *nuti*.[2]

Hymns of praise and collections of more or less separate eulogistic stanza have been composed in all the religious traditions whether theistic or atheistic.

The stotra genre is the expression of devotion and adoration towards a personal guru or various deities representative of the ultimate reality. This tradition of poetic composition has an unbroken history from the time of the *sukta* hymns of the *Ṛg Veda* up to the present expressions of various Bhakti movements.

The *Matsya purāṇa* offers a classification of four types of stotra: *dravyastotram*, *karmastotram*, *vidhistotram* and *abhijanastotram*[3]. Particularly, the category of *karma stotras,* seems to be readily applicable to Buddhist stotra literature, but a deeper analysis reveals that this is not the case. The remarkable aspect of the vast body of Buddhist Sanskrit stotras is the presence of a confessional form of composition wherein the poet reveals his or her own limitations in a kind of psychological self-analysis. Written with all the tenderness of raw emotion and sentiment, Buddhist stotras are rich in human insight and in the acuity of self-awareness. According to Buddhist systems of spiritual development, an individual cannot be successful in *sādhanā*, or practice, without the purification of consciousness. This path of purity, or *viśudhimārga,* involves an integral approach, the combination of the contemplative and reflective aspect of practice with a code of practical conduct. What is to be purified is the relative aspects of consciousness, in which there is an apparent separation between the practitioner and the ultimate reality appearing in the forms of Buddhas and Boddhisattvas. Buddhist stotras are precisely the expression of the path that transcends relative consciousness and leads to the discovery of the ultimate nature, which is, of course, Buddha-nature. Buddhist stotras take a form often similar to the *karma stotras*, offering praises to the deeds of Buddhas and Bodhisattvas.

## Origin of Buddhist Stotras Tradition

It seems that the Buddhist stotra literature begins in the Mahayana tradition. But There is some poetry found in Pāli literature also such as Telakataha Gāthā, Pajjamadhu, Jinacarita, Jinālamkara etc. but they are not in the form of stotra and at the same time, these are from the Sinhali tradition and their dates are much later than the 10th century A.D.

In the Māhayāna tradition, the imaginative approach to the Buddha is quite strikingly different. Followers of the Mahāyāna course uphold that, there are many Buddhas. Gauttama Buddha was one of them. He took birth in a human form as a protector of, and a bestower of loving kindness to, all creatures. This gradual perspective is distinct in its devotional approach to the Buddha and the Stotra form of composition emerges directly from such a view.

One can speculate that the change in Buddhist imagination - and hence in its literature - occurred, at least in part, due to the influence of Vedic religion and a post Vedic Hinduism in India. From the Mahāyāna point of view, the archetypal and imaginative figure of the 'Boddhisattva' is very important. The 'Boddhisattva' is not simply the form of Buddha but an embodiment of a universal power or principle which ever seeks the welfare of all sentient beings. From the Māhayāna point of view, the ending of suffering for all sentient beings is more important than personal enlightenment. This focus on the remarkable figure of the 'Bodhisattva' as an agent of human salvation inspired many Stotras. In this regard, the origin of Hindu Stotras and Buddhist Stotras tradition is virtually similar.

In the beginning of Tantra tradition (6th Century A.D.) a tremendous change happened in Buddhist stotra literature. As we know each Tantra has their personal deity. There are also many mandalas in the Tantric texts. Many god and goddess have their own dwelling place in each mandalas So to praise the deities numerous stotras have composed.

During his visit to India in the 7th century A.D., a Chinese Monk, Itsang, observes that 'in Western India the monks were doing their daily Puja making circles around the Stupa and chanting some Storas with proper accent and tunes'. These chanted Stotras described the many noble qualities of the Buddha. Each of the Stotras contained as many as 10 to 20 verses. It shows that the stotra tradition was the living tradition during that period.

## Stotras in Sūtra Texts (Buddhavachana)

The oldest form of Buddhist stotras is found in the Mahāyāna sūtra texts i.e. **'Buddhavachana'** in different contexts. i.e. Gandṇavyuha, Mahāvastu, Lalitavistara, Saddharmapuṇḍarīka, Samādhirājasutra, Raṣtapālaparipṛcchā, Suvarṇaprabhāsa and Sukhavatīvyuha etc.

Raṣṭapālaparipṛcchā sūtra[4] : In this sutra it is described that the Buddha was once on the mountain Grdhrakuta in the midst of a company of monks and Boddhisatvas, and used to deliver discourses to them on the law. Among the Boddhsisattvas sitting around him, there was one named Prāmodyaraja who stood up and with folded hands recited a hymn in the praise of the Buddha and stood silent after the recitation. There are 353 stanzas in variety of meters. Dodhaka meter is frequently used.

दरिद्रभूतस्य कुरुष्व संग्रहं बद्धस्य मोक्षं कुरु मेऽद्य नाथ।
ससंशयेभ्यो विमर्ति च छिन्द चर्या च मे व्याकुल बोधिमार्गे॥

Suvarṇaprabhāsa sutra[5] : The fifth chapter 'Kamalākarasarvatathāgata stavaparivarta contains hymns of all the Budhas which pass under the name of Kamalakara. A king named Suvarṇabhujendra extolled the spiritual majesty of all the Buddhas (atīta, anāgata and pratyutpanna) by recite them.

शान्तप्रशान्तविशुद्धमुनीन्द्रं सुवर्णवर्णप्रभासितगात्रम्।
सर्वसुरासुरसुस्वर बुद्धं बह्मस्ते स्वरगर्जितीषम्॥

Lalitavistara[6] : In the 23 chapter i.e. 'samstavaparivarta' 11 gods[7] praise Buddha on his enlightenment and request his to preach his new faith to the world.

उत्पन्नो लोकप्रद्याते लोकनाथः प्रभंकरः।
अन्धभूतस्य लोकस्य चक्षुर्दाता रणंजहः॥

Samādhirājasutra[8] : Another name of this sutra is chandrapradīpa sutra. There is stotra entitled 'aryachandrapradipasutra stuti' having 12 verses. It deals with the praising of the subject matter of Samādhirāja. Editor has mentioned this stotra in the Appendix of the same text so it is very difficult to trace that the stotra is the part of the main text or not.

अनिरोधमनुत्पन्नमनविलमनक्षरम्
महायानमहं स्तोष्ये बुद्धज्ञानाभि वाञ्छया॥ १॥
त्राणकं सर्वसत्वानां रात् संसारसागरात्।
संस्थापकं च निर्वाणे शान्ते क्षेमे निरुत्तरे॥ २॥

Saddharmapuṇḍarīka sūtra[9] : In the 24th chapter of Saddharmapuṇḍarīka sūtra there are also stotras praising of Avalokitesvara.

आश्चर्यभूतो जिन अप्रमेयो उत्पन्न लोकस्मि हितानुकम्पी।
नाथोऽसि शास्तासि गुरुसि जातो अनुगृहीता दशिमा दिशोऽद्य॥

Sukhavatīvyuha[10] : In this sutra the Monk Ānanda Dharmākara praise the Buddha with 12 stanzas.

अमितप्रभ अनन्ततुल्यबुद्धे न च इह प्रभा विभाति काचित्।
सूर्यमणिगिरीशचन्द्र आभा न तपित भोसिषु एभि सर्वलोके॥

## Buddhist Stotras in Ka-gyur & Tan-gyur collections

List of 315 Stotras is found in both collections. Subject wise classifications of these stotras are:

### *Ka-gyur*

18 Stotras related to Tantra. Some of the stotras are: Devīkāliprasamsārājatantram, Rogādhipatistotram, Lokastotrapūjākalpamūlatantra.

14 Stotras inside the chapter of Tantric Texts. Some are: Pancatathagata-stuti the 10th chapter in the text of Mañjuśrījñānasatvasya paramārthanāmasamgitī, Stutiparivarta 29th chapter and 30th chapter Sadvijnanastuti is found in the Srijnanatilakayoginitantrarajaparamamahadbhutam nama.

5 Stotras are found in Sūtras texts. Some are: 9th chapter i.e. stutiparivarta is in Arya-astasahasrikaprajnaparamita and Bhagavadratnasamcayagatha.

### *Tan-gyur*

124 Stotras are related to Tantra texts. Some are: Hevajra-stotram of Ratnavajra, Āryatārākurukulla-stotram of Dombiheruka, Vajradaka-stotradandaka-nama of Dharmakirti, aryatarasragdhara-stotram of Sarvajnamitra. Vajravarahitarastotram.

16 Stotras are found inside the commentaries of Tantric Texts. Some are Hevajrapiṇḍārtha Tīkawritten by Ānandagarbha on the text of Hevajratantra. In the beginning there is a stotra namely Kamaeva-stuti. There is commentaries of Advayavajra namely Nāmasamgityupasamhāravitarka on Namasamgiti. Two stotras are found in chapter of 5 and 9 i.e. aarsajnanastuti and panncajnanastutipinartha.

133 stotras are related to Sutra texts. Some are Dharmadhatustava of Nagarjuna, Mahakala-stotram of Vararuchi, Chakrasamvara-stotram of Maitripada.

5 Stotras also found inside the commentaries of Sūtra texts. Some are: there is stotra in chapter nine of Abhisamayalamkara written by Haribhadra on Arya-astasahasrika-prajnaparamita.

At present Buddhist stotras are available in three different forms. 1. Root copies are available in both Sanskrit and Tibetan languages. 2. Root copies are available in Tibetan language only; the Sanskrit copy is lost 3. Root copies are available in Sanskrit language only and the Tibetan translation has not been done.

Beside these there is stotras translated Chinese language also. Some storas are found in Taiso Tripiṭaka. Root copy in Sanskrit language is not available. We do not have much information about the author and time of these stotras. I found there are some stotras in the Catalogue of Buddhist Tripitaka of Bunyiu Nanjio (Published Royal Asiatic Society, Great Britain 1993.) Such as : Manjusri-nama-samgiti and Bhadracaripranidhana.

## Stotras Compiled by Buddhist Acharyas

There are numerous Buddhist stotras found with unknown author. It is very difficult to trace the date etc.

**Nāgārjuna:** (150-250 A.D.) There are 19 stotras ascribed to Nāgārjuna. Such as Dharmadhatustava, Nirupamastava, Lokatitastava, Cittavajrastava, Paramarthastava,

Kayatraya-stotra nama, Satvarahanastava etc. From philosophical point of view Chatustava[11] of Nagarjuna is very famous.

**Ashvagosha:** (1st A.D.)Two Stotras are ascribed to Asvaghosa namely Śatapañcāśat nāma stotra and Gaṇḍī stotra.[12] This Sanskrit text is a small poem with 29 stanzas composed mostly in sragdhara metre. It is a hymn in praise of Gaṇḍī, the Buddhist monastery gong, consisting of a long symmetrical piece of wood; the theme of the poem is the religious message which its sound is supposed to carry when beaten with a short wooden club.

**Matṛcheṭa:** (1st -2nd A.D.) Matṛcheṭa has ascribed to his credit some twelve works.

Famous of his works are Chatu-sataka, Misraka-stotra, Satapancasat and arghyardhasataka. They are praised by the Chinese pilgrim 'Yi- tsing' who spent 671-690 A.D. in India for whom Matṛcheṭa is a famous poet. He writes that those who wants to be a monk they should learn Chatu-sataka and arghyardhasataka. The other name of the Chatu-sataka is Varnarharnavastotra[13] (13 chapters).

**Asaṅga:** (3rd -4th Century A.D.) Dharmakayasrayasamanyaguna-stotram

**Vasubandhu:** (4th -5th Century A.D.) Triratna-stotra ?

**Dharmakirti:** (6th Century A.D.) Buddhaparinirvana-stotram is ascribed to Dharmakirti.[14]

**Chandrakrīti:** (7th Century A.D.) Madhyamakaśāstra-stuti is ascribed to Chandrakrīti. He praises the Madhyamakaśāstra[15] in 14 verses.

**Sarvajñamitra** (8th Century A.D): Tārā-sragdhara-stotram is scribed to Sarvajñamitra. The hymn in sragdhara meter in praise of Arya Tārā in thirty seven verses. As many 96 Buddhist stotras related to Tārā are found in different stotra catalogue.

**Virupada:** Vajrayoginipindartha-stotra, Vajrayogini-stuti-pranidhana

King Harsavardhana (647 A.D.) who under the influence of Chinese Pilgrim Hsuen-Tsang, learned more and more deeply the Buddhism during his last years of his life and composed a Suprabhata-stotra[16], a morning Hymn in praise of Buddha in 24 verses. The poet Vajradatta who lived under the King Devapala (900 A.D.) author of Lokesvara-sataka, the hundred stanza praise of Buddha, Poet become a leaper owing to a curse, he implored lokesvara i.e. Avalokitesvata to help him. But of these the numerous stotras are invoked one after another.

## Tradition of Commentaries

Beside these stotras there are also Commentaries written by different authors. Such as

List of Stotras with Commentaries:

1. Devatishaya-stotra with Comm. by Prajñāvarman
2. Viśeṣa-stava with Comm. by Prajñāvarman
3. Kāyatraya-stotra with Vivaraṇa by Nāgārjuna
4. Sragdharā-stotra[17] by Sarvajñamitra and Comm. by Jinarakṣita

5. Śatapañcāśatka-nāma-stotra by Ashvagoṣa: Comm. by Nandipriya
6. Guṇaparyanta-stotra by Triratna Dasa Comm. Diṅnāga
7. Deśanā-stava by Chandragomin and Comm. Buddhaśānti
8. Srīvajradharasamgītibhagavat-stotra with Comm. by Śāntarakṣita.

**Concussion:** It is well known that stotra literature is a seminal and integral form of ancient Sanskrit literature. Buddhist Sanskrit stotras in particular are often inserted into larger sûtras, the ideas of which they tend to summarize in poetic form. Although the Buddhist Sanskrit stotras comprise a vast area of study, they have been largely unexplored by modern Indian as well as Western scholarship. Some individual stotras have been translated into Indian and Western languages, but no comprehensive study of the Buddhist Sanskrit stotras has been made to date.

### *Notes and References*

1. Verse: 11 Pramārtha-stava by Nāgārjuna
2. *Amarakośa* 1.6. 11
3. Published in Mahayana sutra Samgraha, p. 152 Verse - 292
4. Published from Mithila Vidyapitha, Darbhanga ed. By S. Bagchi p. 24-29
5. Lalitavistara, Mithila Vidyapitha, Darbhanga ed. P. L. Vaidya
6. Suddhavasikayika devaputra, abhasvaradevaputra and brahmakayika deva etc. p. 250
7. Samadhirajasutra, Mithila Vidyapitha, Darbhanga ed. P.L. Vaidya
8. Saddharmapunnḍarīka sūtra, Mithia Vidyapitha, Darbhanga ed. P. L. Vaidya p. 109
9. Sukhavatīvyuha: Mahayana Sutra Samgraha ed. P. L. Vaidya, p. 223
10. Lokatitastava, Achintyastava, Niraupamyastava and Paramartha-satava, Tibetan translation (1914 French Translation by La Vallee Poussin)
11. (Śatapañcāśat nāma stotra: 1910, Fragment edited by Levi, Sylvain; 1916, edited with English Translation by Horenel A. F. Rudolf) There are 13 chapters with mostly sragdhara metre. (Gaṇḍī Stotra: 1913, Edited the Tibetan, Chinese, Russian version by Stael-Holstein, Alexander Von; 1933, restored; English Translation by Johnston, Edward Hamilton).
12. (Varnarharnavastotra: 1905, ed. English Translation by Thomas, Frederick William)
13. (Buddhaparinirvana-stotram : 1973, German Translation by Steinkellner)
14. Published in Baudha-stotra samgraha, Motilal Banarasi,
15. (Suprabhata-stotra: 1888, edited and Russian Translation by Minayeff, Ivan Pavlovitch. 1906: ed. French Translation by Ettinghausen, Maurice Leon
16. (Kāyatraya-stotra: 1896, ed. restored; Chinese Translation; French, Translation. (reprint in Sino-Indian Studies 1945: 108-110)
17. German translation of the Sarvajna-mahesvara-stotra-nama found in Hahn, Michael, *Das Saptamaithunasamyuktasutra, ein Sutra des Ekottarikagama,* Waldschmidt Festschrift (80), p.205-224.

17

# Ecology and its Identity on the Basis of Buddhist Literature and Religion

*Projit Kumar Palit*

The word 'Ecology' signifies the study of human beings, animals and plants in connection with environment. "Ecology deals with the interrelationships of organisms and their environment". So Ecology is a comprehensive term and means physical ecology, mental ecology, social ecology, environmental ecology and above all cosmic ecology, each depending upon the other for survival. A cosmic harmony at the macro and micro levels is tended to formulate a principle of symmetry at the heart of everything. Ecology awareness with scientific experimentation thereby begins. Ecology refers to the harmony in various statuses with interactions of multiple forces in a particle and an antiparticle of the universe. And that harmony prevails on our earth and beyond.

The word 'nature' means everything which is not organized and constructed by man.. It is described as Pakati in Pali and Prakati in Sanskrit. Ancient Indian society ruled out any dichotomy between man and nature. Man and nature are not two separate entitles but are two halves at one circle, man lives in nature and nature to some extent lives in man. Both are parts of the cosmos. The word dhammata and niyama are used in Pali literature as 'natural law on way'. The Vedic risis also drew up a universal law of harmony, known as 'rtam' by which is guided universe. It means a righteous path by which everything in the cosmos moves on. Since everything moves in the right path there is hardly any apprehension of one's causing harm to the other. Any in-balance anywhere is bound to affect this harmony. It provides a sense of security for all the members of the universe resulting in a balance between the whole universes. Hence any undue or untoward activity, either mental or physical, which has been called 'anrta', the antithesis, 'rta' is bound to affect this harmony. Man is a very small part of the cosmos, must be in perfect balance with the whole of it. This is what is known as 'ecological balance' in modern age.

Sakyaputra Gautama appeared as a Buddha in the later Vedic age, when ecological problem as now in the grow, was not known, but the Buddha with deep insight and long experience realized that any physical or mental disbalance of an individual would cause harm to the environment around him. This may speak on the society in which he lives and ultimately may result into the lack at balance in the world and then in the whole universe. So the Buddha laid down rules of conduct for individual (who is the focal point of this 'eco' of home, the natural habitat including man and animal, animate and the inanimate), both for the house holder and recluse. According to Buddhism, changeability is one of the perennial principles of nature. Everything formed is in a constant process of change (sabbe sankhara anicca). Though change in inherent in nature, Buddhism believes that natural processes are affected by the morals of man. If, there is moral deterioration in a man, it accelerates the process of change and brings about changes which are adverse to human well being and happiness. Thus, Buddhism maintains that there is a close link between man's morals and the natural resources available to him.

But western thought and western ethical theories in particular have tended to begin with some notion of the person as an autonomous, rational individual.But the Buddhist conception of ethical agency is that it posits a notion of the self that is both dynamic and developmental. The important key features of Buddhist thought present a radically different notion of the ethical self which is challenges western assumptions of both rationality and autonomy. Buddhist ethics and soteriology do indeed require a significant integrity or rationality of personal identity, yet that identity or individuality of the self is seen as a dynamic karmic continuity rather than as an essential ontological substantiality-as an ongoing *process* rather than an underlying *thing*.

The Buddha was much more concerned to characterize the nature of the self in terms of its end or purpose than in terms of its original cause, seeing the latter question as one of those "unanswerable" (*avyaakṛta*) questions that are not conducive to the task at hand, namely the realization of one's potential for enlightenment and the elimination of suffering. Both these features of the Buddhist conception of the self, the dynamic and the developmental, have significant implications for the relationship of that self to the rest of existence including nature and the environment. But before considering these implications, we must first explore more carefully how Buddhists have traditionally framed their understanding of the self.

The Buddha's teachings was the notion of the non-substantiality of the self, the doctrine referred to in the Pali scriptures *as anattaa* (Sanskrit: *anaatman*) and usually rendered in English as the view of "no-self" or "non-self."

The notion of absolute "self" (*aatman* or *jiiva*) lying at the core of personal identity was one of the central themes of the diverse Upanishadic speculations characteristic of the Age of the Wanderers into which the Buddha was born.While other thinkers of this period also challenged the notion of an essential or substantial self, the Buddha's rejection of an *aatman* was unique in that, unlike the skeptics and materialists of his day, he simultaneously maintained a notion of ethical or karmic continuity, one that persisted not just throughout the life of the individual, but over multiple lifetimes as well. Indeed the Buddha went so far as to assert that his notion of "no-self" was actually necessary to sustain any theory of ethical continuity and efficacy over time. Those among contemporaries of the Buddha who accepted the continuity of karmic efficacy over time felt that it would be quite impossible without a substantial and immutable essence or *aatman* to which the karmic accretions could accrue. If there was no *aatman*, they reasoned, there was nothing that would hold together the series of lives (or even moments within a life for that matter).According the Upanishadic notion about *aatman*- or soul was a virtually everywhere assumption. Yet the Buddha asserted that the supposition of such a idea of essential self-hood was as false as it was unnecessary. He did indeed recognize the necessity of securing the integrity of karmic efficacy, but he felt that positing an essential *aatman* was too high a price to ensure the continuity of the self, a price not only unwarranted, but even detrimental to attaining the esoteric goal as he understood it. The liberation he had realized was, in his view, so utterly transformative, that it could only be obstructed by clinging to any view of a "self," especially one that posited a core or essence that was not subject to change-and hence not subject to transformation. The integrity of personal identity and of ethical efficacy, required not some substantial permanence, he asserted, but only the continuity of the karmic conditioning itself. Here in lies the root of the Buddhist conception of the self, and we can understand the Buddhist idea of how the self is related to its environment only if we fully appreciate the implications of this conception of the self.

According to Buddhism, changeability is one of the perennial principles of nature. Everything formed is in a constant process of change (sabbe sankhara anicca). Though change in inherent in nature, Buddhism believes that natural processes are affected by the morals of man. If, there is moral deterioration in a man, it accelerates the process of change and brings about changes which are adverse to human well being and happiness. Thus, Buddhism maintains that there is a close link between man's morals and the natural resources available to him. This assertion of a cosmic "principle of self-transcendence" as the contemporary Buddhist philosopher Sangharakshita has termed it is one that might well be challenged, to be sure, yet it is one that has remained clear throughout the history of Buddhism. Once we see that Buddhahood is the teleological goal, not just of human existence, but of all sentient existence, we begin to see that the "human self" must be viewed in a much broader perspective. Not only must it be seen as dynamic and developmental; it is by its very nature a being—or rather a *becoming*—that is thus fundamentally trans-human. The Buddhist conception of personal or individual identity, we must now consider the broader cosmological stage upon which the drama of the dynamic and developmental self is played out, for it is this context that brings out the trans-human nature of the self that lies at the heart of this tradition. It is thus not at all inaccurate to describe this system as a Buddhist theory of evolution, as long as we are careful to not to overlook how it differs significantly from the currently prevailing views of biological evolution in the West. While Buddhism recognizes a hierarchy of biological complexification at the level of species, its evolutionary interests focus ultimately on the individual, that is to say on the separate karmic life streams that make their way up the ladder of sentience to reach the point where enlightenment and liberation from the cycle become possible. This process is not only teleological (though not theistic) in a way that most evolutionary biologists would reject, it locates the significant development in awareness or consciousness rather than in biological structure, although the latter are seen as evolutionary expressions of the developing consciousness. The traditional Buddhist approach to recognizing moral consideration for other individuals will necessarily proceed quite differently, whether that consideration is extended to other humans or to other species. Rather than reifying the prevailing sense of an autonomous self-interested individual with its complement of rights, Buddhism seeks to transform the very way which the individual conceives of himself. Traditionally, Buddhist "environmental ethics" has thus been less a matter identifying and securing rights. Rather it has been much more a matter of undertaking a practice of affirming and eventually realizing the trans-human potential for enlightenment. Based as it is in cultivating an ever deeper insight into the trans-species mutuality of sentience and hence potential for enlightenment, Buddhist practice can only express itself as a compassionate, environmental sustaining altruism. Shantideva expresses this eloquently: Just as the body, with its many parts from division into hands and other limbs, should be protected as a single entity, so too should this entire world which is divided [into parts], yet not divided in its nature to suffer and be happy....I should dispel the suffering of others because it is suffering like my own suffering. I should help others too because of their nature as beings, which is like my own being. It has become common place to assert that Buddhism locates the individual in profound inter-relationship with the rest of sentient existence, and ultimately with all of the ecosphere. Most frequently this is argued rather vaguely as an extension of the first Buddhist ethical precept of non-injury or, in a philosophically more sophisticated manner, as an implication of the Mahayana doctrine of emptiness understood as a variety of non-dualism that entails compassionate activity towards all other beings (and the environment that sustains them). This understanding of the emptiness doctrine asserts that, if all things are seen as empty of intrinsic existence, then all things must be seen as interrelated, and the only possible course of action becomes one that seeks to compassionately sustain all of existence.

The "Mahaaparinibbaa.na-sutta" of the *Diigha Nikaaya* relates the Buddha's travels during the final months of his life, a time when he appears to have been particularly concerned to summarize all of his various teachings in terms of a concise and systematic practice. As he traveled from town to town visiting communities of his followers for the last time the most frequently recurring theme of his discourses was the threefold course of training consisting in the cultivation of ethical conduct, meditation and wisdom. This concise formulation of Buddhist praxis is especially useful for our purposes because it clearly stresses the developmental nature of the path. Thus one might well cultivate all three components from the outset of one's practice, the developmental point being that it is only when ethical conduct is firmly established that meditation becomes truly effective, and only through the integrative effect of meditation that the truly transformative power of wisdom becomes possible. The threefold training of Buddhism is the cultivation of greater cognitive and affective concentration or integration, through the practice of meditation. This is the phase of the path in which the Buddha felt humans could begin to develop well beyond the normal human tendencies toward greed, hatred and delusion. The discipline of meditation must necessarily be initially undertaken in a sheltered, isolated environment free from the usual distractions, yet the goal is to cultivate a greater facility of mind and positive emotion that eventually permeates all aspects of one's life. Buddhist meditation in not done for the experience during the meditation session itself, but rather for the transformative effect it has cumulatively.This basic threefold practice elaborated in somewhat more detail in another prominent teaching of the Buddha's last days, the doctrine of the seven factors of enlightenment: mindfulness (*sati*), discrimination of principles (*dhamma-vicaya*), energy in pursuit of the good (*virya*), rapture (*piiti*), tranquility (*passaddhi*), concentration (*samaadhi*), and equanimity (*upekkhaa*). Here we are clearly dealing with the successive cultivation of a set of areteic virtues, specific qualities requisite to the mode of existence no longer constrained by an overly self-referential notion of personal identity. A passage in the *Sa.myutta Nikaaya* that treats these seven in greater detail makes clear the developmental nature of the sequence: "When a monk, thus remaining secluded, recollects and reasons about the doctrine, he initiates the mindfulness factor of enlightenment, which he then develops and perfects. Remaining thus mindful, he discriminates, reflects on and investigates with understanding that doctrine, thus initiating the discrimination of principles factor of enlightenment, which he then develops and perfects...."; and so on until each of the seven is perfected. It is worth also drawing attention to the fact that there is significant emphasis in this list on the process of cognitive and affective refinement in that the fourth through seventh factors are also specific faculties central to the theory of Buddhist meditation. And this point becomes even more evident if we take up the still further elaborated version of the path found in the *Sa.myutta Nikaaya* passage that presents a progressive twelve fold path to enlightenment as an alternative to the reiterative twelve fold cycle of samsaric existence.So far the basic Buddhist doctrines common to all schools of Buddhism, and this has been intentional because there is a characteristically Buddhist approach to trans-human ethical consideration that is part of the core tradition. Yet another source used quite prominently in teaching Buddhist morality in all traditional Buddhist cultures is the collection of *Jaataka* tales, popular fables that recount the earlier lives of the Buddha when he was training as a *bodhisattva* or Buddha-to-be. A central theme of these widely read stories is the list of key virtues perfected by the Buddha during the course of his training, a theme that subsequently became a central pillar of the Buddhist revitalization movement known as the Mahayana. The *Jaataka* list of bodhisattva virtues included generosity, ethical conduct, renunciation, wisdom, energy or enthusiasm (in pursuit of the good), patience or forbearance, truthfulness, resolution, and loving-kindness. And perfections of the *Jaatakas* overlap substantially, in turn, with the six or ten perfections comprising the bodhisattva ideal in Mahayana Buddhism. It is particularly important to stress this continuity in the tradition here, because accounts of the Buddhist perspective on environmental concerns often stress only the Mahayana notion of the interrelatedness of all things, without indicating the extent to which this view is derived from the earlier aspects of basic Buddhism. The

Buddha taught his disciples to have "compassion on all creatures" and "never to destroy the life of any living creature, however tiny it might be." The Karaniyameta Sutta enjoins the practice of metta (loving kindness) towards all creatures, timid and bold, short and long, small and big, minute and great invisible and visible, near and far, awaiting birth and born. While a cattle-butcher is punished for "many hundred thousands of year in purgatory" and layperson is expected to abstain from trading in meat, the Buddhist monks and nuns are to follow an even stricter code so that living creatures are not harmed even unintentionally. Thus the Buddhist tradition advocates fervently against killing and destruction of life in any form. Not even "for the sake of sustaining life would we intentionally deprive any being of life", said the Buddha.

The contemporary Buddhist samgha did realise the intensity of the crisis, a point illustrated by the perception of its nature in the commentary on the Chakkavattisimhanada Sutta. Explaining the pattern of mutual interaction between moral degeneration and environmental degradation, it says, "When humanity is demoralised through greed, famine is the natural outcome; when moral degeneration is due to ignorance, epidemic is the inevitable result; when hatred is the demoralizing force, widespread violence is the ultimate outcome." It echoes the spirit of the Kaliyuga crisis and the consequent transition in Indian history when it adds, "If and when humanity realizes that large-scale devastation has taken place as a result of its moral decline, a change of heart takes place among the few surviving human beings. As morality is renewed, conditions improve through a long period of cause and effect and humanity again starts to enjoy gradually increasing prosperity and longer life." The renewal of morality in a way tantamounts to readjusting the existing pattern of resource use in such a way as to accord centrality to the dual principles of conservation and minimum exploitation of nature.

### *Notes and References*


1. Steven Collins, *Selfless Persons : Imagery and Thought in Theravada Buddhism*, (Cambridge & New York : Cambridge University Press, 1982).
2. Chitkara, M.G.: Encyclopaedia of Buddhism: A World faith. Vol.4: Buddhism and Environment, New Delhi, 2000.
3. "The Bodhisattva: Evolution and Self-Transcendence" Sangharakshita (1983), republished in *The Priceless Jewel*, (Glasgow: Windhorse Publications, 1993).
4. Narayanan, Rajdeva: Ecology and Religion, New Delhi, 2004.
5. Warder, A.K.: Indian Buddhism, Delhi, 1980.
6. Pathak, S.K.: Buddhism and Ecology, New Delhi, 2004.
7. Pandey, K.C.: Ecological Perspectives in Buddhism, New Delhi, 2008.
8. Karmondy, Edward John: Concept of Ecology, Portland, 1996.
9. Yoganaka, S.N.: Dharmajyoti, Bombay, 1994.
10. *Sa.myutta Nikaaya*, 5 vols. (London: Pali Text Society, 1884-98; rpt.) Trans. by C.A.F. Rhys Davids and F.L. Woodward as *Kindred Sayings* (London: Pali Text Society, 1917-30; rpt.)
11. *AA'nguttara Nikaaya*, 5 vols. (London: Pali Text Society, 1885-1900; rpt.) Trans. by F.L. Woodward and Hare as *Gradual Sayings* (London: Pali Text Society, 1932-36; rpt.)

18

# Medico-historical Account of Fruits of Buddhist India

*H. D. Khobragade*

The Buddha is (also) known as the Bhesajjaguru (Master of Medicine). The term, 'Healer' is for Tathāgata. He was the healer of body and mind. He was aware of the viscera. He had observed complete body. He has also stated as to how the body is made up of different elements and how the fruit intake is necessary for the development of a body.

The Buddha had sanctioned medicinal herbs which include fruits to the Order to provide freedom from pains so that it could preserve health to practise the life of purity after warding off sensations of pains and afflictions.

There were renowned physicians and surgeons like Jīvaka Komārabhacca who had performed even major operations and had prescribed medicinal fruits for their patients. He was the famous royal physician and surgeon who was advised to treat the Buddha, His Order and the lay disciples. He treated the people of Magadha suffering from even the then dangerous diseases like leprosy, boils, eczema, consumption and epilepsy with the herbal prescriptions. History indicates that almost all branches of medicine, being studied in the modern world, were studied during the ancient period.

Jīvaka has made a significant contribution to the development of medicine. This tradition continued and even the Emperor Asoka recommended and built hospitals for human beings as well as for animals.

It is said that Jīvaka toured a yojana all around Taxilā, taking a spade in search of non-medicinal plants. He could not find even a single plant without medicinal use. This is indicative of the fact that he had a deep knowledge of the plants and that each plant has medicinal importance.

From the very ancient times the man has had close contact with the fruits in some or other way. It is interesting to note that a large number of fruits grown today had their origin in the same part of Asia that was the earliest home of man. The human beings began to cultivate fruits in good old days, choosing the fruits of the best tastes, largest yield as well as those which were earliest to grow.

Morphologically fruit is a seed bearing portion of a plant and consists of the ripened ovary and its contents. Simple fruits are derived from a single ovary like mango and compound fruits from more than one ovary. The aggregate fruits are formed from numerous carpels of the same flower like strawberry. While composite fruits develop from the ovaries of different flowers of an inflorescence like fig.

There are several thousand drugs- / medicines- yielding plants all over the world. Most of the supply of medicines is obtained from wild plants growing in all parts of the world. The various parts of plants like roots, stems, barks, leaves, flowers, fruits and seeds are used for medicinal purpose. An attempt has been made through this research paper to find out medico-historical account of some fruits.

## Medico-historical Account of Fruits of Buddhist India

From the very ancient times the man has had close contact with the fruits in some or other way. It is interesting to note that a large number of fruits grown today had their origin in the same part of Asia that was the earliest home of man. The man began to cultivate fruits in good olden days, choosing the fruits of the best tastes, largest yield as well as those which were earliest to grow.

Morphologically fruit is a seed bearing portion of a plant and consists of the ripened ovary and its contents. Simple fruits are derived from a single ovary like mango and compound fruits from more than one ovary. The aggregate fruits are formed from numerous carpels of the same flower like strawberry. While composite fruits develop from the ovaries of different flowers of an inflorescence like fig.

The Buddha allowed the monks, if there was reason, to make use of fruits like *vilanga* (*Erycibe paniculata*), pepper or *pippla*, black pepper or *marica*, yellow myrobalan or *haritaka*, beleric myrobalon (*Terminalia belerica*), emblic myrobalan (*Phyllanthus emblica*) The fresh ripe fruits of *Phyllanthus emblica* are largely employed as astringent and laxative medicines. Yellow myrobalon beleric myrobalon (*Terminalia belerica*), emblic myrobalan (*Phyllanthus emblica*) are used in *triphala churn* which is good medicine for almost all problems.[1]

The Buddha prohibited the Order to make use of fruits with seeds. He told the monks to eat the fruits on selective basis as precautionary measures to avoid certain diseases which are caused because of eating seeds e.g. gall stone and kidney stone and to maintain environmental balance. He allowed the Order to eat the following types of fruits.[2]

(a) Fruits damaged by fire

(b) Fruits damaged by knife

(c) Fruits damaged by nail

(d) Fruits without seeds

(e) Fruits whose seeds have been discharged

There are several thousand drugs- / medicines- yielding plants all over the world. Most of the supply of medicines is obtained from wild plants growing in all parts of the world. The various parts of plants like roots, stems, barks, leaves, flowers, fruits and seeds are used for medicinal purpose. An attempt has been made through this research paper to find out medico-historical account of some fruits.

The following fruits are selected:

Pāli: Malura / Bela

Hindi: Bael, Siriphal

English: Bael, English quince

Botanic: Aegal marmelos

Family: Rutaceae

**Aegal marmelos**

This is a tree found in plains and submontane regions of India. The fruits are large, globose, edible and liked because of its aromatic and sweet pulp.

***Medicinal Importance***: The fruit is of great medicinal value. The ripe fruit is aromatic, astringent, cooling and laxative. The unripe and half-ripe fruit is astringent, stomachic, antiscorbutic and digestive.[3] It is best given in sub-acute or chronic cases of diarrhea and dysentery and in irritation of alimentary canal. It is useful adjunct in after-treatment of bacillary dysentery. The ripe fruit is prescribed in intestinal disorders and certain forms of dyspepsia, characterized by alternate constipation and diarrhea. A sherbet/ squash of the ripe fruit is given for chronic intestinal complications like constipation and dyspepsia. It serves as a soothing agent for intestine of patients suffering from chronic diarrhoea and dysentery.[4]

Hindi: Amla

English: Emblic myrobalon

Botanic: Emblic officinalis

Syn : Phyllanthus emblica

Family: Euphorbiaceae

**Phyllanthus emblica**

It is a moderate sized tree found throughout India. It was taken as an object of meditation.[5]

***Medicinal Importance***: The fruit is of great medicinal value. It is one of the richest sources of vitamin C. The fresh fruit is liver tonic, refrigerant, antiscortutic, diuretic and laxative.[6] It is used in fevers vomiting, indigestion, habitual constipation and other digestion troubles. The dried fruit is a good astringent, refrigerant, stomachic, antiscorbutic and blood purifier. It is given in diarrhoea, dysentery and haemorrhage. The infusion of seeds is useful eyewash in ophthalmic diseases. It was also used against eye diseases and back-ache.[7]

Jīvaka Komarabhacca gave Kāka, the slave to eat emblic myrobalan with medicinal part and to drink water.[8]

Pāli: Haritaka
English: Yellow Myrobalan
Botanic: Terminalia citrine
Terminalia chebula
Terminalia belerica

The trees have long been grown in India for their fruits and timber. They occur throughout deciduous forests of India.

The nuts have a tannin content of 30 to 40 per cent.[9]

***Medicinal Importance***: Yellow myrobalan was allowed to be taken by the monks and the nuns in a concoction of broth.[10]

The Buddha prescribed the monks to drink a compound of cow's urine and yellow myrobalan to cure jaundice.[11]

Jīvaka Komarabhacca had cured King Pajjot of Ujjeni of jaundice. He prescribed ghee, but the king had aversion for it. Therefore he boiled ghee and mixed it with medicines which gave a different colour and smell to it. The king drank it and after some hours vomited it out. This left him completely cured of the disease.[12]

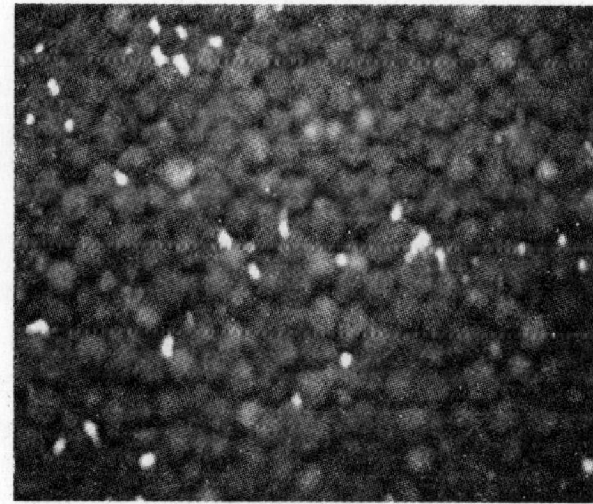

**Piper nigrum**

Pāli: Marica
Hindi:Kalimirch
English: Black Pepper
Botanic: Piper nigrum
Family: Piperaceae

Black pepper is found mostly cultivated in the hot and moist parts of India, Sri Lanka and other tropical countries.

It is a climbing perennial shrub with adventitious roots reaching a length of 30 ft in the wild state.

Its branches are stout, trailing and rooting at the nodes.

Flowers minute in spikes, usually dioecious: fruiting spikes very variable in length and robustness, rachis glabrous.

Fruit ovoid or globose, bright red when ripe one seeded berry-like drupes and about 50 to a catkin. During ripening they change colour from green to bright red and then to yellow. The plants are supported on posts or living trees.

When they are about 2 feet in height, the tip is removed to promote the development of lateral buds. The crop begins to yield in 2 or 3 years and reaches full bearing in 7 years. Propagation is by seeds or cuttings from the tips of the vines.[13]

Seeds are usually globose with testa thin and albumen hard.

Black pepper is one of the most ancient crops cultivated in India and has probably originated in the hills of south western India where it is met with a wild state in the rain forests from north Kanara to Kanyakumari. The pepper vine in its wild state is mostly dioecious and consequently rarely sets fruit. However, under cultivated conditions the fruiting is very much better, since most of the cultivated types are bisexual.

Black pepper consists of the dried, fully developed unripe fruits. It is nearly globular in shape, about 4-5 mm. in diameter with characteristic coat with deep set wrinkles. The freshly harvested spikes are spread on different floors on mats and dried in the sun about a week. During drying the green or red fruits gradually change in colour to dark brown or almost black and their skin becomes tough and wrinkled. The fruits are detached from the stalk by beating the heaped up material with sticks or treading upon it barefooted. The out turn of dried pepper obtained from the green fruits varies from 26-29 % depending upon the type.

***Medicinal Importance***: Pepper stimulates the flow of saliva and gastric juices and has a cooling effect. In modern Indian medicine it is much employed as an aromatic stimulant in cholera, weakness following fevers, coma etc., in stomachic in dyspepsia, as an antiperiodic in malarial fever.[14]

Once Emperor Asoka suffered from a disease which no one could diagnose / cure. His mouth and every pore of his body exuded bad smell. Expert physicians were called in but they all failed to cure him. Therefore the king's young and beautiful wife, Tissarakkhita decided to treat him first with marica.[15] This is indicative of the fact that the girls / women were not prohibited to learn and that she was a doctor.

Pāli: Badarī
Hindi: Ber, Pemdi ber
English: Jujube, Chinese date
Botanic: Ziziphus jujube
Syn. Ziziphus mauritiana
Family: Rhamnaceae

Fruits are edible. The fruit is used fresh, dried or preserved. The bark is used for tanning and the leaves are used as fodder.

***Medicinal Importance***: Once the Buddha suffered from a wind-disease in abdomen at Andhakavinda. Ānanda took a bowl and stood at the door of a physian. The physician's wife saw Ānanda at the; door, went out to meet him; greeted him and asked him as to what kind of medicine was required by him. This is indicative of the fact that the lady was cleaver enough to understand that Ānanda needed medicine. When he said, "For some rice gruel" she thought that the bowl was of the Buddha and she prepared with happiness

**Ziziphus jujube**

and reverence rice gruel with jujube juice and filled the bowl. She prepared and sent other food items required to be taken by the patients suffering from the abdominal wind-disease.[16]

It is stated that the gruel was specifically cooked with jujube; flavoured with oil, mixed with pepper, garlic and *lamajjaka* (the root of *Andropogon muricatus*). Here we understand that the physician's wife was clever to know the need of a person coming to her home and that she also knew as to how to treat the patient. Thus there was no prohibition for the ladies to learn and they were respected in families in the Buddhist India.. In other words the knowledge of medicine was known to her. She might also be a physician. We may presume that the Buddha used to suffer from the abdominal problems at irregular intervals.

Kunal-Jataka (No.536) indicates that there was exchange of hot words between Sakiya and Koliya for sharing of water of the Rohini, when the Sakiya labourers replied, "Nay do you wretched lepers, be off with your children, destitutes and ill-conditioned fellows, who like brute beasts had their dwellings in a hollow jujube tree (kolī). What shall their elephants and horses, their spears and shields avail against us? "------. The Koliyas said, "We will show them how strong we are they dwelt in the jujube trees"-----[17].

Sujāta-Jātaka (No 306) indicates that the fruits were sold in Benares by a beautiful girl in the flower of her youth with a basket of jujube on her head crying, "Jujubes, ripe jujubes, who'll buy my jujube?"[18]

Pāli: Kola, Badara

Hindi: Alucha, Alu bukhar

English: Cola tree, Plum
Botanic: Prunus domestica sub-spp insititia
Family: Rosaceae

**Prunus domestica**

This tree is found in the north India.

Plums are used as fresh fruits, for cooking, jams and canning

***Medicinal Importance***: The words "*yesam rukkhanam phalani paribhunjitva kuttarogo vupasamati*" indicate that the fruits of kola tree had the quality of curing leprosy.[19]

There is an interesting story in Kunala Jātaka about the cure of leprosy. Rama, the king of Benares cured himself in the forest and dwelt in a hollow of Susira tree / Cola tree. Later the discendents of Rama and Sakyan princess inhabited the town built on the spot where the tree stood. The town was, therefore, named Kolanagara and its inhabitants Koliyans.

It is stated that the body of Kokalikan monk broke out with pustules of the size of mustard and was ultimately swollen to the size of *billa* fruit after passing gradually through the transition stages of the size of lentils seeds, chick pea seeds, kola-nut stones, jujube fruit, myrobalan fruit and *vilva* fruit. Ultimately when it was on the plantain leaves, it was of the size of a fish. After that it discharged pus and blood. It seems the dead body was immediately attacked by the carnivorous animals and while eating the small pieces of flesh fell down on a plantain leaf. The pieces of the flesh could have found swollen gradually because of the putrefying action of micro-organisms on them.[20]

***Conclusion***: In the Buddhist India different herbal products like fruits were used for different types of diseases. The procedure is still in practice in remote villages in large scale. We owe our life to the *Bhesajjaguru*, the Buddha and the doctors of the Buddhist India because of whose medicines our generations survived, Brahmans supposed a doctor's profession as a low grade profession and they were even against selling medicines. Reginald S. Copleston in his book entitled 'Theravada Buddhism' has stated 'Medicines may have been already studied, and the sacrificial system led necessarily to some knowledge to anatomy, but the development of Indian Medicine was due to Buddhism.' S R. Goyal in his book 'A History of Indian Buddhism' has mentioned, "Here it may be noted that the credit of having first founded hospital undoubtedly goes to Buddhism".

### *Notes and References*


1. Horner, I. B., 2000, The Book of the Discipline IV (Mahāvagga), p.272
2. Horner, I. B., 1997, The Book of the Discipline VI (Parivara), p.212
3. Meena V. Talim, 1965, Ancient Indian Medicine according to Buddhist Sources, INDICA Vol 2, September, p.92
4. Albert F Hill, 2000, Hill's Economic Botany, p.544
5. Horner, I. B., 1999, The Middle Length Sayings III (Uparipannāsa), p.140.
6. Albert F. Hill, 2000, Hill's Economic Botany, p.567
7. Meena V. Talim, 1965, Ancient Indian Medicine According to Buddhist Sources, INDICA, Vol 2, September, p.96
8. Horner, I. B., 2000, The Book of the Discipline IV (Mahāvagga), p.392-393
9. Albert F. Hill, Hill's Economic Botany, 2000, p.153
10. Horner, I. B., 1997, The Book of the Discipline III (Suttavibhanga), p.245
11. Horner, I. B., 2000, The Book of the Discipline IV (Mahāvagga), p.280

    Meena V. Talim, Ancient Indian Medicine According to Buddhist Sources, INDICA, Vol 2, September, 1965. p.96
12. Ibid, p.96
13. Albert F. Hill, 2000, Hill's Economic Botany, p.590-591
14. Pandey, B. P., 1990, A Text Book of Botany, p.679-680
15. Meena Talim, 1967, Surgery and Surgical Instruments in Buddhist Era, INDICA, March, p.5
16. Horner, I. B., 1998, The Minor Anthologies of the Pāli Canon IV (Vimānavatthu), p.85, 86
17. Francis, H. T., 1990, Stories of the Buddha's Former Births V (The Jataka), p.219
18. Francis, H.T. & Neil, R.A., 1990, Stories of the Buddha's Former Births III (The Jātaka), p.14
19. Bollee, W.B., 1970, Kunala Jātaka, p.2, 80
20. Woodward, F. L., 1997, The Book of the Kindred Sayings V (Saṇyutta-nikāya), p.212

19

# Significance of Buddhist Councils from the Perspective of Applied Buddhism

*Saswati Mutsuddy*

The term *Applied Buddhism* seems to be the idea of the Western Scholars. *Buddhism* signifies the teachings and preachings of Buddha which is concerned with the Gospel of Buddha as recorded in the literature available in Pali, Sanskrit, Buddhist Sanskrit and Prakrit, wherein has been described a very abstruse, complex, learned and lofty philosophy of life or that preserves a kind of rites and rituals founded on the tenets of Buddha and the way of life preached by Him and the term *Applied Buddhism* signifies the applications of Buddhism in the modern way of life or the practical aspects of Buddhism.[1]

In the field of social research there has been clear signals of the development of a modern Buddhist Social Philosophy, which is true at large extent called "*Applied Buddhism*". Though the Buddha did not write a treatise on philosophy or even in the oral teachings, there is, implicit in His teachings, a concern with what may be called world-view, a theory of knowledge, ethics and a social philosophy in a sense the inter-connections between the various divisions of philosophy, which analytically separate, is an important feature of Buddhism. And indeed, "Buddhism is a religion with a philosophy; it recommends a way of life, which follows from its view of life, which is justified on the basis of the philosophy of Buddhism."

However, man can not live without values, and the normative is an essential aspect of the total human existence. In this sense, Buddhism likes most religious and ethical systems. The Buddhist concept of the Middle Way, also called the Noble Eightfold Path is one of the main determinants of happiness and success in Worldly Life. Although, as Padmasiri de Silva observes, this ethical aspects "are deeply rooted in a reflective inquiry about the basis of this way of life and rules of conduct".

From the point of view of the *Applied Buddhism* ethics, the concept Eightfold Path, avoids the extreme of self-indulgence and self-mortification while emphasizing the importance of Right Livelihood, the Fifth Factor in the Path is one of the main determinants of happiness and success in Worldly life. At the same, it is true that the most fateful force in modern life, Buddhist 'Ethos' that would be able to generate desirable social consciousness among people, to replace ignorance with knowledge, greed with generosity, and lack of respect with attributes of compassion and loving-kindness for all forms of life and the environment.

Venerable Piyasilo, in his "*Socioanthropology of Buddhist Prayer*", indicates: the sociologist of religion attempts to accurately show the relationships between religion and other spheres, which might be the applications of Buddhism such as economics, politics and science... Millions of people throughout the world perform rituals; engage in worship or belief in some sort of religion. Many of these contemporary religious activities have always been an important part of continuing traditional cultures.

Therefore, since much of the Asian culture is grounded in Buddhist religion and values, Buddhist socio-anthropology should be able to trace the cumulative working out of the habitual methods and institutions in dealing with the material means of life, in the cultural sequence of a Buddhist bearing; i.e., the *Applied Buddhism* institutions.

## Present requirement of Dhamma Saṇgitī or Buddhist Councils

The three main aspects of the practice of Buddhism are called *Buddha, Dhamma and Saṇgha*. Buddha (which literally means awake) refers to the act of waking up to our real nature and to the truth about suffering. *Dhamma* is the path, the way out of unnecessary suffering. *Sangha* refers to the community or support group which helps mankind on this path. The group becomes what in Buddhism is called a Saṇgha. Stephen Batchelor[2] refers to Saṇgha as a kind of friendship.

This approach to psychotherapy as assisted self-discovery is based on the principles of unity, Organism, mindfulness, non-violence, and body-mind-spirit wholeness. These principles are also an intrinsic part of Buddhist tradition:

(1) **Unity** is the principle that embraces the concept of Oneness and interconnectedness.

(2) **Organism** trusts the wisdom within us all. There is a natural order from which everything unfolds, including healing.

(3) **Mindfulness** is a practice of witnessing present experience in order to bring the light of consciousness to our lives.

(4) **Non-violence** (ahiṇsa) flows naturally out of the first three principles and becomes compassion and loving kindness.

These might be the Principle code of Buddhist Saṇgha and through these they would be able to organize themselves. Through these applications of Buddhism, Saṇgha might be able to show the PATH of proper Buddhism. **The paper aims to fulfill this motto where the significance of Buddhist Councils is conjoined with the *Applied***

***Buddhism***. Buddhist Councils or *Saṇgitis* played an important role systematizing in organizing and Buddhist teachings in the form of Buddhist literature which in due course of time turned out to be one of the richest so far as the religions of the world are concerned. In Pali, the word *Saṇgitī* means singing or chanting collectively. The word comprises ***Sam*** (together) + ***Gi*** (to sing, to chant from the verbal root ***Gi***) + ***ti*** a suffix. So, collectively it means singing or chanting together. These collective recitations which were performed by the monks at all these Buddhist Councils are known as the ***'Dhamma Saṇgitis'***, the Dhamma Recitations.

They are so designated because of the precedent set at the First Buddhist Council, when all the Teachings were recited first by an Elder of the *Saṇgha* and then chanted once again in chorus by all of the monks attending the assembly. The recitation was then judged to have been authentic, when and only when, it had been approved unanimously by the members of the Council. **The real necessity of these councils** had been laid in the *Culla Vagga, chapter xi, viz. Pañcaśatikakhandaka*[3], according to this record the incident which prompted the Elder *Mahākassapa* to call this meeting was his hearing a disparaging remark about the strict rule of life for monks. This is what happened. The monk *Subhadda*, a former barber, who had ordained late in life, upon hearing that the Buddha had died, voiced his resentment at having to abide by all the rules for monks laid down by the Buddha. Many monks lamented the passing of the Buddha and were deeply grieved, however, the Elder *Mahākassapa* heard *Subhadda* say: "Enough you're Reverences, do not grieve, do not lament. We are well rid of this great recluse (the Buddha). We were tormented when he said, 'this is allowable to you, this is not allowable to you' but now we will be able to do as we like and we will not have to do what we do not like.' *Mahākassapa* was alarmed by his remark and feared that the *Dhamma* and the *Vinaya* might be corrupted and not survive intact if other monks were to behave like *Subhadda* and interpret the *Dhamma* and the *Vinaya* rules as they pleased. **To avoid this he decided that the Dhamma must be preserved and protected. So, the first Buddhist Council organized.[4] It is called (the chanting) of the five hundred.**

## First Buddhist Council and Applied Buddhism

In the translator's introduction Prof. Horner states[5] that at the end of section XI, on the council of *Rājagaha*, because exactly five hundred monks were there, it is said that this "Chanting of the discipline", *Vinayasaṇgīti*, is in Consequence called that of the five hundred. Secondly, the author share her view[6] from the commentary of *Vinaya* that Kassapa asked the monks whether dhamma or discipline should be chanted first, and the monks replied: "Discipline is called *āyu*, the life or vitality, of the Buddha's dispensation; while the discipline stands, the dispensation stands. Therefore let us chant discipline first. The same sentiment is expressed in the verse inserted before the *Uddāna*, the key, at the end of Section I of the *Mahāvaṇsa*. The underline notion is that discipline is primarily concerned with sīla or purification of the ways of acting in body and speech and therefore with the first of the three categories into which the whole *sāsana*, dispensation or teaching, is graded.

But at the same time in the text she translates[7] – "Come, let us, your reverences, chant dhamma and discipline before what is not dhamma shines out and dhamma is withheld".

**The approach to the *Saṅgha* of President *Kassapa*** is seems to define as ***Applied Buddhism.*** At that ancient period Buddhism too believed in democracy. As a President of the Council Kassapa might give the order to follow the Saṅgha but he was taking the permission from them to settle the ceremony. The tradition follows the real Buddha's view for which He (Buddha) did not select the leader of Saṅgha and after the demise of Him the ceremony of First Buddhist Council was very significant.

Though Prof. Oldenberg's controversial comment[8] on historicity of the Council continues the dissension of various scholars, but the conclusion might be arranged with the agenda of the Proceedings discussed in the First Council –

(i) Selection of the Venue and the number of participants

(ii) The purification i.e. Arahanthood of the members of the Council.

(iii) Appointment of Upāli as Vinayadhara and ānanda as the Sutradhara;

(iv) Recitation of the Dhamma - Vinaya

(v) The settlement of the Discipline (Vinaya and the Dhamma)

(vi) Confirmation of a particular sermon with its place of promulgation

(vii) To examine the lesser and the minor precepts and the decision thereto

(viii) The disciplinary action (Brahmadaòda) taken against Channa.

Finally, the proceedings were adopted in a democratic way with the approval of the councilors. Even the monks received their seats according to their seniority. It again focused the democracy which regarded the Saṇgha's constitution.[9]

To sum up the agreement of entire discussion, it may be finally same remarked as Dr, S.Barua[10] – (1) The First Council was held, (2) A concise Dvipiṭaka (Vinaya and Dhamma - suttas) was recited by Upāli and Ānanda respectively. (3) Additions to the texts and the narratives of the Council were made gradually in the original account for sectarian interest. As also it was quite natural that in dynamic religious like Buddhism additions to the doctrines were made by the faithful disciples. (4) The omission of the Abhidhamma in the account of the First Council is natural as Dhamma also included in the Abhidhamma. In fact the Abhidhamma is a further extension of explanation of the Dhamma. Pure Abhidhamma works were compiled much later not before the Third Council of Dharmāshoka and especially after the formation of 18 sects.

## Second Buddhist Council and Applied Buddhism

In Translator's introduction I.B.Horner mentioned that the Second Council held at Vesālī a "century" after Gotama's parinibbāna – a century being "no doubt a round number" – is more truly characterized at its end as "a chanting of discipline" than is Section XI. For this chanting by the 700 monks is concerned with ten points of discipline only and whether those could not be relaxed"[11]. The revered monk Yasa, the son of Kākaṇdakā was responsible for the "chanting of discipline" which limited to the ten points (***dasa vatthuni***), was the subject before the Council of Vesālī and that was referring to 'Yasattherassa Saṇgitī', the Recital of the Elder Yasa by various commentaries.

*'Dasavatthunī'* or the ten points or Indulgences described in *Culla Vagga*—

(i) *Siṇgiloṇa Kappa*[12] i.e. 'The Horn-Salt–License' (is it allowable to carry about Salt in a horn with the intention putting it into food, which has not been salted?) Salt like other edibles is condemned in the Pācittiya rule no.38 of the Bhikkhu Pātimokkha[13].

(ii) *Dvaṇgulakappa* i.e. 'The Two-inch-licenses'. (Is it allowable to eat the midday meal beyond the right time, provided only that the shadow has not turned two inches?)[14] It signifies that solid food might be taken not only up till noon; but till the sun throws shadow two inches long. This rule is against Pācittiya No.37.[15]

(iii) *Gāmantara Kappa* i.e. The village-trip-license (Is it allowable for one who has once finished his meal, and refused any more, to eat food which has not been left over, on the ground that he is about to proceed into the village?[16] It is contrary to the Pācittiya No.35 which prevents a Bhikkhu from taking second meal in the same day (offence of overeating).[17]

(iv) *Āvāsa Kappa* i.e. 'The circuit license', (Is it allowable for a number of Bhikkhus who dwell within the same circuit, within the same boundery, to hold separate Uposathas?[18] This practice contravenes the *Mahāvagga* rules of residence in a parish (*sīmā*).[19]

(v) *Anumati Kappa* i.e. The Indemnity license (Is it allowable for a *Saṇgha* which is not legally constituted, to perform an official act, on the ground that they will afterwards obtain the sanction of such Bhikkhus as subsequently arrive?)[20] According to Vinaya rules, the consent may be obtained after the act is passed.This also amounts to a breach of monastic discipline according to the *Mahāvagga* (ix, 3, 5).[21]

(vi) *Āciṇṇa Kappa* i.e. Ṭhe Precedent-License (Is it allowable to do a thing on the ground that "My preceptor has practiced that?") This rule also infringes the monastic order as mentioned in the Mahāvagga.[22]

(vii) *Amathita Kappa* i.e. (The Churn–License) the drinking of buttermilk after meals. This practice is in contravention of Pācittiya No.35 which prohibits over-eating.[23]

(viii) Jalogim-Pātuṇ or the drinking of toddy. This practice is in contravention of Pācittiya rule no.51 which forbids the drinking of intoxicants.[24]

(ix) Adasakam-nisidanam i.e. 'A mat without fringes to sit upon' be permissible for the monk.[25]

(x) Jātarūpa rajataṇ or the acceptance of gold and silver which is forbidden by rule 18 of the Nissaggiya Pācittiya.[26]

These ten points were unanimously rejected by the assembled monks of the council, being declared them as unlawful. A special jury team was considered to take the decision. *Cullavagga* explained:

"Then the Order assembled, willing to investigate that legal question. But while they were investigating that legal question both endless disputations arose and of not one speech were the meaning clear. Then the venerable Revata informed the Order saying: Honoured sirs, let the Order listen to me. While we were investigating this legal question both endless disputations arose and of not one speech was the meaning clear. If it seems right to the Order may settle this legal question by means of a referendum."He selected four monks from the East four monks from Pāvā—of the Eastern monks the *Venerable Sabbakāmin* and the Venerable Sālha and the Venerable Khujjasobhita and the Venerable Vāsabhagāmika;of the monks from Pāvā the Venerable Revata and the Venerable Sambhūta, the wearer of coarse hempen cloth and the Venerable Yasa, the son of Kākaṇdakā, and the Venerable Sumana."[27]

Though the matter of discussion is need not to discuss the member of the jury board, but it need to clear the idea about the republican and democratic form of the council of Saṇgha. There are lot of dissension from the '*DasaVatthunī*' of *Cullavagga* to other version of texts. The historicity of this council uninanimously believed by the various scholars. *Mr.Hofinger* might be the only person who studied the council critically and analytically to decide that these 10 rules include into *Vinaya* in a later composition of it. Again he says that the Vaisali council convened to settle the conflict between the Vajjiputtakas and the rest of community is not a fiction. He adds that the council account is previous to the schism which deviated the Mahāsaṇghikas from the sthaviras. The legend was gradually grown and was accepted by all traditions.[28]

However, the applicability or justifications of these ten controversial points are needed to discuss.

The points like 'Āvāsa Kappa', 'Anumati Kappa', 'Āciṇṇa Kappa', 'Jalogiṇ Pātuṇ', 'Adasakam Nisidanam', and 'Jāta rūpa rajataṇ' are very much applicable or justified for the Buddhist Saṇgha —

The first point: *Āvāsa Kappa*" is justified to protect any schism in the same boundary. If the one place is selected for 'Uposatha', then entire monks should be present in the same place in spite of their different opinion.

The second point: '*Anumati Kappa'* i.e. Indemnity – license is justified to perform legal official act. From this point of view no illegal act would be perform in the Saṇgha.

The third point: '*Āciṇṇa Kappa*', or using customary practices also should be prohibited for the monks.

The fourth point: '*Jalogiṇ Pātuṇ*' is justified not only for the bhikkhus but the justification lies in the entire society. No intoxication means no life hazards in the society. The healthy society gives the birth of healthy citizen.

The fifth point: '*Adasakam Nisīdanam*', from the very point of broadness or show the reverence for the Elder One.

The last one '*Jātarūpa rajataṇ'* is very much applicable. The excess luxurious worldly treasure should not captured by anybody into the world, otherwise it can 'be the life risk.

Except all of these points, '*Siṇgiloṇa Kappa', 'Dvaṇgula Kappa,' 'Gāmantara Kappa', 'Amathita Kappa'* are not applicable or justified for the current society. If there are various types of environmental hazards or complications in the communication, then these rules are difficult to follow by anyone. At the very edge of Global Warming, when there are no control in Tsunami, Hurricane, Femine or Flood, how one should neglect to preserve their food. The accurate time of taking food shows the difficulties in different aspects.Such as 'Food for every man' — is the fundamental right of human being. The said rule (*Dvaṇgula kappa &Gāmantara kappa*) breaks the fundamental rule, to obstruct any monk to take their daily food. The last one, *'Amathita Kappa'* should change from the point of health problem of monks.

Buddha believed in *MajjhimaPaṭiPadā* i.e. The Middle Path. Naturally, no rules should impose anyone. The real application of Buddhism should fulfill then.

**The Fourth, Fifth & Sixth Buddhist Councils**: There are no such traditional accounts of these councils. The traditional Canonical text '*CullaVagga*' gives no information about these councils. The **Fourth Council** was held during the time of King Vaṭṭagāmani Abhaya (101-77) is considered to be the Fourth by the Theravada school though in India, Kaniskas Council was recognized as the Fourth.[29]

**Fifth Council** was held at Mandalaya in Myanmar (Burma). In 1853-78 king Min-donmin arranged this council. The principle object of Fifth Buddhist Council was to promote and purify the dhamma. At the time of Second Anglo-Burmese war, king was fed up and disliked the bloodshed. So, he desired two main theme—Firstly, to modernize the country and Secondly, to hold a Buddhist council to protect and sustain the Buddha Sāsana. But other Theravadin countries like Thailand, Cambodia, Sri Lanka are ignored the synod due to lack of information.The narrative of the synod was preserved in second volume of the Great Chronicle of Burma and the '*Akkhara-Visodhinī*' written in Burmese.Maung Haung Sayadaw, the author of the '*Akkhara-Visodhinī*', himself was active participant in synod. Therefore, it seems that the account of the council as narrated in the above two books are authentic and they agree each other.[30] To fulfill the purpose successfully, king followed the first council's matter which rehearsed by the Theras. To keep the records of Tipiṭaka he took the idea of 'Marble Slab's, this council also known as "*Selakkharārulha*" (recorded in stone); the inscription is called "Mandalay Inscription". The entire Tipiṭaka was engraved on 729 marble slabs composed of the[31] —

| | | |
|---|---|---|
| 1. | *Vinaya Piṭaka* | 111 slabs |
| 2. | *Abhidhamma* | 208 slabs |
| 3. | *Sutta Piṭaka* | 410 slabs |

The preparation, writing, recording, recitation, editing and engraving entire works of the project took five years (from 1857-1861A.D.)[32], with the help of the well-versed bhikkhus. It is said that this great Sangitī was successfully held without any help of other Theravada's Buddhist Countries.

But there are lots of controversies about the location of **Fifth Buddhist Council** which is as follows—

i. According to '*Sangītivaṇsa*'[33] the first three councils were held in India; the Fourth, fifth, sixth and seventh in Sri Lanka and eighth and ninth in Thailand.

ii. The Sinhalese tradition recognized the fifth Buddhist Council which was held in *Alu-Vihāra* or *Aloka Vihara* in Sri Lanka, 450 yrs. after the parinibbāna of the Buddha. But other Theravāda tradition recognized it as another fourth Buddhist Council[34].

iii. There is also mentioned in the Sinhalese tradition about the another council which was held in Ratanapura under the leadership of Venerable Hikkaduve Thera Sumangal in Circa1865A.D.The Tipiÿaka with the commentaries were rehearsed there as before. It continued for five months and Iddamalgaf Basnāyaka Nilame patronized the saṇgītikārakas with food and essential requisites. But the Theravāda countries do not recognized it[35].

According to '*Saṇgitīvaṇsa*'[36], **Sixth council** was also held at Sri Lanka under the patronage of king *Mahānāma*, 956 yrs. after the Master's great decease. In this council, all the commentaries were rehearsed and translated back into *Māgadhi (Pali)* from the Sinhalese language by Buddhaghosa, the great Pali scholar. But according to *"Saddhamma Saṇgaha"*, a Sinhalese compendium of the historical analysis of the councils describes the same happenings but it is silent about the council.

But the another opinion is that the **Sixth Buddhist Council** was inaugurated in May1954 in Rangoon i.e. Yangon, with the collaboration and participation of the scholar monks of different countries like India,Sri Lanka,Nepal,Cambodia,Thailand, Laos and Pakistan.The most Venerable *Abhidhaja Mahāraṭṭha Guru Bhadanta Revata* presided.

The objective of the ***Chaṭṭasaṇgāyana*** is as follows:

i. To revise the texts which contain some miss-spellings and omissions due to repeatedly copying the Tipiṭaka;
ii. To promote the Buddha sāsana and to propagate the teachings of the Buddha abroad
iii. To recite them at the sixth great council
iv. To print these edited Piṭakas in books;
v. To translate them into various languages; and to distribute them all over the world with the object of preserving and propagating the Dhamma.

## Applied Buddhism through Buddhist Councils

The real practice of Buddhism in Buddhist Saṇgha is 'Applied Buddhism', there are some reasons proved the statement—

**Practice of Loving Kindness** is a state of mind in which one person (for example the therapist) sees the other (the client) in a certain way, a way that is nourishing for both. It is a way of perceiving the beauty in the other, seeing the person as a source of inspiration, or perhaps recognizing something that is universally human, something that touches the heart. This way of seeing someone has a receptive quality to it, as if the simple act of taking the person in is a kind of nourishment, a gift. This way of perceiving creates an attitude that is subtly felt by the other person, who somehow knows she is being appreciated, respected, and loved in a spiritual way. People feel safe then to open up, to reveal themselves, to explore themselves. It helps the group to support each person to experience loving presence from both directions. The group becomes what in Buddhism is called a Saṇgha. It refers to Saṇgha as a kind of friendship. *Through this perception—a true friend is more than just someone with whom we share common values and who accepts us for what we are. Such a friend is someone whom we can trust to refine our understanding of what it*

***means to live, who can guide us when we're lost and help us find the way along a path, which can assuage our anguish through the reassurance of his or her presence.***

**Friendship is the sublime path** to Apply Buddhism. At the environment of Globalization, the entire Universe belongs to same platform, through e-connection. Pali canons have been approved at six Buddhist councils. Of them, it is generally observed that —

- ➢ The Fifth Buddhist Council, held in Mandalay during King Mindon's reign, agreed to have *kyauk-sar* (stone inscriptions) of the approved text.
- ➢ the Sixth Buddhist Council, held in *Kava Aye Hlaing Gu* ("World Peace Pagoda Cave"), Yangon in 1954- 56, agreed to print the approved texts of the Pali canons as well as the commentaries and sub commentaries.
- ➢ With the initial sponsorship of TBSA and the devotees of *Dhammananda Vihara, Sayadaw U Silananda* launched two projects[37]
- ➢ CD-ROM for the Pali canons and commentaries approved at the Sixth Buddhist council.
- ➢ Digitized images of the *kyauk-sar* of the text approved at the Fifth Buddhist Council. *Pali Text Society*, London; *Vipassana Research Institute*, Igatpuri, India; *The Corporate Body of the Buddha Educational Foundation*, Taiwan & many other associations are tried their best to preserve Buddhist Canonical & Non Canonical text to publish them.

In **conclusion**, it might be said that **These Fruitful application of Chaṭṭasaṅgāyana** through these publications and various kinds of activities approve the idea of the said council. It might be called ***Action Dharma.*** It is a compelling collection, richly illustrating engaged Buddhist movements and giving fair voice to some of the criticisms against engaged Buddhists and those who study them. It is an extremely valuable work for anyone interested in how Buddhists are dealing with contemporary issues and exploring both precedents for, and the innovations of an ***Action Dharma.E-Sangha and other Online Teachings*** of Buddhism help lay people to know the teachings & preachings of Buddha. Many other organizations like, ***Burma's Mass Lay Meditation Movement: Buddhism and the Cultural Construction of Power, FWBO (U.K),*** *Mlup-Baitong (Engaged Projects in Asia)* is a non-governmental (NGO) environmental organization in Cambodia seeking to conserve natural resources and foster sustainable development, *Wat Plak Mai Lai Forest Monastery* is a densely-wooded forest monastery outside of Bangkok in Thailand, help to promote Buddhism through their different kinds of retreat programme.But at the same time; it is dangerous to proper preservation of Buddha's Teachings. There is a **necessary to organize Buddhist Councils or Saṅgitis**, so the preachings would follow and preserve properly for the Future. The Pali Scholar should be selected to edit the online Pali Canonical and Non-Canonical text to teach those people properly. Then the **significance of Buddhist Councils to Applied Buddhism** serves its appropriate justification.

### *Notes and References*

1. Barua Dipak Kumar, *Applied Buddhism: Studies in the Gos̓pel of Buddha*, Varanasi, 2005, p.1.
2. Ibid, p.8.
3. Poussin Louis De La Vallee, *The Buddhist Councils*, Kolkata, 1976, p.2.

4. Horner, I.B. *Book of Discipline,* Vol.V (Cullavagga), London, 1963, p.406.
5. *Ibid.*, p.xv
6. *Ibid.*, p.394
7. *Ibid.*, p.394
8. (a) It is not history, but pure invention and moreover, invention of no very ancient dates (Vinaya Pitakam vol.1, p.xxvii.)

   (b) In one word, M.Oldenberg believes that all our chapter of the Culla is a "forgery", but a forgery very well done and that the analysis does not permit us to draw from it the conclusions formulated by Minayeff: The Russian savant did not read with sufficient attention the proofs of his admirable book; he would have avoided some mistakes over which his adversary triumphs. (Poussin, p.12f.)
9. Barua, Sumangal, *Buddhist Councils and development of Buddhism*, Kolkata, 1997, p.33.
10. *Ibid.*, p.39
11. Horner, I.B., *The Book of Discipline.* p.xviii.
12. Majumdar, R.C., *Buddhist Councils in Buddhistic Studies*, pp.60-61.
13. Barua, Sumangal, p.50
14. Majumdar, R.C., p.60
15. Barua, Sumangal, p.50
16. Majumdar, R.C., p.60
17. Barua, Sumangal, pp.50
18. Majumdar, R.C., p.60
19. Bapat, P.V., p.42
20. Majumdar, R.C., p.60
21. Barua Sumangal, p.51
22. Barua Sumangal, p.51
23. Bapat, P.V., p.42
24. Ibid., p.42
25. Barua Sumangal, p.51
26. Bapat P.V., p.42
27. Horner I.B., p.424
28. Barua Sumangal, p.58
29. Bapat P.V., p.50 (some other sources believe the date to be 88-46B.C.)
30. Barua, Sumangal, p.131
31. *Ibid.*, p.131
32. a) *Ibid.*, p.133

    b) But in 2500 yrs. of Buddhism, P.V. Bapat, B.Jinananda wrote the year of this council-1871 (B.E.2414). According to him, recitation recording of the Tipiÿaka on marble continued for about five months in the royal palace.
33. Bapat, P.V., p.51
34. (a) Barua, Sumangal, p.126 (b) Bapat, P.V., p.50
35. (a) *Ibid.*, p.127 (b) Bapat, P.V., p.51
36. It is the history of the recital written by the Royal Thai Patriarch named Somdej Phra Vanarat (Bhadanta Vanaratan)
37. *http://www.tbsa.org/*

20

# Essence of Buddhism

*Eknath B. Saharey*

Buddhism is neither merely religion nor philosophy. It does not matter what you call it. Buddhism remains what it is, whatever label you may put on it. The label is immaterial. Even the label "BUDDHISM" which we give to the teachings of the Buddha is of little importance. Secturian labels are hindrance to the independent understanding of truth and they produce harmful prejudices in mans minds. In the third century B.C, the great Buddhist emperor Ashoka of India, following this noble tolerance and understanding, honored and supported all religions in his vast empire. In one of his Rock Edicts No. XII the original of which one may read even today. The Emperor declared 'One should not honour only one's and condemn the religions of others. But one should honour other's religion for this or that reasons. So doing, one help one's own religion to grow and render to the religions of others too. In acting otherwise one digs the grave of one's own religion and also does harm to other religions whosoever honours his own religion and condemns other religions does so indeed through his devotion to his own religion, thinking, I will glorify my own religion.' But on the contrary in so doing he injures his own religion more gravely. So concording is good. Let all listen and be willing to listen to the doctrines professed by others. Once the Buddha visited Kesaputta, town in the kingdom of Kosala. The Kalams resident of Kesaputta told him, there are recluses and Brahmins who visit Kesaputta, explain their own doctrines and despise, condemn and spurn others. We have always doubt and perplexity arises in a matter which is doubtfull, as to who among there prove Truth and who speak falsehood? In reply the Buddha told them- yes Kalams, it is proper that you have doubt and perplexity for doubt has arisen in a matter which in doubtful. Now look you Kalams, do not be lead by reports or its tradition or here say. Be not led by the authority, religious text nor by more logic or inference nor by considering appearances, nor by the delight in speculative opinions, nor by seeing possibilities, nor by the idea, this is our teacher. But O Kalams, when you know for yourselves that certain things are akusals, wrong and bad give them up. And when you know for yourselves that certain things are kussal and good, then only accept and follow them. The Buddha went even further. He told the bhikkhus that a disciple should examines even the Tathagata himself, so that he might be fully convinced of the true value of the teacher whom he followed. This sutta is universally acclaimed as the 'Charter of individual freedom?'

The Buddha was practical teacher and taught only these things which would bring peace and happiness to man. Even so Bhikhhus, of what I have known, I have told you only a little, what I have not told you is very much more. And why I have not told you those things, because that is not useful, not leading to Nirvana i.e. why I have not told you these things. First for all, Buddhism in neither pessimistic nor optimistic, if anything at all, it is realistic. Fortakes a realistic view of life and of the world. The Buddha does not any happiness in life when he says there are sufferings, on the contrary he admits different forms of happiness, both material and spiritual. For lay men as well as for monks. In the Anguttar Nikaya, one of the five original collections in PALI containing the Buddha's discourses. There is a list of happiness (sukkha) such as the happiness of family life and the happiness of recluse, the happiness of sense pleasures and the happiness of renunciation. The happiness of attachment and happiness of the detachment. Physical happiness and mental happiness. It is incorrect to think that Nirvana is the natural result of the extinction of craving. Nirvana is not the result of any thing. Nirvana is the ultimate Truth. If it is ultimate there can be nothing after it. Nirvana means to see the state of things as they are. Nagarjuna clearly says, that samsara has no difference what ever from Nirvana and Nirvana has no difference what so was from samsara. It is propagated and believed that Buddhism is very lofty and sublime that can not be brought into practice by common men and women in today's world of ours. To brings into practice one has to retire from the world to be true Buddhist. This is a sad misconception due to lack of understanding of the teaching of the Buddha, some people run to such hasty and wrong conclusions as a result of this hearing, reading casually something written by same one who has not understand in all its aspects gives only a partial lopsided view of it. The Buddha's teachings does not meant only for Bhikkhus in monasteries, but also for ordinary men and women living at home with their families. The noble Eight fold path is the Buddhist way of life. It is mean for all without any distinction. It would be useless to the masses of man kind if they would not follow it in their daily life in the today's world. If one understands the spirit of Buddhism correctly, one can surely follow and practice it while living the life of an ordinary man. The Buddha was practical teacher. He has practiced himself and then taught only those things which would bring peace and happiness to man. Vacchagotta, the wonderer acetic who met several times to the Buddha asked him several questions and get satisfied. Once he asked Buddha straight forwardly whether there were laymen and women leading the family life followed his teachings successfully and attained to high spiritual status. The Buddha categorically stated there were not one or two nor a hundred two hundred or five hundred, but many more laymen and women leading the family life who followed his teachings successfully attained to high spiritual status. The further stated that true renunciation does not mean running away physically from the world. If one desire to be a Buddhist, there is no initiation ceremony (Baptism) which one has to undergo. If one understands his teachings, convinced that the teachings are the right path and tries to follow, and then one is Buddhist. In fact there are no external rites or ceremonies which a Buddhist has to perform.

Primitive humans found themselves in a dangerous and hostile world. The fear of wild animals, of not being able to find enough food, of injury or disease and natural phenomena like thunders, lightening and volcanoes were constantly with them. Finding no security they created the idea of gods in order to give them comfort in good times, courage in a time dangers and consolation when things went wrong. The Buddhist do not believe in this idea of gods. They believe in Humanity. The Buddha avoids excess and extremesion both followed in a balanced reasonable way without becoming rigid and fanatics. The teaching of the Buddha Centralise on the four Noble Truth, just as the rim and spokes of wheel centre on the hub.

The first noble truth is that life is suffering. To live is to suffer.

The second noble truth is that carving causes all suffering.

The third noble truth is that suffering can be overcome and happiness attained. This is perhaps the most important of the four noble truths. Because in it the Buddha assured us that true happiness and contentment is possible.

The fourth noble truth is the path leading to the overcoming of sufferings entitled as the middle way or majjhima patipada or the noble eight fold path consists of right understanding, right thought, right speech, right action, right livelyhood, right efforts, right mind fullness and right concentration. Buddhism is a way of life and what is essential is to tread the Nobel Eight Fold Path. The Buddha has a code of morality. The Five precepts are basis of Buddhist morality.

The First precept is to avoid killing or harming living beings.

The Second precept is to avoid stealing.

The Third precept is to avoid sexual misconduct.

The Fourth precept is to avoid lying & gossiping.

The Fifth precept is to avoid alcohol and other intoxicating drugs.

There is acute misconception and wrong propaganda on eating meat. It is criticized as violation of first precept. This happened because lack of deep study of the scripture. Buddhist are not necessarily vegetarians. The Buddha himself was not vegetarian. He never teaches his disciples to be vegetarian. Even today there are many good Buddhists who are not vegetarian. By eating meat one does not become impure. In Samyutta Nikaya the Buddha said - being rough, pitiless, back biting, harming ones friends, being heartless, arrogant and greedy makes man impure not eating meat.

Being the immoral conduct, refusing to repay debts, cheating in business, causing divisions amongst people this makes one impure, not the eating meat. Categorically by eating meat one indirectly becomes responsible for killing creatures. But the same is true when one eats vegetables as farmers spray insecticides and poisons so that vegetable should reach on your dinners plates. For manufacturing of soaps, lather bags, hand bags and thousand other products animal are killed. Honesty, generosity and kindness are necessary. It is immaterial whether one is vegetarian or non vegetarian. The Buddha ate pork meat. Be clear he died not by eating pork. The Buddha was 80 years old at that time he passed away and he has been ailing for some time. The reality is that he died of old age. The third precept is to avoid sexual misconduct has a large sense. It means if one are trickery, emotional blackmailing or force and compel same one to have sex, it can be said to be sexual misconduct. Sex should be an expression of love and intimacy between two people and when it is, it contributes to mental and emotional well being. Sex before and even after marriage is not a type of sexual misconduct if there is love and mutual agreement between two people involved. However it should never be forgotten that biological function of sex is reproduction. Buddhism recognizes that sex had several purposes- procreation, recreation, as an expression of love and affection between two people, etc. This being the case, it considers all forms of birth control to be acceptable. Infect, Buddhism would say that in world where the population explosion had become a major problem, birth control is a real blessing.

The fourth precept is to avoid lying means trying to be more truthful & honest. It is also mis-interpreted without knowledge at Dhamma. A Buddhism monk is sitting in a park. He saw a terrified man run past by him. A few minutes later another man carrying knife in hand chasing him came and enquired if he had seen which way the first man has gone. If he has a good reason to suspect that the second man with knife is going to do serious harm to the first. As an ardent, intelligent caring Buddhist he has no hesitation in lying.

Buddhism is supreme philosophy. Philosophy has two words Philo and Sophia. Philo means love and Sophia means wisdom. The philosophy means love & wisdom. Buddhism contains both love and wisdom. This supreme philosophy is given to mankind by the greatest man who ever lived, the supreme Buddha.The Buddhist do charitable work but they don't feel the need to boast about the good they do. They are not after publicity. Those who hanker after publicity cannot be called Buddhist, they can be any one but not the Buddhist.

Buddhism is culture oriented and sober. It is easily accepted by the countries of different culture. Being a message of peace, love, wisdom and happiness to all living beings it spreads crossing barriers, physical, geographical, linguistic and social. One can be truly great, peaceful and peace loving only when he has cultivated five, precepts (pancasila). Truth discovered is subject to change by experiments. Truth of Dhamma does not change according to time and space. Instead of theorizing, the Buddha thought mankind how to live a righteous life by calming the senses and by casting on desires. Practice is important in Buddhism. The Buddhism has a complete system of mental culture. The wisdom of Buddhism founded on compassion has the vital rule of correcting dangerous destination modern science is heading for. Modern psychologist are now deeply interested in the Buddhist analysis of the various factors of consciousness, feelings, perception and volition. It spreads from Laos, Tibet, Bhutan, Sikkim, Nepal, China, and Afghanistan. From Mangolia to Maldives, from Balkh to Bali. There are three main types of Buddhism- Theravada, Mahayana and Vajrayana. Today Theravada is being practiced mainly in- Sri

Lanka, Myanmar, Thailand, Laos & Cambodia. Mahayana is being practiced in India, China, Korea, Taiwan, Vietnam and Japan. Vajrayana is being practiced in Mangolia, Tibet, Laddakh, Nepal, Bhutan & Sikkim.

There is no doubt on that Buddhism is a need of modern world, it is ageless message of loving kindness, compassion, love wisdom, peace & happiness. Peace is one quality which the world is now taking about and which is most desired by world leaders & organization alike.

### *Notes and References*


1. Gahapati Sukha Sutta, Samyutta Nikaya- Published by Vipassana Research Institute, Dhammagiri, Igatpuri (INDIA), Devnagari Publication (1998).
2. Essential themes of Buddhist Scripture- By Ashin Thittila Published by Hope Services, Abindon, Oxfordshire, England (1982).
3. Vide Sutta Nipata, SBE. Vol. 9, Masiny (1983).
4. Vide the Buddha and his teachings. By Narad Thero. Pub by Buddhist Missionary Society, Malaysia (1964).
5. Vinayapitaka- Vipassana Research Institute Dhammagiri, Igatpuri (INDIA) Devanagari Publication (1998).
6. Karl Marks & Buddha Dr. B.R.Ambedkar, Peoples Education Society, Bombay (1958).
7. You and your Problems by Dr. Sri K.Dhammananda Pub. The Corporate Body of the Buddha, Taiwan (1998).
8. What the Buddha Taught by Walpola Rahul, Garden Frasers Gallery Ltd. London and Bedford.
9. The Greatest Man who ever lived (The Supreme Buddha) – Ven. Wargoda Sarda Mahathero Pub. Singapore Meditation Centre.
10. The Tree of Enlightenment by Peter Della Santina Pub. Chico Dharma Study Foundation(1997).
11. Living Legacy of the Buddha By Ven. Acharya Buddharakkhita Pub- Buddha Vachana Trust, Mahabodhi Society, Bangalore (INDIA) (1979).
12. 2500 years of Buddhism, by P.V. Bapat Govt. of India (1956).
13. History of Indian Literature by M.Winternitz, Calcutta (1934).
14. Bodhicaryavatara ed. Shastri Dwarkadas, (1952) Varanasi.
15. Abhidharmakosa ed. Shastri Dwarkadas (1987) Varanasi.
16. Abhidhamma in daily life by Ashin Janakabhivamsa- Pub. The Corporate Body of the Buddha Educational Foundation, Taiwan (1997).

21

# History of Vajrayana Buddhism in Eastern India

*Bikash Mukherji*

The Buddhist Tantras or the Vajrayana form of Buddhism is possibly the last phase of Indian Buddhism, which is broadly divided into two major branches-Hinayana and Mahayana. Mahayana is further divided into two sub branches-Paramitayana (or Sutrayana) and Mantrayana, the latter of which is also called as Tantrayana or Vajrayana and denotes mainly Tantric Buddhism. The Buddhist Tantras, according to some scholars flourished during the period stretching from fourth Century A.D to eleventh Century A.D. Among those Buddhist Tantras, *the Guhyasamaja Tantra* is regarded as the oldest one, while Kalachakra, the latest. The *Kalachakra Tantra* was composed in 11th Century A.D. The tradition avers that the root Tantra *(mulatantra)* was taught by Sakyamuni Buddha in his life time inside the stupa of Dhanyakotaka. The stupa was located at the place now known by the name of Amaravati in the Guntur District of Andhra Pradesh.

It may be noted in this connection that although Mahayana tradition claims that the Tantras were taught by the Buddha but it is difficult to accept that claim. The Tantric Buddhism has in fact no direct connection with the early Buddhism. It seems that Tantric practices current in the masses were accepted by the Buddhists, Hindus and also Jainas and were somehow absorbed in the doctrines of those respective tenets.

Professor Foucher in his *Iconographic Bouddhique* has discussed an illuminated manuscript of *Astasahasrika Prajnaparamita* of 11th century A. D. It contains the illustrations of a number of Mahayana deities worshipped in different parts of eastern India, especially in Bengal. This include Bhagavati Tara of Chandradvipa, Champita Lokanatha, Jayatunga Lokanatha and Buddhardhi Tara of Samatata[1], Chunda of Pattikeraka and Lokanatha of Harikela.

Before discussing in details about Vajrayana Buddhism in Eastern India it is necessary to discuss in brief about Vajrayana Buddhism. Vajrayana Buddhism (popularly known as

Tantrika Buddhism) is a complex and multifaceted system which evolved over several centuries for its final shape.[2] The Vajrayana first came into evidence in 8th century A.D.[3].

The system probably came into existence with its clear exposition in the eight century A.D.The distinctive features of Vajrayana Buddhism are ritual which is used as a substitute or alternative for the earlier abstract meditation. Vajrayana scriptures say that Vajrayana refers to one of the three routes to enlightenment, the other two being Hinayana and Mahayana.

The term "*Vajra*" denoted the thunderbolt, a legendary weapon and divine attribute that was made from an adamantive or indestructible substance which could therefore pierce and penetrate any obstacle or obfuscation. As a secondary meaning, *Vajra* refers to this indestructible substance, and so is sometimes translated as "adamantine" or "diamond". So the Vajrayana is sometimes rendered in English as "The Admantine Vehicle"or the Diamond vehicle.

A *vajra* is also scepter like ritual object,which has a sphere at its centre and a variable number of spokes (depending on Sadhana) enfolding either end of the rod.The *vajra* is often traditionally employed in Tantric rituals in combination with bell or *ghanta*; symbolically *Vajra* may represent method as well as great bliss and bell stands for wisdom, specifically the wisdom realizing emptiness or lack of inherent existence.

Regarding the original location of the Vajrayana form of worship, there are different views as to where in the Indian Sub-continent Vajrayana began. It is stated in a verse of Kalachakra Mulatantra that-Grdhrakute Yatha Sastah (sastra) Prajnaparamitanaye tatha mantranaye prokta Sridhanye dharmadesana i.e. just as the teacher (lord Buddha) offered the teaching of Dharma into the path of Prajnaparamita at Grdhrakuta. Similarly, (he offered teaching) into the path of Mantra at Sridhanya (kataka)[4].Other scholars are of the opinion that it originated in Bengal[5]. Nalanda University in eastern India became a centre for the development of Vajrayana theory, although it is likely that the university followed, rather than led,the early Tantric movement. India would continue as the source of leading edge Vajrayana Practices up until the 11th centuries producing many renowned Mahasiddha.

It is said that Indrabhuti, the oldest known king of Sambalpur (Orissa) founded Vajrayana. From 7th century onwards, many popular religious elements of heterogenous nature were incorporated into Mahayana Buddhism which finally resulted in the origin of Vajrayana,Kalachakrayana and Sahajayana Tantrik Buddhism.

Many celebrated Vajrayana Acharya like Sarah Hadipa, Dombi, Heruka, Tantipa, Luipa, came from so called despised classes. The cult exerted a tremendus influence over the tribal and despised classes of people of Sambalpur Bolangir in Orissa region. It was in 9th/10th century A.D that there appeared seven famous Tantric maiden at Patna (Patnagarh) region was then called Kuanri-Patana. These maidens are popularly known as Satvaheni(seven sisters) namely Gyanadei Maluni, Lahakuti, Luhuruni Nitei Dhobani, Sukuti Chamaruni, Patrapindhi Savaruni, Gangi Gauduni and Sua Teluni. They hailed from the so called low castes of society. Because of their miraculous power and feats, they were later on deified and worshipped by the folk people.

If we examine carefully the tendency and attitude of the Buddhists during the period of our review it would be quite clear that the Buddhists started to merge themselves with the Brahmanical ideas and beliefs. Buddhism as a newly founded system could not have expected to survive and spread over the common people against deep-rooted Brahmanical beliefs unless it was able to show and prove its excellence and superiority over Brahmanism. To influence the common man early and inspire him with awe and reverence for the Buddha was to establish the superiority of the Buddha over popular Brahmanical Gods so long worshipped as the most revered. Prompted perhaps with such an idea the Buddhists who codified and systematized the teachings and words of the Master, long after his Mahaparinirvana, selected Brahma one of the three most important Brahmanical Gods, to the represented as praying for the sermon. In course of time the teacher who was so much against anything connecting with deity and divinity became himself deified in Mahayana and was considered as Lokottara or superhuman. The Buddhist masters with their broadminded receptiveness strengthened by the tendency of spreading over the backward frontier peoples did not hesitate to accept their ideas and deities in their fold. These elements were fully transformed, purged of their primitive crudeness and endowed with sacred symbols. Many of the magic circles of Vajrayana reveal contacts of Buddhism with frontier peoples. The Goddess Ekajata, later considered to be an aspect of Tara is said to have been introduced by Nagarjuna with her liturgy borrowed from Bhota(Tibet) country. The Vajrayanic sects accepted the ideas and intuitions current among the masses and with their tolerant universalism incorporated popular indigenous deities in their *Mandalas* as acolytes of their chief gods. In the process the popular Hindu deities like Indra, Varuna, Mahesvara, Skanda, Vishnu, and even Kama, the god of love, are all admitted wholesale into Buddhism and find their places in the *Mandalas* but as keepers of the quarters. With the diversion of the Buddha's religion to this direction a large number of divine and fiendish beings also found their places in Vajrayanic texts and often they were in female forms and sometime of monstrous appearances in almost all texts of later Buddhism we meet with such beings as Cunda, Amba, Ambika, Dakini, Yogini, Yakshini etc.

The incorporation of Hindu gods and goddesses into Buddhism reached its maximum point with the development of Kalachakra system of the Vajrayana. It is learnt from Kalachakra texts that the Buddhists were faced with a social problem of the infiltration of the Semitic culture and religion and they offered to join hands with the followers of the Brahmanical culture to resist the growing influence of the foreign culture.

It has been stated that the king of Sambhala was very much disturbed to learn that the future generations of both the Buddhists and the Brahmanical sages of Sambhala would accept and propagate the religion of Islam and having killed animals in the name of the Islamic God would eat their meat :

> *Yusmatputrapautradayo mlecchadharmapravrttim krtva Sambhaladi-sannavatimahavisayesu mlecchadharmadesanam karisyanti.Mlecchadevata bisamilla mantrena karttikaya grivayam pasum hatva tatas tesam svadevatamantrenahatanam pasunam mamsam bhaksayisyanti.*

In order to stop this inroad of an alien culture he proposed intermarriage and interdining among the Buddhist and Brahmanical sages and appealed to the sages to assemble under the banner of Lord Kalachakra. Since very ancient time kala (time) has been regarded as the Supreme Lord by many schools. The *Asvamedhikaparvan* of the Mahabharata describes the *wheel of time* in an elaborate metaphorical way to establish that the man who well known the *time* is never deluded and reaches the highest goal. The Lord Supreme, Kalachakra, might have been set up as a non-sectarian God to make it possible for all the warring elements of different religious groups to unite and fight under one banner against the foreign infiltration. The development of this system with abundant incorporation of Brahmanic deities in the *Mandala* might have been a necessity to cause a cultural fusion and offer a united front against the penetration of semitic culture. In order to stop the declining character of Buddhism the Buddhists also borrowed ideas and practices from the developing religious systems of Saivism, Vaisnavism as also the flourishing contemporary Indian religious system as usual foreign elements. Even the Buddhist Tantric system was influenced by Bramanical concept of rites and rituals. The Tantric path described various *homas*, oblations and recitation of mantras. In the Kalachakra Tantra[6] we find interesting account where the Buddha says to King Sucandra:

"I am Indra in the heaven, master of gods and men as well, the sovereign king on the earth, the king of Nagas in the nether world saluted by the families of serpent, going everywhere and the excellent one, I am knowledge, the enlightened one, master of ascetics, the supreme omnipresent, One without change, Vajrayoga of Yogins, Veda and the sacred Omkara came to my refuse, O king, will all devotion."

> *Indro' ham svargaloke tridasanaragurur bhutale cakravarti Putale nagarajah phanikulanamitah sarvagasco'ttamo'ham, Jnanam Buddho munindro'ksharaparamavibhur yoginam Vajrayoga Veda'nkarah Pavitra Vraja mama saranam sarvabhavena rajan.*

Here the verse reminds us of the Vibhuti-yoga of the Bhagavadgita[7] where Sri Krishna describes Himself in an identical manner. Again, Vimaloprabha[8] quotes a mantra from the Rigveda[9] and speaks of the three sacrificial fires, i.e. *Dakshinagni, Garhapatya and Ahavaniya representing respectfully Vidyut and Kravyad with an addition of the fourth Agni, Satya, representaing Jnanagni*[10]. In fact many such borrowings from Brahmanical tradition can be met with in the *Kalachakra Ttantra*.

Kalachakra system and the concept of Kalachakra as the Supreme Lord are two bright examples of the process of cultural fusion as going on in eastern India and they also perhaps confirm that it was not with hatred and aversion that the Buddhists assigned to the Hindu gods posts subordinate to their chief God but it was a historical necessity.

### Notes and References

1. Majumdar, R.C., *History of Bengal*, p.422
2. *Macmillan Encyclopedia of Buddhism*, 2004, pp. 875-876
3. Warder, A.K., 1999, *Indian Buddhism*, p. 466
4. Quoted in the Sekoddesatika p.3

5. edited by Kalpakar Sankaranarayan, *et. al.*, *Buddhism in India and Abroad*, pp.249 ff.
6. *Kalachakra Tantra II*, p.179
7. X,19-38
8. *Kalachakra Tantra,* Vol.II, p.179
9. X. 16.9
10. Vimalaprabha, *op cit*, Vol. II, p.75

22

# Bhikkshuṇīs (Nuns) and their Contribution in Indian Culture

*Sayamtara Jash*

The establishment of the *Bhikkshuṇī-saṁgha* in India during the time of Gautama, the Buddha, is an unparallel event in the history of the gender studies. It is possibly the earliest exclusive foundation of the world that projects the elevation of the status and position of women in general and the nuns in particular. It is still an enigma to the scholars why the Buddha had earlier refused to admit women to the *Saṅgha* or community of celibates (*Bhikkshuṇīs*). The Pāli literature demonstrates that Buddha initially refused his foster mother, Mahāprajāpati Gotamī to be admitted to the *Saṅgha*. Failing to have approval from the great Master, Mahāprajāpati Gotamī then approached Ānanda, disciple of Buddha to plead on her behalf. Buddha, however, turned down his plea to found an Order of nuns. Ānanda, however, persuaded. He reminded that Buddha himself had declared that women are enough for attaining *Nirvāṇa*. The great Master ultimately allowed the Order of the nuns to be found. But the rules of their Order (*Saṅgha*) proclaim that nuns (*Bhikkshuṇīs*) are considered lower to monks. All these rules are elaborately stated in the *Bhikkshuṇī Pātimoksha*.[1]

Our intention is to combine two objects, each forming the counterpart of the other and both of the extraordinary importance, for the studies of women in Buddhism of early India with particular emphasis on the Buddhist *Bhikkshuṇī Prātimoksha*.

However, by recognizing broad parity between man and woman in matters of religion, Buddhism elevated the status of women as liberal reaction against the orthodox *Brāhmanism* of the contemporary period. In fact, Buddhism recognized the individuality and independence of women and their eligibility for salvation in their own right. Formation of the *Bhikkshuṇī Saṅgha* had also an important effect on the position of women in general and especially the Buddhist women. A woman could remain unmarried by becoming a *Bhikkshuṇī*. From widowhood also the women could find a respite in renunciation.

These *Bhikkshuṇīs* came from all walks of life-from palaces, noble families, Brāhmaṇa, Kshatriya, merchant classes, workers, outcaste and even from the harlots. Many women admitted to the nuns Order achieved distinction and enjoyed great prestige and respect in India and abroad also. Saṅghamitra, for example, belonged to the Mauryan royal family, was the first women foreign Missionary in world history, who went to Ceylon (Sri Lanka) and founded there the Order of nuns. She was a daughter of the great Maurya King Aśoka of Magadha in Bihar. Her mother was Vidisādevī, a daughter of a merchant of ancient Vidiśānagar in Madhya Pradesh. She devoted her entire life for the cause of Buddhism and she became a very successful nun who cares for the benefit and happiness of *Bhikkshuṇīs*.[2] The paper is now devoting to throw light on the early life and main activities of some of the prominent nuns who contributed to the cause of the progress and development of the women in general and the nuns in particular.

## Mahāprajāpati Gotamī

Mahāprajāpati Gotamī was born as a daughter of Suppabuddha at the Śākyan village of Devādadaha. She was the younger sister of Mahāmāyā, who died on the seventh day after the birth of Siddhārtha Gautama. After Mahāmāya's death, it is said that, at that time Gotamī had given birth to Nanda Kumāra. Mahāprajāpati took charge of her sister's child and nursed him as her own. After Mahāmāya's death, Mahāprajāpati became the chief queen. She entrusted the care of her own son to a nurse and she herself reared Siddhārtha Gautama. People began to call the prince after her name and thus became Gotama, the child of Gotamī. She was through Mahāprajāpati's request as well as pressure brought to a great extent by Ānanda, the chief disciple of Buddha, that Buddha agreed to admit women in the Order and set up a nunnery for them, although with great reluctance.[3] When Mahāprajāpati was at last admitted into the Order: "she took to meditation exercises under the direct supervision of the great Teacher and soon attained perfection. She lived up to the age of one hundred and twenty years and was declared by the teacher as the oldest and the most experienced of ordained nuns (*rattannunanam*). Buddha did not show any special consideration to her." Buddha held her in the great respect and love is born out by the fact that ".......he paid her visits when she was on her deathbed, and gave suitable discourses after altering the rule that a monk must not go near the bed to a sick nun."

Mahāprajāpati did yeoman service to those women who wanted to join the Order: it was she who secured "Buddha's consent for the formation of the Order of nuns in the Buddhist system, and it was at her instance that several rules were framed for the disciplinary guidance of the nuns. These rules are known as *Bhikkshuṇī Prātimoksha Sūtra*. The *Therīgātha* attributes to her a few *gāthās*, in which she offered her respects to Buddha." It is said that "she practiced the eightfold path and realized that her present body was the last one....."

Although Buddha showed great respect and love to Mahāprajāpati according to some sources it is said that she was aware of the rigours and dominance the monk exercised over the nuns and it is said that when she drew the attention of Buddha he refused to amend the rules. When once again she approached Him, this time through Ānanda to amend the rules so that both the monks and nuns could enjoy equal rights, respect and cordiality between the two and the nuns be treated with respect and not be dominated by the monks, Buddha flatly refused to heed to her request. However it must be recorded that it goes to the credit of Buddha that he took great trouble to remove the misgivings spread by some that she (Mahāprajāpati) took *Prabajjā* and not *Upasampadā*. He went to the extent to declare that he himself was her *āchārya* for *Upasampadā* and that he considered and admired her as a real Brāhmin who was pure in body and mind and did not even have the idea of what a sin is and her character was stainless and fully controlled. It is said that only after this declaration by Buddha she was allowed to approach Buddha for any counseling and arbitration directly without the intervention of any monk, as was the prevailing rule for others.

Similarly as a nun she was always alert about the injustices being inflicted on women. She was responsible for many modifications in the rules and regulations concerning the life of a nun in a nunnery.[4] Finding the practice of nuns being asked to wash the cloths of monks quite derogatory Mahāprajāpati drew the attention of Buddha to this practice and at his intervention it was stopped. Because this type of exploitation was so great that nuns could hardly get enough time for meditations and spiritual practices. In fact, she herself had lived as a nun soon after her entry into the Order she was able to appreciate the difficulties of the nuns. Once when she was sick Buddha went to see her and ask about her welfare: she took this opportunity to convince him how in sickness she was deprived of listening to the scriptural readings (*Dhamma*) since *Bhikkhus* (monks) were not allowed to visit any sick nun nor were the nuns allowed to read these sacred literature to the sick person. Buddha was quick to appreciate her point of view and immediately approved and sanctioned the rule that a nun could read these scriptures to a sick nun since the invalid was not able to move out. So also she was successful in getting the permission from Buddha for the nuns to bathe in any secluded tank / pond / river which were prohibited till then. This act of Gotamī also contributes in enhancing the social status of a woman in the society. She relieved the women especially the *Bhikkshuṇīs* from humiliation and provided them a strong shelter and respectful status in the society. She rendered an excellent service to the cause of nuns and in the development of Buddhist nunnery and her contribution for the cause is still remembered and cherished. It is thus aptly stated that, "After her death she was given a unique honour which was impossible for any ancient Indian woman to receive. The miracles at her cremation rites were second only to those of the Buddha".[5]

## Yaśodharā

The next significant character hailing from the royal family who made a commendable contribution to the field of Indian culture and civilization is Yaśodharā. She was known as Rāhula's mother (Rāhula mātā) and Gautama's wife. She was also called Bhaddākāccanā. According to Buddhaghoshā, she was called Bhaddākāccanā[6] because her skin was like burnished gold (*kāñcanā*), and, in later text, Bimbādevī and, probably, Bimbāsundarī. She was born on the same day as the Bodhisattā. She was married to Gautama Buddha at the age of sixteen. She was placed at the head of forty thousand women given to Gautama by the Śākyans. Gautama, later, left home to homelessness. Afterwards she has born a son who was named Rāhula. According to one account, referred to in the *Jātaka* commentary, Rahula was seven years old, when Buddha left home, he took a last look at his wife from the door of her room. Gautama renounced the world and after attaining *Bodhi* he came back to Kapilāvatthu and preached his doctrine to his clansmen. On the second day of that visit, he begged on the street. Rāhulamāta heard this news and looked out of her window to see if it is true. She saw Buddha and was so struck by the glory of his personality that she uttered eight verses in praise. It was known as, *Narasihagāthā*. On that day Buddha took meal at the invitation of Śuddhodana. Buddha took meal in the palace, and after that all the ladies of the court went to pay him obeisance. But Yaśodharā did not go..... That if she had any virtue in her the Buddha would come to her. Buddha went to her with his two disciples, giving order that she should be allowed to greet him as she wished. She fell at his feet and clasping them with her hands, put her head on them. Śuddhodana stated to the Buddha that from the time he had left home, Yaśodharā had herself given up all luxury and had lived in the same manner as she had heard that the Buddha lived wearing yellow robes, eating only once a day, etc.

According to the version of the *Aṅguttara Nikāya,*[7] she was the chief nun in the possession of supernatural powers (*mahābhinnappattanam*). It is generally believed that she was one of the four disciples of Buddha possessing attainment, the others being Sāriputta, Moggāllana and Bakkula. She expressed her desire for this achievement at the time of Padumuttāra Buddha. *Therī* Yaśodharā played an important role for the spread of Buddhism by initiating several common women folk in religion of the Buddha. She was assigned the chief place among the *Bhikkshuṇī* possessing great supernatural powers, and she also 'attained the six higher powers (*abhijña*).[8]

## Khemā

Khemā, another disciple of the Buddha played an important role for the development of the women folk in early India. The story of her transformation from the proud beautiful wife of king Bimbisāra makes fascinating reading. She was born in Sāgala (identified with Siālkot) in the land of the ancient Madras in N.W.F.P. It is said that she was the daughter of one of the kings of the Punjab and "when she grew up, she had an exquisite appearance with a complexion like metal gold". Tradition avers that "her exquisite beauty attracted the attention of king Bimbisāra, who made her his chief queen."[9] Although Bimbisāra was an ardent devotee of Buddha, but his queen chose not to follow her husband in this respect since she came to know that ".......Lord Buddha condemned infatuation with one's own personal beauty and so she preferred to remain away from him (Buddha) and thus avoid being criticized for her love for beautiful appearance".

There is nothing strange about her behavior since she knew that she was lovely beyond description and was proud of being so. However Bimbisāra tried to pursue Khemā to show respect to the Buddha and follow his teachings as he himself did. Realizing that no amount of persuasion will make the queen change her mind he thought of other means to achieve his object. He took the opportunity of Lord Buddha staying at Venuvana, in Rājagriha, Bihar, and the palace garden which the king himself had given away to the Buddha to convert it into a Buddhist *Saṅgha*. It is known as the famous Buddhist *Saṅgha*-Venuvana Vihāra. Khemā expressed her desire to visit this beautiful garden with all its glory. The king arranged her visit to the garden and asked the party accompanying her to pay homage to the Buddha who was at that time camping at the garden. The queen was not at all interested in visiting Buddha but wanted to return to the palace. The party accompanying the queen took a separate route which had to pass the place where Buddha was camping. In the "meantime Lord Buddha had magically created a woman of exquisite beauty and made her fan him with a palm leaf." The innocent queen while looking out of her carriage saw this scene of beautiful women, much more beautiful than she herself attending on the Lord. She was shocked at the thought that anybody could be much more beautiful than her and slowly got down from the carriage and approached Lord Buddha. She stood there like a statue drinking in the beauty and charm of the women and thought came to her that she herself was not even fit to be the maid servant of such a beauty. The more she looked at the women the more lovely she looked. But suddenly there was transformation in the woman when the Teacher changed the beautiful young lady into matronly middle aged women, then into a wrinkled old hag and ultimately made her fall down on the ground. The lesson had its effect, queen Khemā realized that this is a fate of every living human being including herself and for what she was so proud of when suddenly she heard the voice of Lord Buddha reciting the verse:[10]

> "Those who are given to attachment fall into the stream (of repeated births)
> Like the spider (caught) in the net created by itself.
> One who has no attachment gets rid of this
> Sufferings and goes out by tearing asunder the net".

The Buddhist Pāli literature affords that the queen in her previous lives had accumulated lots of merits and because of this it is said that she obtained '*Arhathood*' immediately. Since she had lost all her interest in the worldly life now she decided to give up this material world and take ordination. Returning to the palace Bimbisāra asked her whether she had met the great Teacher and paid him respects. She calmly replied; 'You have only seen and listened to him only, what you have done is negligible to what I have earned, I have met the real Teacher who I had visualized from such a long time. Permit me, O my Lord to renounce this world and to become a *Bhikkshuṇī*, I beg of you, do me this favor'.

Having received such a logistic response from the queen, Bimbisāra offered his consent for joining the nunnery where it is narrated she became very learned mastering the rules, regulations and related Buddhist śāstras, etc. that ultimately Buddha gave her the highest position among the *Therīs*.

It is said that she acquired such perfection in spiritual knowledge that several scholars and even kings thought it a privilege to discuss with her on spiritual matters. It is said that

Lord Buddha consistently refused to answer a certain question such as whether a *Tathāgata* exists after death. Referring to this once king Pāsendi questioned Khemā to which she persistently replied, "........the Lord has not explained". Pāsendi would not give up and asked, "Why has the Lord not explained?" to which Khemā put a counter question:

> "Let me ask you a question, O king and as it suits you, so explain it. What think you, O King? Have you an account or reckoned or estimator who can count the sand of the Ganges, and say, so many grains, or so many hundred, thousand or hundred thousand grains?"
>
> "No revered one. None can".
>
> ".....Have you an account who can measure the water of the ocean and say, so many measures of water, or so many hundred, thousand or hundred thousand measures?"
>
> "No, reverend one". But why they cannot?"
>
> "Because, Reverend One, the ocean is deep, immeasurable unfathomable.",
>
> "Even so, O king, that body by which one might define a *Tathāgata* is relinquished, cut off at the root, uprooted like a palm-tree, brought to naught, not to arise in the future. Freed from the designation of body a *Tathāgata* is deep, immeasurable, and unfathomable as the ocean."[11]

Further, she explained to the king that the *Tathāgata* after death could not be located by material ingredients (*rupā*) or feeling (*vedanā*) or constituents which composed a being: hence the question of his location after death could not arise..... This exposition satisfied the king, who was highly impressed by her erudition"[12]

## Āmrapāli

Āmrapāli or Ambapali, according to the Pāli legend was found in a mango tree by the Śākyan noble named Mahānamā.[13] It is also stated that as she was born spontaneously of a branch of a mango tree *(amba-rukkhamule opapatika hutva nibbatti)*. This noble man was childless and no wonders he took the child as god-sent and handed her over to his wife who brought her up as her own child. Āmrapāli grew into a beauteous lady of many talents and was coveted by many princes and sons of noble men all over the country. The father was in a fix, since he dared out not go against any of them. So he decided to arrange for a *Svayaṁvara* when Āmrapāli could choose her own husband. On the decided day many princes, noblemen and rich men gathered and all of them desired to see the girl before the actual *Svayaṁvara* took place. According to their wishes Āmrapāli was brought before the assembled guests by her father, "The members were struck with amazement at her beauty and decided unanimously that she should be enjoyed by all (*Gaṇa-bhoga*)". Naturally this decision was a great shock to the father, which father would like this daughter to become a courtesan? At the same time he could not disregard the decision of the guests. As such he was in a fix. At this juncture Āmrapāli herself came to the rescue to her father and agreed to abide by their decision provided that she

1. should be provided with a house in the best locality of the city
2. only one person would be entitled to enter her premises at a time
3. her fees would be very steep- 500 kārshāpaṇas

4. her house could be searched and inspected only after seven days of notice for her enemies or culprits and finally
5. there should be no watch on who came and who went to her house.

The assembled guests agreed to her conditions.

Āmrapāli started the construction of such a fine house in the best locality of the city and it was so beautiful that it became the cynosure of the whole country; she got the walls painted by the best of artists with the portraits of kings, princes, military generals, traders, bankers etc. Once while watching these portraits she came across that of king Bimbisāra and promptly fell in love with him. Strangely at the same time king Bimbisāra had also come to hear about her beauty and talents and was anxious to meet her personally. However the political relationships between the two countries (Lichchhāvis and Magadha) were not at all cordial and so king Bimbisāra was warned against going to Lichchhavis to meet Āmrapāli. However he was so much infatuated by her that he took the risk and came to her with his trusted general Gopā. Āmrapāli sheltered him for seven days taking advantage of her last two conditions in her house. During this period she became pregnant and later gave birth to a son who grew up to be brave dashing young man. However his friends used to tease him for not knowing his father and when his position became unbearable Āmrapāli gave him the signet-ring King Bimbisāra had given to her to be used in case of need. So with the help of the ring the son was united with the father.

After many years he became the disciple of Gautama Buddha and was known as Vimalā-Kondānā. In the meantime Āmrapāli was able to amass large amount of wealth and became very famous. Later she became a lay devotee of Buddha. It is said that she once invited and fed Buddha and all the members of his Order which was much appreciated not only by Buddha but also by the other disciples and finally she presented Buddha with her famous mango grove with all its princely buildings which was later converted into *Bhikkshu Saṅgha*. That was not the end, once she heard her own son give a discourse and she was so much moved by it that she decided to become a *Bhikkshuṇī* and after her ordination she obtained insight into the truth and once she realized the impermanence of the worldly existence attainment of *Arahathood* was but natural. It is also said that she composed many couplets *(Gāthās)*.

In another version it is also said when Āmrapāli invited Buddha and offered him food an act which infuriated her community and she was asked to pay a huge fine to the community and all kinds of pressure were brought upon her to pay the fine. However Āmrapāli remained firm and refused to bow down to the threats. So Lichavis also invited Buddha on the same day to make him cancel the invitation to Āmrapāli. Although Buddha refused to oblige them just to appease them and to ease the tension he spoke to the community about his spiritual message during the feast so it became a spiritual feast from which all benefited. In respect of his diplomatic moves Buddha was a revolutionary as compared to others, specially the conservatives during his time.

Āmrapāli's episode with Buddha is very significant as it reflects the liberal attitude and sense of compassionate feelings of Buddha and the '*Karunā*' (affection and kindness) towards women including the ladies who were known to be courtesans whom many would have preferred to ignore. Āmrapāli's sayings are also mentioned in the *Therīgāthas* which mainly stress on the short lived temporal aspects of life.

Apart from these reputed and well known women personalities we may mention that a large number of Buddhist nuns and lay women followers (*Upāsikās*) have imprinted an indelible mark in the cultural history of India. We may note in this context that in the early Indian inscriptions there are innumerable evidences containing the records of the contributions (*dāna*) of the *Bhikkshuṇīs* (nuns) for the integration of the *Saṁgha* activities with its cultural and traditional bearings. Some of them are like – Bhaddā Kuṇḍalākeśī, Paṭācārā, Viśākhā, Uppalāvānnā, Kisāgotami, Dhammādinnā, Sukkā, Abhirūpānandā, Śelā, Anulā, Cāndā, Sundarī Nandā, Uttarā, Cālā, Upācālā, Vijayā, Sumedhā, Sujātā, Sumanā, Sunitā, and many others who are also immortal for their contributions for the cause of freedom and empowerment of women.[14] Without presenting any further details in this regard it is to be mentioned that the Buddhist Pāli literature of the contemporary period and the *Therīgāthās* composed by the Buddhist nuns describe about the works and activities of some eminent *Bhikkshuṇīs* who have raised the status of women in general, and the nunnery community in particular. In fact, the contribution of these *Bhikkshuṇīs* for the development and enrichment of Indian culture and civilization, especially in the field of gender studies, is immense and can hardly be over estimated.

### Notes and References


1. Akira Hirakawa, 1999, *Monastic Discipline for the Buddhist Nuns: An English Translation of the Chinese Text of the Mahāsaṁghika – Bhikshuṇī Viṇaya*, Patna.
   Roth Gustav, 1970, *Bhikshunī – Viṇaya*, K.P.Jayaswal Research Institute, Patna; Horner, I.B, 1975, *Women under Primitive Buddhism*, Delhi
2. Sohani, S.V., 1971, *Mahāvaṁśa Tika*, Nava Nalanda Publication, Bihar, pp.185-185-192.
3. Oldenberg, H. 1965, *Viṇaya Piṭaka, Mahāvagga and Cullāvagga*, trans. Delhi.
4. Vadekar, R.D. 1939, *Patimokkha, Nissaggiya rule no.17*, Pune, p.9
5. Malalasekera, G.P. 1938, *Dictionary of Pāli Proper Names*, Vol. II. London, p.523.
6. *Manorathapurāṇi*, p.1, 204
7. *Aṅguttara Nikāya*, 1965, Pali Text Society, Vol. I, Delhi, p.25
8. Dutt, Nalinaksha.1971, *Early Monastic Buddhism*, Calcutta, p.105
9. *Ibid.*, p.127
10. Lama, C.R.(ed.) 1982, *Dhammapada, The Dalai Lama Tibeto-Indological Studies Series, Vol.IV*, Central Institute of Higher Tibetan Studies, Sarnath
11. Thomas, Edward J. 1969, *The Life of Buddha in Legend and History*, London
12. *Gathas*. cf. also, *Paramatthadipani, P.T.S.*, pp.207 ff.
13. Majumder, R.C. (ed.). 1990, *The Age of Imperial Unity*, Bombay, Bharatiya Vidya Bhavana, Vol.II, p.568
14. Jash, Sayamtara, 2010, Unpublished Thesis on *Studies of Women in Buddhism as reflected in the Buddhist Pratimoksha*, Visva Bharati.

23

# Jainism: Its Identity on the Basis of Literature and Philosophy

*Asha Mukherjee*

The study of Jainism in general and Jaina Philosophy in particular has not been paid sufficient attention by Indian scholars or by foreign scholars. This research paper aims at arguing against the often maintained view that Jaina and Buddhist philosophy emerged as a reaction against the Brahamanical doctrine of caste and other social evils and that Jainism is offshoot of Buddhism and Hinduism. Instead it is argued here that Jainism is neither an offshoot of Buddhism nor of Hinduism as there is no historical data which can establish this fact. Even before the advent of the Aryans in India we have reasons to believe that highly cultivated society existed along the Ganges around Magadh where Jainism flourished and they had no allegiance to the Vedic authorities. It is an unfortunate fact that Indians had to learn their history from foreign scholars. Most of the text books of Indian history in schools and of Indian philosophy depend upon the erroneous views and are prevalent among the educated Indians.

The origin of this error is to be found in the fact that the founder of Buddhism Goutam Sakyamuni and Mahavira Vardhana the last of the Jaina Thirthankaras were contemporaries. Buddhist literature contains references to Mahavira and his followers, and similarly Jaina literature composed at the time of Mahavira contains cross references to Buddha and his religion. Persons who studied Buddhism first and then the Jain literature came to a hasty conclusion that Jainism must be the branch of Buddhism. Later on some oriental scholars corrected their views and were constrained to accept that Jainism must have been earlier than Buddhism. As a matter of fact Buddha was a younger contemporary of Lord Mahavira. Buddha himself in his conversation with his friend and disciple Sariputta, narrates the fact that he himself in his earlier days was adopting Jaina practice of austerity which he had to give up because of the rigorous discipline which he did not like. The date of Mahavira's *paranirvana,* 527 B.C. is accepted as a land mark in the history of India.

According to *Cambridge History of India*, the 23rd Thirthankara, Lord Parswa who lived, 220 years prior to Lord Mahavira is also considered a historical personage. According to this view Jainism must have been prevalent in India nearly three centuries prior to Gautam Buddha the founder of Buddhism. But we have ground to believe that Jainism was in existence even before Lord Parswa. According to the Jaina tradition Lord Arishtanemi is the 22nd Thirthankara who has said to attain Nirvana on the mount Girnar in Junagarh State, in India which is a place of pilgrimage for the present day Jainas. Arishtanemi was a cousin of Sri Krishna of Mahabharata and his name occurs in Vedic literature as one of the great Rishis. If Sri Krishna and Mahabharata war is accepted on historical ground then we have to accept the history of Arishtanemi also.

According to Jaina tradition there were twenty four Thirthankaras beginning with Lord Rishabha and ending with Mahavira Vardhamana the last three to be personalities of the historic period. The others are of prehistoric age and we need not bother about their history till we know something more than mere tradition. The first Thirthankara Lord Rishabha is considered to be responsible for revealing *ahinsa dharma* for the first time to the world. He was hero of the Iksavaku family. His father was Nabi Maharaja, the last of the Manus and mother Marudevi. Rishabha's period represents a complete change of world conditions. Prior to this the country was called *boga bhumi* where the people were satisfied with all their wants by the mere wish through the help of the traditional *kalpakavriksha*. During the time of Lord Rishabha these happy conditions completely disappeared and the people did not know what to do to have a good way of life. Then they all went to Lord Rishabha praying for help and he shown them the way to good life. He taught them how to obtain food by tilling the soil, agriculture etc. and supply the needy in the absence of *kalpakavrikshas*. He also assigned duty to some for defending and thereby giving rise to first social organization. It was Lord Rishabha who divided the society according to its functions in to three groups, agriculture, traders and soldiers. Later his son Lord Bharata took the charge and Lord Rishabha went in to the forests to perform *tapas*. After attaining *Kevalajnana* he went from one place to another to preach Ahimsa Dharma to the people of the land so that they can also have spiritual relief. Lord Rishabha is known as *adijina* and *adi bhagvana*.

Interestingly, the life of first Thirthankara's is repeated in non-Jaina *puranas* also for example, in *Bhagavatapurana* (V. skanda), *Vishnupurana* and *Vayupurana*. All these Hindu *puranas* maintain that Lord Rishabha preached the doctrine of *ahimsa* after performing yoga for several years. This only shows that Lord Rishabha was worshiped by Jainas and non-Jainas equally as early as in Vedic period.

Vedas include the *Samhitas*, *Brahmanas* and *Upanishads*. Aryans of the Rig Vedic period had to encounter opposition from among the people of the land whom they considered their enemies, who strongly resisted the invading Aryans. We find many hymns referred to a section of the Ikshavakus or Purusha who were in existence in the land long before the Aryans of the Rig Vedic period came into scene these were called *Raghuvamsa- Kshatriya* families, the *Sakya* clan to which Gautama Buddha belonged. Kalidas's *Raguvamsa* is also refers them. All these heroes began their life as normal child, they lived their household lives as *grahastha* after which they completely renounced their worldly attachment and performed *tapas* or *yoga* and then finally discarded their bodies after-realization. This description fully corresponds with the life history of Lord Rishabha the first revealer of Ahimsa to the world.

Therefore we have enough ground to conclude that Rishabha cult must have been prevalent even before the advent of the Aryans and the Rig-Vedic tradition.

The other argument is based on Vedic literature. The Aryans of the Rig Vedic period were resisted by the people of the land called *dasyus* -the slaves or enemies. It seems before the Aryans came they were called enemies and later when they became prisoners of war they were made to work as slaves. These *dasyus* are described as *ayagna, anindra, avrata, anyavrata* and so on. These terms respectively mean those who are opposed to *yagna,* Indra-worship, those that observe a different religious practice and those who do not practice the religion of the Aryans. From these descriptions it is clear that the people of the land were dead against the Vedic institutions of *yagna* or animal sacrifice. The *dasyus* the people of the land are also described to have dark skin and having different language. Therefore they must have been Dravidians who were present all over India at the time of Aryan invasion. Interestingly the Vedic literature uses a term to describe the religion of the *dasyus* who were opposed to *yagna* and Indra worship they were worshippers of *Sisnadeva-* the *linga,* representing the male sex organ. The only meaningful interpretation we could give is that the people of the land were worshippers of nude idol as their God which can be called consistently as *Sisnadeva* which must have been the characteristic of the Rishabha cult and was encouraged by his son Bharata in terms of temple worship. The excavations of Harappa and Mohenjodaro go along with our theory; we have nude images of a yogi considered to be idols used for worship by the people of Indus Valley. Rishabha cult has been prevalent through out the land from Himalayas down to south in Lanka.

According to Jaina tradition the Northern India was completely occupied by five *kshatriya* dynasties namely, the *ikshavakuvamsa*, *harivamsa*, *kuruvamsa*, *ugravamsa* and *nathavamsa* and the people of the land called *vidhyadharas*. The *vidhyadharas* were all followers of Rishabha cult. We find many interesting stories in Jaina *Ramayana*. It clearly states that *vidhyadharas* were followers of Ahimsa and were against any *yagna* within their borders. This explains why in Valmiki *Ramayana Rakshasas* were always against performing *yagna*. Thus people of the land were all followers of Rishabha cult and had a higher form of religion.

There is one more reason. We notice a major shift in Upanishadic period. The people of the land hold that not performing *yagna* is their Dharma and performing *yagna* is a contradiction to Dharma. Prior to that the whole of Vedic culture is *swargakama yajethavyaha* - if you want happiness in *swarga* you must perform sacrifice. But when we turn to the Upanishadic period the idea is entirely different. Prosperity here and in *swarga*-happiness hereafter, both are considered as worthless. One should look for far more valuable than this. What could be the reason for this prime shift? The new culture of *atmavidya* which was championed by the *kshtriya* scholars of the land who lived in eastern part in Gangetic valley defended their *ahimsa* cult and convinced the priest of Kurupanchala. Thus we have the Jaina tradition fully corroborated by non-Jaina Vedic literature in these three distinct historic groups of the *Samhitas*, *Brahamanas* and the *Upanishads*. These facts from the Vedic literature along with the evidences supplied by excavations of the Indus valley would lead us to conclude that the Rishbha cult of ahimsa and the practice of *tapas* and yoga must have been prevalent before the advent of Aryans who sang the hymns of Rigveda. And therefore Rishabha's cult was the most ancient religious cult in India and was practiced before Aryan invasion.

## Jaina Philosophy and its Identity

In Jaina philosophy, great sanctity is attached to all life. Soul is taken as a conscious substance. The word 'Jaina' means a conqueror who has obtained perfect knowledge and absolute freedom from the bondage of *karma*. It specially refers to *tirthankara,* the one who has built a passage through the ocean of births, meaning the teachers of this religion. Sometimes *tirthankara* is also understood to mean the founder of the four *tirthas* or the orders of the monks, the nuns. There were 24 *tirthankaras* of which Rsabha or Adinath was the first, who had conquered their passion and sought liberation. Historically, only the existence of Mahavira is traceable and that of Parsvanatha may be inferred. The essential teachings were canonized only in 3rd century B.C. and were put in writing several centuries later. Bihar was the main center of Mahavira's followers and after the famine in the region a large group of monks left Bihar and migrated to Karnataka. A group however stayed back in Magadh. The one who migrated stuck to the strict regulations became known as *'Digambara'*, the sky-robed, and the later who stayed back and changed their ways due to famine became known as *'svetumbura'*, white – robed. The *'svetambara'*, are further divided in to two sub sects, namely, *deravasi* worshipping the idol in temple and *Sthanakvasi* worshipping their teachers in a monastery. The *Digambaras* were divided into *Terapanthi* and *Bisapanthi* depending on their difference in ritual observance. Jainism found patronage of early rulers like Chandragupta Maurya, Ashoka, Kharvela of Kalinga etc. In order to avoid injury to living organisms agriculture animal husbandry etc. are prohibited in Jainism. Occupations involving less mobility such as those of merchants are more suitable to them. Due to this reason they controlled large business houses related with textiles, grains, machinery and capital investment. Jainas owned textile industry, chemical industry, newspaper, precious metals, jewelry and banking.

Jainas realize that a strict moral discipline is necessary for purity of life. They do not isolate metaphysics from nature of self; behavior cannot be isolated from our metaphysical beliefs. Truth and value are inseparable, without knowing the truth values cannot be realized which is the ultimate aim of philosophy. Therefore metaphysics and ethics are the two sides of the same coin. Samantabhadra goes to the extent of saying without knowing the real nature of things, which is permanency in transistorizes, all moral distinctions between bondage and liberation, *papa* and *punya*, heaven and hell, pleasure and pain will be blurred. (*Jaina Ethics*, Dayananda Bhargava, Motilal Banarasidass,

Delhi, 1968, p. 12). *Nayavada*, represents the most consistent and most logical form of realism in Indian metaphysics. *syadvada* constitutes a comprehensive scheme of complementary methods designed to help the mind in grasping the nature of reality in its unity as well as in its diversity. All evil traits of character, arising out of activity of speech, mind or body have to be eradicated before the attainment of final emancipation.

Every object known to us has innumerable characters besides having positive and negative implications what it is and what it is not. The set of what it is not will always be greater than what it is, which also changes with time. Whatever it is, it is, due to its substantial qualities (*gunas*). There could also be accidental qualities. Consciousness is substantial quality of soul but pleasure, pain, desire are accidental (modes or *paryayas*) to soul substance. Change and permanence both are real. Reality consists of three factors: permanence, origination and decay. Souls have varying degrees and kinds of knowledge. There could be perfect souls, who have attained omniscience or there could be of lower or of lowest imperfect souls, which inhabit bodies in earth, water, air or vegetables. Two to Five sensed are midway between lowest and highest like warms, ants and men. Soul is eternal, but it undergoes change of states. On the basis of one's past actions a jiva enters into a body, *jiva* is not infinite it is not present everywhere but only in the body. Jaina reject the existence of God as the creator of the world, but the notion of worship is quite well accepted in the system. One should worship the liberated or perfect souls, they are God-like and can be prayed or can offer guidance and provide inspiration. Past misdeeds can only be countered by generating strong opposite forces like good thought, good speech and good action within the soul. Therefore everyone must work for his own salvation.

Jainism accepts the dualism between self and non-self; *jiva,* soul and *ajiva*, matter. How the *jiva* joins *ajiva* is a mystery but it is karmic matter, which is the medium between body and soul. The soul has an inherent quality of attracting these particles towards itself. But mere flow of this karmic matter is not an obstacle it is with the four fundamental passions *(kasaya)* anger, pride, deceitfulness and greed *(krodh, moha, kama, lobh)* hold the karmic matter in bondage with soul. This inflow of fresh karmic matter is to be checked (*samvara*). This requires a constant control against trends of mind, deeds and words as may lead to such inflow. One needs to shed of karmic matter, which is already accumulated by the soul by meditation. At the end, the soul that was engulfed in the mud of karmic matter after getting rid of it, shines in its intrinsic purity of infinite knowledge, intuition, bliss and potency. (*Tattvarthasutra*, Banaras, 1952, 1.4). Attainment of right conduct is a gradual process; the aspirant may not be able to achieve the highest ideals at the first stage. He therefore can observe only partial self-control as a householder where as at the stage of monkhood he becomes capable of observing the rules of conduct more comprehensively. So we have two sets of rules of conduct one for householders and the other for the monk.

The role of our intellect, effort, moral teachings as helpers (teachers) are only meaningful if freedom of will is accepted. It makes no sense telling a person what he should do or should not do if he has no choice. The theory of omniscience and the theory of *karman* do presuppose a kind of determinism but they do not come in the way of our efforts to make ourselves moral. Kundakunda says that all of us have two fold consciousness- knowledge consciousness (*jnanacetana*) and action consciousness (*karmacetana*) (*Jaina Ethics,* Dayananda Bhargava, Motilal Banarasidass, Delhi, 1968, p.33).

Knowledge consciousness means the state of absolute freedom from the sense of being an agent of an action. The soul remains in its pure intrinsic, blissful, conscious state. It has no desire to initiate action-a state of supra moral, beyond good or bad- the state of complete freedom. But from practical point of view, it is action consciousness, which dominates. He has passions to choose between good and bad. Here the role of human effort (*purusarthas*) comes in. The two consciousnesses exclude each other and cannot exist side by side. The path to supra-ethical plane of life is only through practical path of morality and not through immorality. The ultimate aim is the complete cessation of all activities and attainment of knowledge consciousness. But it is only his effort and exertion, which brings him nearer to his goal. The self, within self, satisfied with self is the motto of all individualistic systems of philosophy- a kind of inwardness. In general, Indian systems accept that extroversion whether it is due to our incapability of self-control or for the cause of social service, never leads us nearer to the goal. It is rather withdrawal from the outside world, which takes us nearer to self-realization.

Bondage of soul is associated with matter, so it must disassociate itself from matter by *stopping* the influx of new matter into the soul and completely eliminating the matter with which the soul is mixed up. These two methods are called *samvara* and *nirjara*. To remove ignorance one must have the right knowledge. Mere knowledge is useless in itself, it must be practiced which is called right conduct. By *samvara* and *nirjara* soul is liberated by eliminating matter which ties the soul into bondage. The liberation is the joint effect of the three gems right faith (respect towards truth), right knowledge and right conduct.

To ascertain correct knowledge one has to make personal efforts. A practical code of conduct has been provided in this system. Vows compulsory for them were *ahimsa* (abstinence from all injury to life), *satyam* an individual to abstain from falsehood and *brahamcharya,* abstinence from self-indulgence. In total, there are five vows for any Jaina: *Satyam, Ahimsa, Astayam, Brahmcharya* and *Aparigraha.*

*Parigraha* is the result of *mohakarma*, which is the main obstacle to self-realization. *Moha* has two sides- attachment and aversion. The first manifests itself as *parigraha* and the later as *himsa* therefore *aparighraha* is as important as *ahimsa* it is non-attachment as well as non-possession. *Parigraha* includes land, house, coins, gold, maidservants, men servants, jewels, bed and other luxury items. There are some other vows for householders: they are known as *silavratas,* which include three *gunavratas* and four *siksavratas* like restricting the movements of householder in order to avoid violence. (*Jaina Ethics*, Dayananda Bhargava, Motilal Banarasidass, Delhi, 1968, p.128)

According to Jaina, every judgment is to be qualified by word like may be (*syad*). Truth lies in its manifoldness and to make a categorical judgment is to claim that it is only of one kind, which is not only wrong but also being dogmatic according to Jaina theory.

Every judgment only expresses one aspect of reality and is therefore relative to the conditions. Different systems of philosophy present partial aspects of reality. Jaina system insists that we always should use a qualifier to express our view. For example, if it is raining and if I make a judgment "It is raining" then I should say, "May be it is raining" (*syad)* this meant that the space, time, quality etc. under which it is raining. This way of making judgment avoids the possibility of misunderstanding that it is raining, all times and everywhere etc. It emphasizes that the ordinary judgments passed by imperfect minds hold good from particular aspects and circumstances and from that point of view.

## Important contributions of Jaina Philosophy

Firstly, it provides space for difference of opinions and avoids any kind of absolutist stand or conflict. Jainism is accepting a kind of relativism but not skepticism. The approach of Jainism towards opponent is constructive and not destructive. It balances between opposites: practical and transcendental, fate and human efforts, substantial cause and instrumental cause, absolute and relative etc. Jainism argues that our knowledge in material world is limited. One needs to realize that his view does not represent the whole truth about anything and therefore we must learn to appreciate and respect the other's point of views. Secondly, Jainism does not confuse science of spirituality (*moksasastra*) with science of righteousness *(dharmasastra*). The essential nature of *dharma* is different from non-essential beliefs, which change with time and place. Social problems and welfare of the society should not be confused with essential problems of ethics, which is emancipation. Thirdly, it lays emphasis on unity of faith, knowledge and conduct. Jainism is not merely a system of certain code of morality but a religion to be lived in practice. Householders and the monks both have to practice the rules of conduct in their lives. It is neither mere speculative philosophy nor a religion of rituals but a comprehensive system of religion and morality as well as of thought and conduct.

Fourthly, it is the life of a monk, which occupies the central place, as the ultimate aim of life is liberation. Thus complete renunciation of the mundane life and ascetic virtues are the virtues of a higher order for Jaina *Acaryas*.

Fifthly, Jainism is based on diversities as well as equality of life. All souls are equal so man, animal, insects and plant life all are given equal importance while observing ahimsa. Jainism does not accept any kind of distinction based on caste, creed and color.

To conclude, Jainism although originally was a religious movement but it can be regarded as the first example of secularism as it tells us that each view, each point of view has some truth and we must respect that truth, each religion has one perspective out of many and we must respect each perspective. Today, in India, unfortunately, on the name of secularism all the moral and spiritual values are washed away. Secularism does not mean absence of religion and *dharma*. It was never meant that we should banish all moral and spiritual values from our country or that religious and spiritual values should be outlawed from our educational system. It means equal respect for all religions, not equal neglect of all religions.

### *Notes and References*


1. Dayananda Bhargava, *Jaina Ethics*, Motilal Banarasidass, Delhi, 1968.
2. *Tattvarthasutra*, Banaras, 1952.
3. Basham, A.L., 1951, History and doctrines of the Ajivikas, London.
4. Tatia, N., 1951, Studies in Jaina Philosophy, Banaras.
5. Jaini, J.L., Outlines of Jainism, Oxford, 1940.
6. Khadbadi, B.K. *Studies in Jainology, Prakrit Literature and Language*, Prakrit Bharati Academy: Jaipur, 1997,
7. Banerjee, Satya Ranjan, *Introducing Jainism*, Jain Bhawan, Calcutta, 2002,
8. Jaini, P.S., The Jaina Path of Purification, Motilal Banarasidass, Delhi, 2001,
9. Chatterjee, A.K., 1984, *A Comprehensive History of Jainism*, (Vol.-II), Firma KLM, Calcutta.

24

# Jaina Contribution to *Prākṛta* Language and Literature

*Anupam Jash*

Von Humboldt has classified the world languages into four zone and thirteen family, viz., (a) African Zone, which includes (i) Semantic-hemantic,(ii) Vantu (iii) Sudanese and (iv) Bushman family. (b) Eurasian Zone, which includes (v) Malay-Polynesian,(vi) Ural-Altaic, (vii) Chinese, (viii) Dravidian, (ix) Austro-Asiatic, (x) Indo-European, (xi) Caucasian and (xii) Japanese-Korean family. (c) American Zone, which includes (xii) Red-Indian family, and (d) Pacific Zone which includes Malayo-Polynesian family[1]. The Indian Languages are included into the Indo-Āryan family of Euro-Asian Zone.

## The Indo-Āryan Language and *Prākṛta*

Linguists have divided Indo-Āryan Language under three stages from the point of view of their historical development. These are Old Indo-Āryan, Middle Indo-Āryan, and New Indo-Āryan. Each of these three stages of Indo-Āryan Language shows several sub-stages. Prof. Suniti Kumar Chatterjee in his *Origin and Development of the Bengali Language* presents his chronological approach to Indo-Āryan language, which we may describe with the following chart:

| | |
|---|---|
| Old Indo-Āryan | 1500 BC—600 BC |
| 1st Middle Indo-Āryan | 600 BC—200 BC |
| Transitional Middle Indo-Āryan | 200 BC—200 AD |
| 2nd Middle Indo-Āryan | 200 AD—600 AD |
| 3rd Middle Indo-Āryan | 600 AD—1000 AD |
| New Indo-Āryan | 1000 AD— |

This chronology of Indo-Āryan languages, by Prof. Chatterjee has been widely accepted[2]. Old Indo-Āryan contain Vedic *chandas* and classical Sanskrit. Middle Indo-

Āryan contains *Pāli*, *Prākṛta* and *Apabhraṃsa*; in a loose sense all Middle Indo-Āryan are called *Prākṛta* and New Indo-Āryan consists of old Hindi, Gujrati, Bengali, etc. However, an approximate and compact chronological sketch, with no watertight compartments whatsoever, of all literary languages of India can be drawn in the following table:

(I) Vedic and Classical Sanskrit: 1500 BC onwards.

(II) *Prākṛta, Pāli, Ardhamāgadhi, Śaurasenī* etc. 600BC—1000AD

(III) New Indo Āryan: Hindi, Marathi Gujrati etc. 1000AD onwards[3].

Almost all classical Indian languages like *Pāli, Prākṛta* and *Sanskrit* belong to the Indo-Āryan language. Among these *Sanskrit* is the most celebrated classical language of India. Sanskrit was not only spoken as official language among scholars but also was the language of creative writings from the very beginning of the Indian literature. *Prākṛta* is such a language, which has the largest flexibility among all Indo-Āryan languages in terms of direct, denotative and suggestive meanings. Hence, Sanskrit was the refined and cultivated language the medium of speech of the elite, though mainly they used it for literary purpose in those days. *Prākṛta* can be interpreted as the natural language of the masses. When Lord Mahavīra and Lord Buddha having got enlightenment, preferred to preach in the language spoken among common people, in order to popularized their canons among the people, they adopted *Prākṛta* as the medium and then *Prākṛta* came into light. Thenceforth, we get *Prākṛta* developed with many names, viz., *māgadhi, Arhamāgadhi, paiśaci, Pāli, śaurasenī, mahārāṣtri* and *Apabhraṃsa*[4].

Various studies of *Prākṛta* language indicate it as one of the oldest and most popular laymen's language of ancient Indians during early pre-Christian centuries. Mahavira and Buddha popularized it through their sermons and consequently it became a literary language. The major subject matter of this work is related with *Prākṛta* canonical literature spread over many centuries[5].

## The *Prākṛta*

The Sanskrit word *Prākṛta* is derived from *pra-kṛti* (=Nature, and so *Prākṛta*=Natural language). It is the name for a group of Middle Indo-Āryan languages, derived from Classical Sanskrit and other Old Indic dialects[6]. The word itself has a flexible definition, being defined sometimes as, "original, natural, artless, normal, ordinary, usual", or "vernacular", in contrast to the literary and religious orthodoxy of *sanskrtā*. Alternatively, *Prakrita* can be taken to mean "derived from an original," i.e., derived from *Sanskrit*. But there are scholars who believe that *Prākṛta* is older than *Sanskrit*, and it is on the base of *Prākṛta* (original) that the *Sanskrit* (refined) language was made[7]. The term *Prākṛta* (which includes *pāli)* is used for the popular dialects of India which were spoken until the 4th - 8th century, but some scholars use the term *Prakrita* throughout the Middle Indo-Āryan period. Middle Indo-Āryan languages gradually transformed into *Apabhraṃśas* which were used until about the 15th century. *Apabhraṃśas* evolved into modern languages which are equally today spoken by millions of people. The present regional languages of India originated from the various *Prākṛta* languages[8].

## *Prākṛta* Vs *Sanskṛta*

*Prākṛta*, which means 'natural' or 'common', primarily indicates the uncultivated popular dialects which existed side by side with Sanskrit, the 'accurately made', 'polished' and 'refined' speech. The *Prākṛta* then, are the dialects of the unlettered masses, which they used for secular communication in their day-to-day life, while *Sanskṛta* is the language of the intellectual aristocrat, the priest, pundit, or prince, who used it for religious and learned purposes[9].

## Development of *Prākṛta* language

The development of *Prākṛta* language has been classified in three stages:

(1) First stage (600BC-100AD): Inscriptional and Canonical *Prākṛta* language,

(2) Second stage (100AD-600AD): Normal *Prākṛta* language,

(3) Third stage (600AD-1000AD): Modern *Prākṛta* language[10].

The first stage of literary *Prākṛta* is the most important for the studies of Jaina Canons. A large number of inscriptions are also found thought the country in this time. Asokan inscription (300BC), the Hathigumpha inscription of Kalingarāja Khārvela (150BC) is very important documents of this stage. The second stage developed by the writings of Aśvaghosa (100AD), Vararuchi (300AD), Pravarasena and Vakāṭaka (400-450AD). The third stage of *Prākṛta* language up to about 1000AD., but references are available that a variety of *Prākṛta* literature has been written upto the eighteenth century. Thus by the continuous development, *Prākṛta* became literary languages, generally patronized by kings identified with the *Kshatriya* caste, but were regarded as illegitimate by the Brahmin orthodoxy. The earliest extant usage of *Prākṛta* is the corpus of inscriptions of Aśoka, emperor of India. The various *Prākṛta* languages are associated with different patron dynasties, with different religions (mainly Jainism) and different literary traditions, as well as different regions of the Indian subcontinent. The voluminous literature, religious, royal and public patronage give this language a national importance. Moreover, the language was grammatized like Sanskṛta in this period, which led to its standard form and therefore contracted literary nature beyond general public[11].

## Different dialects of *Prākṛta*

When Lord Mahavīra and Lord Buddha preached in this language to the common people, this language was wide-spread. Thenceforth, we get *prākṛtas* developed with many names, since it was current among common people across the country. Consequently different *prākṛtas* came into being with the different names. The *Prākṛta* grammarians give a sketchy description of various *Prākṛta* dialects. These are: (i) *Māgadhī* (ii) *Ardhamāgadhī*. (iii) *Māhārastrī*, (iv) *Śaurasenī*, (v) *Apabhraṃśa*, (vi) *Paiśācī* (vii) *Cūlikā Paiśacī*, and (viii) *Pāli*[12].

## *Prākṛta* as *Ardhamāgadhi*

The native language of *Magadha* country or Bihar or eastern India of today has been called *Magadhan Prākṛt*. Lord *Mahāvīra* belonged to *Magadha* (Bihar) and Lord Ṛṣbhadeb belonged to *Kośala* (U.P.). Both of them are the first and the last *Tirthankaras* of Jaina religion. They delivered their sermons in a language canonically described as *Ardhamāgadhi*, or half-*māgadhi*. *Ardhamāgadhi* language is the mixture of *Māgadhi* and many native languages. It is the co-ordinate form of *Māgadhi* and *Śaurasenī* or *Mahārastri*. *Ardhamāgadhi* has also been influenced by *Sanskṛta*, neighboring native language including *Munda* and *Dravida* ones[13].

## Jaina *Āgama* and *Prākṛta* Literature

The last Jaina *Tirthaṃkara* Lord Māhavīra belonged to *Magadha* (Now, Bihar). When he got enlightenment, he preferred to deliver his preach or sermons in the language spoken among the common people, and he chooses the *Ardhamāgadhi* language. And from then the *Ardhamāgadhi Prākṛta* language came into light. This was an important event in the cultural history of India, because a spoken dialect got for the first time the status of being the medium of religious and ethical preaching and teachings and hence, had the change of being cultivated and the outcome was the appearance of the great *Ardhamāgadhi* Canons (of *Śvetāmbaras*) and the pro-Canons (of *Digambaras*) in later days[14]. The Jain literature includes both religious texts and books on generally secular topics such as sciences, history, and grammar. *Prākṛita-Ardhamāgadhi* literature includes the *Āgamas*, *Āgama-tulya* texts, and *Siddhanta* texts. Composition in *Prākṛtas* ceased around 10th cent AD.

For students of Jainism the Jaina *Prākṛta* literature is a rich source of certain unique material[15]. A huge mass of Jaina literature in *Prākṛta* has grown around the *Ardhamāgadhi* Canon taking the forms of Agamas, *Niryuktis*, *Bhāsyas*, and *Cūrnis* from which arose later vast and varied types of narrative literature: biographies of religious celebrities, legendary tales of didactic motives, illustrative fables, parables, popular romances, fairy tales, *Kathanakas*, *kathākoṣas* etc.

## Jaina Canons

The Jaina Canonical works constitute an important section of *Prākṛta* literature. The preaching of Lord Mahavīra and his disciples have come down to us in the Jaina *Āgamas*, the Canon, in *Ardhamāgadhi*. The *Āgama* contains the following sections: (1) twelve *Añgas*, (2) twelve *Upañgas*, (3) ten *Prakīrnas*, (4) six *cheda Sūtras*, (5) two *Cūlikā-Sūtras*, and (6) four *Mūla sūtras*. (The twelve *añgas*, according to *Digambaras*, are completely lost. But the *Śvetāmbaras* believed that only the twelfth *añga Diṭṭivāda* or *Dṛṣṭivāda*, is lost)[16].

The list of **Añga-sutras** are as follows:

1. *Ācārānga Sutra (Āyārāng).*
2. *Sutrakṛtanga Sutra (Suyagadāng).*

3. *Sthānānga Sutra (Thānāng).*
4. *Samavāyānga Sutra.*
5. *Vyākhyā Prajñapti or Bhagavati Sūtra (Viyah Paṇṇati).*
6. *Jnātā Dharma Kathānga Sutra (Nayadhammakahao).*
7. *Upāsaka Daśānga Sūtra (Uvāsagdasāo).*
8. *Antaḥkṛddaśānga Sūtra (Anatagaddasāo).*
9. *Anuttaroupapātika Dashanga Sūtra (Anuttarov Vaiya Dasao).*
10. *Praśna Vyākrana Sūtra (Panha Vagarnai).*
11. *Vipāka Sūtra (Vivagsuyam)*[17].
12. *Dṛśṭivāda Sūtra (Diṭṭivad):* It was classified in five parts; (l) Parikarma (2) Sutra (3) *Purvagata* (4) *Pratham-anuyoga* and (5) *Chulikā*. The third part, *Purvagata* contained 14 *Pūrvas*. They contain the Jaina religion's endless treasure of knowledge on every subject.

## Anga-bāhya-*Āgamas*

In addition to the twelve *Añga*, there are other canonical literatures (*Añga-bāhya*) which are consisted of *Upānga-sūtras, Cheda-sūtras, Mool-sūtras, Chulikā-sūtras* and *Prakirna-sūtras*.

### *Upāñga-sūtras*

The scriptures, which provide further explanation of *Añga-Āgams*, are called *Upāng-Āgams*. The *upāñga sūtras* are:

1. *Aupapātika Sūtra (Ovavaiya).*
2. *Rajapraśniya Sūtra (Raya Pasen Ijja).*
3. *Jivābhigama Sūtra.*
4. *Prajñāpanā Sūtra (Pannavana).*
5. *Suryaprajñapti Sūtra (Surya Pannti).*
6. *Candraprajñapti Sūtra.*
7. *Jambudveepaprajñapti Sūtra.*
8. *Nirayārvali Sūtra.*
9. *Kalpāvatansikā Sūtra (Kappavadamsiao).*
10. *Pushpikā Sūtra (Puspiao).*
11. *Pushpa Culikā Sūtra.*
12. *Vrashnidashā Sūtra (Vanhidasao).*[18]

### *Cheda Sūtras*

The subject matter described in the *Cheda-sūtras* is the rule of conduct, punishment, and repentance for ascetics. The *Cheda Sūtras* are:

1. *Niśītha Sūtra (Nisiha), 2. Bṛhat Kalpa Sūtra, 3. Vyavahārdasakalpa Sūtra, 4. Dashā Śrūta Skandha Sūtra (Ācārdashā), 5. Panch Kalpa Sūtra, 6. Mahaniśītha Sūtra.*[19]

### *Mūla-Sūtras*

The scriptures, which are essential for monks and nuns to study in the early stages of their ascetic life, are called *Mūla-sūtras*.

1. *Āvaśyaka Sutra, 2. Daśa Vaikalika Sūtra, 3. Uttarādhyayana Sūtra, 4. Ogha Niryukti or Pinda Niryukti Sūtra.*[20]

### *Culikā-sūtras*

The scriptures, which enhance or decorate the meaning of *Añga-Āgamas* are known as *Culikā-sūtras*. These are:

1. *Nandī Sūtra.*
2. *Anuyogadvāra Sūtra.*

### *Prakīrna-sūtras*

Those scriptures describe independent or miscellaneous subjects of the Jaina religion, are *Prakīrna-sūtras*. These are:

*1. Catuḥ Śaraṇa, 2. Ātur Pratyākhyāna (Āyur-Pachakhāna), 3. Bhakti Parijña (Bhatta-pariṇṇa), 4. Sanstāraka (Santhara), 5. Tandulavaitalikā, 6. Chandra-Vedhyaka, 7. Devendra-Stava, 8. Gaṇita Vidyā, 9. Mahāpratyākhyāna, 10. Vīrastava.*

## Commentaries on the *Āgams*

Several commentaries on the *Āgamas* have been written in *Prākṛta*. Those are known as *Niryukti*, *Bhāsya*, and *Cūrni*. *Niryuktis* and *Bhāsyas* are composed in verses while *Cūrnis* are in prose.

### *Digambara Literature*

The *Digambara* sect believes that the *Āgam-sutras* were gradually lost starting from one hundred fifty years after Lord Mahāvīra's *nirvāna*. Hence, they do not recognize the existing *Āgama-sutras* as their authentic scriptures.

In the absence of authentic scriptures, *Digambaras* follow two main texts, three commentaries on main texts, and four *Anuyogas* consisting of more than 20 texts as the basis for their religious philosophy and practices. These scriptures were written by great *Ācāryas* from 100 AD to 1000 AD. They have used the original *Āgama* Sutras as the basis for their work.

### *Ṣatkhand-Āgama*

The *Ṣatkhand-Āgama* is also known as *Mahā-kammapayadi-pāhuda*. Two *Ācāryas*; *Puśpadant* and *Bhutābali* around 160 AD wrote it around 780 AD.

### *Kaṣāy-pāhud or Kaṣāy-prabhṛtā*

*Ācārya Gunadhara* wrote *the Kaṣāy-pāhuda*.

***Four Anuyogas***

1. ***Prathama-anuyoga (Dharma-kathā-anuyoga)*** **- Religious Stories**

   This *anuyoga* consists- Padma-puran, Harivamsa-puran, Adi-puran, and Uttar-puran.

2. ***Charaṇa-anuyoga*** **- Conduct**

   This *anuyoga* consists- Mulachar, Trivarnachar, and Ratna-karanda-shravak-achar.

3. ***Karana-anuyoga (Gaṇit-anuyog)*** **- Mathematics**

   This *anuyoga* consists - *Surya-prajñapti, Chandra-prajñapti, Jaya-dhaval-tika*, and *Gommata-sāra*.

4. ***Dravya-anuyoga*** - Philosophy

   This *anuyoga* consists of the following texts, written by *Ācārya Kundakunda*, which contain philosophical doctrine, theories, metaphysics, *Tattvajñana*, and like literature. The texts are: *Niyamasāra, Panchastikāya, Pravachanasāra*, and *Samaya-sara*[21].

## Historio-Cultural Contribution of non-*Āgamic Prākṛta* literature

A good deal of *Prākṛta* literature has grown beside the non-canonical literature. These may be divided in several classes:

### 1. *Lyrical Anthologies*

A collection of some 700 *gāthas*, the *Gātha Sattasatī*, attributed to *Hāla* is a good *Prākṛta* lyrical anthology. The themes of the *Sattasatī* are drawn from rural life. The village folk, the foibles of love, sentiment of erotic are narrated in touching manner. Another *Prākṛta* lyrical anthology is the *Vajjālaggā* of *Jayavallabha*. The subjects of the verses are grouped into three human ends—*dharma, artha* and *kāma*[22].

### 2. *Narrative literature*

The narrative literature of the Jainas in *Prākṛta* is vast and rich. This literature served the purpose of folk literature also. We find the origin of the folk literature in *Vasudevahiṇdi* for the first time[23]. Some other of the narrative literature are: *Triṣaṣṭi-Śalākā-Puruṣa-caritra*, by Hemacandra, is the biographies of sixty-three great men who are the celebrities of Jainism. *Paūmacariya*, a Puranic epic composed by Guṇādhya in 4 A.D. *Kumārapāla-Pratibodha*, a legendary tale of king Kumarapala written by Somaprabha, in c.1195 AD. Another important literary work of this century is the *Surasundarīcariya*, written by Dhanesvara in 1095V.S. this work is actually the love story of a Vidyadhara prince in 4000 *Prākṛta* verses. *Kathākosha*, of Jinesvara written in *Prākṛta*, in 1052 AD, is one of the most celebrated Jaina *Prākṛta* works on popular stories[24].

### 3. *Classical Kāvya and Campū*

There are stylistic *Kāvya* and prose romances in *Prākṛta* literature. The *Setubandha* or *Dahamuhavaha* by Pravarasena deals with the incident of *Rāmāyana*. *Gaūdavahokavya* by Vākpatirāja (c.733) celebrates the historical elements of the Gaūda King. *Kuvalayamālā* (c.779) of Uddyotanasūri is a book on romance in *Prākṛta*. This supplies useful politico-historical material. The *Līlāvatī* by Kutūhala is a stylistic, romantic *kāvya*. But this is no longer available in the original. *Mahavīra-Carita* by Gunacandra gives a traditional account of Mahāvīra's life, in a charming *kāvya* style.[25]

## 4. *Philosophical treatise*

*Prākṛta* literature, as we all know, is one of the varied source-materials of Indian Philosophy, specially of Jaina Philosophy. Other than the Āgamic texts there are huge texts elucidating the philosophical doctrine of Jainism, such as : *Dhavalā, Jayadhavalā, Mahadhavalā* commentaries. There are other commentaries such as *kama-Payadi* by Śivaśarman, *Pañcasañgraha* by Candṛṣi, *Gommaṭasāra* by Nemicandra. Siddhasena Divākara's *Sanmati-Tarka-Prakarana* (4th cent.), in *Prākṛta*, gives authentic and critical exposition of many different philosophical streams of India prevailing before his times. This is a comparative work philosophical trend of different religions, written by one of the early Jaina logicians. This brilliant treatise elucidating mainly the Jaina epistemology and logic. Devasena deals with various topics of Jainism in his *Bhavasañgraha*, *Ārādhanāsāra* and *Tattvasāra*[26].

## 5. *Political treatise*

*Nītivyākyāmṛta* of Somadeva (10th cent.) is an excellent treatise on the science and art of politics in India. Different Jainas *cāritras* and *Purāṇas* often touch the politics, through which we get information about current political theories, origin of different dynasties etc. *Ādipurana* of Jinasena (9th cent.) deserves such attention and appreciation.[27] It has been called an encyclopedia of the Digambara religion[28]. In this text, Jinasena's knowledge regarding the various *janapadas* is remarkable. A treatise on the duties of warriors and the art of governing is also found in this book[29].

## 6. *Grammar*

There are useful grammar written in *Prākṛta*. Some of these are: *Prākṛta-Vyākaraṇa* or *Siddhahemaśabdānu Śāsana* written by Ācārya Hemacandra, is devoted to the *Prakṛta* grammar, According to Kielhorn, it is 'the best grammar of the Indian middle ages'. Vararuci, Canda Markaṇdeya are the other great grammarians of *Prākṛta* language and literature.[30]

## 7. *Lexicons*

Only two *Prākṛta kosas* or lexicons have been discovered up to now. One of which is *Deśīnāmamāla* (also called *Ratnāvalī*) written by *Ācārya* Hemacandra and other is *Pāiya-lacchī-nāma-māla* written by Dhanapāla. *Deśīnāmamāla* written by *Ācārya* Hemacandra, has practically no rival in the Indian literature. It has 783 verses, divided in eight chapters and arranged according to the initial letter of the words. *Deśīnāmamāla* considers those *Deśī* words, which are not derived from Sanskrit, and also not found in Sanskrit lexicons. Those words, which are used in standard *Prākṛta* from times immemorial are considered as *Deśī* by Hemacandra[31]. *Pāiya-lacchī-nāma-māla* written by Dhanapāla presents a list of *Prākṛta* synonymous words. It is also a great work in *Prākṛta* lexicon[32]. The famous Jaina writer Dhanapāla composed this text in the Vikrama Samvat 1029 corresponding to the 1072 A.D[33]. Besides the authors of the Deśikosa referred above, Hemacandra, refers some other authors of *Prākṛta kośas*; we know nothing about them except the reference of *Ācārya* Hemacandra in his *Deśīnāmamāla*. Among them, 1. Devarāja, is the author of a metrical kośa in which he gave the meanings of *deśi* words in *Prākṛta* language. 2. Drona was a author of a *Prākṛta* lexicon, 3. Pādaliptācārya, 4. Rāhulakah and 5.Silānka also wrote Deśikosa, but we know nothing about them or of their works[34].

## 8. *History and Cosmology*

*Tiloyapaṇṇatti* of Yativṛṣabha (2nd cent.) is an early *Prākṛta* text on cosmology. This work throws light on many things such as nature, shape, size and divisions of Universe, ancient geography, politics, history of ancient India, commencement of Śaka rule, their dynastic chronology & eras, Jaina doctrine, puranic traditions and so on. This is also very useful for studying the development of mathematics, in ancient times. *Aṅgavijja* written by an unknown author/s, is a *Prākṛta* work of importance for reconstructing India's history of the first four centuries after Christ[35]. This work has been fittingly described as the treasurehouse for the cultural history of India of the early Christian period[36].

## 9. *Morality and Ethics*

Another significant aspect of *Prākṛta* literature is its high moral tone. *Śravaka-vidhi* by Dhanapāla is a short *Prākṛta* verse treatise on the lay life. There was another *Prākṛta* verses, *Sīra-Vicāra* and *Dharma-ratna-prakaraṇa* by Sānti-Sūri, which tract on the qualities of the ideal layman and ideal monk. It is the earliest literary sources for the 21 *śravaka-guṇas*[37]. Nemicandra's *Pravacana-sāroddhāra* is also a *Prākṛta* verse compendium of Jaina ethics. For the medieval period the last major *Prākṛta* work on Jaina ethics is the *Śrāddha-dina-kṛtya* by Devendra[38]. These literatures teach laymen as well as monks the eternal values and lessons.

## Conclusion

*Prākṛta* language and literature are very valuable for a complete and first hand knowledge of the ancient Indian culture[39]. The significance of *Prākṛta* sources is that they are connected with almost every phase and part of this vast country. These works do not restrict to only one or two subjects or to only religious philosophies but embrace various branches of literature such as poetics, politics, grammar, logic, dialectics, astronomy, astrology, medicine, cosmology, epigraphy, etc. these sources are highly critical, standard, authentic and contain abundant historical information[40]. As the Jainas have produced their vast literature in these languages from very ancient times, they have certainly played a very important part in the development of the different languages of India[41]. Prof. A.N. Upadhye has truly said, "Indian linguistics would certainly be poorer in the absence of *Prākṛta* literature, for on its lap have grown the modern Indian languages. *Prākṛta* literature goes a long way in helping to add important and significant details to our picture of Indian culture and civilization"[42].

## *Notes and References*

1. Jain, N.L. *Scientific Contents in Prakrta Canons*, P.V.R. Institute, Varanasi, 1996, p.8-12.
2. Misra, S.S. *Date of Second Middle Indo-Āryan: A Fresh Chronological Estimate*, in '*Jain Vidya and Prākṛit*', (ed. By Jain, G.C.), Sampurnananda Sanskrit Unversity, Varanasi, 1987, p.221-23.
3. Khadbadi, B.K. *Studies in Jainology, Prākṛit Literature and Language*, Prakrit Bharati Academy, Jaipur, 1997, p.298.
4. Sharma, Dinanath. *Problems in Learning Prakrit language*, in *Contribution of Jainas to Sanskrit and Prākṛit literature*, ed. By J.B. Shah, SCE Research Center, Ahmedabed, 2008, p.133-135.
5. Jain, N.L. *Op.Cit.*, p.10.
6. Daniels, Peter T., *The World's Writing Systems*. Oxford University Press, London,1996. p.377.
7. Woolner, Alfred C. *Introduction to Prākṛit*. Delhi: Motilal Banarsidass, Delhi, 1999. p.3.
8. Dalal, Roshen. *The Penguin Dictionary of Religion in India*, Penguin Books, Delhi, 2006, p.369.
9. Upadhye, A.N. *Prākṛt Language and Literature*, in '*The Cultural heritage of India*', (Vol.V), ed. Suniti Kumar Chatterji, The Ramakrishna Mission Institute of Culture, Calcutta, 2001. p.164.
10. Jain, N.L. *Op.Cit*, p.25.
11. Jain, N.L. *Op.Cit*, p.25.
12. Sharma, Dinanath. *Op.Cit.*, p.133.
13. Jain, N.L. *Op.Cit*, p.22-23.
14. Khadabadi, B.K. *Op.Cit*, p.297.
15. Dixit,K.K. *On studying the Prakrit Literature*, in '*Prakrit Studies*', L.D.Institute, Ahmedabad, 1978, p.38.
16. Banerjee, Satya Ranjan. *Introducing Jainism*, Jain Bhawan, Calcutta, 2002, p.18.
17. Nahar, P.C. & Ghosh, K.C. *An Encyclopaedia of Jainism*, Sri Sai Satguru Publication, Delhi, 1996, p.xxxii.
18. Ibid., p.xxxiv.
19. Ibid., p.xxxv.
20. Ibid., p.xxxv.
21. Jaini, P.S. *The Jaina Path of Purification*, Motilal Banarasidass, Delhi, 2001, p.78-81.
22. Upadhye, A.N., *Op.Cit.*, p.172-3.
23. Gopani, A.S. *Some Aspects of Indian Culture*, L.D. Institute, Ahmedabad, 1981, p.57.
24. Chatterjee, A.K. *A Comprehensive History of Jainism*, (vol.-II), Firma KLM, Calcutta, 1984, p.208-9.
25. Upadhye, A.N., *Op.Cit.*, p.178-9.
26. Ibid., p.181.
27. Jamindar, Rasesh. *Historio-Culture Contribution of Jaina Ācāryas through Prākṛit Sources*, in '*Prākṛit Studies*', L. D. Institute, Ahmedabad, 1978, p.34.
28. Winternitz, M. *A History of Indian Literature*, Vol-II, Delhi, 1972, p.498.

29. Chatterjee, A.K. *A Comprehensive History of Jainism*, (Vol.I), Firma KLM, Calcutta, 1978, p.306.
30. Upadhye, A.N., *Op.Cit.*, p.182.
31. Ramanujaswami, P.V. (intro.), *The Desi Nāmamāla of Hemacandra*, ed. by R. Pischel, Bombay Sanskrit Series, No. xvii, Bhandarkar Oriental Research Institute, Poona, 1938, p.3.
32. Upadhye, A.N., *Op.Cit.*, p.182.
33. Chatterjee, A.K., *A Comprehensive History of Jainism*, (Vol.I), Firma KLM, Calcutta, 1978, p.164.
34. Ramanujaswami, P.V. (intro.), *The Desi Nāmamāla of Hemacandra*, ed. by R. Pischel, Bombay Sanskrit Series, No. xvii, Bhandarkar Oriental Research Institute, Poona, 1938, p.12-14.
35. Jamindar, Rasesh, *Op.Cit.*, p.34.
36. Chatterjee, A.K., *A Comprehensive History of Jainism*, (Vol.I), Firma KLM, Calcutta, 1978, p.256.
37. Williams, R. *Jaina Yoga*, Motilal Banarasidass, Delhi, 1998, p.9.
38. Ibid., p.13.
39. Choudhuri, G.C., *Prakrit studies: Some Problems and Solutions*, in '*Prakrit Studies*', L.D.Institute, Ahmedabad, 1978, p.159.
40. Jamindar, Rasesh, *Op.Cit.*, p.34.
41. Roy, Ashim Kumar. *A History of The Jains*, Gitanjali Publishing House: New Delhi,1984.
42. Upadhye, A.N. *Op.Cit.*, p.183.

25

# A Study of Islamic Literature of Shah Waliullah Muhaddith Dehlavi

*Muhammad Ismail*

Shah Waliullah was born at Phulat,[1] a small village near Delhi, in 1703. In 1707 Aurangzeb, the great Mughal Emperor, breathed his last and centrifugal tendencies became rife and rampant in the country. Shah Waliullah's father was Maulana Shah Abdur Rahim,[2] a celebrated scholar of his time and was associated in the compilation of the famous compendium of Muslim Law, the *Fatawa-i-Alamgiri*. His seminary *Madrasah-i-Rahimia* at Delhi was a veritable centre of Muslim learning in those days and became the nucleus of a revolutionary movement for the reconstruction of religious thought in Islam.[3] Shah Waliullah received his education in this institution and he was in his teens when he himself started teaching there. Then he went to Arabia and sat at the feet of eminent scholars of Hejaz. In a treatise he has given an account of the scholars and saints whom he met in the Hejaz.[4] He received his *sanad* from Shaikh Abu Tahir b. Ibrahim of Medinah. On his return to Delhi on July 9, 1732, he gave up teaching in routine manner and concentrated on training advanced scholars in different branches of religious learning and spent most of his time in writing books. His seminary thus turned into a centre for the intellectual and religious resurgence of Islamic sciences and for organizing a country-wide movement for the dissemination of religious knowledge and for infusing a new spirit of religious enquiry and investigation and preparing people for replacing a social system, which had outlived its utility, by a system more democratic in spirit and more progressive in outlook. Reacting to the political situation of the country which was suffering at the hands of new powers which had created disturbed conditions all around, he persuaded contemporary princes and rulers, particularly Ahmad Shah Abdali, Najib ud Daula and Nizam ul Mulk, to exert themselves in setting right the chaotic conditions.[5]

In view of the services rendered by Shah Waliullah for the revival of Islamic spirit all over the world, he is rightly recognized as the 12th century (Hijra) Mujaddid in Islam. During the 18th century, Muslims of India were divided into sections and sub-sections and the majority of them had very little to do with Islam. The spirit of Islam was forgotten. The Ulama, who were the upholders of Islam, were spending their time and wasting their wisdom by engaging themselves in hair-splitting arguments over interpretation of the findings of their respective imams which only resulted in petty feuds and mutual rivalries. For revival of Islam, Shah Waliullah desired to present Islam in its true form which does not admit extreme rigidity and reserve as depicted by the then theologians and the misguided mystics (Sufis) and to break away from the old order, replacing it by the new one to meet the requirements of the time.[6] He felt the inevitability of resurgence of a movement to eradicate evil and enjoin good and dispense justice as enshrined in the Holy Qur'an. To achieve this end, he raised the slogan "back to the Qur'an and Hadith."

The reformist endeavors of Shah Waliullah starts with the Holy Qur'an as the basis. He translated the Qur'an into Persian which was then the language of the elite Muslims in India. His books on exegesis and Qur'anic Studies include *Fathur-Rahman, al Fawz al Kabir and Fath al Khabir.* Thus he brought out a revolutionary change into the practice of the sheer conventional reading of the Qur'an, without knowing its meaning.

The Sunnah of Prophet Muhammad (PBUH), being the second source of Islamic Shari'ah, caught utmost attention of Shah Waliullah. He firmly believed that, for the restoration of a decadent community to its original state of dignity and honour, it was necessary to revive the science of tradition and dispel confusion from it wherever it occurs. With this objective in view, he instituted an academy, Darul Hadith, the first of its kind in South Asia. He popularized the study of Apostolic traditions and prepared commentaries on the *Muwatta* of Imam Malik, known as *Musaffa* and *Musawwa* and *Sharh Tarajim Abwabi Sahih Bukhari,* which, he thought, embodied the spirit of early Islam and could be instrumental in imbuing the thought and personality of contemporary Muslims with the spirit of the Sunnah.

Shah Waliullah laid the foundation of a new *ilm-i-kalam* in his *Hujjatullahil Baligha*, which is unique and indeed an encyclopaedia of religious sciences. His magnum opus *Hujjatullahil-Baligha,* which ranks with *Ihya-i-Ulum al-Din* of Imam Ghazzali as a classic on the religious philosophy of Islam,[7] ushered in the dawn of a new era in the intellectual history of modern Islam. The task before the modern Muslim is to rethink the whole system of Islam without completely breaking with the past. As such Allamah Iqbal was justified in holding the view that Shah Waliullah was the first Indian Muslim who felt the urge of a new spirit in him.[8] This makes all efforts to understand him and his thought relevant to the needs of present Day Muslim society.

Islamic literature written by Shah Waliullah has been arranged subject-wise in the following pages. His works, both printed as well as in manuscript forms are briefly introduced below:

## (i) Qur'anic Studies

1. *Fath al Rahman Fi Tarjamat al Qur'an (Persian)*

It is a work on the holy Qur'an in the Persian language. The rendering is neither too leteral nor to idiomatic. Marginal notes are occasional and brief. The translation was made with a view to facilitating the Qur'anic study to those Muslims who were not well-versed in Arabic. The work was started in 1719 and completed in 1743. It was reprinted by Matba' Hashmi, Meerut-1869; Matba Faruqi, Delhi, 1294; Lucknow-1902; Taj company, Lahore, 1986.

2. *Al-Fawz al Kabir fi Usul-al-Tafsir (Persian)*

This work deals with the principles of *tafsir* (exegesis). He divides the entire text of the Qur'an into five topics.

(1) *al-Ahkam,* or the commands; (2) *Mukhasamah* or contention with four classes of people: polytheists, Jews, Christians, and the hypocrites; (3) *Tazkir bi Ala'i Allah,* or remembrance an account of the gifts of Allah; (4) *Tazkir bi Ayyam Allah*, or reference to the past history of mankind; and (5) *Mu'ad*, or an account of death and life after death.

The question of tansikh or the abrogation of certain injection of the Qur'an has been discussed in detail. Shah Waliullah believes that the number of such commands cannot be more than five in total.[9] (Published by Matba' Ahmadi, Hooghli, 1249/1834; Matba' Mujtabi, Delhi, 1898; Maktaba Salafia, Lahore, 1951; Qadimi Kutub Khana, Karachi, n.d. Urdu translation; by Qashid Ahmad Ansari, Delhi, 1963; by Muhammad Salim Abdullah; Karachi, n.d.; Lahore, n.d. Arabic translation by Muhammad Aizaz 'Ali, Deoband, by Salman Husaini Nadvi, Lucknow; Abu Sufiyan Miftahi, Mau; English translation by Jalbani, The Principles of the Qur'an commentary, Islamabad, 1985).

3. *Fath al Khabir bima la budda min hifzi Ilm al Tafsir (Arabic)*

It is a short treatise on the essentials of tafsir (exegesis). The work originally forms the fifth chapter of the al-Fuaz al-Kabir. The work contains a discussion on the causes of the revelation of the injections of the Holy Qur'an.[10] In this work the author has made an extensive use of the Sahih al Bukhari and other books on the hadith to explain the difficult and Archaic words and phrases of the Qur'an. (Published by: Matba' Ahmadi, Hooghly, 1834; Nawal Kishore, Lucknow, A.H. 1314).

4. *Al-Muqaddama fi Qawanim al-Tarjamah (Persian)*

This is a short treatise on the principles of translation. All important aspect, of the topic have been systematically and brilliantly discussed in it. It is an important aid to scholars engaged in translation of the Qur'an into different languages. It was written in 1738.

5. *Tawil-al-Ahadith Fi Rumuz Qisas al Anbiya (Arabic)*

This work highlights the rational interpretation of extraordinary and miraculous incidents connected with the lives of the prophets mentioned in the Qur'an. For example, the birth of Prophet 'Isa (Jesus), the crossing of the Nile by Moses, and the bodily change of the

Israelis into monkeys have been explained rationally.[11] (Published by: (edited by Qasmi, Hyderabad, Sindh, 1966. Urdu translations: Matba Ahmadi, 1899, al-Rahim 3:12 (May 1972); A Mystical Interpretation of Prophetic Tales by an Indian Muslim: Shah Waliullah of Delhi's *Tawil al Hadith* E.J. Brill. Leiden, 1973).

6. *Muqaddama Dar Fann-iTarjamah (Persian)*

The work is also known as *Al Muqaddama Fi Qawanin al-Tarjamah*. It is included in *Fath al Rahman*. The latter is more *extensive* which exists only in the manuscript form. The Urdu translation is available.

7. *Zahrawain (Persian)*

The work contains translation of suhrahs *al-Baqarah* and *Al-i Imran*. The work is in manuscript form. It could be part of *Fath al Rahman*.

## (ii) Hadith Studies

1. *Al-Musawwa fi Ahadith al-Muwatta (Arabic)*

The work is a commentary on the *Muwatta* of Imam Malik composed in the Arabic language. This book also aims at bringing about a compromise between the differences of the Hanafis and the Shafi'is. Shah Waliullah, therefore, explains the traditions contained in this book with a greater stress upon the rulsings of Imam Abu Hanifa and Imam Shafi. (Published by Matba' Murtaza) Delhi, 1293 and 1347; Makkah, n.d. and Hyderabad, Sindh. Urdu translations: al-Rahim 1:5 (October 1263 and 6 November 1963).

2. *Al-Musaffa fi Ahadith-al-Muwatta (Persian)*

The work is a precious commentary on the *Muwatta* of Imam Malik. In this work Shah Waliullah tried his best to find a formula for creating conciliation and compromise among different schools of Sunni *Fiqh*. For this purpose he wanted to select a collection of Traditions which would be acceptable to all the schools. Shah Waliullah, therefore wrote a commentary on it, explaining the Traditions by way of Ijtihad (fresh interpretation). The work was edited after the death of Shah Waliullah, in the year 1179/1766. (Published by: Matba Faruqi, Delhi, 1293/1876; Matba' Murtazavi, Delhi 1993; Muhammad Ali Karkhana Islami Kutub, Karachi, 1980. Incomplete Urdu translation in al-Rahim 1:5 (October 1963; by Syed Abdullah, Matba Ahmadi, Kolkata, 1294 A.H.)

3. *Arba'un Hadithan Musalsalat Bi al-Ashraf Fi Ghalib Sanadiha (Arabic)*

It is a small collection of forty Traditions (Ahadith) on the authority of Abu Tahr Kurdi, which contain almost all the fundamentals of Islam. (Published, at Saharanpur, 1292/ 1875).

4. *Al-Durr al-Thamin fi Mubashshirat al-Nabi al Amin (Arabic)*

This short treatise contains a collection of those Traditions which, the author claims, were either related to him by the Prophet (pbuh) in a dream directly[12] or had reached him from his father or a teacher. (Published at Saharanpur 1292/1875), Urdu translation, Matba' Mujtabai, Delhi, 1899.

5. *Al-Fadl al-Mubin fi al-Salasil min Hadith al-Nabi al-Amin (Arabic)*

This short treatise deals with the authorities of the Traditions of the Prophet (pbuh). The work is also called Musalsalat.[13] (Published, at Saharanpur, 1292/1875).

6. *Al Nawadir min Ahadith Sayyid al-Awa'il wa-al-Awakhir (Arabic)*

This short reatise deals with rare Traditions of the Prophet Muhammad (pbuh). (Published, at Saharanpur, 1292/1875).

7. *Sharh Tarajim Abwab al-Bukhari (Arabic)*

This short treatise contains a critical study of the chapters of Sahih Bukhari, a famous collection of Traditions made by Imam Bukhari. This work is enriched by illuminating annotations.[14] It was written in 1145-46/1732-33. Published at Hyderabad (Decean), 1949; Asahh al-Matabi'a, Delhi, n.d., and Matba Nur al Anwar, Arah, Bihar, n.d.

8. *Irshad 'Ala Muhimmat 'Ilm al-Isnad (Arabic)*

This short treatise deals with the authorities of the Traditions of the Prophet Muhammad (pbuh). The work has been published several times.[15] (Published by: Matba' Ahmadi, Delhi, 1307/1889 and Sajjad publishers, Lahore, 1960).

## Works on Islamic Fiqh (Law)

1. *Iqd al-Jid fi Bayan Ahkam alIjtihad Wal Taqlid (Arabic)*

The book deals with the problem of *ijtihad* (independent investigation) and *taqlid* (blind imitation). The work is divided into five chapters. In the opinion of Shah Waliullah it would be wrong to believe that the door of ijtihad is closed now. He thinks that anyone who is qualified as a Mujtahid can exercise it. According to him, the necessary qualifications of a *mujtahid* are a through knowledge of the *Qur'an, Hadith,* the rulings of the earlier doctors of law, Arabic language and a capacity to take inferences from the sources concerned. However, a lay man is advised to follow one or the other of the four schools of law. Blind conformity is undesirable, but it is not altogether forbidden, especially these days when the qazis (jurists) have become worldly-minded, hence they cannot be expected to dispense justice. (Published by: Matba Siddiqi, Bareilly, 1309; Maktaba Salafia, Lahore, 1965; Matba Mujtabai, Delhi, 1344/1925 along with its Urdu translation: Translations: Silk Marwarid 1310; Muhammad Abdul Shakur Faruqi, Lucknow, n.d.: Sajidur Rahman Daud Rahbar).

2. *Al-Insaf fi-Bayan Asbab al-Ikhtilaf (Arabic)*

The work is a history of the evolution of the four schools of *fiqh* or the Islamic law. The causes that led to their foundation are traced in the differences of opinion over various problems of Islamic law among the early Muslims. It would be wrong to believe that a Muslim must follow one or other school of law. One may do so, and indeed in certain cases it is advisable, but the rulings of the earlier jurists should never be taken as Divine revelations. They can be rejected if they contradict Hadith. (Published by: Matba' Mujtaba', Delhi, 1308/1891; Matba' Siddiqi, Bareilly, 1307; edited by Qashid Ahmad Jalandhari,

Lahore, 1971, edited by Mohiuddin Khatib, Cairo, 1960; edited by Abdal Fattah Abu Ghudda, Beirut, 1977-78; Urdu translations; Kashshaf by Muhammad Abdullah Baliawi, Lucknow, 1886, Wassaf by Muhammad Abdul Shakar Faruqi, Lucknow, 1910; *Ikhtilafi Masail Mein Itidal ki Rah,* Rampur, 1932, Markazi Maktaba Islami, Delhi, 1973).

### (iii) Tasawwuf

1. *Al-Qawl al-Jamil (Arabic)*

The book deals with the practical aspect of Tasawwuf, such as the qualifications of a preceptor, essential to be observed for the training of novices of the path etc. The work also contains an account of practices peculiar to various Sufi orders. The healing power of the Qur'anic verses has been emphasized. The practice of writing amulets is approved. Amulets and extraordinary recitations from the Qur'anic verses have been given for almost every physical and mental disease. (editions: Matba'al-Jamaliya, Misr 1290: Matba Nizami, Kanpur, 1291; Urdu translations by Khurram Ali Bilhauri, Bombay, n.d., entitled *Shifa al'Alil,* Delhi, n.d., Mohammad Sarwar, Lahore, 1946; entitle *"Tasawwuf Ke Adab wa Ashghal Aur Unka Falsafa".*

2. *Al-Tafhimat al-Ilahiyah (Arabic and Persian)*

This work is a collection of articles and letters written to various novices of the Sufi path. Each article deals with different aspects of Tasawwuf, as perceived by the author through his personal experiences. The problem of ontological monism *(Wahdatul-wujud)* and phenomenological monism *(Wahadat al-Shuhud)* has been discussed in a letter to Afandi Ismail, wherein an attempt has been made to reconcile both of these doctrines. The book also comprises Shah Waliullah's address made to almost all the sections of his community, reminding them of their negligence towards the duties enjoined upon them by their religion and the law of the land. (Published by: Majalis 'Ilmi, Dabhel, 1355 H: Madinah Press, Bijnore, 1936; Hydrabad Sindh, 1973).

3. *Ham'at (Persian)*

The work deals with the historical development of Islamic Tasawwuf. He gives an account of the mystical experiences of the Sufi Saints of Islam, along with his own judgement. According to Shah Waliullah, a journey on the spiritual path does not exempt a novice from the observance of Shariat. The work was completed in October 1735/Jamadi-al-Akhir 1148.[16] (Published by: Lahore, 1941, edited by Qasmi, Hydrabad, Sindh, 1964. Urdu translations; Muhammad Sarwar, *Tasawwuf Ki Haqiqat Aur Uska Falsafa-i-Tarikh,* Lahore, 1964 and 1999; Maktaba Rahmania, Deoband, 1969).

4. *Sata'at (Persian)*

It is a short treatise on Sufi philosophy. It also deals with the life after death and the system of Divine manifestations working in the universe:[17] (Published by: Matba' Ahmadi, Delhi, 1307; Karachi, 1939; edited by Qasmi, Hydrabad, Sindh 1964; by Muhammad Matin Hashmi, Lahore, 1986; English translation by Jalbani, Hydrabad, Sindh, 1970, and Kitab Bhavan, Delhi, 1981).

5. *Lamhat (Arabic)*

The work is a small treatise devoted to the discussion of Sufi philosophy. It contains an exhaustive treatment of philosophical terms and subjects like *Wujud* (being), *al-Shakhs-al-Akbar* (The Great Body), *Hazirat-al-Quds* (Holy Fold), etc.[18] (Published by: edited by Qasmi, Hyderabad, Sindh, n.d. English translations by Jalbani and D.B. Fry. *Sufism and the Islamic Tradition: Lamhat and Sata'at* of Shah Waliullah of Delhi, London, 1980).

6. *Fuyud-al-Haramain (Arabic)*

It deals with the spiritual experiences he had obtained, through visions at the holy precincts of Makkah and Madinah. The work affords valuable material for the novices of the Sufi path.

7. *Altaf al Quds Fi Ma'arif Lataif al Nafs (Persian)*

The work deals with the philosophy of *Tasawwuf.* (Published by: Matba'Ahmadi, Delhi, 1307, along with Urdu translation by Abdul Hamid Sawati; Gujranwala, 1964; English translation by Jalbani and pendelberry, entitled 'The sacred knowledge', London, 1984.

8. *Al Qasida al-Lamiya (Arabic)*

It features at the conclusion of the 11th observation in *Fuyuz al Haramayn.*

9. *Al Intibah Fi Salasil Auliya Allah wa Asanid Warithi Rasullah (Persian)*

The work deals with Sufi practices by various Sufi Silsilahs. (Published by: Matba'Ahmadi, Dehli, 1311; Maktaba Salafiya, 1969 *"Ithaf al Nabih"* being the abridgement of its two chapters).

10. *Al Khayr al-Kathir (Arabic)*

The work highlights on the philosophy of *Tasawwuf.* Compiled by Shah Muhammad Ashiq Phulati in 1161/1847. (Published by: Madinah Barqi Press, Bijnore, 1352, Majlis 'Ilmi, Dabhel, 1354; Cairo, 1974; English translation by Jalbani, Hydrabad, Sindh, 1974).

11. *Al-Maqala al Waziya Fi al Nasiha (Persian)*

The work contains authors instructions for the profit of disciples and relatives. (Published by : Matba' Mutiur Rahman, Delhi, 1268; Matba' Masihi, Kanpur, 1273).

12. *Al-Budur al-Bazigha (Arabic).*

The work is a sequel to *Hujjatulla al Baligha.* It is an encyclopaedic work on the philosophy of *Religion* and *Tasawwuf.* (Published by: Majlis 'Ilmi, Dabhel 1354; Hyderabad, Sindh 1970. Urdu translation by Qazi Mujibur Rahman, Lahore, 2000 and English translation by Jalbani, Islamabad, 1985).

13. *Lama'at (Perian)*

14. *Shifa-al-Qulub (Persian)*

15. *Sharh Hizb-al-Bahr (Persian)*

16. *Sharh Ruba'iyatain*[19] *(Persian)*

17. *Fath-al-Wudud li Ma'rifat-al-Junud (Arabic)*

18. *'Awarif (Arabic)*

## (iv) Philosophy of Islam

1. *Hujjat-Allah al-Balighah (Arabic)*

Shah Waliullah is particularly known for his work *Hujjat-Allah-al-Balighah*. The work is a scientific study of sociological, religious and ethical problems. Circumstances compelled Shah Waliullah to write this book and he presented a rational explanation of the tenets of Islam. The book is divided into two parts. The Ist part consists of scholastic discussions. His observation in the Introduction that he believes in the truth of Islam in the light of reason and logic is manifest throughout its pages. The polemic starts with the metaphysical discussions, and is followed by social philosophy which is divided into different systematic stages called *irtifaqat*. In the second part the dogmas of Islam are rationalized. It ends with a review of the history of the Muslims. The author has made an extensive use of the Traditions of the Prophet which has made the book, an authentic collection of Hadith. The terminology used in this work is almost the same as found in the classical literature on philosophy, scholasticism and Tasawwuf. (Published by: Matba' Siddiqi, Bareilly, 1286; Bulaq, Misr, 1296/1877; Idara al-Taba' al Muniriya, Cairo, 1352/1833; Multazim al Taba' wa al Nashr, Dar al Kutub al Hadith, Cairo, 1952-1953; Kitab Khana Rashidiya, Delhi, 1953. Urdu translations: Abu Muhammad Abdul Haq Haqqani, Asahha al Matabi; Karachi, n.d., titled Nia'matullah al-Sabigha; Khalid Ahmad Israeli, Kitab Khana Islami, Lahore, n.d. titled: Ayatullah al-Kamilah; Abdur Rahim, Ahsan brothers, Lahore, n.d. also translated in to English, Bengali and many other languages and published.

## (v) Islamic Scholasticism

1. *Qurrat al-'Ainain fi Tafdil al-Shaikhain (Persian)*

The work was composed at the instance of Khwaja Muhammad Amin, a favourite pupil of Shah Waliullah. The central theme of the book is Shi'a-Sunni controversy over the excellent attributes of the Companions of the Prophet, but as the title of the book indicates, only the case of first two caliphs, Abu-Bakr Siddiq and 'Umar Faruq, has been dealt with in it. Shah Waliullah, tries to establish on the basis of historical evidences that the order of succession of these two early caliphs was best suited to the interest of the Islamic state of Madinah. Citing the opinion of the Prophet about both of them, he explains that they deserved the position they held, and that the charges levelled against them were not justified. In the end, he gives his own opinion by relating a vision of his in which he contacted the souls of the four Caliphs in the *Hazirat al-Quds* (the Holy Fold) where the souls of the most perfect men meet with the Great Soul.[20] Shah Waliullah found that the spiritual state of the first two Caliphs resembled more the state of *Nabuwwat* (Prophethood) while that of the later two resembled the state of *Walayat* (Sainthood). That is why the succession of Abu Bakr and 'Umar Faruq falls nearer to the period of the Prophet (pbuh) and that of 'Usman and 'Ali take place later. (Published by: Matba' Mujtabi Delhi, 1320; Matba' Rozana Akhbar, Delhi, 1899; Maktaba Salafiya, 1976. Urdu translations; by Ahmad Ali, 'Alavi Press, Lucknow, 1296; Mufid Am Press, Agra, 1295).

2. *Al-'Aqidat al-Hasanah (Arabic)*

This is a short treatise on the religious beliefs of Shah Waliullah. The *'aqa'id,* or beliefs, expounded in it are in fact, those which are commonly expressed by the sunnis. (Published by: Matba Ahmadi, Delhi, n.d. Urdu translation; Matba' Rozana Akhbar, Delhi, n.d. commentary entitled, al Aqida al Hasana by Mohammad Owais Nagrami).

3. *Muqaddamat al-Sunniya Fi al Intisar Li Firaq al Sunniya*

This is a short treatise written in defence of the Sunni beliefs.[21] The work is the Arabic translation of Mujaddid Alf Thani's Persian tract *Radd-i-Rawafid.* (Published by Abu-al-Khayr Academy, Delhi, n.d.).

## (vi) Polemical literature and History

1. *Izalat al-khafa 'An khilafat al-Khulafa (Persian)*

This is an important work on the justification of the order of the succession of the first four Caliphs of the Prophet (pbuh). Shah Waliullah has presented the Sunni viewpoint regarding the Caliphs referred to above and his discussions are well balanced. (Published by: Matba' Siddiqi, Bareily, 1286/1869; Suhail Academy, Lahore, 1976: Qadimi Kutub Khana, n.d., Urdu translation by Muhammad Abdul Shakur Faruqi, Insha Allah, Hamidur Rahman Faruqi, Instiyaq Ahmad Deobandi, Karachi, n.d.).

## (vii) History

1. *Surur al-Mahzun Fi Siyr al Amin al Mamun (Persian)*

It is a Persian translation of *Nur-al-Uyun fi Talkhis al-Siyar al-Amin w al-Mamun* of Ibn Sayyid-al-Nas,[22] a brief biography of Prophet Muhammad (pbuh). (Published by: Matba' Mujtabai, Delhi, 1308; Karachi, 1358. Urdu translation by Maula Baksh Chishti, Sitara Hind, Delhi, 1315, titled *al Kanj al Maknun;* by Ashiq Ali, al-Zikr al-Maymun, Matba, Muhammadi Delhi, n.d. (Ayn al'Uyan by Abul Qasim Ibn Abdul Aziz Haswi, Tonk, 1271.

2. *Anfas-al-'Arifin (Persian)*

This is a family biographical book of Shah Waliullah. He has given biographical notes on his fore-fathers and his teachers at Makkah and Madinah, together with a brief sketch of his own life. It is a collection of the following seven tracts: 1) *"Bawariq al Wilayah";* hagiology of Shaykh Abdur Rahim), 2) *"Shawariq al Marifa";* hagiology of Raza Muhammad)' 3) *"Al Midad Fi Ma'athir al Ajdad";* hagiology of Shah Waliullah's ancestors)' 4) *"Al-Nabazat al Ibrizia fi al-Lata'if al-Aziziyah";* hagiology of Shaykh 'Abdul Aziz and his family); 5) *"Al-'Atiyah al-Samadiya fi Anfas al-Muhammadiya";* (hagiology of Shaykh Muhammad Phulati); 6) *"Insan al 'Ayn fi Masha'ikh al-Hara mayan";* hagiology of the teachers and leading authorities of Makkah and Madinah); 7) *"al Jaz al Latif fi Tarjamat al-Abd al-Da'if"*; (a brief sketch of his own life). (Published by: Matba' Mujtabai, Delhi, 1335: Karachi, 1358; Urdu translations; Muhammad Faruq, Qadiri, Lahore, 1974, 1998; Maktaba al Falah, Deoband, n.d.; Muhammad Asghar Faruqi, Lahore, 1977.

## (viii) Maktubat

1. *Shah Waliullah Ke Siyasi Maktubat (Persian)*

The work is a collection of Shah Waliullah's letters which he wrote to various politically influential persons, including the Mughal king and Ahmad Shah Abdali. These letters have been selected from a collection of Shah Waliullah's letters made by Shaikh Muhammad 'Ashiq and his son, 'Abdur Rahman, in two volumes. The first volume contains 281 and the second volume 77 letters. Out of these 358 letters, 26 are of political nature, which have been presented in book form by Prof. K.A. Nizami, Delhi, 1950.

2. *Letters contained in Hayat-e-Wali (Arabic)*

These letters are eleven in number and were selected from a large collection which was in possession of the author of Hayat-e-Wali.[23]

3. *Letters contained in Kalimat-e-Tayyibat*[24] *(Persian and Arabic)*

These letters are twenty four in number and were written to Mirza Mazhar Janjanan, Khwaja Muhammad Amin, Shah Abu Sa'id, Shaikh Ismail bin 'Abdullah Rumi and others. These letters contain mystical and philosophical discussions.(Published by Matba' Mujtabai, Delhi 1909).

4. *Majmua' Makatib*

The work was written by Abdur Rahman Ibn Shah Muhammad Ashiq Phulati (Persian). The work is in the manuscript form. (Urdu translation: Nadir Maktubat-i-Hazrat Shah Waliullah Muhaddith Dehlavi by Nasim Ahmad Faridi, Phulat, 1998. Introduction by Nisar Ahmad Faruqi).

5. *Maktubat al Ma'rif,*

(Published by: Matba' al-Ulum, Saharanpur, 1304; Matba' Mujtabai, Delhi).

6. *Maktab Madani*

The work is included in *Tafhimat-i-Ilahiya.* Urdu translation by Muhammad Hanif Nadvi, Lahore, 1965.

## (ix) Poetry

1. *Sarf Mir (Persian)*

The work is a persian translation in verse form by Mir Jurjani (d. 1413) for the education of his son Shah Abdul Aziz (b. 1746) The work was completed in 1752, and Published by Matba' Mohammadi, Lahore, 1293).

2. *Diwan of Shah Waliullah (Arabic)*

His *Diwan* of Arabic poems compiled by Ishaq b. Muhammad 'Irfan of Bareli (d. 1234 A.H./1818 C.E.) is now in possession of the Library of Nadwatul-'Ulama Lucknow.[25]

3. *Persian Poems Contained in Hayat-e-Wali and Kalimat-e-Tayyibat*

A large number of Persian verses of Shah Waliullah are found in *Hyat-e-Wali* and *Kalimat-e-Tayyibat*.

4. *Atyab al-Nagham fi Madh Syed al-Arab w –al- 'Ajam (Arabic)*

The work contains *Qasidah Baiyah* and *Qasidah Hamziya* and their Persian commentary by Shah Waliullah. The work was completed on 24 Rabi al Thani 1156/17 June 1843. (Published by: Matba' Mujtabai, Delhi, 1308, Translated into Urdu by Pir Muhammad Karam Shah Azhari, Lahore 1985).

5. *Al-Qasidah al Hamziya Fi al-Madih al Nabawiya (Arabic)*

The work contains poems in praise of the Prophet Muhammad (pbuh). It was composed in 1147/1745. (Published by: Matba Mujtabai, Delhi, 1308. Translated into Urdu by Pir Muhammad Karam Shah Azhari, Lahore, 1985).

## Works on Miscellaneous

1. *Al-Sirr-al-Maktum fi Asbab Tadwin-al-'Ulum (Arabic)*

A short treatise which was written at the request of Shah Waliullah's two disciples, Mullah Aman Allah and Mullah Sher Muhammad.[26] The work is printed and deals with various branches of knowledge.

2. *Risala-e-Danishmandi (Persian)*

It is a small treatise which deals with methods related to teaching and writing.[27] (Published by: Matba' Ahmadi, Delhi, 1899. Urdu translation by Muhammad Sarwar, Lahore, 1964) Arabic translation by Muhammad Akram Nadvi, 1403).

3. *Wasiyyat nama (Persian)*

It is a short treatise on the beliefs of the author.

In addition to the above, Dr. Mazhar Baqa[28] has given a list of the following works on, Shah Waliullah:

1. *al-Itisam*
2. *Waridat*
3. *Nihayat al-Usul*
4. *Al-Anwar al-Muhammadiyya*
5. *Fath al-Islam*
6. *Risalah Dar Radd-e-Rawafid.*
7. *Kashf –al-Anwar*
8. *al-Tanbih Ala Ma Yahtajn Ilaihi al-lMuhaddis wa al-Faqih.*

9. *Asar –al-Muhaddisin*
10. *Risala fi Mas'alah 'Ilm al-Wajib*
11. *Risalah al Dehlawi*
12. *Al Anfas al Muhammadiyya*
13. *Mansur*

Some scholars wrote books and pamphlets on controversial issues and attributed them to Shah Waliullah. Such books are as follows:

1. *Qurrat-al-Ain fi Ibtal- Shahadat-al-Husain*
2. *Jannat-al-Aliyyah fi Manaqib-al-Mu'awiyyah*
3. *Qawl-e-Sadid*
4. *Ishara-e-Mustamarrah*[29]
5. *Tuhfat al-Muwahhidin*
6. *Al-Balagh al-Mubin*[30] *(Persian) on Tasawwuf (Matba' Mujtabai, n.d.).*
7. *Faiz-e-'Am*[31]
8. *Risalah-e-Awa'il*[32]
9. *Mayajab Hifzuhu-al-Nazir*[33]

## Islamic Literature of Shah Waliullah in Chornological Order

The works of Shah Waliullah are discussed above subjectwise. Now a summary account of his Islamic Literature in the chronological order is given below.

**First Phase:** Shah Waliullah's Pre-pilgrimage Works (1703-1732)

1. *al-Qasidah al-Lamiyah (Arabic)*
2. *al –Qawl al-Jamil Fi Bayan Sawa al-Sabil (Arabic)*
3. *Fath al Rahman (Persian)*

**Second Phase:** During Shah Waliullah's stay in the holy cities of Makkah and Madinah (1713-1732).

1. Al-Muqaddama al-Sunniya Fi al-intisar Li Firaq al-Sunniyah (Arabic)

**Third Phase:** After Shah Waliullah's return from Makkah and Madinah (1732-1739)

1. *Al-Durr al-Thami'n Fi Mubashirat al Nabi al-Amin* (Arabic)
2. *Al-Nawadir Min Ahadith Syed al-Awail Wa al-Awakhir* (Arabic)
3. *Al-Musalsalat Min Hadith al-Nabi* (Arabic)
4. *Arb'un Hadithan Musalsalat Bi al-Ashraf Fi Ghalib Sanadiha* (Arabic)
5. *Irshad 'Ala Muhimmat 'Ilm al-Isnad* (Arabic)

**Fourth Phase** (1740-76)

1. *Sharh Tarajim Abwab Sahih al-Bukhari* (Arabic)
2. *Altaf al-Quds Fi Ma'arif Lataif al-Nafs* (Persian)
3. *Fuyud al Haramayn* (Arabic)
4. *Anfas al 'Arifin* (Persian/Arabic) Collection of the seven tracts:

5. Bawariq al Wilayah
6. Shawariq al Ma'rifah
7. al-Midad Fi Ma'athir al-Ajdad
8. al-Nabazat al Ibriziah Fi al Lata'if al-Aziziya
9. al-'Atiyah al-Samadiyah fi Anfas al-Muhammadiya
10. Insan al 'Ayn fi Mashayikh al-Haramaun
11. Al Juz al Latif fi Tarjamat al 'Abd al Da'if
12. *Hujjatullah al-Baligha* (Arabic)
13. *Hama'at* (Persian)
14. *al-Intibah Fi Salasil Auliya Allah wa Asanid Warithi Rasulullah* (Persian)
15. *Tawil al Ahadith Fi Rumuz Qisas al-Anbiya* (Arabic)
16. *Fath al-Rahman Fi Tarjamat al-Qur'an* (Persian)
17. *Atyab al-Nagham Fi Madh Syed al 'Arab wa al-'Ajam* (Arabic)
18. *Al-Qasidah al-Hamziyah Fi al-Madih al-Nabawiyah* (Arabic)
19. *Muqaddama Dar Fann-i-Tarjamah* (Persian)
20. *Hawami* (Persian)
21. *Sat'at* (Persian)
22. *Al-Musawwa Min Ahadith al-Muwatta* (Arabic)
23. *Al-Khayr al Kathir* (Arabic)
24. *Al-Fawz al Kabir Fi Usul al-Tafsir* (Persian)
25. *Fath al Khabir bima la budda min hifzi' Ilm al Tafsir* (Arabic)
26. *Qurrat al-Aynain Fi Tafdil al-Shaykhain* (Persian)
27. *Sarf Mir* (Persian)
28. *Al Maqalah al-Waziyah Fi al Nasihah* (Persian)
29. *Al Insaf Fi Bayan Asbab al-Ikhtilaf* (Arabic)
30. *Iqd al Jid Fi Bayan al-Ahkam al-Ijtihad wa al-Taqlid* (Arabic)
31. *Lamahat* (Arabic)
32. *Al-Budur al Bazighah* (Arabic)
33. *Al-Tafhimat al-Ilahiyah* (Arabic/Persian)
34. *Izalat al-Khafa 'An Khilafat al Khulafa* (Persian)
35. *al Musaffa* (Persian)

***Note:*** Some other important works on the life, thought and works of Shah Waliullah are as follows: Maulana Gilani, *Tazkirah Shah Waliullah Muhaddith;* Dr. Athar Abbas Rizvi, *Shah Waliullah and his Times;* J.M.S. Baljon, *Religion and Thought of Shah Waliullah;* Ghulam Husain Jalbani, *Life of Shah Waliullah;* Abul Hasan Ali Nadvi, *Tarikh Dawat Wa Azimat,* Ismail Godharvi; *Shah Waliullah Dehlavi,* Dr. Baqa Muzhar, *usul Fiqh Aur Shah Waliullah;* Maulana 'Ubaidullah Sindhi, *Shah Waliullah Aur Unka Falsafa; Shah Waliullah Aur Unki Siyasi Tahrik; Shah Waliullah Aur Qur'an Wa Hadith;* Maulana Manazir Ahsan Gilani, *Tazkirah Hazrat Shah Waliullah;* Muhammad Rahim Bakhsh, *Hayat-Wali;* A.D. Muztir, *Shah Waliullah: A Saint Scholar of Muslim India;* Abdul Qayyum Mazahiri,

*Shah Waliullah Muhaddith Dehlavi;* Dr. M. Yasin Mazhar Siddiqi, *Shah Waliullah Dehlavi, An Introduction to His illustrious Personality and Achievements;* Dr. Abdul Ali, Role of Shah Wali Allah as Renovator of Islam with special Reference to Tasawwuf. (Published in Bulletin of the Institute of Islamic Studies,, 2004 Dept. of Islamic Studies, A.M.U., Aligarh).

## *Notes and References*

1. For a detailed biography, see *Qaul al-Jili wa asrar al Khafi* by Maulana Muhammad 'Ashiq. The only Manuscript of this work is preserved in a library at Kakori, Near Lucknow, See *Shah Waliullah kay siyasi Maktubat,* ed., by K.A. Nizami, 2nd Edition, Delhi; for a short autobiographical account, see *Al Juzw al-latif fi tarjamah-i-Abd al-Za'if,* Delhi, 1355 A.H. (Published by the Matba'i-Ahmadi, Delhi). For other biographical details vide, a) *Hayat-i-wali* by *Maulavi Rahim Bakhsh (Afzal-ul-Matabi;* Delhi, 1319 A.H.); b) Shah Waliullah No. of al Furqan (Bareilly. 1360 A.H.); c) Shah *Waliullah aur unki Siyasi Tehrikh* by Maulana Obaidullah Sindhi, Sind-sagar academy, Lahore.
2. For detailed account of Shah Waliullah's Ancestors, see *Anfas al-'arifin* by Shah Waliullah, Delhi, 1355 A.H.
3. It is true to say that Shah Waliullah believed in the dynamic nature of Islam. His appeal to the theologians of his day was to cast aside conservatism and study Islam as a living faith, capable of guiding the destinies of men in all circumstances and under all climes. He says, "the simple people of our age are totally indifferent towards it (Ijtehad). Like camels they have strings in their noses." (*Musaffa,* Vol. I, P. II.) In the same book he exhorts them to think afresh over the problems that arise from day to day.
4. Shah Waliullah, *Insan al Ayan Fi Mashaikhil Hara mayen,* Ahmadi Press, Delhi.
5. See, *Shah Waiullah kay siyasi maktubat,* ed. K.A. Nizami, Delhi, 1950.
6. Jalbani, G.N., *Teachings of Shah Waliullah,* Lahore, 1978, p. 03
7. Maulana Shibli Nomani, *'Ilm al-Kalam,* Ma'arif Press, 1939, p. 117.
8. Iqbal, Muhammad, *The Reconstruction of Religious Thought in Islam,* rep. Lahore, 1944.
9. The five verses that stand abrogated to Shah Waliullah, are found in the Qur'an in chapters given as under. (i) ii, 180; (ii) X, 65; (iii) xxii, 52; (iv) xxviii, 12; (v) xxix, 2. *al Fauz al Kabir,* Lahore, pp. 15-16.
10. Introduction to *Fath al-Khabir,* by Shah Waliullah, p. 43
11. Shah Waliullah, *Tawil al-Ahadith,* pp. 9, 47, 63, 101, etc.
12. Mazhar Baqa, *Usul-e-Fikh aur Shah Wali Allah,* Islamabad, 1973, p. 66, F.N.2.
13. *Ibid.*
14. For detailed review see Ghulam Mustafa Qasimi, *'Shah Wali Allah Ki Talifat per ek Nazr'*, al-Rahim, May 1966, p. 875.
15. *Ibid.*
16. *Hama'at,* Hydrabad, 1964, p. 135.
17. 'Introduction' to an English Translation of *Sata'at,* by Jalbani, Hyderabad, 1970.
18. *Lamahat* has been translated into English by Jalbani, Hydrabd, 1970.
19. The work is a commentary on two couplets of Khwaja Baqi Billah, *Hayat-e-Wali,* p. 246.
20. Shah Wai Allah, *Sata'at,* Hydrabad, 1964, p. 42.

21. A manuscript copy is possessed by the Kutub Khana Sa'idiyya, Tonk, vide Dr. Mazhar Baqa, op.cit., p. 71.
22. Dr. Mazhar Baqa, op.cit., p. 69.
23. Rahim Bukhsh Dehlawi. *Hayat-e-Wali,* Lahore, 1972, p. 371.
24. Abul Khair Muhammad bin Ahmad, *Kalimat-e-Tayyibat,* ed. Hafiz Muhammad Fazal ur-Rahman, Delhi, 1309 A.H.
25. Dr. Fazle Mahmud, *A Study of Life and Works of Shah Waliullah,* p. 47.
26. Shah Waliullah, *al-Sirr-al-Maktum fi Asbab Tadwin –al-Ulum,* Delhi, 1903.
27. Shah Waliullah, *Risalah-e-Danishmandi,* ed. Zahirud din Sayyid Ahmad Waliullah, Delhi, 1903.
28. Dr. Mazhar Baqa, *Usul-e-Fiqh aur Shah Waliullah,* pp. 71-73.
29. An illuminating discussion on the false attribution of Books at Nos. 1-4 is given by Muhammad Ayyub Qadiri in his article *'Shah Wali Allah Dehlawi se Mansub Tasanif,' al-Rahim,* June 1964, pp. 18-26.
30. Works at Nos. 5-6, also bracketed with those at Nos. 1-4 by Muhammad Ayyub Qadiri (op.cit.).
31. It is a short treatise of Shah 'Abdul 'Aziz; see, Dr. Mazhar Baqa, op.cit., p. 74.
32. The author of this treatise is Shaikh Muhammad Sa'id son of Shaikh Muhammad; see, Dr. Mazhar Baqa, op.cit., p. 75.
33. This work was written by the disciples of Shah Waliullah who is referred to by the author as Shaikhuna (aur Shaikh); see, Dr. Mazhar Baqa, *op.cit.*, p. 75.

26

# Sufism and the Position of Man in the Universe: A Reflection in Religious Viewpoint

*Md. Sirajul Islam*

Present age is an age of Science and Technology. Science provides us an unimaginable comfort in the various fields of life. This advancement helps us to remove all types of bigotries that strengthens logical outlook. The scientific work of this present era is largely devoted to establishing the autonomy of the biological sciences as forming a separate realm, independent of physics or matter on the one hand and the science of mind on the other. But in the traditional age, the discussion about matter, life and mind were deeply entangled together as to be hardly distinguishable and that was recognized as a cosmological aspect of the universe. Greek natural science mainly was based upon the principle that the nature is the saturated or permeated by mind. Their world of nature was considered as a world of bodies in motion, where the vitality of soul was integrated. They also believed about the existence of mind as a rational faculty in human body. Accordingly, the world of nature is not only alive but also intelligent, it is not only a vast animal with a soul or life of its own, rather a rational life of its own. The universe is neither given in experience nor it is a mental construction. What is given is always something occupying some part of time and space. Obviously, the entire universe includes more than our perception that is super-sensual. It contains many abstract possibilities that are not ostensively comprehensible and that are to be realized only.[1] According to them, the mutual participation psychical element (soul) and intellectual activity (mind) helps to regulate physical organism (body) of human being. Naturally, the notion of psychical and intellectual kinship with the body is a strange to us. More sharply we can say that Socrates was the first philosopher who first made a departure from nature and penetrated to the world of mind. The previous thinkers before Socrates were basically laid emphasis upon the natural theory. But in the hands of Plato, Aristotle and Descartes the discussion concerning nature got second position. Even Aristotle who treats the soul as an *entelechy* as organic bodies of intellect (nous), in some sense it is a part of the soul (*Anima*). Descartes, the father of modern Philosophy appreciated the body- mind distinction and asserts body is one substance and mind is another and each works independently of the other according to its own laws. But an anatomist he connected these two by affirming the functions of pineal gland, which he thinks as the organ of union of body and soul. Not only he, but Berkeley, Kant, Hegel all have spoke in the same way "that mind makes nature" and nature is a by product of the autonomous and self existing activity of mind. All experiments, however, invariably failed to show any evidence to the motion of the earth relative to the ether. You may glorify the unity of the world or the interconnectedness of the things without denying the physical science which denying some aspects of the world that are independent of others.[2]

But the Greek cosmology and the modern view of nature are not same. The Greek cosmology was based upon the analogy between the macrocosm nature and the microcosm man, as man is revealed to himself in his own self-consciousness. The modern view of cosmology is basically analogical and an endeavor to expressed all things mechanically. This modernist view of cosmology is stress upon the appearance and change. Sufi spiritualists say, it is true the world is a state of continuous motion and change, but true nature of change can be apprehended only whenever the unchanging substance is appreciated, otherwise not. Therefore, the concept of matter and mind has emerged.[3]

The materialists believe in the primacy of matter and primordial substance of the physical world and regarded energy as the product and the changing form of matter. The energists claim that on the contrary, energy is he primary and eternal substance of the physical world. And matter is the changed and compressed form of energy. In opposition to both groups, Einstein proclaimed that an experiment in a darkened room proves that neither matter nor energy is the primary and true source of the world of being. These two interchange each other in such way as to prove that they are the alternating manifestations of an invisible and unknowable essence that some times shows it self in the form of matter and some times in the form of energy. The only task of Physics is to examine these twin manifestations of the super sensible being.[4] Sufi spirituality holds, man's relation with the universe may be considered as the unity of nature with meta-nature, sensible and super sensible permanence and impermanence. Mir Damad a notable Muslim Philosopher divided world into three kinds. First is the world of essence and Attribute; the second, is a "Atemporal World" (al-'alam al-Dhari), which is the space for pure archetypes (al-mujarradat) and the third is the "Temporal World" (al-'alam al-Zamani), which is the space for daily events, created beings. There is a hierarchical relationship among these three worlds. The everlasting world encompasses the A temporal and the Temporal. The temporal world is the weakest and least enduring of the three. As temporal events are contingent upon time that is there is a time – when they were not and they were produced and brought into being in time. The same contingency governs the hierarchical order of *sarmad* (everlasting), *dahr* (atemporality) and *zaman* (temporality).[5]

Religions structures the universe as a vast cosmic eco system, an intricate network of symbiotic relation among inter dependent parts, in which each part has a specific function to perform that contributes to the whole system. Religions establishes each part in its proper place and ensure that every aspect of the cosmic system is properly balanced and co-ordinated with every other aspect of this contributes the maximum to its own evolution and to the evolution of the whole system. The principle of religion can be found operating in the multiple levels corresponding to the various planes of existence. At each level of organic unity structured in which the separation of functions among the various classes of beings is clearly defined, specific functions or needs of activity being assigned to each class of beings in accordance to its inherent nature.

Religion is a cosmic ordering principle, finds expression on the human plane in the ritual, social and moral orders, particularly as represented in the religion. Religion possesses both ontological and normative principles, includes both nature and law or substance or code of life. Religion is an innate condition of external and internal function of nature of man. Code ensures about heavenly power in the individual's inherent duty where virtues are unavoidable.

## Sufism

Sufism is a kind of religious movement that integrated phenomenal, cosmological and psychological aspects of human being and at the same time. Sufis are aspiring to comprehend the divine traits of this universe in a very systematic way. Before describing about the man and his life in the universe I think, it is essential to state some thing about Sufism. Hence, at the outset we will discuss concerning Sufism then and the other points of this topics.

### *What is Sufism*

Sufism is a mystico-spiritual movement in Islamic Religion, initiated by some pious Muslim devotees against the dictatorship of some tyrannical Muslim caliphs as well as the social injustices of the then Muslim society. After the demise of the holy Prophet Muhammad (S) some Caliphs of the Muslim States utilized Islam enormously to fulfill their personal interests and they have performed wrong/evil deeds in the name of Islam. Some strict God feared Muslim personalities were not satisfied by the activities of those Caliphs. In this intention they distinct themselves from the grips of them remain aloof completely from their political domain. But it does not mean that spirituality was absent in Islam. In the Middle-East long before the advent of Islam there were many mystic circles those who were basically engaged to worship God through unsurpassed love and austere practices, namely, *rabbun, bakkun* etc. They did not emerge from any single race or religious creed. Their main intention was to establish loving relationship with the Reality, which ultimately elevates them into a mystical experience. The influences of these pre-Islamic mystics are predominant in the various parts of the Middle- East even today. After the emergence of Islam these spiritual and mystical devotees absorbed with the Quranic ideals and took distinct name as ***Sufi***. Sufism is also an egalitarian spiritual movement in Islam. Sufis are not hesitating to accept the reasonable portion of thoughts and practices of other faiths and cultures in their domain. Historically, it is very natural that under some socio-cultural circumstances the Sufis have absorbed many concepts and doctrines of other races or religions, which were not prevalent in Islam. In the due course, Sufism fragmented in many orders (*silsilahs*) and made little differences from one order to another and took various names to designate their master, like *Dervishes*, *Pirs, Faqirs, Sufis* etc. This tendency of Islamic spirituality made the difficulties to perceive a universal feature among these distinct groups. However, they all followed some common features and ideals in maintaining their specific distinctions. Thereafter, these spiritual groups have fused in Islamic spirituality and all have been acquainted as Muslim devotees. In fact, Sufism has taken nearly 200 years to absorb with Islam. The term Sufi was first applied to Abu Hashim Kufi, who died about 776AD, hence, historically it is evident that the term Sufi was not been utilized before that period.[6] But it is quietly erroneous to think that spirituality was not prevalent in Islam, rather, it was impregnated in a latent form in Islam prior to the emergence of Sufism. Though the term "Sufi" is not found in the Holy Quran, however, numerous synonymous terms are visible in it, which are deeply related to spiritual experience of Islam, like, *Muqarrabun* (Proximity to god), *Salehin* (pious man), *Faqirun* (mendicants), *Sadeqin* (Truthful man), *Saberin* (patient man), *Abrar* (Virtuous man) and so on. Now we are going to indicate some instances from the holy Quran which will strengthen the authenticity of our thought about specification / mysticism.

a) "*Wa nahnu aqrabo ilaihe min hablil warid*"[7] i.e. For we are nearer to him than his (devotee) jagular vein.
b) "*aina yasrabo bihal* muqarrabuna"[8] i.e. a spiring from the water where the drink those nearest to God.
c) "*innal abrara la fi nayeemin*"[9] i.e. Truly the righteous will in bliss.
d) "*wa yukallamunnasa fil mahde wa kahlam wa minas salehim*"[10] i.e. he shall speak to the people in childhood and in maturity and he shall be (of the company) of the righteous.
c) "*innallaha ma'assaberin*"[11] i.e. Indeed God is with those who in patiently preserve.
f) "*illa man atallaha be qalbin salehin*" (Quran) i.e. nobody will reach to God unless his soul is pure.
g) "qadaflaha man tazakka" (Quran)i.e. he will be rewarded whose soul is clean and pure. Not only in the holy Quran but also in the Hadith Prophet (S) himself provided vivid instances concerning the spiritual as well as mystical ideals in Islam. He spent good deal of time at cave Hira, he himself preferred night vigil, supererogatory prayer which are highly resembled to spirituality. Beside this, his *"miraj"* (nocturnal ascension) is undoubtedly a spiritual as well as highly mystical one. The aesthetic aspect of Islam is based on simplicity and good deal of life. Here a spiritual anchorite is aspiring for absolute communication with divine Reality for attaining Truth. The hypothesis on which it rests that the human soul and divine soul become united with unflinching transcendental pleasure or bliss. In Arabia, Islamic spirituality was generally known as *"Tasawwufa"*, which later on popularly acquainted as "Sufism" in Persian land. After the admixture of Sufism with Islam it has got special impetus in the Islamic fold and became popular among the common Muslim masses. The traditions of Prophet Muhammad(s) made some special impact upon them in addition to their specific codifies and principles and Sufis were wanted to exist within the protection of Islam so that they can avail same status in it. The emergence of Prophet Muhammad(s) changed the socio-religious life of entire Middle East and took a new shape disparaging irrational

bigotries in human life and society as well. Before the emergence of Islam, almost the whole Persia was of the Zoroastrian faith although there were some Jews, some Christians and some spiritual mystics. According to some scholars that the people of last section were engaged in esoteric practices which followed the inner truth in every Semitic religious traditions. During the period of devotion an anchorite is come into the nearer to God. The supreme goal of a Sufi mystic in same as the mystics of other religions. Their utmost call for God basically an unsurpassed loving relationship between divinity and devotee, highly resemble to the *premalila* of the Vaisnavite cult of Hinduism. The sum mum bonum of the Sufi anchorite is to unite his finite soul with the infinite Entity, which is called in Sufi terminology *'Fana – Fillah'* (annihilation in God) and *'Baqa – Billa'* (persistence in God) as an everlasting fellowship.

Therefore, Sufism is an inner *(Batin)* movement of soul by which the finite/ carnal soul becomes pure and perfect through the systematic training and exercises. He believes, God shows His majesty upon him in order to test the sweetness of the spiritual faith and love.

Rumi says-

*" ekhtelaf-e khalq aj nam uftad chun be ma'anyraft aran uftad*
*aj nazar gah ast aye magaz ujud ekhtelaf - e- mumin wa gabar wa yahud"*

i.e. The difference among creatures comes from the outward form(nam) When we penetrate into the inner meaning (ma'na) there is peace.

Oh! Marrow of existence! It is because of the point of view in question that there has come into being differences among the Muslim, Zoroastrian and Jew.[12]

Sufism is spiritual journey; it is a journey from mundane sphere to the heavenly sphere. It is therefore, necessary to examine man's relation with the universe that surrounds him in the light of the question of change and permanence. His process of becoming is self-evident. Contemporary man bewildered concerning the sense of permanence in relation to the universe.

## Man and Sufism

Man and his position in Islam as well as in Sufism is a subject of endless controversies. Some say man is considered as the *vicegerent of God* (*khalifah tullah*) in the world. Some others also are saying that man is a *slave of God* (*bandah*), hence, he is nothing but an instrument of eternal fate.[13] According to the holy Quran man was created by the hands of God *(khalaqal Adama beyadehi)*[14] and he gave him life and spirit by breathing into him with His own breath.[15] He (God) created man, out of a (mere) clot of congealed blood.[16] In another verse He again depicts the same idea as Man We did create from a quintessence of clay then We placed him as a (drop of) sperm in a place of rest firmly fixed; then We made the sperm into congealed blood; then of that clot we made a (fetus) lump; then We made out of that lump bones and clothed the bones with flesh.[17] The lowly origin of the animal in man is with the high destiny offered to him in his intellectual, moral and spiritual nature by his most bountiful creator. Again the holy Quran says, and we will show them Our signs in the horizons and in themselves.[18] In the Tradition the Prophet maintains, He (God) created Adam in His image (*Khalaqal Adam' ala suratihi*) and He taught Adam the names[19] and became master of all creatures. He is composed of body, mind and soul and each need to be integrated on its own free will, love and the power of individuation. Although, the body is a most outward aspect of man, having its own objective existence and mode of action, it is not the greatest obstacle to obtain integration. Man is usually contemplative as well as active creatures that possess spiritual and phenomenal capabilities. Both state that man is a microcosm in the universe. Islam has indeed assigned a very high place to man and Sufism, however dwelt intently upon the various aspects of man. They believe the operations of divine omnipotence are carried out on man. Moreover, he comes to realize the cosmic dimension of his being, not in quantitative but in a qualitative and symbolic sense. Generally, Sufis apprehend world as a veil (*hijab*) it needs unfold through will power, experience and self-awareness. According to Sufism, existence of human being is therefore, harmonious order that is endowed with life, will, sensation and purpose, just like a vast and absolute man (man accompanied with the attributes of God). To put it differently, if we take a man endowed with awareness, creativity and purpose, exemplary to the utmost degree in all of his aspects, and then enlarge him to the utmost degree, then he will appears to us as a pious personality.

Man whenever attains divine attributes becomes Godlike and then his all activities are to be considered as the activities of God. Generally, The relationship of man with God is natural and meta-natural and same as that of light with lamp that emits it. It is also the same as the relationship between individual's awareness of his limb and the limb itself; his perception is not separate from limb, and still less, the limb itself. At the same time, the limb itself, without his consciousness of it, it is meaningless corpse. So Sufis does not believe in pantheism, polytheism, Trinitarians outlook or dualism, but only in strict monotheism (*Tawhid*). *Tawhid* represents a particular view of the world that demonstrates a universal unity in existence, a unity between three separate hypotheses – God, nature, and man – because the origin of all there is the same. All have the same direction, the same will, the same spirit, the same motion, and the same life. The Prophet Muhammad says, God resides in the hearts of the faithful and that is the real throne of Him (*qulubul mumenina arsh Allah*). Another popular tradition is ' God says, heaven and earth contain Me not, but the heart of my faithful servant contains me.[20] In cosmological viewpoint, Tawhid being divided into two relative aspects: a) the unseen and b) manifest. These two terms correspond in current usage to the sensible and the supersensible. The supersensible object is beyond observation and experiment and is hidden from our sense perception. This does not indicate the form of dualism; rather it is a relative classification. It is an epistemological and logical interpretation, not only accepted but also applied by science too.

The materialists believe in the primacy of matter as the primordial substance of the physical world, and regard energy as the product and the changing form of matter. The claim, energy is the primary source and substance of all things and matter is the changed and compressed form of energy. In response to this view Einstein proclaimed that an experiment in a darkened room proves that neither matter nor energy is the primary and true source of the world of being. The two interchange with each other in such a way as to prove that they are the alternating manifestations of an invisible and unknowable essence that some times shows itself in the form of matter and some times in the form of energy. The only task of physics is to examine these twin manifestations of the one super sensible being.

The worldview of Sufism is naturalistic. They say the manifest world, is composed of a series of signs (*ayat*) which possess various norms (*sunan*). The use of the word sign depicts various meanings. Here the oceans and trees, night and day, earth and sun natural beauty and man himself are the sign of the Reality. The term sign is the sense of tangibility it represents manifestation, not only in physics but all the sciences concerned it as the tangible world- phenomenon, translated in Persian *padida* or *padidar* and in Arabic as Zahira, phenomenology. Both are based upon Absolute Truth. What is knowable, and accessible to our experience, knowledge and sense perception, is appearance and not being. It consists of the outer and sensible manifestations and traces of a primary, unseen and super sensory Reality. Physics, Chemistry and Psychology can examine, analyze and render knowable these outer manifestations and sensible indications of the true essence of the world and the soul. Science deals with the signs, indications and manifestations of being, because sensible nature is the amalgam of these signs and manifestations. The concept of this sign in Sufism is closer to the approach of modern science as well as the ancient mysticism. Sufi concept of *wahdat al wujud* (unity in being) and *wahdat as suhud* (unity in witness) are very analytical. Sufis interpreted it in the sense of unity of nature and Meta- nature. It linked between phenomenal aspect as well as heavenly aspect of the universe. The Light verse of the holy Quran (24:35) also depicts the same notion, illustrates this concept of being, since it illustrates the special relationship between God and the world. There is a contradiction between man and nature, spirit and body, matter and mind sensible and super sensible, but it is inevitable and normal to apprehend the contradictory categories as a whole.

The creation of man that is the essence of spiritual destiny and attributes of the human race. In this regard the Holy Quran says, man in the biological sense, it uses the language of the natural sciences, mentioning sperm drops of clotted blood, fetus etc that are mentioned earlier. The Quranic statement signifying that man is compounded from the spirit of God and putrid clay that is similar to the assertion of Pascal in his book *Two Infinities*, that man is a being intermediate between two infinities: infinity of lowliness and weakness and infinity of greatness and glory. The similar idea is also found in the holy Quran, like – "*laqad khalaqnal insane fi ahsane taqwim, summa radana hu asfala safelin*" i.e. We have indeed created man in the best moulds then do we abase him (to be) the lowest of the low.[21] In the existential view point man is free and responsible will occupying a station intermediate between two opposing poles-God and Satan. The combination of these two opposites, the thesis and antithesis, which exist both in man's nature and his fate, create motion in him, a dialectic, ineluctable and evolutionary movement, and a constant struggle between the two opposing poles in man's essence and his life.[22] In the world of the mind, it is impossible for an object to be hot and cold at the same time or to be large and small at a time. In Meta -nature, however, this is not only possible, but actually obtains. The intellect cannot conceive of a being simultaneously dead and alive, because death and life cancel each other out, but in Meta-nature death and life exist with each other and within each other, they are the two side of the single coin. Hence Hadrat Ali the 4th Caliph of Islam and the door of Sufism says, "The breath of life itself is a progress toward death."[23]

And in fact we see that man known to us as risen so far in brilliance of spirit, splendor, beauty, awareness, virtue, purity, courage, faith and generosity, and integrity of character, that he leaves us amazed. No being material or immaterial, angel or jinn, has the capacity for similar growth. At the same time, we see other men who in their vileness, impurity, weakness, ugliness, cowardice and criminality have descended lower than any beast, microbe or demon. Man may attain the infinite in vileness, ugliness and evil just as does in perfection, nobility and beauty. One extremity of man is that he touches God, the other, the devil whatever he prefers. Man is situated between two absolute possibilities, each situated at two extremities. He is a highway leading from "minus to the power of infinity" to "plus to the power of infinity." Facing him, traced out across the plain of being, is a highway leading from an infinitely vile minus to an infinitely exalted plus. He is a free and responsible will; he is both a will obliged to choose and the object of his own will and choice. To use the terminology of Brahmanism, he is the way, the wayfarer and the wayfaring. He is engaged in a constant migration from his self to clay to his divine self that is why, God ordered to the angels to bow down to man (Adam).

Man, this compound of opposites, is a dialectical being, a binary miracle of God. In his essence and life-destiny, he is an "infinite direction," either toward clay or toward God. The holy Quran repeatedly discuss the creation and composition of man, as it is scientific and not philosophical. No element of God is exit in him. God exists in him as a potentiality for which man can reach perfection. So the holy Quran says, truly we are God's and to Him we shall return."[24] *On account of man's dualistic nature he is in the continuous motion. His life is the stage for a battle between two forces that results in a continuous evolution toward perfection. Men have a choice and engage in constant becoming. He is in infinite migration, a migration within himself. Religion is, therefore only a path not an aim, its aim is to attain truth only. We are using religion as an aim, hence it creating problem in the society.*

## Sufi Psychology

Sufism integrated various doctrines like- metaphysics, cosmology, sociology, eschatology, psychology etc. Sufi psychology is mainly based on the Quranic ideas. Man is a composition of body (*jism*) and soul (*ruh*). In this regard the Bengali Sufi singers (faqiri cult devotees) say, "*jaha nai bhande taha nai brahmande*" i.e. whatever is not in this body that is not in the universe. The body of the devotee helps him a lot to attain psychological perfection. In astonishingly they again asked to the people, " *tintala ei ghar khanite bas kariche kon jana ! tar at khupri nai daraja.....* " i.e. who resides in this three stairs building! It has eight cells and nine doors...The second part of him is keenly related to his psychological and divine element. The life of a man will not be considered as a complete until and unless we discuss something about his psychological aspects. Moreover, his psychical structure helps to realize the soul from its own knots after illuminating its darkest aspects through rigorous practices in the inner journey of his soul. Hence, the term "Sufi psychology" is probably a deceptive one, because it implies that there is relatively homogeneous doctrines of the psyche that majority of the Sufis believe as an important factor. As for the doctrinal aspect of Sufi psychology, the human soul is the faculty of many planes that united systematically. Sufi psychology is basically a discussion of nafs, *qalb* and *ruh.*[25] The nafs is the lowest principle of man. The *qalb* is something higher than the *nafs* and the *ruh* is called spirit the purified soul. Thye reputed Sufi al Kharraz states that *nafs* and *qalb* the element *tab*,"nature" the natural function of man.[26] Nuri the celebrated Sufi says that man's heart possess four different aspects as per the holy Quran, like, *sadr* (breast),connected with Islam (39:23); *Qalb* (heart) is the seat of *Iman* (49:7;16:106); *Fuad* (higher category of heart) connected with *Ma`rifa* (gnosis) (53:11) *Lubb* (inner most heart) is the real seat of the *Tawhid* (3:109).[27] However, Sufis have lay emphasis upon Latif-*e-Sitta* (The six subtleties) that is the most pertinent parts of Sufi psychology. The *latif-e-sitta* is related to Nafs, *Qalb, Sirr, Ruh, Khafi*, and *Akhfa*. These six *lataif* (sing: *latifa*) designate various psycho spiritual "organs", or sometimes, faculties of sensory and super sensory perception. In general, *Sufic* development involves the awakening of soul in a certain order of these spiritual centers of perception that lies absolute peace in the mind of the devotee as well as the whole universe. In Sufism, the term *"mauta qabla an tamauta"* i.e. die before you die is an important slogan, where carnal soul, (*al-nafs al-ammarah*) elevate man in the state of spiritual stage. The second category of soul in Sufism is called *al-nafs al lawwamah,* the soul that is higher than the former one. The third category of soul is called *al-nafs al mutmainna*, i.e. the satisfied or purified soul. In the Quranic terminology this soul is also called *al-ruh*. Through latifa a Sufi can fit himself to attain divine knowledge (*marifat*) and then he become familiar as an *arif* (gnostic). Sufi psychology elevates man beyond the empirical, earthly self that helps him to apprehend the wholeness of human state as integrated whole. The goal of a spiritual man is a journey through the cosmos and ultimately beyond it. From the psychological point of view, it must be remembered that Sufism contains a complete method of curing the illness of the human soul. They believe, only the higher can know the lower; only the spirit can know the psyche and illuminate its dark corners and crevasses. Only the man whose soul and psyche becomes integrated and illuminated has the right to cure the others.[28] Sufis interpreted different spiritual states in the level of their consciousness on which they occur intuitive knowledge of the divine, like, a) kashf *–e-kauni*, it manifest in the state of dreams and clairvoyance as a pious action and purifications of the lower soul. b) kashf –e-ilahi, is a state of hidden thought acquired after constant polishing the heart of a devotee. c) kashf-e-aqli, lowest grade of intuitive knowledge. d) kash-e-imani, is a state of perfect faith where a devotee attains divine proximity.[29]

## Sufi Concept of the Universe

Sufis believe, from the metaphysical and cosmological viewpoint there are several elements of permanence in the relationship between man and the universe. The foremost element is the cosmic environment that depicts the idea that men is not an ultimate Reality and merely possess the character of relativity. Logically is evident that things are not absolute must be relative. There is another logical point is emerge here that how this relativity can be apprehended? Relativity can only be apprehended through the knowledge of Absolute. In the universe, the absolute is always absolute and the relative is always is relative and no amount of significant change is possible to each other. The changing pattern of the universe implies logically its permanent feature and change can only be apprehended in terms of the permanent. Sufis say, Absolute (*mutlaq*) can be understood in the notion of relative (*muqayyad*) or vice-versa. It is the nature of the universe that it mutable and in a state of continuous movement/ motion. The very realization of the universe is that the changing pattern of created order (*al-khalq*) implies the awareness of truth (*al-haq*) that transcends it generally. To realize the relativity of man needs metaphysical and phenomenal distinction of the things/subjects. Another most important element of permanence is the relation of man in the universe as the manifestation of the absolute in the relative as the form of symbols (*rumuz*). The symbol is not to be understood as a man made convention, rather it is an ontological reality manifested by God (Absolute) to man. This symbol bears hierarchic order of the universe and the multiple structures of beings. Man seeks to ascertain permanence in his life through inward evolution. He believes in the evolution of his mind and sees his position as the mere reflection of his divinity that is permanent and unchanged. Sometimes it is called the uniformity of nature that integrate time and the process of creation in the image of eternity.[30] The knowledge of the universe illumines soul of the devotee, which yearns for union with God. This universe is the emanation of God and man seeks real not reflection of the real.[31]

Sufis understand the entire universe as a totality of seven skies or heavens, in their terminology that is called *Sab Sama* (seven skies or heavens). They are: 1) *Alam –e-Hahoot* (Realm of He-ness). It can also be supposed of as the Realm of pre-existence, i.e. the condition of the universe before its formation. It is equated with unknowable God's essence and named *Alam-l-Hahut, the* world of "He-ness"; etymologically, Arabic root word for God with attributes of manifest Absolute is al-Lah or "the Divinity" and *Hu* ("He") for Unmanifest Absolute is, naked essence of Godhead, nothing can be said about Him. 2) *Maqaam*-e-Mehmood (Place of the extolled). The residing place of Prophet Mohammad (Place be upon him). Beyond this lies the unperceivable. 3) *Alam – e-Lahoot* (Realm of Divinity). The Realm of Divinity is that region where incalculable unseen tinny dots emerge and expand to such a large circles that engulfs the entire universe. This realm is also known as *Tajalliat* (The Beatific Vision) of the Circle of the Beatific Vision. These countless circles are the bases of all the root causes of the universe. These very circles give rise to the species (or kinds of non living) of the universe. This whole circle is known as the *Ghaib-ul-ghaib* (Unseen of the Unseen). The final boundary of the human knowledge and understanding is called *Hijab-e-Mehmod* (The Extolled Veil), which is the extreme height of the *Arsh* (Supreme Empyrean). It is that ascent for which the human perception could train itself for the cognition of the Extolled Veil and beatific Visions of the attributes of God that are operative in there *Nehr-e-tasweed* (The Channel of Black draught / Darkness) whose last limit is in the Realm of Divinity, is the basis of the unseen that feeds *Rooh-e-Azam* (The Great Soul). 4) *Alam –e-Jabaroot* (Realm of Omnipotency). The stage when the universe is constituted into features is known as the Realm of Omni potency. *Hijab-e-Kibria* (The Grand Veil) is the last limit of this realm. *Nehr-e-tajreed* (Channel of Abstraction) whose last limit is The Realm of Omni potency feeds *Rooh-e-Insani* (Human Soul) with its information. 5) Alam – *e- Malakoot* (Angelic Realm). When the characteristics of the species and their individuals descend from the Realm of Omni potency, separate consciousness comes into being; this stage is called the Angelic Realm. Its last limit is called *Hijab-e-Azmat* (The Great Veil). *Nehr-e-Tasheed* (Channel of Evidence) whose last limit is Angelic Realm, feeds *Latifa-e-Qalbi*. Ibn Arabi a celebrated Sufi inserted a sphere between *Alm-e- Jabarut* and *Alm –e- Malakoot* as a sphere called *`Alam al Mithal*, where the existentialization takes place into the high ambition (*himma*) and the prayers of the sufi devotee reach in the high in order to set spiritual energies that bring the possibilities into actual beings.[32] 6) *Arsh-e-Mulla* (The Divine of Throne). The limiting boundary through which no one but the very nearest to God can pass. The above-mentioned realms (Alam-*e-Malkoot, Alam-e-Jabroot* & *Alam-e- Lahoot*) are its levels of functioning. 7) *Alam –e-Nasoot* (Realm of Humans). When the features further descend and come out of the limits of the angelic realm, foundations of the tangible world of matter are being laid, which is known as *Alam-e-Nasoot*. It includes the material realm (most of which humans can see) and all the normally visible cosmos is included in it. *Nehr-e-Tazheer* (Channel of Manifestation), whose last limits *Alam-e-Nasoot*, feeds *Latifa-e-Nafsi*. Human Realm is categorized as under: One *Kitab*-al-thousand *Hazeere* (Galaxies), each one has 13 billion Solar systems, out of which 1 billion solar systems have life on one of their planets Each star has 9,12,13 planets around it. On every planet (that has life on it), life exists in three different planes of existence. These include Plane of Angels, Plane of *Jinns,* and Plane of Humans. On the other hand it is surrounded by another realm known as *Alam-e-Araf* or *Barzakh* (Astral plane) where humans stay after the die (when the connection of soul breaks with the physical body). Humans can also visit astral realm during sleep (in dreaming state) or during the period of meditation.

These *Sab'a Samawat* (The Seven *Skies*) are similar to the Seven Valleys in the *Bahai* Faith, these are the boundary of material Realm. The seven skies can be thought of as 7 energy levels or 7 levels of enlightens. At the end of 7th sky is the height known as the *Baitul mamoor* (Inhabited Dwelling). After which the station *Sidartul Muntaha (Lote* Tree) can be attained, which is the last limit of the fight of the most angels. The most important element in man's relation with the universe is his existential situation in the hierarchy of universal existence (*maratib al wujud*). This notion depicts from the holy Quran as – '*inna lillahe wa inna ilaihe raje'un*" i.e. Indeed! We are from Allah and indeed we are returning to Him.[33] With respect to the absolute and all the states of being that comprises the universe. Man is what he has always been and always will be, an image of the Absolute in the relative that cast into the wave of becoming in order to return this becoming itself to being. The ontological existence of man in the total scheme of things is forever the same and all other aspects of him in the universe as studied in the cosmology may change either apparently or violently.[34] The perfect man is he who is realized in himself all the possibilities of being and becomes the model of everybody. The descent of the universal spirit into matter and the purgative ascent of man out of matter have been the beliefs of the Sufis throughout the ages. Jili says, successive stages of divine manifestation is *ahadiya* (oneness), *huwiya* (he-ness) and *aniya* (I-ness).. In essence man is a cosmic thought, which assumes flesh and connects Absolute Being with the universe. The perfect man is present at all times under different names. He is intermediate between the creator and the creatures, in him all divine attributes are manifested and become a pure soul (*ruh al quds*).[35]

I regard materialism is a fashion; it is a world-view that regards the universe as a discordant assemblage full of disunity, contradiction, and heterogeneity, possessing a variety of independent and clashing poles, conflicting tendencies, variegated and unconnected desires, reckonings, customs, purposes and wills. Sufi concept of man and the universe is an essential integral approach that delineates complete integration and unity in the universe as a whole. This integration is an essential aspect of Islamic ideals. The man who has achieved integration possesses some specific characterstics discernible only by those who are capable of observing all creatures as his own.

The present world is in a crucial stage, every moment we are in the nerve tension and severe dread for total destruction. Therefore, the primary quest for us is not for bread but for existence. Hence, the scholars of all circles are thinking- *how this present world is to be saved?* Utilization of deadly weapons invented by science never is considered as the clue of peace and happiness in the society. In the crisis of the society a scientist may appealed to the people on the humanitarian ground for preserving peace, solidarity and unity of the society. Science does not have within itself any inherent leverage by which it can prevent its exploitation by human impulse and passion. Since science can produce great results, its exploitation can also be great. It is now well recognized that the development of science should be supplemented by enormous development of human goodness. Now, the present world is searching for universal unity, integrity and solidarity. Material prosperity of the science provides us enormous comfort and utility but not universal good and peace. It has no mechanism for generating peace and goodness independent of religion. Similarly religion has no technology to create machine or computer for generating peace and goodness independent of science and it has no technology to avoid agony and misery of the people of the universe with out any help of scientific investigation. Science cannot afford to be value neutral; it can build a bridge between knowledge and value. This is one of the important gates by which science and technology can enter into the domain of ethics and spirituality is the real life of man that encompasses all aspects of human beings through which the reality of the universe can be apprehended. Therefore, the great poet Sa'di says-

> *"ashqan bar hameh 'alam keh hameh 'alam aj ust"*[36]
>
> i.e. I am (man) in love with the whole universe because it comes from Him.

### Notes and References

1. Morris R Cohen, Studies in Philosophy and Science, (Henry Halt and company, New York, 1949), p.17.

2. *Ibid*., pp. 22-25.
3. Seyyed Hossein Nasr, Sufi Essays,(George Allen and Unwin Ltd., London, 1972), p.87.
4. Morris R Cohen, *op. cit*., pp. 216, 226, 231.
5. Seyyed Hossein Nasr and Oliver Leaman, History of Islamic Philosophy, Part-I & II, (Routledge, London, New York, 1996), pp.613, 1040, 1041.
6. Md. Sirajul Islam, Sufism and Bhakti- A Comparative Study, (The Council for Research in Values and Philosophy, Washington, D.C., 2004), p.5.
7. The Holy Quran, L: 16.
8. Ibid., lxxxiii:28.
9. Ibid., lxxxiii:22.
10. Ibid., iii:46.
11. Ibid., ii:153.
12. Seyyed Hossein Nasr, Sufi Essays, *op. cit*., p.123
13. Annemarie Schimmel, Mystical Dimensions of Islam, (The University of North Carolina Press, Chapel Hill, 1975), p.187.
14. The Holy Quran, xxxviii: 75.
15. Ibid., p. xv:29, xxxviii:72.
16. Ibid., xcvi:2.
17. Ibid., xxiii:12-14.
18. Ibid., xli:53.
19. Ibid., ii:31.
20. Annemarie Schimmel, *op. cit*., p.190.
21. The Holy Quran, xcv: 41.
22. Ali Shariati, The Sociology of Islam, p.89.
23. Ibid., p.89.
24. The Holy Quran, xxiii: 60.
25. Sharda, S.R., Sufi Thought, (Munshiram Manoharlal Publishers Ltd., New Delhi, 1980), p.27.
26. Annemarie Schimmel, *op. cit*., p.191.
27. Ibid., p.192.
28. Seyyed Hossein Nasr, Sufi Essays, op. cit., pp.46, 47.
29. Annemarie Schimmel, *op. cit*., pp.192-193.
30. Seyyed Hossein Nasr, Sufi Essays, *op.cit*., pp. 89-91.
31. Umaruddin, M., The Ethical Philosophy of Al-Ghazzali, (Aligarh Muslim University, Aligarh, 1962), p.96.
32. Annemarie Schimmel, *op. cit*., p. 270.
33. The Holy Quran, ii: 165.
34. Seyyed Hossein Nasr, Sufi Essays, *op. cit*., p. 93.
35. Shustury, A.M.A., Outlines of Islamic Culture, (Bangalore, 1954), p.405.
36. Seyyed Hossein Nasr, Sufi Essays, *op. cit*., p.159.

27

# Indigenous Mystic Elements in Kashmiri Sufi Poetry

*Meem Hai Zaffar*

Kashmir has been a highly advanced seat of learning since ancient times. It has been at the cross currents of many cultures and religions. The spiritual and intellectual landscape of the Valley has always been a nodal point for different parts of the world like Iran, Central Asia, China and Arabia for exchange of scholarly ideas on religion, philosophy, art and literature. But for the distinctive identity and the survival of any cultural tradition, it is essential that it should have its roots in the soil of a world view which should be so broad, deep and rich, that it could nurture and sustain that culture for a considerable period of time and also assist it in maintaining and extending its space.

Kashmiri culture has been founded and nurtured by those saints, called *Rishis* and *Sufis* in whose name Kashmir is still known as *Rishwari* (abode of *Rishis)*. The foundational layers of Kashmiri cultural tradition are informed by the world-view which comprises mainly the intense intellectual and spiritual labour of these *Rishis*.

From the 6th century A.D to the 11th century A.D, Kashmir was considered to be the seat of learning and knowledge, in this part of the world. Throughout the Indian sub-continent it was known as *S'ardapith* i.e. the abode of *Sarasvati*, the Goddess of knowledge. The 4th Buddhist Council was held here during the 7th Century A.D. Holding of this council in the Valley is a proof of the fact that Kashmir held the position of centrality from the point of view of the development of knowledge and learning, although geographically it happens to be on the margins of the sub-continent.

## Buddhism and Shaivism

In Buddhist thought *Nirvana* is possible only by removing the wrong knowledge about self and realizing the principle of non-self or *Shunya*, whereas in *Shaivism* the recognition of self itself, which is the sole and ultimate reality, is the only way to liberation. Buddhism was divided into two sects: *Hinayana* and *Mahayana*. *Hinayanees* are of the view that an individual should concern himself with his own *Nirvana* and that is possible if he follows the righteous eight-fold path as shown by Buddha. But *Mahayanees* are of the view that individual *Nirvana* is of little significance unless and until the realized one aims at and attempts for the *Nirvana* of all his fellow beings. They advocate that although Gautama had attained enlightenment, he came back to his fellow men as Buddha to assist them in attaining enlightenment. The *Shaivistic* approach to liberation is informed by the principles of *Mahayana* Buddhism. The enlightened one has to come back to the society for the enlightenment of one's fellow beings and this is corroborated not only by the life and message of Lal Ded and Nund Rishi, who are considered as the pioneers of Kashmiri Sufi poetry, but also by a long line of Sufi Saint Poets who succeeded them.

The etymological meaning of the word 'Śiva' is `good`. According to Śaivism the ultimate and the eternal reality is 'Absolute Good'. The Universe is the manifestation of the Absolute Good or Śiva. This Absolute Good is an infinite, eternal and conscious light, which is also manifested through space and time and all that is contained within space and time. So, the Universe is a manifestation of the absolute reality and this reality is absolute conscious light. Man is also a ray of the same light. The goal and purpose of human life is to recognize this absolute and eternal reality.

Self-recognition is the ultimate intrinsic value for *Śaivism*. Since all creation has only one origin and source, there is no question of inequality among humans on the spiritual plane. But to realize this value man has to strive very hard. *Śaivism* as propounded and propagated during the medieval times in Kashmir is not only an academic and intellectual pursuit but essentially a spiritual course of action for seekers of the truth and self knowledge. This is amply proved by the very person of the saint poet Lal-Ded who transformed her earthly existence into Heavenly Being by treading the path of the spiritual discipline. Her poetry forms the foundation not only of contemporary Kashmiri literature but also that of culture as a whole. As stated earlier Kashmir produced great thinkers and Spiritual practitioners from the 6th century A.D to the 12th century A.D but all their works are in Sanskrit language. After the advent of Islam in Kashmir around this time Kashmiri people gradually lost their hold on the language due to various political, social, religious and linguistic reasons; and whatever intellectual heritage their predecessors had bequeathed to them, became inaccessible to them. With the passage of time a gulf emerged between the pre- Islamic Kashmir and the Islamic Kashmir; but Lal-Ded is the most significant historical bridge that connects the two shores of this gulf very effectively. She was the product of the creed preached by Vasugupta in the 9th century and the philosophy propounded by Abhinavahgupta in the 10th and the 11th centuries. Her poetry was not written down during her life time. It was because of her power to move that people heard her and formed her words into chants and mantras which continue to be sung even today. She revolted against all the oppressive structures which' stifle and kill the human spirit and critically interrogated practices of inequality and injustice that were current during the times. In one of her famous *Vaakhs* she hits the nail on the head by taking us to the roots of all conflict: inequality, oppression, lack of respect for one another's belief, dogmatic thought etc. In addition to all this the *Vaakh* contains a very profound spiritual message, It reads:

*Śaiva chhuy thali thali rav zaan*
*Mov zaan heund ta musalman*
*Trukay chhukh ta panun paan prava zaan*
*Soy chhay sahebas zaine zaan*

*Śaiva is everywhere— know Him as the sun*
*Know not the Hindu different to the Muslim*
*Know your self; if wise, as a ray of that sun*
*That alone is the way to saheb*[1]

The key concepts of this *Vaakh* 'Shiva' and 'Saheb' occurring respectively in the first and the last lines of the *Vaakh* belong to two different religio-spiritual and linguistic traditions; one indigenous and the other which came from outside but was destined to become the dominant tradition in the times to come. Writing about Lala's poetry a modern scholar comments on this *Vaakh*;

> Apart from the obvious idea of breaking down religious barriers by invoking the image of the sun shining upon every one without distinction, notice how seamlessly Lal-Ded hangs the Islamist valance of saheb to the apparent shaivite reference to Śaiva. The verse enacts in its own syncretic idiom, the religious, mystic and linguistic synthesis it advocates.[2]

Almost all the basic features of *Shaivism* are woven in the mosaic of Lala's verses and all the principles of this spiritual practice can be delineated in her poetry. She abhorred the dogmatic religious rituals and practices and was quite outspoken in condemning them, she says:

*Deev vatta divar vatta*
*Petha bon chhuy ikavaath*
*Pooz kas karakh hutta batta*
*Kar Manas tu pavanas sangath*

*The idol is but stone; the temple is but stone,*
*From top to bottom all is stone,*
*What is it you worship, O stubborn Pandit?*
*True worship must bind the vital air of the heart to the mind.*[3]

And again:

*The thoughtless read the holy books.*
*As parrots in their cages recite Ram, Ram.*
*Their reading is like churning water.*
*Fruitless effort ridiculous conceit.*[4]

Here are some of the Vaakhs that give us an idea of the path that Lal-Ded traversed and the destination she reached.

*In life I sought neither wealth nor power,*
*Nor ran after the pleasures of sense,*
*Moderate in food and drink, I lived a controlled life;*
*Patiently bore my lot, my pain and poverty,*
*And loved my god.*[5]

*Slay the murderous demons,*
*Lust, anger and greed;*
*Or aiming their arrows at you, they will*
*Surely shoot you dead.*
*Take care, feed them on the self-restraint*
*And discrimination of the self;*
*Thus starved, these demons will become powerless and weak.*[6]
*O fool, right action does not lie*
*In observing fasts and ceremonial rites*
*O fool, right action does not lie*
*In providing for bodily comfort and ease*
*In contemplation of the self alone*
*Is right action and right counsel for you.*[7]
*Realisation is rare indeed:*
*Seek not afar, it's near by you.*
*First slay desire, then still the mind,*
*Giving up vain imaginings;*
*Then Meditate on the self within,*
*And lo! The void merges in the void.*[8]
*My guru gave me but one precept*
*"From without withdraw your gaze within*
*And fix it on the Inmost self."*
*Taking to heart this one precept,*
*Naked I began to dance.*[9]

These Vaakhs give us an idea of the spiritual discipline that Lal practiced and prescribed for us. Now let us see the fruit of this spiritual labour:

*Would you understand what oneness is?*
*It has turned me into nothingness.*
*Though He is one, alone, and All,*
*Yet I am caught in the war of Two*
*Though He has neither colour nor form,*
*Yet I am caught in his wondrous forms.*[10]
*Whatever work I did became worship of the lord*
*Whatever word I uttered became Mantra.*
*What this body of mine experienced became.*
*The sadhana! Of saiva tantra.*
*Illumining my path to paramsiva*[11]
*Thou wert absorbed in Thine own Self,*
*Hidden from me;*
*I passed whole day in seeking thee out.*
*But when I saw Thee in mine own self,*
*O joy! Then thou and I*
*Disported ourselves in ecstasy.*[12]
*Here there is neither word nor thought,*
*Transcendent nor non-Transcendent here.*
*Vows of silence and mystic mudra-s*

*Cannot gain you admittance here.*
*Even saiva and shakti (tattva-s) remain not here.*[13]

*I traversed the vastness of the void alone,*
*Leaving behind me reason and sense,*
*Than came upon the secret of the self;*
*And, all of a sudden, unexpectedly,*
*In mud the lotus bloomed for me.*[14]
*Like a tenuous web Siva spreads Himself,*
*Penetrating all frames of all things,*
*If while alive, you cannot see Him,*
*How can you see Him after death?*
*Think deep and sift the true Self from the self.*[15]

The last two Vaakhs are a bold statement that absolute reality can and is to be realized in this very life. Notice the interrogative emphasis in the two lines:

*If while alive you cannot see Him,*
*How can you see Him after death.*

And relate it to the last line of the earlier Vaakh which reads:

*In mud the lotus bloomed for me.*

Through spiritual effort one has to realize the blooming of the flower upon the dirty ground covered with litter, mud and dirt i.e. some thing valueless (representing human body). One has to begin with brute matter, the lower *prakrti,* the manifested universe in order to realize the higher self within (the flower) and thence to immerse in the lake of immortality *(lay Ka'rmas amritsars)* that is absorption in the Divine (to quote her oft repeated phrase) void merging in the void *(shunyas shunyaya millith gav).*

## Sufism

After Lal-Ded the first Muslim saint poet of Kashmir Sheikh Noor-ul-din-Wali popularly known as Nund Rishi is considered along with Lal-Ded the fountainhead of all subsequent Kashmiri Sufi poetry, which considers this world as a play field where we have our time of fun and frolic, of our allotted sunshine and shade. But, however absorbing the world may be, we are warned not to forget our eternal **Home**, the blessed presence of God. Thus the goal is defined. Lalla-Ded calls it ***Mukti*** or release from the bondage of the cycle of birth and death, by self recognition which implies God recognition. Nund Rishi speaks of everlasting bliss in Heaven as a result of spiritual evolution and reabsorption in Him who is the source of all existence. The most attractive feature of this faith is the assurance that the goal is attainable by anybody who observes a certain code of conduct and adopts the path scrupulously avoiding the way layers, viz., inordinate greed, attachment to worldly goods, anger, pride and conceit. Through the beautiful medium of their poetry the saint poets have shown the path. The message transmitted through the aesthetic device of Rasa leaves an indelible mark on our psychological and spiritual space. Nund Rishi is all adoration for Lal-Ded and the spiritual tradition she bequeathed to us and he prays thus:

*Tami Padma:npo:rachi Lalei*
*Yami galei amrit chiva.*
*Soy sa:ni avta:r lvalei*
*Suy ma var ditto: diva*
*(It was) Lalla of Padmanpora*
*Who drank, in long draughts, nectar divine;*
*A beloved Avtar she was to us, too:*
*May Thou, Lord, bestow a similar boon upon me!*[16]

On examining the shalook, (Shruk in Kashmiri) we find the key concepts therein are: *Amrit*, *Avatar*, *Var* (vardhana) and *Deev* or *Devta*. All these concepts are indigenous and belong to the linguistic, cultural and spiritual tradition of pre-Islamic Kashmir and the Sheikh by celebrating the rhythm and music of these concepts in a new complex religio-political and socio-cultural scenario demonstrates as to how much deeply and firmly is he rooted in his soil.

Nund Rishi is called the Alamdar-i-Kashmir (Flag Bearer of Kashmir) as he assimilated and propagated a synthesis of the two spiritual traditions one the indigenous and the other imported which had become popular among the people of Kashmir lately. His greatness does not lie only in the fact that in a new religio-socio-politico milieu he nurtured the spiritual heritage of Kashmir; rather his real greatness is exhibited in his life long effort for making the spiritual and cultural values of the tradition an integral part of the collective consciousness of Kashmiri speaking people and he worked for creating and enhancing the social space for these values. He also enriched this tradition by new encounters and spiritual experiments; expanded and refocused it in a thought provoking way even for those who had come with the new message and some of whom were unduly proud and considered themselves culturally and spiritually superior to the natives. There is a popular story in Kashmir, to the effect:

> *When Nund was born he would not suckle at his mother breast and refused to be drawn to feed itself for three days. At this crucial juncture the wandering saint Lal-Ded came to the rescue of the worried mother of the newly born. She took Nund in her lap and put her dried breast into his mouth and asked, "When you were not shy of being born, why are you shy of suckling now?" The infant started suckling at the breast of the saint and the story goes that milk oozed out of the breast and fed the infant.*

This is a mystical or metaphorical rendering of the fact that the spiritual tradition of Kashmir was transmitted from Lal-Ded to Nund Rishi.

Nund Rishi or Shiekh-ul-Alam also holds the view that this universe is the manifestation of the Ultimate Reality and he also like Lal-Ded is a staunch believer of Oneness of Being. He has articulated and expressed this experience in many of his *Shalooks*. One of them reads;

*Thou art the butcher, thou the slaughtering blade;*
*Thou art the vendor, Thou the customer too.*
*The one There, is the One Here;*
*Omnipresent, he occupies all space:*

*The pedestrian and the charioteer are one,*
*The invisible He, behind the scenes.*[17]

He too has realized the fruitlessness of dogmatic religious rituals and practices in the process of spiritual evolution; and says:

*If seven times bathing where to bear any fruit*
*The fish and crocodile alike would behave*
*If God were gladdened when we famish with fasts*
*Never would the destitute put rice in the pot.*[18]

And again;

*Their plate and tongue wore out with reading*
*And writing tired out their hands*
*Still they lost not their attachment to the world*
*Neither care nor counsel prevailed over them.*[19]

For Nund- Rishi also recognition of the self is the ultimate value, but its realization presupposes great spiritual evolution. The biggest hurdle in this process is the ego; the, 'I' and the psychological constructs that originate from it.

Nund says:

*My ego is an Elephant run amuck*
*Me has he trampled under his heavy foot;*
*You may feed him on broth, again and again,*
*Full of pranks is the captivating animal!*
*Out of a thousand, hardly one escapes,*
*Otherwise, all have been crushed by him*[20]

The journey might be tedious, but the goal is achicvable; and in keeping with his cultural and spiritual tradition he also marks a path for the realization of this value. See the following *Shalooks*:

*He does not judge thee by thy dialectics,*
*The spiritual condition does He observe.*
*Meditate on God with tongue stuck to thy palate,*
*Thus will the King Swan be drawn into thy net.*[21]

*Call not the self bad:*
*Thou hast to deal with it, always:*
*Within bounds, shouldst thou restrain the self,*
*God is attained by recognizing it.*[22]

*I ferried my boat without an oar,*
*I slayed Vanity, Greed and Attachment,*
*And looked for the Lord, with an undivided mind:*
*Thus did I recognize my own soul.*[23]

*I looked for Him in the Bhavans and six directions,*
*Neither any mark nor clue did I come upon:*
*I enquired of the Mullahs and the Hermits:*
*Hearing me they only bemoaned (their ignorance).*
*As I subdued my logic and doubts,*
*Lo! I found Him all-pervading and myself naught.*[24]

From the last two *Shalooks* we can infer that self recognition is not possible through discursive and logical knowledge rather one can proceed on this path only when one gives up all the observational, logical and rational means and supports of knowledge. According to *Shaiva* system human effort can be effective only to the extent of washing out *Kārma mala* and *Māyiya mala* but for washing out *Ānava mala* Grace of God is required. At this stage all possible human supports are to be given up and one has to ferry one's boat without any oar; as the poet has said in the *Shalooks* referred to, above. Nund Rishi's vision is not much different from that of Lal-Ded. But his song had a new feel as it was a synthesis of Śaivite and Islamic rhythms. Just ponder over this *Shalook;*

*Poz yod bo:zakh pa:ntsh namu:rakh*
*Nata ma:z namu:rakh soy chhem nema:z*
*Shivasta Shunyahas yod myul karakh*
*Seduy soy chhay vahantar nema:z.*
*If you listen to truth, curb the five;*
*Otherwise, you bend the body and call it "Nemaz"!*
*If you unite Siva and the void,*
*That is the inner Nemaz, indeed.*[25]

The concept of Nemaz is not to be found in Lal-Ded; but *Shiva* and *Shunya* (void) are the warp and the weft of her spiritual experiences. Now contemplate for yourself how Nund preserves and enriches the tradition. To unite *Shiva* and the *Shunya* (void) is the real Nemaz. With what ease have the concepts belonging to different spiritual traditions been intermingled and what a fantastic rhythm they create. The spiritual experience of the saint has highly recharged these concepts and the terms connoting them appear to be dancing. A divine light emanates from this dance which is so sharp that it pierces not only one's eyes but the heart also. Nund is creating and evolving new norms of beauty a new aesthetics. He is a *Rasik* also and by celebrating *Sringar* he illuminates the path both for himself and for others;

*A lover is he, who burns with love,*
*Like gold will glitter his own self,*
*The one, who's heart is afflicted with love,*
*Will surely attain the infinite self.*[26]

When the unification of *Shiva* and *Shunya* is effected through the Nemaz of love, the goal is attained;

*Close by me stood He, and I by him,*
*Relaxed felt I by His very side,*
*Wrongly had I looked for him in alien lands*
*(When) I found solace within my self.*[27]

The spiritual and aesthetic values that have come down to us by the word of mouth through *Guru-Shisha parmpara* from Lal-Ded and Nund Rishi, have been a great source of inspiration for all our Sufi poets even to this day. With their own spiritual experiences they have broadened, deepened and enriched this tradition. The characteristic feature of this tradition has been the spiritual approach to the problems of life. The concept of religion is more comprehensive, it is cosmopolitan in essence. Freedom from prejudice and narrow mindedness is the hall-mark of this culture. The whole corpus of Kashmiri Sufi poetry revolves round the experience of self recognition, *pratyabhijñā* or *Irfan-i-Dhãt* which is considered the ultimate purpose and function of human existence. Let us have a brief diachronic view.

After Lal-Ded and Nund Rishi who belong to the 14th century there is a vacuum in the history of Kashmiri poetry that extends almost up to the last decades of the 18th century. During these three hundred years we come across only three names; Haba-Khatoon, Habibullah Nowshahri and Rupa Bhawani the first two belong to the late 16th century and the early 17th century, while Rupa Bhawani belongs to the 17th century. Haba-Khatoon was a romantic poet and most of her verses have come down to us. The other two are Sufi poets but not much of their poetry is available. Rupa Bhawani who was born more than two hundred years after the death of Nund Rishi rekindles the same fire with her verses:

*Churn the milk of the mind, your Self the churner,*
*Locate the Primal Point and sound. Break it down with the power of mediation.*
*Heat the butter of knowledge,*
*Spiritually empowered, you will find the ghee.*[28]
*With these ingredients, a yagya I perform,*
*Offering the oblation of my own organs*
*The flames that rise are Your own effulgence.*
*In them my essence revealed, I stand as myself, finally.*[29]

This concern for the realization of the centre of one's being, one's true identity, reveals her roots in the tradition.

There might have been poets during these three centuries who's compositions have not been able to survive the harshness of times, but after the 18th century we have a galaxy of Sufi poets who's verses are a witness to the depth and strength of Kashmiri spiritual tradition. Momin an early 18th century poet sings:

*Realize unity and transcend duality.*
*Recognise thyself, from within you.*
*Leave six, four, nine and seven behind;*
*Drive your horse ahead.*
*One is manifesting His oneness.*
*Recognise thyself, from within you.*[30]

His contemporary *Sucha Kral* celebrates the oneness of being in his poetry saying:

*O ! Myself who am I?*
*All is He, I am just a pretext.*
*Nothingness there was; there was some thing.*
*What Does Nothingness signify?*
*I did not realize, everything is He.*
*The Lord was himself, in my home.*
*Whom shall call a friend; whom an enemy?*
*All is He, I am just a pretext.*[31]

And again:

*Don't count you and me.*
*This is a vain delusion.*
*Duality mars can't you see?*
*This is a vain delusion.*[32]

One of the significant and authentic voices of the early 19th century is Shaha Gafoor, who's poetry is greatly permeated by the concepts drawn from *Śaivistic* thought. Here is a quote:

*Nothing is to be gained from birth and death.*
*Fuse your consciousness with so hum.*
*Transcend the self and realize the lord.*
*Be with the real and you shall be the real.*
*To realize the lord ego has to be killed.*
*Fuse your consciousness with so hum.*[33]

His younger contemporary Shamas Fakir sings:

*In the brook, flows the source of the brook,*
*From where did the source come?*
*Turn your gaze within; you shall realize the 'One'.*
*From where did the source come?*[34]

Here is another quote:

*I am nothingness, he is the Being.*
*How shall nothingness communicate with the Being.*
*I perceive only nothingness on all sides.*
*How shall nothingness communicate with the Being.*[35]

And again:

*Transform consciousness into jüãna,*
*jüãna shall unite with the Lord.*
*She (Lal) went to pray in the Karmic Sansar,*
*In the idol house of the Dharma shastra.*
*When lal-united cosmos with the self,*
*jüãna united with the lord.*[36]

The whole process of Lala's transformation has been reproduced rather re-enacted artistically in these verses and as a consequence thereof the path of knowledge has been illuminated for the seeker.

Coming to the 20th century I shall talk about three representative poets of the tradition. These are Samad Mir, Ahad Zargar and Bimla Raina. Samad Mir who died in the year 1958 had no formal education and was an illiterate. Zagar died in the year 1984 he was, semi-literate. Bimla Raina is in her sixties and lives at Jammu, she studied up to the high school. Although not highly educated in the formal sense of the term, these poets are quite well versed in their cultural and spiritual tradition which has survived through the word of mouth. Unfortunately the most of the products of our new education system are quite uneducated when it comes to their own cultural and spiritual tradition.

Samad Mir is quite at home in both the spiritual traditions one indigenous and the other Islamic and their syntheses which he inherited. In order to create an appealing colour scheme and new designs in the fabric of his poetry, he draws upon the tradition creatively. Here is an example:

*Die in life and realize Ha and Hu*
*Recite Om Su, recite Om Su*
*One, who transcends doubt, leaves anger and vacillation*
*Ram Rahim become indistinguishable for him*
*One who burns the self that hates, becomes Sãdhu*
*Recite Om Su, recite Om Su.*[37]

Notice how the terms *Ha, Hu, Om, Su Ram Rahim* and *Sãdhu* are aesthetically blended and how they enhance the beauty of the text. The intense spiritual experience of the poet enables him to use words in totally new arrangements, giving birth to unexpected shades of meaning. Here is yet another example of his powerful expression.

*With his ego dissolving cry, Mansoor,*
*Did not respect the limitations of the path even once,*
*He did not hide in the safe abode.*
*Since then every fibre of my being is on fire.*[38]

The fire that burns the poet, is at the same time the source of light and warmth for him as well as for others. In order to enlighten oneself and the others one has to burn oneself. That is the message of the Sufi.

Ahad Zargar is one of the most significant signatures of the contemporary Kashmiri Sufi poetry. He has great command over language. Like Samad Mir he is well versed in the spiritual ethos of Kashmir and by his contribution has definitely enriched the tradition. Some of his poems ignited controversies in the conservative religious circles of the valley, and some clerics even issued fatwas against him. But threats and fatwas notwithstanding he continued to articulate and express himself in the same controversial but piercing idiom. Here are some extracts:

*I am the hidden secret of both the interior as well as the exterior.*
*To whom shall I bow, and for whom shall I perform the 'Nemaz'.*
*I am the ultimate grace of both the mosque and the temple.*
*I am the worshipper, but I am the one worshipped.*
*I am the chain of birth and death.*
*And it is me again who is to play the game of love.*[39]
*In the absence of Nothingness, there is no possibility of Being.*
*Nothingness is all pervading.*
*But if Nothingness is mere Nothingness,*
*Who has deluded me?*
*Realize Nothingness within yourself,*
*Dance round nothingness like a moth.*
*Keep your heart awake with Nothingness.*[40]

Now you can yourself appreciate the kind of language the poet is using. Here is yet another instance of his creative use of language:

*Upon the dark throne sits the dark king*
*On the dark gate is the dark gate keeper*
*And the army of the General is also dark*
*The dark city is ruled by the king Indera*
*The dark fairies are playing the music*
*In the dark city there is the echo of dark music*
*In the dark ocean there are dark gems*
*The dark diver is in search,*
*So that he can lay his hands on the dark pearls*
*Ahad Zargar came with a dark gift*
*Wearing a necklace of dark pearls*
*He has made a heap of dark jewels*[41]
*Rig Veda Yajir Veda, Sam Veda are the robes of sanyasees,*
*My master pointed to the four Vedas*
*Yogis demonstrated the method of jūāna,*
*Realize the essence of air, earth, fire and water*
*Transcending clouds of passion unite with the essence.*[42]

Ahad Zargar is a prolific poet. It is not possible to comment upon all the aspects of his poetry in such a brief presentation, still the writer has made an effort to discern the aspects of his poetry that relate him to the synthetic spiritual tradition of Kashmir.

Bimla Raina who is a living poet composes in the style and form of Lal-Ded. She calls her compositions Vaakh. Not only the form of her compositions but her language also resembles that of Lal-Ded. Some literary critics opine that her language is archaic, consequently they disapprove of it. But the present writer is of the view that form and content are inseparable in poetry. The kind of themes Bimla ji is articulating and expressing demand the kind of language she is using. She is also quite creative in the matter of using language. In the first instance it may appear that the language used is archaic, but when one delves deep in the universe of her poetic compositions, one realizes that appearances are deceptive. There is nothing archaic about the language Bimla ji is using. Her poetry springs from the depths of her being and it gets its form as well as content from the creative process it undergoes. Here are some of her Vaakhs.

*Through arguments vehement, you will not reach him.*
*The one, who is immanent, yet fixed and still.*
*Warnings He sends you through your heart and pulse.*
*And judges, who can absorb and how much.*[43]
*I cleansed my mind of envy, aversion and prying,*
*And underwent the penance of going through the mill;*
*Gave up selfishness and learnt to worry for others;*

*Thus I got to know,*
*How to offer myself at the altar of love.*[44]
*Drink the nectar of love sip by sip*
*And the heart will bloom lotus like*
*Thoughts of duality will melt away*
*And never will your mind restless be*[45]

## Conclusion

This is no surprise that an echo of Lal-Ded is discernible in these Vaakhs. Even non-Sufi or secular contemporary Kashmiri poetry draws heavily from Lal-Ded and relates itself to her. Lal-Ded is as alive today as she ever was; and so is the message of her life. Let me close this presentation with two Vaakhs of Bimla ji that remind us of the lesson that Lal-Ded had learnt and we along with the poet may make an effort to learn:

*Listen to the strings of your own heart,*
*Shutting barring all doors and windows,*
*Tune them and wait for the music within.*
*He Himself is the musician.*[46]
*The Guru told me, "go inwards,*
*Hold Him tight within your heart,*
*Read but the lesson that Lalla did"*
*Every pore of my body chants "Om Om".*[47]

### *Notes and References*

1. Kaul Jayalal (1973): Lal Ded, Sahitya academy, New Delhi-p.107.
2. Mattoo Neerja (Oct, 2006): A Fresh Look at Some Kashmiri Women poets – article presented at a seminar organized by the Institute of Kashmir Studies, University of Kashmir.
3. Kaul, *op.cit*, p.110.
4. Ibid, p.104.
5. Ibid, p.98.
6. Ibid, p.101.
7. Ibid, p.107.
8. Ibid, p.118.
9. Ibid, p.97.
10. Ibid, p.129.
11. Ibid, p.134.
12. Ibid, p.133.
13. Ibid, p.132.
14. Ibid, p.122.
15. Ibid, p.115.
16. Parimoo, B.N (1984): Nund Rishi Unity in Diversity, J&K academy of Art, culture and languages, Srinagar,,p.106.
17. Ibid, p.19.
18. Ibid, p.269.
19. Ibid, p.286.
20. Ibid, p.72.
21. Ibid, p.129.
22. Ibid, p.267.
23. Ibid, p.127.
24. Ibid, p.126.
25. Ibid, p.159.

26. Ibid, p.305.
27. Ibid, p.126.
28. Saqi, Moti Lal ed.(1984): Sufi Shaari, Academy of Art culture and Languages, Srinagar, p.69.
29. Ibid, p.68.
30. Ibid, p.121.
31. Ibid, p.78.
32. Ibid, p.78.
33. Ibid, p.121.
34. Ibid, p.121.
35. Ibid, p.122.
36. Ibid, p.127.
37. Ibid, p.89.
38. Ibid, p.91.
39. Ahad Zargar (2007): Kulyat Ahad Zargar, K. A Zargar, Srinagar, p.58.
40. Ibid, p.58.
41. Ibid, p.69.
42. Ibid, p.71.
43. Arvind Gigo trans. ed. (2007): The Silence within, n-p- Search, new Delhi, p.49.
44. Ibid, p.53.
45. Ibid, p.54.
46. Ibid, p.55.
47. Ibid, p.44.

28

# Dara Shukoh: The Sufist

*Sukumar Bhattacharya*

The philosopher-prince Dara Shukoh, the eldest son of the Mughal emperor Shah Jahan, was the embodiment of pluralistic culture. While he failed to succeed in statecraft and war, he devoted the greater part of his time and energy to carry on pursuits including literary ones for the promotion of socio-religious peace as also proper understanding and harmony between different communities by way of meaningful dialogue to create an atmosphere of mutual appreciation. In this regard he partly reflected his illustrious great-grandfather Akbar's attitude. This distinguished liberal thinker with an artistic bent of mind significantly contributed to the furtherance of the cause of spiritualism in India.

Dara Shukoh, a lifelong scholar and mystic philosopher, while devoting himself to theosophical studies, came into close contact with a number of Muslim and Hindu saints and became greatly interested in Sufism. His Sufistic leanings made him interested in mysticism of other religious systems. His association with Muslim and Hindu mystics like Mulla Shah Muhammad, Shaikh Muhibbullah, Shah Dilruba, Baba Lal and Jagannath Mishra also contributed to this aspect of religious rapprochement. While retaining full allegiance to the Prophet Muhammad and the Holy Quran, he saw the vitality of reconciling Islam to the socio-cultural progress in India and the world at large. The Sufis as the Islamic Unitarians may be seen to aim at the doctrine of *Tawhid* (Unity of God or Divine Pantheism) after obtaining a true knowledge of His Unity. While searching for the doctrine of *Tawhid,* Dara Shukoh studied translations of the Jewish, Christian and Brahmanical scriptures. Like other Muslim theosophers, he was greatly under the influence of Neo-Platonism.

The death of his infant daughter in 1634 greatly shocked Dara Shukoh and his wife Nadira Begam. Greatly bereaved, they strove for spiritual solace and got it from the celebrated Sufi mystic saint Mian Mir of Lahore who belonged to the Qadiriya order established by Abdul Qadir Gilani. Incidentally it may be stated that though at the family level Dara had inherited association with the Chisti sect of the Sufis with Khwaja Muinuddin Chisti as the patron-saint of the Mughal dynasty, he eventually dissociated himself from the Chisti order to join the Qadiriya sect. But as Mian Mir before long died, Dara could not become his disciple. His association with Mian Mir and his order helped him to believe in the primary superiority of the esoteric to the exoteric path of Islam and also of the concept of *Hama-u-st* (All is He) to the notion of *Hama-az-u-st* (All is from Him). His liberal aspiration was to replace exoteric Islam by esotericism as a lively moral force among the enlightened Muslims. He come to encounter considerable opposition from the orthodox *Ulama*. His estrangement from the *Ulama* may be regarded as a logical conclusion. He truly felt that the religious exclusivity as upheld by the *Ulama* ran counter to the vital interests of a multicultural county like India. In his poems Dara, while glorifying the Qadiriyas, came to challenge the *Ulama* regularly.

Dara came to be very intimately associated with Mulla Shah, a disciple of Mian Mir. With his broad intellectual attitude Mulla Shah was a great pantheist with an exalted humanistic mental faculty. Dara's initiation into the Qadiriya fraternity was greatly shaped by Mian Mir and Mulla Shah. After initiation Dara named himself as Qadiri and Hanafi. He became Mulla Shah's disciple. Of course, Dara's first religious instructor was Mulla Abdul Latif Sultanpuri of the Punjab. His interest in the Qadiriya sect was first roused by his subsequent teacher Shaikh Mirak, and his association with Mian Mir later came to deepen it. Eventually Dara came to regard the five major Sufi sects in India - Qadiriya, Naqshbandiya, Chishtiya, Kubrawiya and Suhrawardiya – to have a pivotal role in all mundane and spiritual affairs.

Dara's piety was well reflected in his intellectual pursuits. Between 1639 and 1646 he produced three Sufistic works, *Safinat-ut-Awliya, Sakinat-ut-Awliya* and *Risalaṣ-i-Haqnuma,* covering a significant phase in the development of his spiritualism. The *Safinat-ul- Awliya* deals with the lives of Indian and non-Indian Sufis. We come across a detailed study of the life and teachings of Mian Mir and his disciples in the *Sakinal-ul-Awliya*. Unlike the first biographical work, the second one no doubt exclusively treats of the saints of the Qadiriya sect in India but marks the furtherance of spiritual search. As held by Dara himself, it was divine stimulus that enabled him to write the *Risala-i-Haqnuma* to throw light on Sufistic practices. It will reflects on his character and personality. The components of Sufism were hardly expressed in a more interesting and understandable manner by any other scholar within such a limited space. According to Dara, this production is based on the standard works of Sufism like *Fusus al-Hikam* and *Futuhat al- Makkiyya* of lbn al-Arabi and *Kitab al–Luma* of Abu Nasr al-Sarraj. He held that the pattern of Sufism as delineated by him was in keeping with the religious living of the Prophet. He viewed that the attainment of sainthood (Fakirism) depended not on individual endeavours or performances but on Divine Grace. Dara dealt with the Sufi concept of planes of existence. As pointed out by him, some Sufis thought of four planes of existence: *Alam-i- Nasut*. (the Physical Plane or the World of Sensation and Perception), *Alam-i-Malakut* (the Astro-mental Plane or the World of Spirits), *Alan-i-Jabrut* (the Celestial Plane or the World of *Bliss*, Unity and Satisfaction) and *Alam-i-Lahut* or *Alam-i-Hawwiyat* (the Plane of Thatness or the World of Absolute Truth). But other Sufis come to count five planes, distinguishing *Alam-i-Misal* (the World of Analogies) form the *Alam-i-Malakut*. In his *Risala-i-Haqnuma* Dara offers an interesting portrait of the four planes, while intimating his personal experience in this respect. As felt by him, a mystic can hardly find the *Alam-i-Lahut* (the World of Divinity) as his abiding plane. The *Alam-i-Nasut* being the right place for the human being, the mystic completes his journey when he comes back to the *Alam-i-Nasut*.

In championing the eclectic tradition as a Sufist Dara Shukoh sought to find a common ground for Islam and Hinduism and wrote the *Majma-ul-Bahrain* (Mingling of Two Oceans) as the first fruit of his comparative study of these two religions. Though it is not definitely known when it was actually written, it is generally held that it was composed possibly in 1650-1656. Dara's great purpose in this work was to show the identity of the ideas of Hindu cosmogony with those expressed in the Quran. As he saw it, the difference between the Hindus and Muslims in respect of attaining the knowledge of God lay in words. Precisely speaking, the conflict was linguistic and expressional. In this composition Dara sought to trace the basic principles of the concept of Creation as stressed by Hinduism and Islam. He strongly felt that his studies would greatly benefit the 'elect' of the Hindu and Muslim societies. Indeed his original way of thinking served to stress the commonality in the Indian society. Thus Dara Shukoh came to produce the first thoughtful scholarly work in the way of mutual understanding and appreciation. Incidentally it may be noted that while in his *Majma-ul-Bahrain* Dara Shukoh sought to find out the Sufistic and Upanishad co-relations in terms of beliefs and practices, the elite of the Indian Muslim society came to practically identify the Vedanta with Sufism.

In his thirst for *Tawhid* (Divine Unity) Dara Shukoh produced the *Sirr-i-Akbar*, the Persian translation of 52 Upanishads, as an important scholarly work. That his theosophical views were moving around the Advaita Vedantic philosophy is also well evident in his choosing for Persian translation such other Sanskrit compositions as *Bhagavad-Gita*, *Yogavasistha* and *Prabodhachandrodaya*. He considered not only the Quran but also the Vedas as the Word of God' (*Kalam-i-Ilahi*)

The orthodox Muslims regarded Dara Shukoh's pantheistic views as un-Islamic. As a reply to this criticism he wrote in 1652 *Hasanat-ul-Arifin*. Though it is a minor work, it significantly throws light on his religious ideas and spiritualism. The pantheistic disposition is also well reflected in the *Tariqat-ul-Haqiqat,* a tract written by him in mixed prose and poetry. Dara who never deviated from outward conformity to the Islamic faith can hardly be accused of apostasy. Of course, he might not have followed the practices of praying and fasting as orthodox Muslims like Aurangzeb had done. His views on the basic points of the Islamic faith hardly differed essentially from those of the orthodox Muslims except on the issue whether God-Knowing *Arifs* (gnostics) can be exempted from submission to the rules of religious discipline (*Shariyat*). Unlike the moderate Sufis, he viewed that after the *Haqiqat* (the Dawn of Truth) an *Arif* would be free from the rigours of the *Shariyat*. Like Akbar the Great Dara Shukoh as an outstanding Islamic thinker of India showed great moral courage in expressing his religio-spiritual convictions.

Dara Shukoh, a very learned prince of the Mughal dynasty, was the greatest Indian scholar of his times. As a distinguished philosopher-theosophist he played a significant role in the evolution of spiritualism in India. This great advocate of impartial asceticism rejected religious arrogance and ritualism to strive for reconciliation and peace. The liberal influences of his times were well reflected in his philosophical erudition. His literary activities were closely related to the evolution of spiritualism. As a distinguished Sufi of his times he was a great champion of the principle of *Wahidiyya* (Unity-in-Plurality) to promote socio-cultural progress in India with her multiple religio-spiritual traditions.

### *Notes and References*

1. Ali, Hafiz Md. Taher- *Impact of Sufism*, Santiniketan, 2003.
2. Ali, Maulana M.- *The Religion of Islam*, Lahore, 1936.
3. Ali, S.A., *The Spirit of Islam,* London, 1952.
4. Arberry, A.J.- *An Introduction to the History of Sufism,*London,1942.
5. ———*Sufism : An Account of the Mystics of Islam,* London, 1950.
6. *The Cambridge History mof Isla*, Vol. II, Cambridge, 1970.
7. Dahnhardt, Thomas- *Change and Continuity in Indian Sufism,* New Delhi, 2002.
8. De, Amalendu- *Islam in Modern India,* Calcutta, 1982.
9. Dey, Amit-*Sufism in India*, Calcutta, 1996.
10. Hasrat, Bikrama Jit – *Dara Shukoh: Life and works*, New Delhi, 1982.
11. Mohanta, D.K. (Ed)-*Islam and Philosophy*, Kolkata, 2007.
12. Nicholson, R.A.-*The Mystics of Islam,* London, 1914.
13. ———*Studies in Islamic Mysticism,* Cambridge, 1921.
14. ———*The Idea of Personality in Sufism,* Cambridge, 1923.
15. Qanungo,K.R.- *Dara Shukoh*, Vol.I, Calcutta,1952.
16. Rizvi, S.A.A.- *A Hisfory of Sufism in India*, Vols. I & II, New Delhi, 1986 &1992.
17. ———*Muslim Revivalist Movements in Northern India in the Sixteenth and Seventeenth Centuries,* Agra, 1965.
18. Schimmel, A.- *Mystical Dimensions of Islam*, North Carolina, Chapel Hill, 1975.
19. Sell, E.- *Religious Orders of Islam*, Madras, 1908.
20. Sen, K.M.- *Medieval Mysticism of India*, London, 1931.
21. Subhan, J.A.- *Sufism: Its Saints and Shrines*, Lucknow, 1960.
22. Titus, M.T., *Indian Islam,* Madras, 1938.
23. Trimingham, J. S.- *The Sufi Orders in Islam*, Oxford, 1971.

29

# Islamic Literature in Kerala

*T. Abdul Rasak*

The term 'Islamic literature' has generally been used to mean the literature on Islam and its teachings; it includes the literature on the Holy Quran like its commentaries, the prophetic tradition and the Islamic jurisprudence and way of life; it also includes the literature on Islamic history and personalities. However, of late, the term has also been applied to the creative literature written with an Islamic perspective, thanks to the Islamic revivalism of the 20th century. It is true that Islam brought radical changes, along with others, to the fabric of Arabic literature since its emergence in Arabia in the early 7th century. Since then, Islamic literature, in both its denotations mentioned here, has been brought out not only in Arabic, but in other languages too consequent upon the advent of Islam to other cultures.

Kerala had been having trade relations with Arabia well before the emergence of Islam. The significant presence of Arabs-primarily traders- on the Malabar Coast has been recorded in many Roman and Tamil sources. They were encouraged to settle and set up trading outposts and factories by the local kings. One version, though not the historically accepted one, of the origination of the word 'Kerala' is that it is from Arabic *khairullah* meaning 'the blessing of the God'; Arab travelers named it so thanks to the natural beauty and prosperity of Kerala.

Kerala society was so connected with Arabia that the waves of renaissance Islam caused in Arabia after its emergence in the early 7th century was felt in Kerala soon. The Arab traders brought Islam to the Malabar Coast of Kerala, built mosques, married local women and built their homes there. They were not resented by the local populace or the rulers; rather they were respected. It is believed that Cheraman Perumal who was the ruler of Kerala in the 9th century was attracted to Islam in his old age and sailed for Mecca to embrace it.

Islam paved the way for increased cultural interaction of the Arabs with Kerala. Historians unanimously opine that there were peaceful co-existence with those who converted to Islam and others.

Malik Ibn Dinar is the first missionary who propagated Islam in Kerala. He, along with a delegation of forty-four came to Kerala in the later half of the 7th century and created the first Muslim settlement at Kodungallur in the present Thrissur district of Kerala. The indigenous people got easily attracted to them thanks to the message of brotherhood they preached and the simple life they led.[1] Over the centuries, a Muslim community steadily arose in Kerala either through religious conversion or marital relationship between Kerala women and the Arab traders. They flourished in the Malabar[2] region of Kerala. They were known as *Mappilas.*[3]

The Islamic literature emerged in Kerala over the centuries can linguistically be categorized into three: one, the literature in Arabic; two, the literature in the hybrid language of Arabi-Malayalam[4] ; and three, the literature in Malayalam, the local language. All these three linguistic categories of Islamic literature in Kerala throughout the ages have mostly been literature on Islam and not creative writings in an Islamic perspective. This research aims to analyze the latter two categories of Islamic literature in Kerala.

***Islamic literature in Arabi-Malayalam:*** Developed in 8th century by the Arab immigrants to facilitate written communication with indigenous community, the Arabi-Malayalam hybrid script, by the course of time, evolved into a language having its own identity. It prospered in terms of literary output too; with a repertoire of more than five thousand works in prose and verse, both Islamic and otherwise, it has left a rich heritage to Kerala culture. Its literature not only became popular among the Muslims of Kerala but also had a great impact on Malayalam literature too.

The verse works in Arabi-Malayalam, generally known as 'Mappila songs', are songs replete with poetic elements and rhythm; they are devotional in nature and comprise of the following: panegyric poems on Muslim saints (*Malappattukal*); martial songs on the history of wars waged in the early period of Islam (*Padappattukal*); and epics on the life of the prophets and other great personalities in Islam (*Qissappattukal*) and eulogies on them (*Madh Pattukal*).

***The panegyric songs:*** These are the poems extolling the praiseworthy events in the life of the holy saints in utmost devotion. There are a good number of panegyric poems in Arabic-Malayalam; the most popular among them are *Muhyiddin Mala, Badr Mala, Rifai Mala, Nafisat Mala, Mamburam Mala, Malappuram Mala*, and *Mahmud Mala*. Right from the beginning, these songs have been well assimilated to the folklore tradition of the Malabar Muslims.

*Muhyiddin Mala* is the first poetic work composed in Arabic-Malayalam. It was written in 1607 AD in full-fledged Arabic-Malayalam script by Qazi Muhammad, an Islamic scholar and a former *qazi* of Kozhikode.[5] It tells the miraculous tales of Sheikh Muhyiddin of Jilan in an irrational and unconvincing style and contains superstitious beliefs on him. However, it also contains ideas promoting communal harmony, peaceful co-existence and secular values. It is worth mentioning here that in December 2008, Kendra Sahitya Akademi organized a symposium on *Muhyiddin Mala* at Kozhikode (Calicut) where the speakers stressed the contributions made by the 400 year old poem to Malayalam literature.[6] This work, in fact, is the foundation of Arabic-Malayalam literature; other panegyric poems have been composed emulating *Muhyiddin Mala*. Each of these poems has been composed collecting data from authentic works on the history of Islam; some even acknowledged the names of the source works. These poems were meant to shed light on the holy saints of Islam and to create an urge in the mind of the reader to learn more about them and to make him follow their path.[7]

There are over 50 martial songs in Arabic-Malayalam, the most prominent ones being *Badr Patappattu, Uhd Patappattu, Makkam Fath, Futuhussam, Hunain Patappattu, Khandaq Patappattu* and *Khaibar Patappattu*. As the titles indicate these narrate the early wars Muslims were forced to fight for survival in the hostile situation of Arabia. Moyinkutty Vaidyar(1852-1892), who is considered to be the best ever genius in Arabic-Malayalam literature, made a remarkable contribution to this genre. He has expressed in marvelous Mappila songs the great events in the history of Islam like *Badr, Uhd* (the battles Prophet Muhammad, along with followers, was forced to fight for self defense) and *Hijra* (the migration of the Prophet and followers from Mecca to Medina to save themselves from the persecution of the Meccans who were hostile to Islam initially). *Badr Patappattu* (1876) is widely acclaimed as the author's masterpiece and is undoubtedly the best work in this genre. Chakkeeri Ahmed Kutty, another leading figure in Arabic-Malayalam literature, too expressed the battle of *Badr* in a marvelous Mappila song. *Futuhussam* is a martial song written by Chettuvayi Pareekkutty. Besides being devotional in appeal, these works kindled in the audience a sense of Islamic history and a spirit of rebellion against the British.[8] These songs have been a source of inspiration to learn history even for those who are least inclined to it. Moyinkutty Vaidyar's songs are very much studied and discussed in the literary and cultural circles of Kerala.[9] They have also attracted the attention of the western linguistic researchers; Vaidyar's *Badr Patappattu* along with his *Badr al-munir Husn al-jamal*, a romantic piece in mappila songs, has been translated to English and published in *Indian antiquity*.

These songs induced awareness among the Muslims of Kerala about religion, language and poetry. However these songs, as they were in Arabic-Malayalam script, have not been considered a part of Malayalam literature. The later generation of poets, however, started writing mappila songs in Malayalam script itself. As a form of entertainment, mappila songs do have popular appeal in Kerala and are practiced and enjoyed by people cutting across religious identities; they have found a pride of place in Malayalam films too. Owing to its mass appeal, a popular Malayalam television channel conducted a reality TV of mappila songs in 2009 and some other Malayalam channels followed suit.

**Prose works**: Islamic literature in Arabic-Malayalam prose dates back to the 10th century. As the script was developed by the Arab-Muslim immigrants in Malabar in the 8th century for missionary purpose, producing Islamic didactic literature was a need of the hour. But, unlike the works in verse, the early works in prose have not been passed through oral tradition; they have not been preserved as manuscripts either. So these works have not come to light.

The history of Islamic prose works in Arabic-Malayalam starts from the establishment of the first Arabic-Malayalam printing press in 1867 at Tellicherry in the present Kannur district of North Kerala. Following suit, Arabic-Malayalam printing presses were started in different places of Malabar region like Ponnani, Tirurangadi and Valapattanam.

The first translation and commentary of the holy Quran in Kerala, *Tarjama Tafsir al-Quran* (Meaning of the Interpretation of Quran), was written in Arabic-Malayalam by the immensely rich and generous Muhyiddin bin Abd al-Qadir, alias Mayinkutty Elaya of the *Arakkal* royal family of Kannur depending on the 15th century Arabic commentary *Tafsiral-Jalalayn*; started writing in 1855, the work was completed in six volumes in 1869. Having made a hundred copies of it by copyists at a cost of Rupees one lakh of the time, the author himself circulated the manuscripts free of cost among the nobility and Islamic scholars of Malabar; a few copies were also given to certain mosques. It was printed and published in 1870. The second translation in Arabic-Malayalam appeared only after a century in 1959; that was *Tarjumanul Quran* (The Meaning of the Quran) in 6 volumes by K. Umar Moulavi[10] (1917-2000) of Veliyankode in Trichur District of Kerala.[11] Both these works are not available in print now.

A good number of works have been written in Arabic-Malayalam on the biography of Prophet Muhammad, prophetic tradition (Hadith), history of Islam and Islamic jurisprudence as well. The most prominent among them are: *Akhbar Ahmadiyya* (The Message of Muhammad) by Chalilakath Muhammad Musliyar; *Al-Sirat al-Nabawiyya* by Mulampath Kunhamu; *Tuhfat al-saimin* (on Islamic fasting) by mammad Musliyar.

Translations from Arabic constitute major bulk of Islamic literature in Arabic-Malayalam prose; most of the authentic Arabic books on Islam have been translated to Arabic-Malayalam well before the emergence of the printing press. Among them is the noted work on the history of Islam in Kerala, *Tuhfat al-Mujahidin* of Zain al-din al-Makhdum translated by K. Musan Kutty. (Interestingly, the Arabic *tarjama* for 'translation' means prose in Arabic-Malayalam). Many of these have not seen the light of the day as the manuscripts have either been lost or spoiled due to lack of preservation.[12]

Arabic-Malayalam had a considerable presence in Islamic journalism too. The noted social reformer and Islamic scholar Sanaullah Makti Tangal had published an Arabic-Malayalam journal about 110 years ago. The other prominent Islamic journals were *Al-Islah* edited by the nationalist leader E. Moidu Moulavi, *Al-Islam* edited by the social reformer Vakkam Abdul Qadir Moulavi, *Al-Irshad* edited by K.M. Moulavi and *Al-Murshid* sponsored by the Kerala Jamiyyath al-Ulama, an Islamic organization.

Right from the inception of the *madrasa*[13] education system in the 1950s, the major religious education organization of Kerala *Samastha Kerala Jamiyyath al-Ulema* has been publishing in Arabic-Malayalam primary level Islamic textbooks for their 6000-odd *madrasas* spread across Kerala. In addition to this, periodicals too are being published. Thus Arabic-Malayalam is still survives in Kerala especially in Malabar. With the exception of this, the Muslim community has switched over to the Malayalam script since a few decades and the language of Islamic literature has been replaced by pure Malayalam. Thus Islamic literature made its way to the mainstream Malayalam literature.

## Islamic literature in Malayalam

As Arabic-Malayalam was the popular language of written communication of Kerala Muslims for centuries, Islamic literature had a late appearance in Malayalam, say, in the 1940s only. Though the Muslim scholar and reformer Sayyid Sanaulla Makti Tangal had written about 30 works in Malayalam before this, they haven't gained popularity even among the Muslim community because of the domination of the Arabic-Malayalam script.

The holy Quran is the sacred book and fundamental source of Islam. Obviously, its translation and commentary find a pride of place in the Islamic literature in Malayalam too. The first translation of the holy Quran into Malayalam appeared in 1963; it is *Parisuddha Quran Paribhasayum Vyakhyanavum* (Translation and Commentary of the Holy Quran) by C.N. Ahmed Moulavi (1905-1993), a progressive Islamic scholar known for his rational approach. As it can be understood, this work caused uproar in the Islamic circles of Kerala because of the highly controversial views of the author like denying the miracles of the Prophets. This work and the controversies it created were, undoubtedly, the motivating factor for the emergence of the later translations of the holy Quran.

The second work of translation is that of Muttanisseril Koyakkutty Moulavi[14] (b. 1925) from Kayamkulam in south Kerala. Named *Parisuddha Quran Malayala Paribhasha* (Malayalam Translation of the Holy Quran), it was published in 1967 in a user-friendly compact size.

The composition of a voluminous commentary of Quran, a result of 17 years' dedicated effort started in 1960, was completed in 1977 by Muhammad Amani Moulavi partially assisted by PK. Moosa Moulavi and A. Alavi Moulavi. Named *Amani Moulaviyude Paribhasa* (Amani Moulavi's Translation) after the author, it was published in twelve volumes; later second edition came out in six volumes. What makes it distinct from the earlier two commentaries and the later ones is that it gives the translation of each word of a verse and then that of the entire verse; this method facilitates anyone literate in Arabic to learn the Quran without another's help. This commentary has been prepared consulting fourteen Arabic commentaries of the Quran.

The world famous commentary of the holy Quran in Urdu, *Tafhimul Quran*[15] (Understanding the Quran) by well known Islamic thinker and reformer Sayyid Abul A'la Maududi(1903-1979) has been translated into Malayalam by the same name; it has been published in six volumes by Islamic Publishing House, Calicut; first volume appeared in 1972 and last one in 1998. This work is a loose translation preserving the tone, spirit and effect of the Quran intact. Its abridged version in Urdu *Tarjuma-e-Quran* (Translation of the Quran) by the same author has also been translated into Malayalam and published in a single volume in 1988. These two works are distinguished by a lucid style and eloquent language.

Two Arabic commentaries of the Quran have also been rendered into Malayalam. The first one is a 15th century work, *Tafsir al- Jalalayn* (commentary by two Jalals)[16] composed, as the title itself suggests, by Jalal al-Din Abd al-Rahman al-Suyuti and Jalal al-Din Ahmed al-Mahalli rendered into Malayalam by K. Abdulla Moulavi, Mattool (1917-1977). The second one is *Fi Zilal al-Quran* (In the Shade of the Quran), a commentary or rather, as the name suggests, an appreciation of the Quran by the well-known 20th century Egyptian scholar and writer Sayyid Qutb (1906-66). The most popular among the Arabic commentaries of the Quran, it has been rendered into Malayalam by V.S. Salim and Kunhu Muhammad Pulavath, edited by Dr. Muhyiddin Alwaye and published by Manas Foundation, Aluva, Cochin in twelve volumes; its first edition came out in 1995 and last one in 2004. This work succeeds in conveying to the reader the literary beauty and aesthetic appeal of the Quran.

*Fathur Rahman fi Tafsir al-Quran* is a translation and commentary of the Quran written by K.V. Muhammad Musliar Kuttanad (d. 2000), an orthodox scholar. *Vishuddha Quran Sampurna Paribhasa* (A Complete Translation of the Holy Quran) is a joint work by Abdul Hamid Madani and Kunhi Muhammad Parappur Madani published in 1991. This has later been recognized and published by King Fahd Complex for the Printing of the holy Quran, Medina, the official agency for printing and publication of the Quran in the Kingdom of Saudi Arabia. *Al-Quran* is a translation by Hafiz P.H. Abdul Gaffar Moulavi (b. 1958); it has been published by the largest publishing house of Kerala, D.C. Books, Kottayam.

In addition to these, two poetic renderings have also come out in Malayalam. One is *Amrithavani* by K.G. Raghavan Nair of Ottappalam in Palakkad district of Kerala published in 1997 by Islamic Publishing House, Calicut. The other one is *Divya Dipti* (The Divine Light) by Konniyur Raghavan Nair of Konni in Pathanamthitta district of Kerala published in 2000 by Samanwayam Books, Calicut.

It is worth mentioning here that despite the proliferation of translations and commentaries in Malayalam, the Quran, however, has not had much impact on Malayalam literature.[17]

***Mappila songs in Malayalam:*** As mentioned earlier, Mappila songs, for centuries, were used to be written in Arabic-Malayalam and have not been considered as a part of mainstream Malayalam literature. However, this attitude had changed as some modern poets dared to compose Mappila songs in the Malayalam script. The pioneer among them is T. Ubaid who was a song composer as well as a poet. P.T. Abdur Rahman and M.A. Kalpetta are the two who followed suit, the former being a well-known poet in Malayalam literature. Thereafter, a series of composers started composing Mappila songs in Malayalam, the most successful among them being U.K.Ibrahim Moulavi alias Abu Sahla who expressed Islamic thought through Mappila songs in a forceful style. His historical songs like *Nuh Nabiyum Samudayawum* (Prophet Nuh and his community) and *Musanabiyum Firawnum* (Prophet Moses and the Pharoah) have been widely acclaimed. Abu Sahla's songs have been published in a collection named *Vihayassinte Virimaril* (In the Vastness of the Sky).

Despite the fact that there are many talented Muslim writers in Kerala who have contributed to Malayalam numerable short stories, novels and plays written in the backdrop of the Muslim life in Kerala, few of them wrote in an Islamic perspective. The noted man of letters of Malayalam, Vaikom Muhammad Basheer is an exception to this. Islamic values and concept of the universe do reflect in most of his writings. The plays *Kandam Becha Coat* (The patched Coat) of T. Yusuf and *Maruppachcha* (The Oasis) of B. Muhammad have Islamic plots. The poet Ponkunnam Syed Muhammad's *Mahammadam* (On Muhammad) is an epic on the life history of Prophet Muhammad. The well-known poet Yusuf Ali Kecheri has also composed many poems having Islamic themes. T. Ubaid and P.T. Abdur Rahman are two other poets worth mentioning here. The poet Muhammad Kutty Elambilakkode has published a collection of Islamic poems titled *Kokila Ganam* (The Song of the Cuckoo). The poet Abdul Hayy Edayur is another noteworthy figure in this field who has composed many poems for children. He has also versified the biographies of Prophet Muhammad and his companion Umar bin al-Khattab.

A good number of Islamic works have been translated into Malayalam from Arabic, Urdu and English. Among the prominent English works in translation are: *Islam between East and West* by Alija Ali Izzat Begovic, *The Road to Mecca* by Muhammad Asad and *The Preaching of Islam* by Sir Thomas Arnold.

During the last few decades, some Islamic publishing firms have come up in Kerala publishing a good number of books in Malayalam. The most prominent among them is The Islamic Publishing House(IPH) based in Calicut. Having had a humble beginning in 1945, this firm has grown to be the largest Islamic publishing centre in South India. It has already published more than 500 books authored by scholars and thinkers from India and abroad on topics as varied as the Quran, the Hadith, history of the prohets, Islamic jurisprudence, history, social science, comparative religion, travelogues and children's literature. Having an intellectual appeal, most of these works present Islam as a complete code of life and not simply as a religion of certain customs and rituals.

The Islamic Encyclopedia project of the IPH is a significant milestone in the literary and publishing history of Kerala. The topics related to Islam and Muslims are categorized according to the Malayalam alphabetical order. A collaborative effort of almost 200 authors, the encyclopedia will have 12 volumes of which 10 have already come out.

Compared to the rest of India, Islamic literature has a wider readership in Kerala thanks to its higher literacy and a good reading culture. It is not confined to the intellectually elite, but rather reaches the masses and is read by people cutting across different strata of the Muslim society.

### Notes and References

1. Kunhi, P.K. Muhammad, 'Islaminte agamanm keralathil', in *Kerala Muslim Navothana Charithram,* Ed: T.K. Ubaid (1998), Calicut, pp. 9-13.
2. Malabar comprises of the districts of Palakkad, Malappuram, Kozhikode, Wayanad, Kannur, and Kasargode districts and Chavakkad Taluk of Trichur district of present Kerala state. The

name is a combination of Malayalam *mala* (mountain) and Arabic *barr* (land), meaning mountainous land.

3. There are different versions on the origin of this word. The most convincing one is that it is an honorific title that would have been applied by natives of Kerala to welcomed and respected Arab immigrants; according to this version, the word is derived from Malayalam *Maha Pilla*, meaning "great child". Other versions are that it is derived from ancient Malayalam *pillai* (son-in-law or bridegroom) refering to the marriages of local women to the Arab immigrants or from Arabic *ma fallah*, meaning "not a farmer", as the Arabs were, in contrast to the agrarian society of Kerala, not farmers. Ronald E.Miller, *Mappila Muslims of Kerala*, Madras: Orient Longman, (1992), pp.30-31. Cf. Kunhi, PK Muhammad, *op. cit.* By the course of time it became a distinctive term to refer to the Muslim community of the Malabar region of Kerala where it flourished.
4. It is Malayalam written in a modified Arabic script that can account for all Malayalam sounds and still represents Arabic words in the original script in order to preserve correct pronunciation. Different scholars have dated the origin of the script differently; estimates vary from 1500 years ago to 1000 years to about 500 years ago. (See: Karassery, M.N., "Arabi-Malayalam" in *Arabic in South India*, Ed. Dr. E.K. Ahmed Kutty, Dept. of Arabic, University of Calicut, 2003, p. 129). However, it has been used for didactic purposes by Malabar Muslims right from 9th century when the local language Malayalam didn't have a unified script. The script was the chief medium of religious education for the Malabar Muslims till recent times. Having linguistic features distinct from both Malayalam and Arabic, it grew to a language having its own identity. As it has been used by the *Mappilas* of Malabar, it was known as *Mappila* language and its literature as *Mappila* literature. In addition to Malayalam, it has words from Arabic, Persian, Urdu, Sanskrit, Kannada and Tulu languages either in their original or adapted form. It has been the vernacular of the *Mappilas* in the Malabar region of Kerala stretching northward from Kodungallur to Kasargode. (see: Abu, O., *Arabi-Malayala Sahitya Charithram*, Kottayam: SPCS,1970. p. 7). The necessity for a mode of written communication for religious teaching in the absence of a unified script for Malayalam necessitated developing this hybrid script. Over the ages, it became the language of choice for Malabar Muslims. Though they opted for the Malayalam script since a few decades, Arabic-Malayalam still survives.
5. Abu, O., *Arabi-Malayala Sahitya Charithram* (Malayalam), Kottayam: SPCS (1970), p. 17.
6. The noted Malayalam critic and a former professor of Malayalam at the University of Calicut, Prof. Sukumar Azhikode, among others, attended the symposium and said that right from the beginning the poem had an internal feel of Kerala. He added that the poem was an antidote to the mutual hatred that existed among people now. According to Prof. Azhikode, people even now ignored the secular thoughts that were so explicitly mentioned in *Muhyiddin Mala*. (For a report of the symposium see *The Hindu* dated December 03, 2008).
7. Abu, O., *op. cit.* p. 77.
8. Karassery, M.N., 'Arabi-Malayalam', in *Arabic in South India*, Ed: Dr. E.K. Ahmed Kutty, (2003), Calicut, Dept. of Arabic, University of Calicut. pp. 127-133.
9. The Dept. of Culture, Govt. of Kerala has started a centre named after Moyinkutty Vaidyar at his birthplace, Kondotty in the Malappuram district of Kerala; the centre aims to study and promote Mappila songs and culture.
10. *Moulavi* and *Musliar* repeatedly figuring in this article are honorific titles for a Muslim religious scholar in Kerala; while *moulavi* is used for the scholars of the progressive reformist

groups, *musliar* is used for those of the traditional orthodox group. Both, in meaning, are equivalent to a *maulana* in the rest of the country. *Tangal*, another term peculiar to the Kerala Muslims, is an honorific title applied to a descendant of the Prophet Muhammad; in this sense *Sayyid* is used in the rest of India.

11. Later this work has been rendered to Malayalam and published in a single volume.
12. Abu, O., *op. cit.* p. 130.
13. In Kerala *madrasa* means a part-time Islamic school where school going children attend for about two-hour morning or evening classes. Unlike the rest of the country, full-time *madrasas* do not exist in Kerala.
14. Muttanisseril Koyakkutty Moulavi has also translated into Malayalam *Muqaddima* (The Prolegomena), a 14th century work dealing with philosophy of history written by the North African historian Ibn Khaldun.
15. This is a legendary work that has been rendered into most of the Indian languages, English, Arabic, Persian, Pushtu, Turkish, Japanese, Thai, Sinhalese, and Russian as well.
16. The same work, as mentioned earlier, has also been rendered into Arabic-Malayalam well before.
17. This is despite the fact that Arabic language had a great impact on Malayalam especially in terms of its vocabulary. According to Hermann Gundert(1814-1893), the German missionary and scholar and the first authentic lexicographer in Malayalam, around 3000 words of Arabic origin are there in Malayalam. The religion of Islam also had a deep impact on the culture of Kerala.

30

# Tagore's Concept of Religion in *Arogya* (*Convalescence*): A Quest

***Mohit Chakrabarti***

Rabindranath Tagore's *Arogya (Convalescence)* is a unique creative contribution. Pregnant in soul-stirring in-depth vision of life and experience, it heralds the glory of the religion of fullness and poignance, serenity and reverence for the victory of man. Apart from the fact that it is one of the most mature creations of Tagore, it conveys a new promise of life vibrant with catholicity of vision and serenity of perfection. Joy and sorrow, freedom and freshness, erudition and experience are so intermingled in the poems that one cannot but look into the inner world of consciousness and beyond that. All these amply contribute to his unique concept of religion—the religion of man—where transcendence and transfer, transparency and Truth serve as characteristic components.

The very first poem which represents the essence of religion as Tagore conceptualises is an outcome of his serene experience in life on the fusion of Truth and Joy as the most thrilling and living entities in human life. It is an image of images which religion presents one with the inner realisation of beauty and grandeur. A positive approach to life thus nursed in religion of the right message of the Victory of Man is the greatest reward from the All Serene. Truth shines with all its splendour and grandeur. It sustains. It brings forth endless joy, the worthiest dividend with which one is blessed and carries forth the modest words of gratitude with the vision of the Ever Luminous:

*E dyulok madhumoy, madhumoy prithibir dhuli,*
*Antare niyechhi ami tuli*
*Ei mahamantrakhani*
*Charitartha jeebaner bane.*
*Dine dine peyechhinu satyer ya-kichhu upahar*
*Madhurase kshay* nai tar.
*Tai ei mantrabanee mrityur sesher prante baje*

*Sab kshati mithya kari ananter ananda biraje.*
*Sesh sparsa niye yaba yabe dharaneer*
*Bale yaba tomar dhulir*
*Tilak parechhi bhale,*
*Dekhechhi nityer jyoti duryoger mayar adale.*
*Satyer anandarup e dhulite niyechhe murati*
*Ei jene e dhulay rakhinu pranati.*[1]

Pleasant is this heaven, pleasant is the earth's dust,
Upon my heart have I recast
This great vow
The message of life did bestow.
Day by day the gifts of truth did I receive whatsoever
Decay in the present juicy form will ne'er favour
This message of vow on the edge of death so creates
The joy of the endless makes all loss futile and permeates.
When I shall depart with the last touch of the earth,
I shall say the dust from my path
Has adorned my forehead
The halo of the Eternal have I seen in the mystery of dismay shrouded.
The joyous form of Truth in this dust has taken the image,
Knowing this, I salute the dust on the earth's stage.

[Translated by me.]

Tagore adores beauty not in mere appearance but deep from his religious vision where beauty turns into spirituality in all essence of inwardness. He welcomes the ever new in the image of beauty that is both in form and appearance and at the same time formless thereby welcoming a shift from reality to spirituality in naturalness and spontaneity. The bridge he creates between the earth and the mind of man is just to herald the glory of the Eternal Man everywhere. in his serene vision one comes across this poetic grandeur:

*Param sundar*
*Aloker snanpunya prate.*
*Asim arup*
*Rupe rupe sparsamani*
*Rasamurti karichhe rachana,*
*Pratidin*
*Chiranutaner abhishek*
*Chirapuratan veditale.*
*Miliya shyamale nilimay*
*Dharanir uttariya*
*Vune chale chhayate alote.*
*Akaser hritspandan*
*Pallave pallave dey dola.*
*Prabhater kantha hate manihar kare jhilimili*
*Van hate vane.*
*Pakhider akaran gan*
*Sadhuvad dite thake jivanalakshmire.*
*Sav-kichhu sathe mise manusher ptitir paras*

*Amriter artha dey tare,*
*Madhumay kare dey dharanir dhuli,*
*Sarvatra vichhaye deychiramanaver singhasan.*

The most beautiful
Is adorned in the holy morning
Of the bathing of light
The unending formless
With the touchstone of infinite forms
Is creating the images of appreciation,
Everyday
The welcome of the ever new
At the altar of the ever old.
With unison of the green and the blue firmament
The scarf of the earth
In light and shade goes a-weaving.
The heartbeat of the sky
Does throb from leaf to leaf.
The morning's necklace sparkles
From forest to forest.
The unaccountable songs of birds
Go on thanking the goddess of the affluence of life.
The touch of human love
Does bring forth the meaning of nectar in fusion with all,
Turns the dust of the earth pleasant
And spreads the throne of the Eternal Man everywhere.[2]

[Translated by me.]

Tagore's religion welcomes the Eternal Man in the vision of joy that stands for fullness and gratitude. It shows the avenues of inner appraisal of nature that enlivens and renews our promises to live. Tagore unfolds this religion par excellence through his unique experience:

*Mukta vatayanprante janasunya ghare*
*Vase thaki nisthavdha prahare*
*Vahire shymal chhande uthe gaan*
*Dharanir praner ahavan;*
*Amriter utsasrote*
*Chitta bhese chale jay digabnter nilim alote.*
*Kar pane pathaive stuti*
*Vyagra ei maner akuti,*
*Amulyere mulya dite phire se khunjiya vanirup,*
*Kare thake chup,*
*Vale, ami anandita, chhanda jay thami,*
*Vale, dhanya ami.*

On the edge of the open window, in the lonely parlour
I remain seated in the silent hour.
Outside, in the rhythm of the green, songs herald
The beckoning of the life of the world.

Towards the flow of the origin of eternity
The mind floats in with the horizon's bluish spree.
To whom adoration is to be sent
Is the eager mind's only incumbent.
On he seeks in the image of words the priceless to pay,
Not a word does he say.
Glad am I, he murmurs, rhythm comes to a stop,
Says he, the harvest of thanks I crop.[3]

[Translated by me.]

The religion of the self identified in the Supreme Self is an altogether new experience with which Tagore remains outstanding and extraordinary. His self-learning of religion out of feelings that speak the language of man is a religion where the living drama of human life is movingly portrayed in the vast panorama of creation and farewell to earth:

*Virat sristir kshetre*
*Atasvajir khela akase akase*
*Surya tara laye*
*Yug-yuganter parimape.*
*Anadi adrisya hate amio esechhi*
*Kshudra agnikana niye*
*Ek prante kshudra dese kale.*
*Prastaner anke aj esechhi yemani*
*Deepsikha mlan haye ela,*
*Chhayate padila dhara e khela mayar swarup,*
*Slath haye ela dhire*
*Such duhkhanatyasajyaguli.*
Amid the vast creation
The game of fireworks throughout the sky
Goes on along with the sun and the stars
In the yardstick of age beyond age.
I have also come from the endless and the invisible
With a trifling splinter of fire
At one end in a small space and time.
Come as I have today in the act of departure,
The flame of the lamp turned pale.
The reality of enchantment of this play is revealed in shadow.
Slowly the dramatic costumes
Of happiness and sorrow become loose.[4]

[Translated by me.]

The religion of the Ever New by inviting the young is an altogether new dimension where Tagore perhaps has no parallel. The religion of beauty as he appreciates is born of this spontaneous welcome to the change of nature which denotes the change of the mindset in the efflorescence of the Ever New. This is what Nature as an exponent of vibrant religion teaches us. Tagore adroitly expresses this vision of religion in terms of beauty:

*Palas anandamurti jeevaner phalgundiner,*
*Aj ei sammanhiner*

*Daridra velay dile dekha*
*Yetha ami sathihin eka*
*Utsaver prangan-vahire*
*Sashyahin marumay teere.*
*Yekhane e dharanir prafulla praner kunja hate*
*Anadrita din mor niruddes srote*
*Chhinnavrinta chaliyachhe bhese*
*Vasanter seshe.*
*Tavuo to kripanata nai tava dane,*
*Youvaner purna mulya dile mor diptihin prane.*
*Adrishter avajnare kara ni swikar,*
*Ghuchaile avasad tar,*
*Janaile chitte mor labhi anukshan*
*Sundarer abhyarthana, naviner ase nimantran.*

*Palas* is the emblem of joy of the spring of life,
Today to one bereft of honour
In his poor hours you met
Where I, the companionless, am alone
Out of the courtyard of ceremonies
On the sandy shores of the desert sans crops.
Wherefrom the boisterous garden of life of this earth
My unwelcome days towards streams lost
Like torn sheets are gone a-floating
At the end of the spring.
Even then, your gift is beyond austerity
The full price of youth you have offered in my heart sans lustre
The aversion of providence you denied not,
Her tiredness you did ameliorate,
Conveyed me and so am I all the time
Prized with the welcome of Beauty, the invitation of the young.[5]

[Translated by me.]

The religion of beauty as Tagore advocates above in terms of his experience of rich perception of inwardness by 'recognition of beauty' reminds one of how he realises truth and beauty:

> In the history of aesthetics there also comes an age of emancipation when the recognition of beauty in things great and small becomes easy, and when we see it more in the unassuming harmony of common objects than in things startling in their singularity. So much so, that we have to go through the stages of reaction when in the representation of beauty we try to avoid everything that is obviously pleasing and that has been crowned by the sanction of convention. We are then tempted in defiance to exaggerate the commonness of commonplace things, thereby making them aggressively uncommon. To restore harmony we create the discords which are a feature of all reactions. We already see in the present age the sign of this aesthetic reaction, which proves that man has at last come to know that it is only the narrowness of perception which sharply divides the field of his aesthetic consciousness into ugliness and beauty. When he has the power to see things detached from self-interest and from the insistent claims of the lust of the senses, then alone can he have the true vision of

the beauty that is everywhere. Then only can he see that what is unpleasant to us is not necessary unbeautiful, but has its beauty in truth.

When we say that beauty is everywhere we do not mean that the word ugliness should be abolished from our language, just as it would be absurd to say that there is no such thing as untruth. Untruth there certainly is, not in the system of the universe, but in our power of comprehension, as its negative element. In the same manner there is ugliness in the distorted expression of beauty in our life and in our art which comes from our imperfect realisation of Truth. To a certain extent we can set our life against the law of truth which is in us and which is in all, and likewise we can give rise to ugliness by going counter to the eternal law of harmony which is everywhere.[6]

The quest for religion as the inseparable component of beauty becomes more explicit in self-confession. Tagore frankly admits the role of beauty as the religion of all religions of life and work, erudition and edification, where joy and sorrow, victory and defeat, fear and death—all are the positive aspects of self-assessment and self-fulfilment. The pleasant blessings of beauty bring forth religion as natural and spontaneous as day-to-day happenings of life. As he presents us with his enriched experience of the realisation of beauty:

*E jeevane sundarer peyechhi madhur asirvad,*
*Manusher pritipatre pai tanri sudhar aswad.*
*Duhsaha duhkher dine*
*Akshata aparajita atmare layechhi ami chine.*
*Asanna mrityuur chhaya yedin karechhi anubhav*
*Sedin bhayer hate hay ni durval parabhav.*
*Mahattama manusher sparsa hate hai ni vanchita,*
*Tander amritavani antarete karechhi sanchita.*
*Jeevaner vidhatar ye dakshinya peyechhi jeevane*
*Tahari smaranlipi rakhilum sakritajnamane.*

The sweet blessings of beauty have I received in this life,
In the urn of human life do I have the taste of His very drinking pipe.
In unbearable sorrowful days
Known have I the self that unhurt and unbeaten stays.
The day when I have felt the shadow of death in sight,
I faced not defeat meek at the hands of fright.
Ne'er was I from the touch of the greatest men debarred,
Their message of nectar in the heart I have treasured.
The favour of the God of life that I have received in the life of mine
With grateful mind that memorandum do I entwine.[7]

[Translated by me.]

For a journey to the inner world of serenity amidst 'the marriage of darkness and light' as Tagore envisions, one is prepared for a sombre consciousness of the beyond. The Truth Eternal as the emblem of religion that guides and guards against all constraints of time and action, beckons man for the journey beyond:

*Nakshatrer santikshetra aseem gagan*
*Yetha dheke rekhe dey dinasrir arup sattare*
*Sethay karate labh satya apanare*
*Kheya dey ratri paravare.*

Where the infinite sky the sphere of the blessings of the stars
Covers up the formless existence of the beauty of the dahy
Truth to be attained there itself
Oars on in the sea of night.[8]

[Translated by me.]

Is the Light Eternal the signal for fusion with the Ever Joyful? Where is the Paradise of consciousness? Wherefrom does it come, and how? As a mystic visionary, the Eternal Spirit as Tagore envisions the great soul in terms of the Upanishads prepares for 'being true within';

*Ya atma apahatapapma vijaro*
*Vimrityurvisokohvijighotsohpipasah*
*Satyakamah satyasankalpah sohanveshtavyah sa vijignasitavyah.*

The great soul who is within me, who is beyond age and death and sorrow, beyond hunger and thirst, He who is true in thought and action, Him we must seek, Him we must know.

This seeking and knowing him is not seeking and knowing outside oneself. It is knowing through becoming, receiving through being true within.

As man is essentially a spirit, this principle of unity holds good in all departments of his life.[9]

Profoundly blessed as he is with spiritual calmness of mind and passions crystallised with the antidote of religion that emancipates man from being battered and obscured under the spell of drab materialism, Tagore wants the blessings of silence:

*Kshane kshane mane hay yatrar samay vujhi ela*
*Vidaydiner 'pare avaran phelo*
*Apragalbha suryasta-abhar,*
*Samay yavar*
*Sanmta hok stavdha hok, smaransabhar samaroha*
*Na rachuk soker sammoha.*
*Vanasreni prasthaner dware*
*Dharanir santimantra dik mouna pallavsambhare.*
*Namiya asuk dhire ratrir nihsavda asirvad*
*Saptarshir jyotir Prasad.*

Oft do I think as if the time for adieu has come
Cast the veil on the day of farewell
Of the light of the controlled setting sun
Let the parting time
Be peaceful and silent, let not the assembly of condolence
Create the illusion of bereavement.
Let the rows of forest of the door of departure
Proclaim the message of peace of the world with the assembly of leaves.
Let the silent blessings of the night—
The offerings of the halo of the seven saints—
Come down.[10]

[Translated by me.]

Realisation of the self in and through joy as Tagore strongly believes has its illumined efflorescence in his quest for religion. He is quite aware of the fact that he has already been blessed with the mark of victory in the sacred fountain light of consciousness derived from the religion of joy, the religion of Truth. The portrait of the ideal man in the vision of freedom as Truth—*mukti*—in creative consciousness, in joy beyond where the religion of man is glorified with unison and creativity.[11] He finds no difference between his soul and the touch of joy which he receives in the heartland of light:

*Aloker antare ye anander parasan pai*
*Jani ami tar sathe amar atmar bhed nai.*
*Ek adi jyotiutsa hate*
*Chaitanyer punyasrote*
*Amar hayechhe abhishek*
*Lalate diyechhe jayalekh,*
*Janayechhe amriter ami adhikari*
*Param amir sathe yukta hate pari*
*Vichitra jagate*
*Praves labhite pari anander pathe.*

The touch of joy that in the heart of light I receive
Know I that my soul no difference does conceive.
From an ancient lustrous source
In the holy current of conscious course
Initiated have I been
On the forehead, the mark of victory was given,
It has informed that the source of nectar I know
With the Great I, I can unite and glow
In this world of wonder
In the avenue of joy I may enter.[12]

What, then, is Tagore's quest for unison with the All Serene —a quest for religion *par excellence*? Here is his incomparable and significant answer:

*E amir avaran sahaje skhalita haye yak,*
*Chaitanyer subhra jyoti*
*Bhed kari kuhelika*
*Satyer amrita rup karuk parkas.*
*Sarva manusher majhe*
*Ek chiramanaver anandakiran*
*Chitte mor hok vikirita.*
*Sangsarer kshuvdhatar sthavdha urdhaloke*
*Nityer ye santirup tai yena dekhe yete pari,*
*Jeevaner jatil ya vahu nirarthak,*
*Mithyar vahan yahasamajer krittim mulyei,*
*Tai niye kangaler asanta janata*
*Dure thele diye*
*E jammer satya arthaspashta chokhe jene yai yena*
*Seema tar perovar age.*

Let the cocoon of this self unmask
The bright halo of consciousness
Express the eternal form of Truth
By piercing the mist.
Let the light of joy of a Man Eternal
Amid all men
Be enkindled in my mind.
Beyond the silent world of worldly grievance
Let me behold the blessed form of the Eternal.
Whatever is amply meaningless and critical in this life
Whatever embodies falsehood in the sham value of the society,
Leaving aside all beggarly and
Troubled crowd
Let me know the true meaning with my vivid eyes
Prior to crossing the bar.[13]
Do we follow the footprints of the Poet?

## *Notes and References*

1. Tagore, Rabindranath: *Arogya, Rabinda-Rachanavali,* Government of West Bengal, Calcutta, 1983, Vol. III, p.821.
2. *Ibid.,* pp.821-822.
3. *Ibid.,* p.825.
4. *Ibid.,* pp. 826-827.
5. *Ibid.,* pp. 828-829.
6. Tagore, Rabindranath: *Sadhana,* Macmillan India Limited, New Delhi, Macmillan Pocket Tagore Edition, 1983, pp.119-120.
7. Tagore, Rabindranath: *Arogya, Rabindra-Rachanavali,* Government of West Bengal, Calcutta, 1983,Vol. III, p. 838.
8. *Ibid.,* p. 839.
9. Tagore, Rabindranath: *Man,* Andhra University Press, Waltair, 1991, p. 48.
10. Tagore, Rabindranath: *Arogya, Rabindra-Rachanavali,* Government of West Bengal, Calcutta, 1983, Vol. III, p. 839.
11. Tagore characteristically elucidates this concept elsewhere: "Our greed diverts our attention to materials away from the supreme value of truth which is the quality of universal being. The gulf thus created by the receding stream of the soul we try to replenish with a continuous stream of wealth, which may have the power to fill but not the power to unite and recreate. Therefore, the gap is dangerously concealed under the glittering quicksand of things, which by their own weight cause a sudden subsidence while we are in the depth of sleep.

    The real tragedy, however, does not lie in the risk of our material security but in the obscuration of Man himself in the human world. In the creative activities of his soul Man realizes his surroundings as his larger self, instinct with his own life and love. But, in his ambition, he deforms and defiles it with the callous handling of his voracity. His world of utility, assuming a gigantic proportion, reacts upon his inner nature and hypnotically suggests to him a scheme of the universe which is an abstract system. In such a world there can be no question of *mukti,* the freedom of truth, because it is a solitary fact, a cage with no sky beyond it. In all appearance, our world is a close world of hard facts; it is like a seed with its tough cover. But, within this enclosure there is working our silent cry of life for *mukti,* even when its possibility is darkly silent. When some huge, overgrown temptation tramples into stillness, this living aspiration, then, does civilization die like a seed that has lost its urging for germination. And this *mukti* is in the truth that dwells in the ideal man. —*The Religion of Man,* George Allen & Unwin Limited, London, 1951, pp. 72-73.

12. Tagore, Rabindranath: *Arogya, Rabindra-Rachanavali,* Government of West Bengal, Calcutta, 1983, Vol. III, p. 839.
13. *Ibid.*, p. 840.

31

# 'Sāvitrī' as a Religio-literary Composition

*Raghunath Ghosh*

It is a remarkable fact that Sri Aurobindo, the philosopher and *yogī* is also a poet. In consonance with his philosophy of integralism, as a part, he has wielded an intense art-form, developed an integral style and word-power to match his experience and vision. This statement is true of his poetry in general and the *Sāvitrī* in particular. Like his philosophy, the material of his poetry is provided by a developing pattern of spiritual experiences and realizations. Hence the poetry of Sri Aurobindo is to be understood in terms of the notion of poetic integralism, i.e. the universe of poetry lying beyond ordinary creative intelligence. Sri Aurobindo's poetry is generally called 'overhead poetry' or the poetry of the over mind. The over mind, in terms of Sri Aurobindo's philosophy, is nearest to the identity of being and becoming, the super mind the sovereign truth – consciousness. From this plane of expression and vision, word and rhythm become at once intense and immense to the utmost. The overhead utterance is marked by a value and form in which all the realities of the subordinate planes fuse in something diversely ultimate, and variously transfigured by an inmost oneness with the cosmic harmony and with the supracosmic mystery. Language in such an atmosphere becomes *mantra*. Sri Aurobindo's poetry has shown how and when *mantra* is possible. 'A gate of dreams ajar on mystery's verge.'

Most of the studies of Sri Aurobindo's poetry have been undertaken with reference to the poetry of Europe. This is but natural, since he wrote in a European language. But it is also a fact that a great bulk of his literary criticism is devoted to studies into Sanskrit literature. Sri Aurobindo has written extensively on Vyāsa and Vālmīki, on Kālidas, whose *Vikramorvaśīya* and *Kumārasambhava* he rendered into English. It is true that Sri Aurobindo's perspective of literary criticism has always been that of world-literature, yet he always stressed the fact that the poetry of *mantra* has been found in the *Vedas*, the *Upaniṣads* and the *Bhagavad Gītā*, besides elsewhere. He also wrote *Vāsavadattā,* modeled on the drama by Bhāsa. The chapter on Sanskrit literature of Sri Aurobindo's *Foundations of Indian Culture* is an instance of writing the history of the literature in a creative manner. In the circumstance it is surprising that no discussion is undertaken by way of evaluating Sri Aurobindo's poetry in the light of religious and aesthetic standpoints. And it is precisely to this task that I propose to address myself.

## II

The Sanskrit rhetoricians have laid importance on the use of *Alamkāra* in a *kāvya*. According to Dandin, the attributes or merits or excellences that go wholly to adorn or embellish *kāvya-s* are called *Alamkāra* (figure of speech)[1] Vāmana also admits the use of *Alamkāra* as the cause of poetic beauty. The word *Kāvya*, as Vāmana observed, applies strictly to word and sense embellished with *guṇa-s* or excellences and *Alamkāra-s* or poetic figures.[2] Sri Aurobindo also used series of similes and other *Alamkāra-s* in his *Sāvitrī*, perhaps keeping their theories in view. When Aswapathy, Sāvitrī's father, realized the higher harmonies of Consciousness, the unity of the truth and idea has been described by a beautiful simile:

"There was no gulf between thought and fact; ever they replied like bird to calling bird."[3] We come across many such passages where he used different figures of speech,

> "As a star unaccompanied moves through heaven
> Unastonished by the immensities of space,
> Travelling infinity by its own light,
> The great are strongest when they stand alone."[4]

As an evidence of the use of *Rūpaka Alamkāra* in which Sri Aurobindo shows his par excellence, the following passage may be quoted:

> "Offered to the daughter of infinity
> His passion-flower of love and doom she gave."[5]

Let us consider the reasons for Sri Aurobindo's writing the *Sāvitrī* in a poetic language but not in a language of prose. The poetic feelings of Sri Aurobindo refused to be rendered in a language of prose. The reason for this is found in *Dhvanyāloka* where Ānandavardhana says : "Poetic language .... is different from the language of prose; it arouses in the reader echoes and feelings in a word, aesthetic experience-foreign to prose, whose value is purely informative and didactic. The words in a prose text have, according to Indian linguistics, two or, in the view of some writers, three powers, of which the chief-one is the power of denotation *(abhidhā)*, the faculty, that is, of denoting a given object. Clearly, the power to arouse aesthetic experience cannot be reduced to this.[6] From this statement it is known that the power of denotation *(abhidhā)* which is prominent in prose cannot give rise to the aesthetic excellence, and hence poetic language in which the suggestive meaning is prominent is necessary. Denotation is based upon words alone. The suggestiveness depends on both words and senses.[7] Sri Aurobindo also emphasizes on the suggested meaning of the *Sāvitrī*. Through this poetry Sri Aurobindo tries to suggest that just as Sāvitrī does one can also be the abode of knowledge, religion, love, emotion, power and yogic experience and can transform oneself into Divinity. And after bringing down the Supramental consciousness in oneself one can conquer Death, the king of decay, and can prepare in this world firm footing of an immoral world, full of bliss where there is no suffering, no injustice, after constructing a bridge over the inaccessible ocean situated in the midst of heaven and earth. This is the message of the *Sāvitrī*. The epic opens with the description of the first flush of self-consciousness from the sleeps of unconscious, which is symbolized as Dawn (*Uṣā*). The Divine Consciousness (*Bhāgavatī Cetanā*) comes to this kingdom of ignorance in order to make Her manifested and gives her Divine glimpses. But after noticing that this world, full of ignorance, is not prepared for Her absolute manifestation, She returns to Her own abode. At last Divine Mother comes to this world as an incarnation and She is named 'Sāvitrī' who conquers Death, the main obstacle to bring the Supramental power and consciousness. The Dawn indicates or suggests the arrival of Supra-mental consciousness in this mortal world. "The poet of *Sāvitrī* stands as the maker of a new age of poetry as of life and literature. Its appearance in these days of distress and deviation brings new hope. Let us salute the Dawn, that 'harmonises with the dawns that shone out before and those that now must shine.'

The king of Aśvapati who was childless performed austerities and sacrifices for a longer period of time to have a child. When his performance of sacrifices matured, the goddess Sāvitrī appeared before him from the sacrificial fire and being pleased agreed to offer some boons. As per his boon Aśvapati was blessed with a daughter called Sāvitrī (as per the name of the goddess). In course of time Sāvitrī grew up and the king arranged her marriage with prince Satyabān, the son of king Dyumatsen, who was living in the forest. When the parent approved this marriage, Narada disapproved it after knowing that Satyabān, though brave, intelligent, generous etc., was destined to die after one year. But Sāvitrī determined to marry in spite of knowing this and ultimately the marriage took place. Just after one year or so Satyabān wanted to go to the forest to fetch sacrificial wood. Thinking the probable danger Sāvitrī wanted to give him company, she was not allowed after considering many things. Due to having strong will-force Sāvitrī at last accompanied him in the forest. After cutting wood Satyabān had experienced severe pain in the head and Sāvitrī offered her lap to put his head. Within a short while Satyabān had fallen eternally asleep and saw the God of death (Yama) waiting for her husband. She found that Satyabān's soul separated from his physical mortal frame was taken by the God of death. Sāvitrī had opened a dialogue with Yama and followed him until he became pleased. Ultimately the God of death had to surrender to Sāvitrī being pleased on her devotion to her husband and argumentation with him. He commited to offer her some boons, one of which was the restoration of her husband's life. In this way Sāvitrī had won the death and came back to the hermitage with her husband Satyabān.

In Sāvitrī Sri Aurobindo has tried to show the symbolic presentation of ideal woman. In this peace of literature we get an ideal image of a woman who becomes victorious to Yama, the God of death, which symbolically suggests the victory of love over death[8].

Sāvitrī is painted by Sri Aurobindo as a devoted wife towards her husband and she acts as per sweet will of her husband. The term 'Sāvitrī' was derived from the word '*savitā*' meaning the Sun. The power of the Sun is called '*Sāvitrī*' because it protects, creates, and maintains the universe. Sāvitrī is described in such a way that she is an incarnation of Divine Mother who is entrusted with liberating an individual from the clutches of Death. It suggests that the Divine Mother can transform Death to the immortality. It is described in the following way:

*'The Mighty Mother sits in lucent calm.*
*And holds the eternal child upon her knees,*
*Attending the day when he shall speak to fate.'* [9]

Sāvitrī is a warrior-woman who becomes glorious in encountering Death. She has destroyed Death and brought Immortality for a man. It is Sāvitrī to whom *a choice is given between life and death.* She prefers to conquer Death with the help of her will-force and love. It is *a right to love and live.* Sri Aurobindo believes that it is only love, which can be a bridge between a man and God. It is the force of disintegrity or bliss of perfect union. Sāvitrī is very much brave due to having genuine love towards her husband and hence Sri Aurobindo metaphorises her as '*The Flame*' 'who can destroy even death'.

It is Yama who for the first time comes in contact with 'Mighty Mother' who is a *claimant of Immortality* and an *embodiment of the Flaming Truth.* This is a kind of worship of the Mother Goddess even by the Lord of Death. '*Let deathless eyes look into the eyes of Death... transform earth's death into immortal life*'.[10]

On request of Yama the Divine Mother has exposed herself and given him supreme enlightenment. It is described as '*Eternity looked into the eyes of Death*'. Sāvitrī, in fact, performs Yoga through which she 'goes' down to her heart to know her own self and finds out different levels of consciousness. In spite of knowing her husband's death within one year she marries him challenging her own fate. Because she is over confident that she will be in a position to change her destiny. It is said: "*My fate is what my spirits' strength can make/ My fate is what my spirits' strength can bear//*"[11].

The purpose of *yoga* of Sāvitrī is in order to know the real nature of herself. She gradually comes to know the course of evolution from Matter to Mind and the existence of psychic being. Through such meditation and concentration she knows herself and comes to know that she lives in Infinity.

Sāvitrī, the conscious Prakṛti, conquers Yama (the king of death) in debate i.e., by wisdom and fearlessness and in this way she is able to bring Satyabān back to life. Satyabān has been transformed to *someone possessing the Truth, which is the literal meaning of the term.* The term '*Aśvapati*' means 'the Lord of Life'. The term '*Aśva*' means 'horse' symbolizing life-energy. Hence Aśvapati has been painted by Sri Aurobindo as *the aspiring soul of man.*[12]

The *Yoga* of Aśvapati has been interpreted by Sri Aurobindo as a symbol of human soul having descended on this earth from Divine heights and on the way of realizing the self and the world.[13] Aśvapati's *yoga* is for the divinization of his physical being. In Sri Aurobindo's philosophy this human body is much significant in the phenomenon of the realization of the Divine. Even the mortal body can be transformed to a Divine one.

Hence, his devotion to God is to divinize his physical being *(annamaya koṣa)* at the initial stage. After this stage his soul is free from ignorance. As soon as it is free from ignorance, it becomes the substratum of a higher knowledge, power and bliss. Aśvapati has performed sacrifice to obtain a child, which is interpreted as his journey towards the occult world. This journey is only to do welfare of all people. At the end of this rigorous *sādhanā* he meets the Divine Mother and prays her to come down to this earth to save the humanity and to reduce a man's suffering[14]. Being satisfied on his austerity the Divine Mother has committed a boon to the king that she will grace the earth through her human manifestation- *"A new light shall break upon the earth, a new world shall be born, things that were promised shall be fulfilled"*[15].

Sāvitrī is the Divine Mother who is Prakṛti. In the form of a seed she is in the form of Truth. She is the constructed bridge between man and God. Sri Aurobindo describes:

*"She is golden bridge, the wonderful fire*
*The luminous heart of the unknown is she*
*A power of silence in the depths of god;*
*She is the force, the inevitable word,*
*The magnet of our difficult ascent.."*[16]

The descent of Sāvitrī, the Mother Goddess, on the earth may be fruitful if there is a genuine aspiration on the part of human consciousness. Aśvapati's *yoga* is meant for his perfection. His upward journey is for the descent of Sāvitrī on this earth. From the death of Satyabān it is to be presumed that the death is inevitable in one's life and it is due to one's ignorance and suffering. The conquer over death and getting back to the life shows that there is a life which is purified as well as transformed.[17]

When Truth dictates life and mind aspires for the Divinity super-mind reveals. Our Matter, Mind and Life will be radically transformed when there is the manifestation of supra-mental consciousness. These matter, mind and life will act as the vehicle of Truth and God. When mind aspires for the Divine light, the body will carry out the forces of the Divine. Ultimately a man will be able to conquer death.

Sāvitrī in the form of a wife loyal to her husband has got power through which she snatches her husband from the cluster of Death. On the other hand, Sāvitrī in the form of Divine Mother provides immortality to a man after removing Death. In both the cases it is possible through love and devotion. Love has got an enormous power even capable of removing Death. This message we receive from Sāvitrī.

The whole *Kāvya* i.e. *Sāvitrī* is full of suggestion or *Dhvani* which is described as a soul of *Kāvya* by the Sanskrit rhetoricians.[18] According to Anandavardhana, the suggestion or *Dhvani* can give a logical account of the poetic procedures to the satisfaction of the creative poet. In a successful *Kāvya* there must be a prominent *(angī) Rasa*. When *Rasa* is principal, it is called *Dhvani*. When *Rasa* is subsidiary, it should be called as *Rasavadalamkāra*, but not *Dhvani*. So, *Dhvani* is the quintessence of poetry and *Rasa* is the quintessence of *Dhvani*.[19] In the *Sāvitrī* there is prominence of *Dhvani* and hence, there is *Rasa*.

Both Sri Aurobindo and the Sanskrit rhetoricians advocate that aesthetic experience or *Rasa* is impersonal, disinterested and universal delight. That is to say, a successful *Kāvya* always conveys us a spiritual or super-sensuous *(lokottara)* pleasure. From the sentences – 'your enemy is dead' 'your son is born', we may have some sort of pleasure which is purely this-worldly but no spiritual and hence, these sentences can not be treated as *Kāvya*. The cause of the spiritual pleasure is the object of knowledge if there is existence of suggestion followed by the presence of *Guṇas* and *Alamkāras* and absence of defects.[20] Moreover, joy is always spiritual as it is in the nature of spirit. Every form of pleasure is the manifestation of the spirit, which is supported by Upanisadic statement – *"Ānando brahmeti vyajānāt"*. The same idea has been expressed in the *Bṛhadāraṇyakopaniṣad* where Yajñavalkya said to Maitreyi that no indeed for the husband's sake the husband is dear to the wife, but for the same of the self, the husband is dear."[21] There is a great difference between aesthetic experience and spiritual experience attained through contemplation upon the Non-dual Reality. Art experience cannot remain for long time and it ceases when the factor essential for this experience are withdrawn. On the other hand, the spiritual experience is permanent and hence, if it is attained, it does not cease.[22] That is why, Abhinavagupta compares this feeling (i.e. aesthetic experience) to the feeling due to the realization of Brahman.[23]

Sri Aurobindo also advocates the same view. According to him, beauty is of the Divine, "It is in truth seeking, as in religion, for the Divine, the All-Beautiful in man, in nature, in life, in thought in art for God is Beauty and Delight hidden in the variation of his masks and forms."

Like Abhinavagupta Sri Aurobindo also accepts the view that beauty belongs to Self and an object seems to be beautiful due to having the same Self within us. How can this beauty be realized? Sri Aurobindo says - 'The soul of beauty in us identifies itself with the soul of beauty in the thing created and feels in appreciation in the same divine intoxication and uplifting which the artist felt in creation.'[24]

The artistic creation is capable of giving us disinterested delight and is necessarily the genius work. It comes out from something deep within which calls down the word, the vision, the light and power from a level above the normal mind, (i.e. overmind). The joy of the Self cannot be realized through the mind 'limited by intellectual activity, practical utility and the externals of life.' The creation of beauty in poetry, as Sri Aurobindo has observed, does not come within the purview of the reason. The beauty in poetry cannot be created through infrarational power, but it comes through suprarational power or by vision. This view or suprarational power can not come from an ordinary mental platform, but it comes from the plane of over mind. The poetry which embodies suprarational beauty or vision and which comes from the over mind is described as *Mantra*. So, we might characterize the *Sāvitrī* as *Mantra* in poetry, or the poetry of vision.

The derivative meaning of the term *'Mantra'* also shows that reason of the infrarational stage of mind is of no use in the state of *Mantra*. The derivative meaning of the term *'Mantra'* is as follows: *'Mananāt trāyate iti Matraḥ'* (i.e. That which saves us from making reflection is called *Mantra*). The *Manana* is a kind of mental phenomenon, which, when in respect of a particular meaning of word there is doubt as to the conflict with other *Pramāṇas*, causes knowledge in the form of *Tarka* which becomes a promoter in removing that doubt.[25] That is to say, when a man tries to examine through his intellect that which he through his intellect that which he has known from other sources is called *Mantra*. The *Sāvitrī* is a *Kāvya* which does not provide a person having ordinary mental platform with any scope for examining it through his independent reason. As this *Kāvya* is a product of Suprarational mind, the poetic excellences cannot be realized through the ordinary mind and hence, the process of reflection or *Manana* is not possible so far as the '*Sāvitrī*' is concerned. As it saves an individual from doing reflection or *Manana,* it is called *Mantra*.

That poetry cannot be defined in terms of ordinary human logic has been accepted by Viśvanātha, the celebrated Sanskrit rhetorician. According to him, poetry is a peculiarly unworldly phenomenon, an extraordinary creation of a supernatural, super normal genius and hence, it cannot be governed by the rules of ordinary human intellect. In ordinary life sorrow comes from sorrow, fear follows fear, but in the world of poetry we find pleasure deriving from the painful, horrible and terrible situations.[26]

For Sri Aurobindo, poetry is the spontaneous overflow of the powerful feelings. It is not possible for a poet to give a logical account in respect of using a particular word or phrase to the critical intellect. It should be clearly borne in mind that no purpose is involved in the use of same phrase or some words repeatedly by a poet, but it is to a great extent spontaneous. A critic of the *Sāvitrī* once wrote a letter to Sri Aurobindo enquiring as to why the word 'great' is repeatedly used in the line about the 'great unsatisfied god head' (*Sāvitrī,* p. 19). In response to this, Sri Aurobindo says that his poetry is the spontaneous overflow of his feeling. "He does not himself deliberately choose or arrange word or rhythm but only sees it as it comes in the very act of inspiration. If there is any purpose of any kind, it also comes by and in the process of inspiration ... Thus I can not tell you for what purpose I admitted the repetitions of the word 'great' ..."[27]

The above mentioned notion of Poetry had been accepted by Ānandavardhana and Abhinavagupta also. The sorrow of the first poet at the separation of the curlew couple took the shape of a verse.[28] When Vālmīki was affected by noticing the killing of the loving curlew at the hands of the hunter, his sorrow became boundless. And it so stirred him, as to give rise to the impassioned song (*Śloka*). Abhinavagupta has tried to analyze the case in the following way. The sage has no personal sorrow, but the sight of bird's sorrow stirs his aesthetic contemplation of universal sorrow which spontaneously overflows in metrical form.[29]

Poetry comes from the over mind and hence, it described as *Mantra*, having the power of vision. The poet or *kavi* is seer (*ṛṣi)* and can foresee Truths in the womb of the future (*krāntadarśī)*. Without some kind of *yoga* a poet can neither realize, nor visualize what is going to happen in near or distant future. The yogic and poetic experience of Sri Aurobindo has been reflected in his *Sāvitrī* and hence, it becomes a successful poetry. So it is essential for a poet to rise to moments of yogic experience so that he can speak of Truths. That is why, Vāmana, the Sanskrit rhetoricians, prescribes *Avadhāna* as a principal factor of the creation of a successful poetry. Now, let us explain the term '*Avadhāna*'. One pointed concentration is called *Avadhāna*. It is, in other words, complete cessation of thoughts in respect of this-worldly objects. Only the concentrated mind can find the objects of description as such.[30] But Vāmana mentions clearly that our concentration will be limited to object of description alone. But Sri Aurobindo says that *yoga* is union with the Supreme Being. If poet is united with Supreme Being he will see all future objects as such. But Vamana is in favour of the acceptance of the phenomenon of concentration over the object of description only. All objects of description, I think, are the manifestations of the *Saccidānanda*. If a poet has been united with the Supreme Being, all the objects of descriptions will be revealed to him as they are. So, Sri Aurobindo's view that a poet should have union with the Supreme Being is more logically intelligible.

Vision is the characteristic feature of a poet. That is, a poet must be a seer and revealer of truth. The greatest poets are endowed with a 'large and powerful interpretative and intuitive vision of Nature and life and man.' Homer, Shakespeare, Dante, Vālmīki and Kalidasa are endowed with this fundamental characteristic i.e. greatness.[25]

The poet's vision is reflected in the *Sāvitrī* and its language is the language of the poetry of the Subjective Age. "True, the voice indeed, the poem is dominated by the voice." Therefore, the *Sāvitrī* can throw a flood of light on the destiny of man.

## III

It will have been seen by now that however intimate Sri Aurobindo's position has been with some of the leading figures of Sanskrit poetics; there are ways in which he could be said to have marked large departures. These are important in many ways. First, we may point to the fact that Sri Aurobindo's concept of poetry as *mantra* is something novel in the history of Indian poetics. Or to put the matter in other words, no philosopher in India before him brought poetry to bear upon philosophy in a measure and function of the aesthetic delight is linked by him directly to *śruti,* that particularly the thesis that the Reality to *Ānanda*. This point has been hinted at by such thinkers as Abhinavagupta, but hardly in the overt manner as Sri Aurobindo does. Thirdly, Sri Aurobindo has reinterpreted the concept of *rasa* in Upanisadic lights, namely, that *rasa* is the taste and essence of things as they are. Accordingly, the experience of *rasa* becomes an experience of *Ānanda,* though in a mortal measure. The difference, according to Sri Aurobindo, between aesthetic *rasa* and divine *Ānanda* is only a matter of degree, the one is a dwarfed image of the other. Thus poetry becomes related to Truth, and not a semblance (*Sahodara*) of Truth. Hence Sri Aurobindo has forwarded a new aesthetics based upon his concept of Reality as conscious-force and delight. The notion of the planes of expression corresponds to the notion of the dimensions of the evolving mind. Thus poetry remains a cognitive affair all through. An allied point is about the role of imagination in man's spiritual or creative life. Imagination, for Sri Aurobindo, is something which is not non-intelligent, it is a sort of seeing intelligence, and it is this fashion that the poet is a *rsi* or seer. The divine intelligence has been spoken of in the Vedas as *Kavi*, and the deeper implications of this epithet has been exploited by Sri Aurobindo in such a way as never before. And lastly, he has made poetry a vehicle for communication of spiritual truths. In so doing he was a Vedic thinker in our age. This could not perhaps be said of any other thinker of Sanskrit poetics in the same sense. Sri Aurobindo would have endorsed Sankara's view that art is a form of worship – *Nirajanavidhih (Saundaryalahari*, verse – 100). This is because the ideal of art, the Beautiful, is one with the Divine.

## Notes and References

1. "Kavyasobhakaran dharmanalamkaran pracaksate."
   *Kavyadarsa*, 2nd chapter.
2. "Kavyam grahyamalamkarat." *Kavyalamkarasutravrtti* 1.1.1. "Kavyasabdoyam gunalamkarasamskrtayoh sabdarthayorvartate.
   Commentary on *Kavyalamkarasutravrtti* – 1.1.1.
3. *Savitri*, p. 371 (Sri Aurobindo Ashrama).
4. *Ibid.*, pp. 522-23.
5. *Ibid.*, p. 9.
6. *An Introduction to Indian Poetics*, p. 78, Macmillan.
7. "Evam tavadvacakatva-danyadeva vyanjakatvam; Itasca vacakatva – vyanjakatvasyanyatvam yadvacakatvam Sabdaikasrayamitattu sabdasrayamarthasrayam ca sabdarthayordvayorapi vyanjakatvasya pratipaditatvat." *Dhavanyaloka* Ch. III, p. 202, (K. Krishnamoorty).
8. Mishra, D.S., *Poetry and Philosophy in Sri Aurobindo's Sāvitrī*, p.4, 1989.
9. *Sri Aurobindo' Centenary Library*, Vol-29, p.661, Pondicherry.
10. Reddy, V. Madhusudana, *Seven Studies in Sri Aurobindo*, pp.95-96, Hyderabad, 1989.
11. Ibid, p.96
12. Purani, A.B., *Sāvitrī: An Approach and a Study*, pp.203, Pondicherry, 1952.
13. *Ibid*, p.5.
14. Mishra, D.S., *Poetry and Philosophy of Sri Aurobindo's Sāvitrī*, p.20, New delhi, 1989.
15. Purani, A.B., *Sāvitrī: An Approach and a Study*, p.6, Pondicherry, 1952.
16. *Sri Aurobindo Centenary Library*, Vol-29, p.661, Pondicherry.
17. *Poetry of Sri Aurobindo* by Sri S. Ghosh, P. 43 (Chatuskon).
18. "Kavyasyatma dhvaniriti..." *Dhvanyaloka*, p. 1 (Krishnamoorthy).
19. "Vacyavacakarutvahetunam vividhatmanam Rasadiparata yatra sa dhvanevisayo matah." "Pradhane'nyatra vakyarthe yatrangam tu rasadaya- h Kavye tasminnalamkaro rasadirite me matih." *Dhvanyaloka*, 2/4-5.
20. "Ripuste mrtoh purtaste jatah ityadi vakyarthe jnanajanyahladasya na lokottaratvamiti na tatra Kavyatvaprasaktih. Yadrsahiadan pratyarthanam Karanata ca vyanga vaisistyena dosasama nadhikaranaguna-lamkarasadbhavasampaditacarutvena ca sambhavati." Commentary on verse no. 10, cu-I, *Kavyadarsa* (K.Roy Edition).
21. "Na va are patyuh kamaya patih priye bhavatyatmanastu kamaya patih priyo bhavati". *Brhadaranyakopanisad*, 4/4/6.
22. *History of Sanskrit Poetics*, p. 388 by P.V.Kane.

23. "Parabrahmasvadasabrahmacaritvam castvasya rasasvadasya", *'Locana'* on *Dhvanyaloka*, p. 200, Jagannath Pathaka.
    *The Human Cycle*, p. 135, (Sri Aurobindo Ashrama).
    *The Human Cycle*, p. 134 (same edition)
    *The Future Poetry*, p. 342, Sri Aurobindo Ashrama.
24. *Ibid.*
25. "Mananam nama Sabdavadharite' rthe manantaravirodhasankayam tasnnirakaranankulatarkatmakajn-anajanako manasavyaparah.
    *Vedanta paribhasa*, p. 213 (By Swami Madhavananda).
26. "Hetutvam sokaharasadergatebhyo loka samsrayat, Sokaharsadayo loke jayantam nama laukikah, Alaukikavibhavatvam praptebhyah Kavyasamsrayat. Sukham Sanjayate tebhyah sarvebhyo' piti ka ksatih."
    *Sahityadarpana* – 3/6-7.
27. *Letters on Sāvitrī*, pp. 839-40 (Sri Aurobindo Ashrama).
28. "Kraunvncadvandvaviyogotthah Sokah slokatvamagatah." *Dhvanyaloka* 1/5.
29. "Krauncasya dvandvaviyogena sahacarihananodbhutena sahacaryadhvamse northito yah sokah..."
    *Locana* on *Dhvanyaloka*, p. 86 (same edition).
30. "Cittaikagryamavadhanam." *Kavyalankarasutravrtti*, 1.3.17.
    "Vahirindriyavyaparaviramanmananso vahvarthaparaktiravadhanam.
    Avadhanasya prayojanamabhidhatte. Avahitamiti. Arthan pasyati.
    Abhinavapatharthanaprativandhamullikhatityarthah."
    Commentary on *Kavyalamkarasutravrtti*, on *Sutra no. 1.3-17*, p. 91 (ed. by Dr. Basu).

32

# Sri Aurobindo and Whitman: A New Religious Wisdom

*Sarani Mondal and Goutam Ghosal*

Sri Aurobindo devotes three chapters in *The Future Poetry* to speak of the Romantic Poets, whom he calls "The Poets of the Dawn", finding a deeper religious sense in them. He obviously finds a new consciousness in these poets and a distinct effort to go beyond the mere intellectual sense in search of a poetry "whose task is to render truth of the Spirit by passing behind the appearances of the Sense and the intellect to their spiritual reality" (FP- 111). He differentiates between the spirit of the religious poetry and this new sprit of spiritual poetry and finds a link between the Romantics and the Sufis and Vaishnava poetry. But then, Walt Whitman pleases him the most in his search for the poetry of spiritual incantation in the English language.

Sri Aurobindo does not offer many examples. The purpose of our paper is to find out the examples following his clues. Let us start with Wordsworth. Sri Aurobindo appreciates the early poetry of Wordsworth and finds him lacking in the inspired speech in his later poetry. He blames his stress on intellect which obstructed the visional stuff in his later poetry.

> In the end the poet in him died while the man and the writer lived on; the moralist and concentred thinker had killed the singer, the intellect had walled up the issues of the imagination and spiritual vision...A certain number of his shorter poems rank among the greatest things in poetry and this number is not inconsiderable. But elsewhere he rises high, sometimes astonishingly high, for a few lines but cannot keep long to the high poetic expression and sometimes can sink low and sometimes astonishingly low, even to bathos and triviality, especially when he strains towards an excessive simplicity which can become puerile or worse.
>
> (FP-117-118).

Obviously, Sri Aurobindo sees the disappearance of a poet and the entry of a mere teacher in verse because the intellectual mind becomes too predominant in the later

Wordsworth. But which are those shorter poems Sri Aurobindo wishes to place "among the greatest things in poetry"? He was certainly meaning the Lucy poems (G.T: 179-182) and the poems like "The Solitary Reaper" (G.T: 255) and "By the Sea" (G.T: 273). Later in his life, in a letter to K.D. Sethna, Sir Aurobindo remembers four lines from "The Solitary Reaper" while talking of the subtle something in the highest poetry. We are temped to quote Sir Aurobindo's words, which precede those four lines.

> We can feel perhaps the Spirit of the universe lending its own depths to our mortal speech or listening from behind to some expression of itself, listening perhaps to its memories of
>
> Old, unhappy, far-off things
> And battles long ago

Or feeling and hearing, it may be said, the vast oceanic stillness and the cry of the Cuckoo.

> Breaking the silence of the seas
> Among the farthest Hebrides

We may select, for example, the first eight lines of the sonnet, "By the Sea" which speaks of that bare grandeur of the early poetry of Wordsworth and that charm of the revelatory speech. These eight lines will clarify why Sri Aurobindo calls Wordsworth "a seer of the calm spirit in Naturc, the poet of man's large identity with her and serene liberating communion" (FP- 118). There is no trace of the teacher in verse in these eight lines of the poem. Instead, we have the exact adjectives expressing the realization of the magic hour, the great twilight, which has flared up the poet's indwelling spirit. The adjectives are also interlinked. The evening is beautiful, clam and frcc. True sense of beauty can only be perceived when we are calm. There is a feeling of great liberation now and that is why the word "free" is an automatic choice. The 'holy time' in the poem immediately takes us to Sri Aurobindo's phrase 'golden evening' in his poem "Evening" (SABCL-5:46). Both the phrases highlight the importance of the hour. The mind becomes calm and quiet at this juncture of day and night. The adjectives 'calm' and 'quite' are related but not synonymous. Sri Aurobindo explains in a letter the distinction between 'clam' and 'quite'. (*Letters on Yoga*, SABCL Vol-13, pp. 641- 42).

According to the Indian seer-poet, 'calm' is *Sthirata* and quiet is *acancalata*. The work 'breathless' is a supplement to 'calm' and 'quiet'. The phrase 'breathless in adoration' is a miracle of exactitude. Nature at this juncture of day and night is aspiring to God and in her adoration she has become so quiet that no sound of her breath can be heard in this holy hush. It is a marvelous silence, which is intensified by the slow downward movement of the 'broad sun'. There is no sound from the sinking sun.The last word in the quatrain is 'tranquility'.

The second quatrain continues the note of calm, quiet and tranquility. The incantatory style is obvious in the first two lines, which have no colour, no ornamentation, no outward glow. Let us listen to the bare revelatory lines reflecting the sublime consciousness of Wordsworth:

> The gentleness of heaven is on the Sea:
> Listen ! the mighty being is awake... (GT: 273)

Talking of the future poetry, Sir Aurobindo emphatically stresses the value of revelation, which is direct sight, *dristi*. It is this power that Wordsworth loses in his later poetry. That is why Sri Aurobindo sees the later Wordsworth "petering out" "like a motor car without petrol" (SABCL: Vol-9: 521).

At another place, he has shown us the strength of Wordsworth, his moments of glory, which diminished in his later life. He tells us clearly why Wordsworth lost his sight then:

> At the beginning, he struck in the midst of some alloy full into his purest vein of gold. His earliest vision of his task was the right vision, and whatever may be the general truth of his philosophy of childhood in the great Ode, it seems to have been true of him. For as intellectuality grew on him, the vision failed, the first clear intimations dimmed and finally passed, living behind an unillumined waste of mere thought and moralizing. (SABCL:Vol-9:120).

Sri Aurobindo believes that the thing, which the poet sees and feels, not what he opines, is the real theme of his poetry. Judged from this standard the first eight lines of "By the Sea" exemplify real poetry, the poetry of a superior consciousness. What Sri Aurobindo appreciatively says of him in *The Future Poetry* is perfectly applicable to the first eight lines of "By the Sea":

> But it is in the Nature-strain of which he is the discoverer that he is unique, for it is then that the seer in him either speaks the revelatory thought of his spirit or gives us strains greater than thought, the imperishable substance of spiritual consciousness finding itself in sight and speech. (FP-117)

Sir Aurobindo tells us clearly that Coleridge, despite his eye for the supra-physical worlds, does not see the highest things. He has at best an eye for the middle world, where we the occasional reflections of a refined consciousness. Let us refer to Coleridge's "Frost at Midnight" wishing the reader to see the poet's consciousness verging on the borderline of Silence.

Sri Aurobindo does not speak quite enthusiastically about Coleridge, but positively refers to his three poems, (he does not name the three), where the poet is able to keep the intellectual mind "in abeyance". Sri Aurobindo further says, "It is indeed just over the mystic border that his sight penetrates and to its most inferior forms". But, one must remember Sri Aurobindo's special demands from mystic poetry, which he himself writes. The positive words are to be noted with care, because he is after all writing about the poets of the dawn. Coleridge, according to Sri Aurobindo, catches the mystic lights falling upon the surface earth, but "it is caught with a truth and intensity which makes magical the scenes and movements of the earth life and transforms light of physical nature into light of supernature". Sri Aurobindo observes the refinement in Coleridge's presentation of the "middle worlds' and finally accepts the visional stuff in his poetry calling it a "superlative power" within "narrow limits" (SABCL-9: 972: 124).

Coleridge comes to the poetry of silence in "Frost at Midnight", which breathes an air of silence throughout. For that real stuff, one must turn to Sri Aurobindo's mature poetry. In "Frost at Midnight", the lonely poet is watching his baby in the cradle. All the members of the cottage are in deep slumber. It is snowing. There is no wind. Only the flickering flame of the fire and the shrill cry of the owl create a contrasting note in that grim silent night. The sleepless night transports the poet into his own childhood days. Then we see a backward movement through the lanes of memory. Slides of past memory flash before his eyes one by one: his school days, his "birth-place", the "old church-tower", "the bell" and "the music on a hot fair day". He remembers how he enjoyed all those little wonders of life. Here we get a clue to Wordsworth's poetic theory: "emotions recollected in tranquility". The poet recollects his long buried emotions in absolute solitude. Although he is working under the spell of a simple Romantic nostalgia, he comes close to the borderline of true silence, may be half-aware of what he is doing.

The soft breathing of his child brings him into the present moment. The face of his child amuses him with tender gladness. Here the movement of he lyric becomes futuristic. The poet starts thinking about the future of his child. He dreams that his baby will grow up in close contact with Nature. He will run like the wind by the brook. He will observe the different objects of Nature and will also experience the bliss of the Eternal spirit. God is immanent in Nature. We just need to realize him. God is our real teacher. He moulds our spirit and shapes us. There is a powerful aloofness in the poet. He seems to have been very quiet when he wrote the poem. Was he on sedative, opium? From the yogic point of view this is quite natural. Was he conscious that he was just circling around the entry point of the poetry of silence?

In thinking of Nature as a positive influence on the developing spirit of man, he passes by a supreme secret. He wishes his son to grow up amidst sun and shower. He wishes his son to love all the seasons and aspects of Nature: the "red breast Robin", "the mossy apple tree", "the tuft of snow hanging from the branch", the frost and the soft moon. The concluding lines restore again the mood of silence. The moon has an obvious contribution to the poetry of silence. The meditative mood is unmistakable, be it the effect of sedative or any natural yoga. The lyric is a stream of consciousness, occasionally rising from a depth of thought to the sudden moments of revelation. Sri Aurobindo draws our attention to Coleridge's "spontaneity of conversation or rather monologue" (9: 124), which makes it an easy guess for us that this poem might have been one of the three he mentions in *The Future Poetry*. The true poetry of silence is different. Let us listen to the Master:

> The voice that only Silence' ear has heard
> Leaps missioned from an eternal glory of Day.
>
> (*Sonnets*: 1980 & 1999: 38)

To most readers, this will be less interesting than Coleridge's poetry. But there are readers, who have either felt the experience or have an inkling of that vast silence.

Unlike this poetry, the spiritual note is quite strong in Shelley's poetry and Sri Aurobindo has no hesitation in calling him the most rich in spiritual substance of all the Romantic poets of the 19th century England.

> A greater poet by nature than almost any of these, Shelley was alone of them all very nearly fitted to be a sovereign voice of the new spiritual force that was at the moment attempting to break into poetry and possess there its kingdom … He is a seer of spiritual realities, much more radiantly near to them than Wordsworth has, what Colridge had not, a poetic grasp of metaphysical truths, can see the forms and hear the voices of higher elemental spirits and natural godheads than those seen and hard by Blake…
>
> (FP – 122-23)

As Sri Aurobindos calls *Prometheus Unbound* his supreme effort and one of the masterpieces of poetry (FP-124), we shall try to see why Sri Aurobindo rates it so high as great poetry. For Shelley, love is the central idea of life and a key to the great future of mankind. Asia, the heroine of the poem, is a Mother-Force, a half-clear vision of Sri Aurobindo's Sāvitrī who fights against Death with her flaming love for the earth. Shelley's concept of love, like Sri Aurobindo's, is related to the concept of suffering. This idea of suffering becomes clear in his treatment of the figure of Prometheus in Act I of the play. Love never comes easily to a person. It comes through suffering. It is a great realization. Love stands against Ego. Love is humility. Thus, we see the adamant Prometheus growing humble when he listens to his own voice cursing Evil (*The Dhammapada* constantly cautions us against the impulse to hit back).

> For I hate no more
> As then ere misery made me wise

This wisdom is the growth of love in man, the growth of the sleeping Christ or the psychic being. In the poem, Saturn is good principle, Jupiter is Evil, Prometheus a great regenerator doing what Sri Aurobindo would have called "A God's Labour". Asia is the symbol of Love, which saves the earth from the clutches of Evil (Jupiter). Demogorgon is the symbol of life force, a neutral force, who is made positive by Asia or the power of love. Demgorgon dethrones Evil (Jupiter) at the start of Act III. And them comes the songs for the golden age. The concept of the World Mother saving the earth had been faintly known to the poet of *Prometheus Unbound* before the composition of *Sāvitrī*. Like Sāvitrī, Asia too becomes conscious of her inner voyage in Act II, Scene II, of *Prometheus Unbound*.

> My soul is an enchanted boat
> Which like a sleeping swan doth float
> Upon the silver waves of thy sweet singing ….

Prometheus and Asia, Purusha and Prakriti, the psyche and the epipsyche principle, according to Carlos Baker, have resolved to collaborate for the creation of a new world.

In Keats, Sri Aurobindo sees a new fire of aspiration, which is not a direct quest for the Divine, but an indirect all for the Divine through the medium of Beauty.

> All the other high things that interested his great
> equals, had for him no interest; one godhead
> only he worshipped, the image of divine beauty,
> and through this alone he wished to see Truth
> and by her to achieve spiritual delight
> and not so much freedom as completeness.
>
> (*SABCL*-9: 130)

Sri Aurobindo finds an evolution of the consciousness of Beauty in Keats, a kind of gradation of beauty starting from the sensuous and ending in the Ideal Beauty. I quote again from Sri Aurobindo:

> And he saw her in three of her four forms, sensuous beauty, imaginative beauty, intellectual and ideal beauty. But it is the first only which he had entirely expressed when his thread was cut short in its beginning; the second he had carried far, but it was not yet full-orbed: towards the third and highest he was only striving ... (ibid)

Sensuousness is predominant, but sensuous beauty is not a satisfactory ideal for Keats. He has an eye on a better beauty.

Keats' inspirational style has a magical quality, and in such magic utterances we sense his passion for the divine idea of beauty. There are lines in Keats which clearly reveal a quest for something beyond. The last two lines from "To Psyche" may be cited:

> A bright torch, and a casement ope at night,
> To let the warm love in ! (Blunden: 261)

In the same poem, Keats suddenly discovers a feeling of "wide quietness". Sri Aurobindo's appreciation of Keats' oft-quoted lines from the Nightingale ode is again not a traditional praise:

> ... magic casements, opening on the foam
> Of perilous seas, in faery lands forlorn. (Ibid: 257)

He finds a suggestion of the infinite in these lines. This is poetry of incantation and magic.

In "Terror of Death", (Ibid: 396) Keats exhibits at least at one place a faint idea of Ideal Beauty.

> When I have fears that I may cease to be
> Before my pen has glean'd my teeming brain,
> Before high-piled books, in charact'ry
> Hold like rich garners the full-ripen'd grain;
> When I behold, upon the night's starr'd face,
> Huge cloudy symbols of a high romance,
> And think that I may never live to trace
> Their shadows, with the magic hand of chance;
>
> And when I feel, fair Creature of an hour !
> That I shall never look upon thee more,

Never have relish in the fairy power
Of unreflecting love then on the shore
Of the wide world I stand alone, and think
Till Love and Fame to nothingness do sink.

There are three levels of fear in the poem. The first stanza records the tension of the "teeming brain" and the "full-ripen'd grain". In the second quatrain, Keats' fear lies in a more serious sense of missing. He will not be able to see the huge "cloudy symbols" of a 'high romance'. This is a flickering perception of th: Ideal Beauty through the senses. In the third quatrain, his concentration is on love and the last two lines contain a sense of despair. But there is just one instance of Keats' perception of the divine beauty in the poem. That is in the second line of the second quatrain.

In "Hyperion" Keats foreshadows Sri Aurobindo's theory of spiritual evolution. The basic message is not complex. Sri Aurobindo's celebrated maxim – "we do not belong to the past dawns, but to the noons of the future" (SABCL-13: 1970: 8) – sums up the essence. In Book II, Oceanus' long speech summarises Keats' whole idea of the Titans and the significance of the defeat. While Book I is an expression of agony and strife, Book II is a clarification and a solution as well. Oceanus insists on the value of endurance and acceptance and then he makes clear the eternal law of evolution:

As Heaven and Earth are fairer, fairer far
Than Chaos and blank Darkness, though once chiefs;
And as we show beyond that Heaven and Earth
In form and shape compact and beautiful,
In will, in action free, companionship,
And thousand other signs of purer life,
So on our heels a fresh perfection treads
A power more strong in beauty, born of us
And fated to excel us ... (Blunden: 284)

The exact nature of spiritual evolution was unknown to Keats; he could only feel that the new power would be more strong in beauty.

...'tis the eternal law
That first in beauty should be first in might ... (*Ibid*: 284)

Oceanus believes that the fall is an inevitability according to the law of nature. The force of thunder is not the reason. Oceanus expresses Keats' world view. The present leaves the past behind.

Another race may drive
Our conquerors to mourn as we do now. (*Ibid*: 284)

As 'Hyperion' is the document of Keats' final maturity, we are led to believe by the speeches of Occanus that Keats is a futurist like Sri Aurobindo. He welcomes the beauty that belongs to the better race, the beauty that is ever on the move through repeated deaths. Man is a transitional being – Sri Aurobindo claims. He clarifies Keats' idea indicating the conclusive journey of the human soul. In Whitman, Sri Aurobindo virtually found his real predecessor.

Whitman grew up during the great renaissance of American literature, during the heydays of literary Transcendentalism, observing closely the works of Emerson, Thoreau, Margaret Fuller and the authors from the anti-Emersonian school of Transcendentalism, which was critical about Emerson's dependence on literature to express Transcendentalism. Sri Aurobindo too returned to India from England in the wake of the nineteenth century Bengali renaissance. Both Whitman and Sri Aurobindo were aware of the native sources. Behind Whitman stood Emerson and the other Transcendentalists. And in 1893, Sri Aurobindo could still see behind him the towering presence of Sri Ramakrishna, the great spiritual nationalist of India.

Emerson's literary aim focused on uniting the seer and the sayer, vision and literary expression. Quite naturally, Whitman's sympathy lay with the literary Transcendentalists, the school of Emerson. And he had long prepared for his masterpiece, which later created history in 1855. Even till his death in 1892, he went on adding more leaves to his precious *Leaves of Grass* and was deliberate in his search for a dynamic divine slowly manifesting on earth. We see the reflection of the same idea later in Sri Aurobindo, especially in his post-1895 lyrics.

Unlike Whitman, Sri Aurobindo depended largely on the Indian scriptural tradition and became ecstatic when he found the essence of that tradition in Whitman's poetry. Coming back to India from the West after Whitman's death, Sri Aurobindo wished to go deep into the roots of his own culture. As he discovered the lost poetic code, he simultaneously discovered Whitman in an Indian context and also in the context of the poetry of the future. Spirituality is not India's sole property, because she had only preserved its many secret principles. Spirituality belongs to man in the universe; every individual can have access to the secret areas of consciousness. The English language was like Sri Aurobindo's mother tongue and he was thinking of making it more plastic to help in the growth of a global awareness to the deeper spiritual aspects of life. He saw in Whitman a pioneer of the future poetry and wished to follow his track in his own search for a new poetry and a new poetic credo. Unlike Whitman, he was a conscious yogi and stayed aloof even when he participated in various political and social activities. God came to Whitman early in his life. He was not well off and was brought up in an essentially religious environment. He imbibed the simple faith from his mother. Sri Aurobindo grew up in an intellectual culture and he came of a well to do family. He did not like the restrictions of religion put upon him by his Christian patrons. He found God rather late in life but stuck to Him very intensely in his post-1895 lyrics. He had steered clear of religion as a student in England, but he discovered a new God in Baroda. All his love now turned towards this newly discovered God.

Unlike Whitman's, Sri Aurobindo's theory of poetry is one-pointed in its stress on the discovery of *mantra* or incantation along with the explanatory notes on the higher planes from which poetry of the future will be written. A close look at Whitman's *Prefaces* and other notes on poetry will reveal Whitman's awareness of poetry as an inspired art, an art that is a product of intuition and vision. When Whitman says in the 1855 Preface that the poet is "no arguer", he simply anticipates Sri Aurobindo's theory of poetry as revelation, where the intellectual mind has a very little role to play. "The greatest poet does not moralize or make application of morals ... he knows the soul". (*Preface,* 1855) Sri Aurobindo too speaks of a kind of poetry, which will be different from preaching, thinking and philosophizing. He goes back to the ancient Sanskrit poetry to verify the true role of a poet, which has nothing to do with teaching and philosophy. The ancient Sanskrit word "Kavi" meant the person who could simply saw and sing.

> The Kavi was in the idea of the ancients the seer and revealer of truth, and though we have wandered far enough from that ideal to demand from him only the pleasure of the ear and the amusement of the aesthetic faculty, still all great poetry preserves something of that higher truth of its own aim and significance.
>
> (*SABCL* 9: 1972: 29)

Whitman was aware of this basic role of the poet, that is, to provide his readers with sight. And the "inner sight" must be "intense in him before he can awaken it in us" (*Ibid*: 29-30). He certainly had this deliberate motive and it is curious that his poetry itself expressed this theory quite often. The poetry of vision is also the poetry of listening, the search for the ultimate word, which is a sudden discovery. And it goes beyond all analysis. The revealed word is the *mantra*; the seer-poet discovers it in his soul. Whitman's practice was wonderfully fused with his theory:

> A word then, (for I will conquer it)
> The word final, superior to all,
> Subtle, sent up – what was it? – I listen .... (Reader's Edition: 252)

Like Sri Aurobindo, Whitman was also deliberate in his motive. He wished to discover the "Kosmic" in his poetry. When he said "the poetry of the future aims at the free expression of emotion (which means far, far more than appears at first)" (Louise Pound: 341), he was anticipating Sri Aurobindo's theory of poetry without intellectual obstruction. Whitman himself suggested within bracket its great implications. Sri Aurobindo sheds light on this free emotional element with a wonderful phrase in *The Future Poetry*. He calls it "the soul of the emotion".

> ... it is not the mere emotion itself the poet seeks, but the soul of the motion, that in it for the delight of which the soul in us and the world desires or accepts emotional experience.
>
> (*SABCL* 9: 1972:15)

This spiritual emotion, which rises in the heart of the seer, may be spontaneously expressed in the lyric form.

Both the poets deal with great issues like democracy and the enlargement of democracy for the spiritual unity of mankind, the spiritual journey inward and upward, death, love, immportality, rebirth and renewal, the world and the individual, God and cosmic consciousness. Both the poets go beyond the parochial national feeling in search of a glorious future of man. Whitman comes back to his self from the world outside; Sri Aurobindo goes from inside out, from the inner self to the external world. The American poet had thought of the integration of the material and the spiritual in *Leaves of Grass* well ahead of Sri Aurobindo, who came later to systematize the idea. Here is Whitman, the poet of integral life, speaking in "Starting from Paumanok".

> I will make the poems of materials, for I think they are to be the most spiritual poems,
> And I will make the poems of my body and of mortality,
> For I think I shall then supply myself with the poems of my soul and of immortality. (Reader's Edition: 18)

Sri Aurobindo takes up the idea from 1895 onwards to codify the theory of Divine life on earth and to reframe the theory in terms of lyric poetry, which he believes to be the most inevitable form of future poetry. A brief example from his lyric poetry will speak of his effort:

> The body with increasing soul to fill,
> Extend Heaven's claim upon the toiling earth
> And climb from death to a diviner birth
> Grasped and supported by immortal Will.
>
> (*SABCL*, Vol-5: 61)

The "immortal Will" is the Divine will, already concealed in Matter. God himself will grow up from below and descend from above into the material life. Sri Aurobindo confirms Whitman's faith in the joint collaboration of the body and the soul and he wishes to light "Heaven's fire" "in the breast of the earth". (*Ibid*, 102) Both the poets are in love with this earth and they extend their arms to embrace her. Death has always been feared, but both the poets face it full square in search of an immortal existence. Whitman struggles against it with a gesture of courage. Sri Aurobindo's challenge is bolder. For both, however, death is an entry into a new world. Whitman is ecstatic in "Night on the Prairies":

> I was thinking this globe enough till there sprang out so noiseless around me myriads of other globes.
>
> (Reader's Edition: 452)

Sri Aurobindo goes straight into the arms of God and discovers his deep, deathless being.

> No power can slay my soul; it lives in Thee.
> Thy presence is my immortality.
>
> (*SABCL*, Vol-5: 143)

He grows in an intense love for the Divine and feels a great release from the bondage of death:

> Time voyages with Thee upon its prow –
> And all the future's passionate hope is thou.
>
> (*Ibid*: 154)

Both the poets know that death is not the end of the road and that life moves on. They speak of an eternal pilgrimage, an eternal walk ahead pressed by a great feeling of love. It is a motiveless love. They do not seek for return. They are just fascinated by the power of love. They are under a magic spell. This love erases all tension, the tension of death and nothingness, which bothers most human beings. Whitman bathes into a queer ecstasy of freedom as he says:

> Love, that is day and night .... Love, that is sun and moon and stars,
> Love, that is crimson, sumptuous, sick with perfume,
> No other words but words of love, no other thought but love.
>
> (Reader's Edition: 470)

Love is the pulse of all, the keynote of existence. Sri Aurobindo uses the force of love deliberately as an antidote to death. In both, it is synonymous with humility. When the small self is dead, the true self creeps in from the deepest depths of our being and occupies all the parts of our being. The small "I" grows into a vast entity, the cosmic "I", egoless and free. At least at the time of writing certain lines, Whitman leaves behind his small self and feels identified with the whole of the universe, hearing and seeing God in every object.

> I hear you whispering there O stars of heaven,
> O suns – O grass of graves – O perpetual transfers and promotions,
> If you do not say any thing how can I say any thing? (*Ibid*: 87)

He lives and breathes in God and it seems as if he is reborn in the Indian poet to carry forward his limitless aspiration for God. What Sri Aurobindo says on cosmic consciousness is perfectly applicable to Whitman's lyrics:

> In it we live as we lived before in the ego-sense, active, more and more in contact, even unified more and more with other minds, other lives, other bodies than the organism we call ourselves, producing effects not only on our own moral and mental being and on the subjective being of others, but even on the physical world and its events by means nearer to the divine than those possible to our egoistic capacity. (SABCL, Vol-18: 21-22)

This cosmic consciousness is quite real to Whitman. He does not imagine it in *Leaves of Grass*. He has expressed what he has felt. He as felt the great liberation of the individual being and has become the universal individual. This cosmic consciousness is not a static awareness. It is dynamic and moves towards what Sri Aurobindo calls the supramental realization.

This advanced cosmic consciousness has created some distance between Sri Aurobindo's poetry and the common reader. Also, as we have already said, he has suffered from the problem of objective correlative and has sought to solve the problem by being a bit too expository in the sonnets and lyrics of his mature years, when he was rising from height to height in the spiritual hemisphere and was moving towards the Supermind (a plane above the mind of present humanity, which will create the next species beyond man). But this he could do only by following the expanding "I" of Whitman. The same "I" evolves in Sri Aurobindo's poetry and creates a sort of bare glory. Not as charming as Whitman's, yet his lines are no less interesting:

I have gone out from the universe I made,
And have grown nameless and immeasurable. (SABCL, Vol-5: 33)

Does it really communicate? How does it really feel to grow into the "nameless" and the "immeasurable"? This is still a problem for spiritual poetry proper (as contrasted with the mystic poetry of sweet and hazy awareness), which seeks to record the direct seeing or feeling of Truth-consciousness. Whitman, the mystic poet, is quite within our perception as he stimulates the secret aspiration in us. But, Sri Aurobindo goes too far out, although basically he follows the track Whitman had prepared before him. If the Romantics had been the poets of the dawn for Sri Aurobindo, then he certainly found in Whitman a brilliant sunrise moving towards the future noons.

### *Notes and References*

1. Sri Aurobindo, *The Future Poetry*, Sri Aurobindo Ashram, Pondicherry, 1994 (FP).
2. Sri Aurobindo, *The Future Poetry*, SABCL-9, Sri Aurobindo Ashram, Pondicherry, 1972.
3. See Sri Aurobindo's Action, Pondicherry, June, 2007 for the whole essay on cobridge by Sarani Mondal.
4. Sri Aurobindo, SABCL-23, Sri Aurobindo Ashram, Pondicherry, 1970.
5. Palgrave, F.T., *The Golden Treasury*, Oxford University Press, Calcutta, 1998.
6. Sri Aurobindo, SABCL-5 (*Collected Poems*), Sri Aurobindo Ashram, Pondicherry, 1972.
7. Edmund Blunden (ed.) *Selected Poems*: John Keats, Rupa & Co, Calcutta, 2001.
8. Sri Aurobindo, SABCL-13 (*Essays on the Gita*), Sri Aurobindo Ashram, Pondicherry, 1970.
9. Sri Aurobindo, *Sonnets*, Sri Aurobindo Ashram, Pondicherry, 1980, 1999.
10. Sri Aurobindo, SABCL Vol-18 (*The Life Divine)*, Pondicherry: Sri Aurobindo Ashram, 1971.
11. Leaves of Grass Norton Critical Edition, New York: Norton, (eds) Harald Blalget and Scullgy Brodley, 1973.
12. Leaves of Grass. Reader's Edition, (eds) Blodget & Bradley, London: University of London Pres, 1965.
13. 1855, Preface from Norton Critical Edition.
14. Walt Whitman, "Poetry Today in America", from Walt Whitman: Democratic Vistas and other frose, ed. Louise Pound, Doubbday, New York: Doran and Company, 1935.

33

# Supreme Morality of Chikuro Hiroike: Its Relevance in Contemporary India and Abroad

*Sib Ranjan Misra*

Chikuro Hiroike (b.1866), an eminent philosopher is widely recognized as an architect of the philosophy of Supreme Morality. This philosophy was examined from the standpoint of personal experiences of his life and stands the test from the standpoint of history of mankind.

Supreme morality contains the essence of the following great moral system; 1)that of Amatrasu Onikami, the heavenly ancestress of the Imperial house of Japan 2) that of Confucius of China 3) that of Sakyamuni of India 4) that of Jesus Christ and 5) that of Socrates of Greece. The simply speaking, it suggests that we have to put aside selfish instinct or egoism and in its place in our minds' Divine Benevolence'. Egoism is principally due to instinct of self-preservation. Supreme moral demands faithful and sincere efforts without any desire for reward – a kind of determination formed itself within to renounce self completely.

Endeavour has simply been made here first to reflect on the basic concepts and principles of Supreme Morality of Chikuro Hiroike-1, its relationship with India, religious teachings and then try to articulate relevance of different tenets of supreme morality in contemporary world.

## Section One

As we know, moralogy is a science of morals. It is a positive and synthetic science. It is positive, simply because the analysis conforms to the principles of empirical observation, classification and then, explanations. It is synthetic because it synthesizes the teachings of the sages along with relevant data available on modern science.

It is also important to note that supreme morality is distinct from conventional morality. Traditional morality is not complete by itself.. It is pertinent to be in agreement with true divine spirit. Otherwise, our conduct may be motivated by our own personal wisdom and certain pre-natal activities, but not by the true spirit of benevolence. He did not believe in artificial regulations and man-made laws. This may involve improper elements.

Supreme morality suggests that we have to put aside selfish egoism and in its place in our mind Divine Benevolence. Egoism is principally due to instinct of self-preservation. This instinct moves us in selfish and egoistical way. Greed, arrogance, false pride etc are the outward expression of man's egoistic spirit. The Supreme Morality suggests the removal of ones own egoistic instinct to follow the Divine Law, of placing our duty over all in the spirit of benevolence, integrity, discretion and deference. With all these, our spiritual life will be enlightened and they attain salvation. Once Divine law of nature is adapted, the inessential components for human existence disappear. Supreme morality is to come up to a state of culture from the civilized state.

Morality was used merely as a matter of personal conduct for one's soul's salvation. But Supreme Morality, as developed by Dr. Hiroike is chiefly concerned with public or collective aspect-from the stability of the individual to the welfare of the community at large. It is the public aspect of morality which has been neglected so far in the past.

Dr. Hiroike presented five principles of supreme morality abstracted from the teachings of great Sages of the world like -Socrates, Jesus Christ, Sakyamuni and Confucius as follows:

01. Self-renunciation : It is important for us to do away with ego-centric self which will lead us to the improvement of our character and personality.
02. Acceptance of belief in the Benevolence of God—God is equated with reality. It is not something as absolute. God is the creator who is personal and to whom prayer may be addressed. We must develop a spirit of benevolence and love towards all living creatures to nourish everything for others which is the way to our real happiness.
03. Precedence of our Duties over Rights—The rights of man should be preceded by the performance of his duties.
04. Respect for Ortholinons - Line of Succession—Greek word-meaning sacred thread—essential to express our gratitude and to repay our debts to the Ortholinons of the present and the past—we are the inseparable part of the whole of creation—an identification of the SELF with the evolutionary stream - leads to the mutuality of loyalty to the stream in recognition of benefits conferred-rationalized: we cannot start from the void -- so, to take account of the common store of experiences --so the thread Ortholinon runs through personalities-and cohesion will not be achieved without it
05. Enlightenment and Salvation—We have to develop in ourselves the spirit to pray for the happiness of others by transplanting the above four principles in their spirit. The good we do to others confers a reciprocal benefits to us and at the end all are united with God.

## Section Two

The ethical thought in the Bhagavat Gita is here pertinent to analyse the similarity in the concept of supreme morality with the fundamental teachings in the Hindu philosophy, precisely lessons in the Gita, in a very simple way.

The teachings of the Bhagavat Gita have for its starting point the misery of mundane existence. The soul is viewed as trapped in the cycle of rebirths because impeded empirical consciousness deludes it into imagining that it is dependent on the body and that it undergoes all the sufferings of finite existence. Essentially, the soul is quite independent of the body; but as it is ignorant of its true nature, it remains a prisoner in the "this perishable, unhappy world." In the light of the human predicament, good or evil are defined in relation to the soul's release from or resignation to the weary round of rebirths. Release leads to the attainment of Nirvana. Theologically, the goal of life is union with Iswara (God) and Morality provides the foundation on which the superstructure of the holy life culminating in Nirvana is built.

What is the nature of Gita's ethics? Let us narrate simply as follows.The opening scene pictures Arjuna standing in his chariot between the armies of the Kauravas and Pandavas.. Seeng all his kinsmen standing arrayed, Arjuna is overcome with grief and utters these words of distress to the charioteers

"My limbs collapse, my mouth dries up, there is trembling in my body and my hair stands on end --I do not desire victory, O Krishna, nor kingdom, nor pleasure-"

Arjunas depression is my form of self-indulgent pity which prevents him from doing his duty because it will harm his kith and kin.

Such sentimentality incurs the rebuke of Krishna who exhorts him to act bravely. "Yield not to this impotence, O Partha, for it is not proper for the Abandon this petty weakness of heart and arise, O opressor of the foe."

It is true that these words of Krishna are a clarion call to action and therein lies the main thrust of the Gita's ethical teachings.

Karma is evil and should be abandoned because it leads to rebirths by making a shrewd analysis of human behaviour. It does not stop with karma, but goes beyond karma to kama. Behind the deed lies the desire. Aversions and attachments determines a man's behavior, therefore, a man's real enemies are not actions but passions. Actions are only the motor manifestations of the impulse to love or to hate. The implication of this analysis is that the power to bind one to continued existence resides not in karma but in kama. Once desire removed from the deed, the deed loses its fateful sting. He who knows this is wise. Gita expresses it:

"Having no desire, with his mind and self-controlled, abandoning all possessions, performing actions with the body alone, he commits no sin

He who is content with what comes by chance, who has passed beyond the pairs (of opposites), who is free from jealousy and is indifferent to successes and failures, even when he is acting he is not bound".

The above analysis of action as the extension of desire, along with the inference that detached actions per se have no binding power, brings one to the conclusion that what is ethically required is not "renunciation of action " but "renunciation in action. " The Gita's expression of detached activism is karma-yoga. Karma -yoga treats the act as an end in itself and not as a means to another end". In action, only hast thou a right and never in its fruits. Let not thy motive be the fruits of action, nor let thy attachment be to inaction". In Karma Yoga, while it does not abandon activity, it preserves the spirit of renunciation.

The crux of the Gita's teachings refers to acting without attachment (Niskama karma) to the fruits of action. People are to act, Arjuna is assured but always without interest or purpose (Artha). The theme of 'dis-interest " or non-attachment is a common cross-cutting thread in many classical Hindu ethics combines continuous with diversity. Hindu ethics are not fixed, static and unchanging substances - a state of ceaseless flow down the ages. The evolutionary character of Hindu ethics gives it a contemporary relevance. Being open to change, its principles can be adapted to contemporary ethical situation.

Precisely because the liberated person has put all vestings of egoism behind, he has attained a state of mind where without regard for personal benefit, he acts out of a free compassion for other beings.

This is exactly the state achieved by Arjuna in the Bhagavat Gita. Perplexes over the terrible implications for himself and his kinsmen, if he is to perform his warrior's duties, Arjuna is unable to act until in a series of religious encounters, he learns from Krishna that one's true self is not strained by moral good or evil. This instruction frees him to do his duties and thereby help sustain the cosmic -moral order. Far from being antinomian or immoral, therefore, these teachings of "detached action (Niskama karma), as Max Weber observed, is one of the loftiest achievement of Indian moral and religious thoughts. According to Hindu tradition, ultimate redemption requires one to attain the conscentious that full liberation (Moksa, Nirvana) is open only those who transcend attachment to Samsara, the karmic realm of merit or demerit.

On the surface, all these teachings appear to undermine the significance of morality and moral striving and if it is true that at one time or another teaching, such as these have been taken to antinomian conclusions.

In essence, the basic ideas of Supreme Morality have significant similarity between the Niskam karma as enunciated in the Gita and Dr. Hiroikes ideas on morality.

## Section Three

In this section we shall make an attempt to see how the basic fundamental ideas of Supreme Morality is relevant in contemporary world. A dispassionate study of today's world events reveal that people are being battered by a variety of recent crises and concerns such as inter-state rivalry, religious fanaticism, an increasing trade deficit, a rise in the rate of unemployment, regionalism, floundering economy etc. corruption which is found abundantly in countries of widely varying ideology, economic conditions or social development is another issue of serious concern. Corruption is both an individual and structural phenomenon.

Against this backdrop, an analysis about how the basic principles of Supreme morality which Dr. Chikuro Hiroike enunciated could be looked upon as a viable strategy.

As it is already mentioned, we live today in a world of imperfections. We recognize people are facing a variety of crises and concerns that are agitating the minds in the contemporary world like how to create national or international integration/to create borderless economic structure

- ➢ how to minimize the imbalance or inequality in economic development among different countries
- ➢ how to address the issues like trade deficit, declining rate of unemployment/economic slowdown bankruptcy etc
- ➢ how to take care of global issues like environmental degradation
- ➢ how to promote the creation of common international value or culture system
- ➢ how to reduce conflicts that generate from ethnic or religious issues etc

All these need to be addressed.

At the same time,we also witness-all the ethics and values are under attack traditions are subjected to ridicule moral standards have slipped to an appalling degree -openly advocating hedonism belief in God is evaporating etc.

It is first of all pertinent to understand its relevance in the context of international relations, because even the national situation of a country today is not exclusively determined only by its own domestic factors/values. International factors play a role precisely in a globalized regime.

Dr. Hiroike is a global man. He was not lacking in world views on different issues even though he talked about the spirit /strength of nationalism.

But if we look at the world today, the strength and spirit of nationalism is gradually eroding for different reasons. One, we witness today the proliferation of different international organizations /trading blocks, irrespective of geographical or national territorial boundaries.

Two, globalization regime and mass communications have impacted on our outlook towards international understanding.

Again, there are some problems of global significance like environmental crisis which calls for international collaboration

But doubts are there about their effective functioning.

Dr Hiroike was sceptic about effectiveness of institutions like League of nations, Disarmanent conferences, non-war treatise etc for the attainment of absolute peace security and happiness of human kind. This is, he believed, because of the collisions of interests between groups and also lack of cultivation of one's fortune 'with supreme virtue /lack of spirit of enlightenment of members of each group. He maintained that it is impossible to organise a true social organisation i.e. a social unit if the human beings do not restrain their selfish instincts.

He, therefore, suggested-'solution lies in – the enlightenment of the people by means of supreme morality' and to practise the ortholinon principle. National ortholinon should be integrated with the international ortholinon.

Dr. Hiroike recognized the 'economy' and morality are not contradictory rather complementary.. (Treatise Part 3 pp 208-209)

Hiroike made a critical study of the fundamental economic ideas developed by economists like Adam Smith, Menger, Marx etc. He observed ' economic ideas of Smith were built upon the individual self-interest/egoism '. He did not agree with the criticisms levelled against the capitalists by Marx...

The heterodox system together with liberalism, socialism and capitalism have stimulated human desire and so, destructive. So, it is better to accept orthodox learning. We shall be able to build a society with security, peace and happiness by organized, constructive, steady, eternal and peaceful means.

He was not in favor of the rapid expansion or quick enlargement of a nation or an enterprise. Rather he suggested expansion in 'the natural course of events' through inner control by means of morality.

If it is developed quickly, he argued, many people may tend to join the enterprise out of their own exclusive selfish interest and may cause sufferings to many others within and outside the particular enterprise. (Treatise Part3 p 598)

He also maintained---' In every country from government offices, schools, firms, banks and private houses to roads, bridges and entertainment facilities---are made far more grand, magnificent and normal than the practical living capacity of the people can sustain and this necessarily results in the increase of national expenses, taxes and living costs.' (A Treatise of Moral Science part 3, p 207)

This is how excess capacity or surplus production is generated. And the role of the multinational corporations is pertinent to understand.

The implications of this are vast and varied.

Quantitative expansion of production may lead to-- over-production, over-saleable, in the market and consequently fluctuations in market prices take place. Excess production, as we see today, is creating a problem of disposable issue. Blunt indiscriminate industrialization emits pollutants and aggravate? global environmental crisis and also create a society of consumerism. We have institutionalized wasteful consumption. The replacement of home electronics product is often encouraged even they are usable. The principle of more and more is believed to be a case of human alienation by depriving human goodness from humankind. There should be definite limit to growth. We listen sometime to the idea of MOT TAI NAI in Japan. The existence of unutilized capacity is undesirable.

Incidentally, it is pertinent to note that Dr.Hiroike was not approving the plucking of flowers from his garden and throw them or did not allow cutting of trees from his garden. He was conscious about the impact of all these activities even though, the science of ecology was not born in proper form that time..

Besides theoretical aspect of economics, Dr Hiroike suggested some ideas about management based on the principles of moralogy.

Dr Hiroike maintained that

'The company is not a place for struggling for money or other material benefits: but a holy place for managers to educate and help workers and for people to educate them.' (Hiroike 1986-a Treatise on Moral science Part 3. p.550).

He identified three features

Firstly, Character as capital

Character, implies both mental and human abilities-it is scholarship, intelligence and ability. It is the result of the accumulation of moral practices -by the parents, ancestors of each person.

He believed that the company is for human development and salvation. To foster and grow men of higher character. Necessarily, a manager is to try for happiness of the employees. In this way, he cultivates direct benevolence. Enlightened in this way, employees will also conform to the manager's mind and do their best.

Again, what is indispensable for the manager is always to nourish human abilities necessary for the development of the enterprise. Because an enterprise may fail simply because 'of its ignorance of the trends of the age' (Treatise, Part 2, p.81). We cannot safely live in the past. 'As the teachings of the sages are the natural law of the universe, things (goods and service) are the appearance of its principles and the concrete method of dealing with these things productive method have to be improved, according to the evolution of human spirit.

This is where the issue of innovation emerges.

Thirdly, Triadic Justice

The business activities should take care of the interests of all sides-self, the other party and the third party.

In Treatise, Part 3, p 59 supreme morality intends to enlighten all people concerned with the same principle: the seller the buyers and all others merchants, users, capitalists, workers etc even if whose interests may be in opposite position. The purpose is to give peace and happiness to everybody. Otherwise, it will create problems and instability.

Key points: to cultivate character may be enumerated as follows.

- To think of the future of the employees
- To enlighten each party all by supreme morality (if we do not, we lack respect for humanity --cannot cultivate the spirit of benevolence)

Corporate Social Responsibility (CSR) is now a widely talked about issue.

Companies/management are required to see the world beyond their companies.

An enterprise for its sustainable development needs a solid support and co-operation of the people and society around it.

It is to take care of the interests of the society to provide essential commodities at reasonable prices to look into the interests of customers, employees, stackholders stockholders etc. and to help society and nation for improving moral level.

There is a need to reexamine and reconstruct the nature of behaviour of business organizations.

Lock-outs? strikes lay-offs, bankruptcy, corruption have become the order in the business world or economic world today.

The form of economy that we see today has been substantially impoverished by the distance that has grown between economy and morality.

It is difficult to organize a true organization, social or economic unless the human beings restrain their self-instlnct.

Dr Hiroike believed - 'man's moral sense 'is the most important factor in preventing recurrence of such troubles as financial panics, trade depressions, lack of credit and bankruptcies—" (The Characteristics of Moralogy and Supreme Morality Hiroike, 1966) So, he called upon to develop economic systems and industrial and economic organizations on the firm foundation of supreme morality and on the basis of the principles on natural sciences.

Today, we witness corruption in different areas. Corruption is the manifestation of imperfect social system. It can be found in countries of widely varying ideology,economic conditions or social development. In its wildest connotation, it includes improper and selfish use of power and influence. On the root cause of corruption,Adam smith maintained – "the disposition to admire, almost to worship the rich and the powerful and to despise or at least to neglect persons of power and mean conditions is at the time the great and most universal cause of the corruption of our moral sentiments."

Liberalisation process is one that affects both the ideological outlook as well as values orientation. Of the individuals in a manner that makes man more inclined to act in the interests of private benefits. In fact, liberalization meant to many liberalization from all ethical and moral bindings and compunctions. The whole set of values from which the society stands committed is under threat of displacement in the name of liberalisation and opening of the country. With the increasing pressure of demonstration effect and the strong desire to keep up with the Jone's, people today are generally compelled to enter into the world of corruption even by breaking the moral or ethical boundary. And consumerism and commodity fetishism started and people are induced to acquire more of everything by means fair or foul. The breakdown of traditional values and religious sanctions against unfair means made corruption generally acceptable and universal.

True, the ideas and principles of Supreme Morality developed by Dr Hiroike were under the restrictions of time. But even then, there are certain fundamental principles which will make enormous contributions, if rightly followed, to the creation of a society with deep human kindness and a world with peace,security and happiness.

## End Notes

1. Chikuro Hiroike (1866-1938) started his career as a local teacher in Nakatsuin,the Southern island of Kyusu. In his mid-twenties, he moved from Nakatsu to Kyoto where he deepened his study in history. Hiroike accomplished great scholastic feats in every field. On August 17,1926 he completed Treatise on Moral science: A First Attempt to establish Moralogy as a new science. The magnum opus was published in 1928 and it laid the foundation for moral education in schools and society in Japan.

## References

Crawford C.S., 1974, The evolution of Hindu Ethical ideals Firma K.L. Mukhopadhyaya, Calcutta.

The Institute of Moralogy 2001, Chikuro Hiroike -The Father of Moralogy, The Institute of Moralogy Chiba Prefecture Tokyo Japan.

The Institute of Moralogy 2000, Towards Supreme Morality 1-4 volumes 1966 Chiba prefecture.

The Institute of Moralogy 1966, The characteristics of Moralogy and Supreme Moralogy, The Institute of Moralogy Chiba Prefecture Tokyo Japan.